Informers Up Close

Informers Up Close

Stories from Communist Prague

MARK A. DRUMBL
Class of 1975 Alumni Professor of Law
Director, Transnational Law Institute
Washington and Lee University
and
BARBORA HOLÁ
Senior Researcher, Netherlands Institute for the Study of Crime and Law Enforcement
Professor, Department of Criminology, Vrije Universiteit Amsterdam

OXFORD
UNIVERSITY PRESS

OXFORD
UNIVERSITY PRESS

Great Clarendon Street, Oxford, OX2 6DP,
United Kingdom

Oxford University Press is a department of the University of Oxford.
It furthers the University's objective of excellence in research, scholarship,
and education by publishing worldwide. Oxford is a registered trade mark of
Oxford University Press in the UK and in certain other countries

Published in the United States of America by Oxford University Press
198 Madison Avenue, New York, NY 10016, United States of America

British Library Cataloguing in Publication Data

Data available

Library of Congress Control Number: 2023951785

ISBN 978–0–19–285513–8

DOI: 10.1093/oso/9780192855138.001.0001

Printed and bound by
CPI Group (UK) Ltd, Croydon, CR0 4YY

Dedicated to the +

Preface and Acknowledgements

A stream of stars shared so much with us and brightened our skies with their ideas and input. In no particular order we thank: Tim MacDonnell, Alex Klein, Krzysztof Jasiewicz, Patrick Bergemann, Cynthia Horne, Kjell Anderson, Kieran McEvoy, Luke Moffett, Sarah Nouwen, Kevin Hearty, Patryk Gacka, Thijs Bouwknegt, Maartje Weerdesteijn, Paul Morrow, Conor O'Reilly, Mark Rush, Marina Aksenova, Justyna Granacka, Rebecca Sutton, Veronika Bílková, Russ Miller, Eszter Salgó, Heather Conway, Christina Li, Jon Eastwood, Alan Norrie, Diane Marie Amann, Christoph Sperfeldt, and Solange Mouthaan. A very special thanks goes to Richard Wilson for hosting a workshop at the University of Connecticut with such incredible participants and friends and conviviality, including Christian Lance-De Vos, Jocelyn Getgen, Jamie Rowen, Lara Nettelfield, Lawrence Douglas, and Devin Pendas.

A stellar team of research assistants, led by the indomitable Jenna Mueller, ironed out many knotty wrinkles and added much finesse. Anna Jordanová did an amazing job searching through the immense mass of the StB archives, helping us with our informer selection, and compiling initial file-stories. In addition to Jenna and Anna, thanks go to Zach Zimmermann, Natalia Micheli, Jack Perryman, Kevin Rodriguez, Dominique Cravins, Eliška Mocková, and Lucie Pěntáková.

Appreciation also goes to the many unnamed interlocutors, placed in person and ethered in the virtual, who over this book's brilliant writing trajectory participated in events hosted all over this big, brassy, bold world: Sarajevo (thank you Mirza); North Macedonia (thank you Andrej); Prague, Edinburgh, Florence, Riga, Birmingham, Belfast, Copenhagen, London, Lexington, Mexico City (twice: thank you Juan, Leigh, Beatriz); Osgoode Hall Law School (thank you Palma and Heidi); Leeds University (thank you Elies); Western University (thank you Valerie); John Cabot University in Rome (thank you Silvia); NUI-Galway (thank you Shane); William and Mary University (thank you Nancy); VU Amsterdam and Center for International Criminal Justice (thank you Joris, Maarten, and Gabriele); Institute of International Relations in Prague, the US State Department; and at gatherings of the American Society of International Law (Mid-Year Meeting (2020, online)), Law & Society Association (2020, online), European Society of Criminology (2020, online), Dutch Society of Criminology (2021, online), and Southeastern Association of American Law Schools (Amelia Island, Florida, 2021). The early input of five anonymous reviewers kindled and ignited our journey. And thanks to those folks who sat down with us for riveting interviews, coffees, meetings, and discussions in London, Chicago, New York, Philadelphia, Brno, Prague, and at the

National Czech and Slovak Museum in Cedar Rapids, Iowa. And while forgettable, the FNs opened our eyes and made the malicious side of informing seem very real.

A little lark paper turned into a committed book journey in April 2020, as we became scrambled pixellations in on-screen boxes, as events cancelled in cascades. At one such event, which shifted at the last minute from Toulouse to Zoomtopia, we looked at each other's rectangle and Mark sent a chat that said: 'Well, this is a project that can be written during a pandemic, no? So let's do it as a full book and let's have something to look hugely forward to', and Barbora gave a smile and a thumbs up, and so it was, so it has been ... and we did it ... and that's why we thank the ERCP Toulouse for that initial sparkly nudge.

Barbora would like to recognize her parents, Michaela and Jiří, whose stories (but also half-stories and silences) of growing up and living in Communist Prague triggered and inspired her throughout this book journey. *Děkuji za všechno mami a tati!* Mark would like to thank Michelle, Paul, Luke, and Irma for all their love, support, patience, and humour; while his father Hubert passed away right at the very start of this writing path in December 2019, his spirit lives in it as it does in all of Mark's days; and lastly, Mark wishes to recognize his godfather Antonín, who also rests in peace, for his memorable path from Brno to London to the RAF Battle of Britain then onwards to Montréal, through Vienna. Thank you for the electric way you spoke of Czechoslovakia. And Mark and Barbora would like to recognize each other. The journey of co-authoring this book—of getting 'up close' to informers, emotions, stories, irregularities and dimensions, sentiments and words, swirls and twirls, homelands and new frontiers, mirrors and windows—has been an unforgettable adventure. The closing passages of Evelyn Waugh's *Brideshead Revisited* burst colourfully:

> Something quite remote from anything the builders intended has come out of their work; something none of us thought about at the time; a small red flame—a beaten-copper lamp of deplorable design relit before the beaten-copper doors of a tabernacle. It could not have been lit but for the builders and the tragedians, and there I found it this morning, burning anew among the old stones.... I quickened my pace ... 'You're looking unusually cheerful today.'

The Francis Lewis Law Center at Washington and Lee University, School of Law, provided generous financial support to this project on many levels: Funding for research assistants, workshop organizing (many thanks to Erica Ingersoll and Terri Byrnes), and sabbatical leave for Barbora at Washington and Lee and for Mark at Queen's University Belfast. The NSCR pitched in as well.

An educational website that serves as an accessible companion to this book for readers and educators is located at http://www.nscr.nl/Informers-Up-Close. Please contact either or both of us with any related inquiries.

Contents

Glossary of Terms

Agency work: Recruitment and management of informers by the Czechoslovak State Security Police (*Státní bezpečnost* (StB)).

Cadre screening: Official screening for employment and study purposes whereby Czechoslovak citizens were assessed for their social fitness based on their family background, political views, and public (and private) conduct and statements.

Charter 77: Civic dissident initiative named after a document (The Charter 77) published in Czechoslovakia in January 1977 which critiqued the government for failing to implement some of its international human rights obligations.

Conspirational flat/apartment: Private residences or other premises which their owners or users provided to the StB for their meetings between officers and informers.

Czechoslovakia: Czechoslovakia was formed as an independent state on 28 October 1918, when it declared independence from the Austro-Hungarian Empire. Czechoslovakia consisted of the historical Czech lands (Bohemia, Moravia, and Czech Silesia) and Slovakia. In 1948, Communists took over power in Czechoslovakia. The Communist regime lasted until 1989. During the forty years of Communism, Czechoslovakia also underwent subtle name changes. The initial official title 'Czechoslovak Republic' was changed into 'Czechoslovak Socialist Republic' in 1960. In 1969, the former unitary state was changed into a federation consisting of the Czech Socialist Republic and the Slovak Socialist Republic, but the official state name remained the same. In 1990, following the demise of the Communist regime, the country's name was initially changed into 'Czechoslovak Federative Republic'. After Slovakian protests regarding the conjoined name, the country was renamed as 'Czech and Slovak Federative Republic'. Czechoslovakia ceased to exist on 1 January 1993.

Czechoslovak Crown: The currency (*československá koruna*, Kčs). Czechoslovakia joined the International Monetary fund on 18 December 1946. At that time, the exchange rate between the Kčs and the $US was set at 50:1. On 1 June 1953, further monetary reform was initiated in which the exchange rate was set at 7.2 Kčs to 1$US. At this point a controlled rationing system of foreign exchange funds was introduced. This system remained in place until the end of 1990. In 1957, an official non-commercial exchange rate was introduced for foreign currencies. As of September 2023, the exchange rate on open exchange markets between the Kč (Czech crown) and the $US is approximately 22:1.

Czech Republic: Following the dissolution of the Czech and Slovak Federative Republic on 1 January 1993, the Czech Republic (also referred to as Czechia) and Slovakia were established as its two successor independent states. In this book we use the full, formal country name—the Czech Republic (in Czech *Česká republika*) and not its shortened version—Czechia (in Czech *Česko*). Both names are currently listed as the country names in the UNGEGN List of Country Names. Czechia became effective as a name only as of 17 May 2016.

De-conspiration: When an StB informer exposed the contact with the StB (and hence their informer status) to somebody else.

Former (or past) people: Individuals or groups of individuals considered 'enemy elements' according to Secret Order of the Minister of Interior No 1 of 3 January 1959. The StB compiled lists of the former people. Many were landowners, *petit bourgeois*, proprietors of small businesses, or *kulaks*. In 1964 the term 'former people' was replaced by Order of Minister of Interior No 10 of 17 February 1964 with the term 'an enemy person'.

Ideological diversion: Undermining and distraction of the population through the dissemination of anti-Communist ideas. According to the StB, such diversion was frequently attempted by foreigners from the capitalist West.

Informer: The term we use to refer to all categories of StB secret collaborators, including agents, informers (as one of the sub-categories used by the StB until 1972), residents, owners of conspirational flats, confidants, and candidates for secret collaboration). The typology of informers and its development within StB internal guidelines is discussed in Chapter 2, Section III.B.

Junák: The Czechoslovak Scouts organization, which was disbanded by the Communists in 1948. Some of its members were persecuted by the regime.

Kulak: Wealthy peasant or farmer who employed labour or possessed real estate and machinery.

Normalization: The period of Communist rule in Czechoslovakia in the 1970s and 1980s.

Operation Danube: The invasion of Czechoslovakia by four Warsaw Pact armies on 20–21 August 1968 which ended the liberalizing period of the Prague Spring.

Parasitism: A criminal offence stipulated in the 1956 amendment of the 1950 Czechoslovak Criminal Code. This offence, which endured on the books throughout the remainder of the Communist era, in essence established a duty to work and was deployed to prosecute individuals who lacked a 'proper' job, such as those who did business without required permits, sex workers, moneylenders, or gamblers.

Person of interest: Individuals on the StB's radar screen either because the StB suspected them to be potentially hostile toward the regime or because the StB picked them for secret collaboration.

Prague Spring: A brief period of political liberalization amid Czechoslovak Communist governance in 1968 which was quashed by Operation Danube.

Reactionist elements: Individuals who (actually or allegedly) failed to identify with the Communist regime.

Realization: Implementation or termination of an operation by the StB. Can also refer to 'realization of a person', meaning for instance their interrogation, prosecution, or arrest. Persons who StB informers had informed upon were at times 'realized'.

Samizdat: A form of dissident activity in which individuals reproduced censored and underground publications, often by hand or mimeograph, and passed the documents from reader to reader.

Sokol: A gymnastics organization that was based upon the principle of 'a strong mind in a sound body'. During Communism, the Sokol movement was suppressed by the regime. Some of its members were imprisoned or exiled.

Stalinism: A harsh period of the Czechoslovak Communist regime between 1948 and 1956.

Velvet Revolution: A relatively non-violent transition of power and overthrow of the Communists in Czechoslovakia by mass protests in November 1989.

List of Abbreviations

ABS	The Security Services Archive (*Archiv bezpečnostních složek*)
BRD	The Federal Republic of Germany, 'West Germany' (*Bundesrepublik Deutschland*)
ČEDOK	The Czechoslovak Travel and Transport Agency (*Československá cestovní a dopravní kancelář*)
ČSM	The Communist Party Youth Union (*Československý svaz mládeže*). In 1969 the ČSM was replaced by the SSM.
ČSSR	The Czechoslovak Socialist Republic (*Československá socialistická republika*)
DDR	The German Democratic Republic, 'East Germany' (*Deutsche Demokratische Republik*)
DM	The German Mark (currency) (*Deutsche Mark*)
Kčs	The Czechoslovak Crown (currency) (*československá koruna*)
KSČ	The Communist Party of Czechoslovakia (*Komunistická strana Československa*)
PTP	Special battalions formed to detain and re-educate 'politically unreliable' soldiers (*pomocné technické prapory*)
SNB	The National Security Corps (*Sbor národní bezpečnosti*)
StB	The State Security Police (*Státní bezpečnost*)
TNP	Forced labor camps (*tábory nucené práce*)
SSM	The Communist Party Youth Union, which replaced ČSM in 1969 (*Socialistický svaz mládeže*)
ÚDV	The Office for the Documentation and Prosecution of Communist Crimes (*Úřad dokumentace a vyšetřování zločinů komunismu*)
USSR	The Union of Soviet Socialist Republics
ÚSTR	The Institute for the Study of Totalitarian Regimes (*Ústav pro studium totalitních režimů*)
VB	The Public Security (*i.e.* ordinary police) (*Veřejná bezpečnost*)

Translations

All translations from all Czech (or on rare occasion Slovak) documents (or films) into English (whether StB files, official oral history projects, or secondary sources) have been directly made by Barbora Holá and in the cases of some StB files by Anna Jordanová.

1

Introduction

Becoming More Informed About Informers

She deceived me from start to finish;
Nothing was ever what it seemed.
She could make me think that ash was flour.[1]

François Villon
The Testament (*Le Testament*) (1461)

Snitch. Fink. Snoop. Rat. Turncoat. Mole. All these derogatory terms refer to one character: the informer. Indeed, informers evoke visceral public reactions. Names such as Judas Iscariot and Benedict Arnold remain fixed metaphoric points of reference for treachery. Informers morally vex the human imagination and occupy a nettlesome positionality in law, policy, and ethics. One of the seminal discussions of legal philosophy—the Hart/Fuller debate on legal positivism and natural law—anchors itself in the 'grudge informer', namely, a wife who was having an affair and got rid of her husband by telling Nazi authorities that he had privately slandered Hitler.[2] Informers have caught the eyes of countless authors, musicians, and filmmakers. Overwhelmingly, their works depict informers as baleful characters or, at

[1] François Villon, *Poems* (David Georgi tr, Northwestern University Press 2013) 73, Stanza 67, lines 689–691.

[2] In 1949, the wife was criminally prosecuted for her conduct. A German Court of Appeals had to decide whether she should be punished for denouncing her husband, who had returned from the war front in 1944. See Judgment of the Provincial High Court and Court of Appeal [Oberlandesgericht] of 27 July 1945, OLG Bamberg in SJZ 1950, 207. The husband had indeed mocked Hitler. The wife argued in her defence that her actions were lawful under Nazi law in force at the time. The German court nonetheless found her guilty of illegally depriving her husband of his liberty under an 1871 law that remained on the books throughout the Nazi period. It ruled that the Nazi laws about informing, upon which the wife relied to justify her reporting of her husband, were 'contrary to the sound conscience and sense of justice of all decent human beings'. HLA Hart, 'Positivism and the Separation of Law and Morals' (1958) 71 Harvard L Rev 593. Hart chided this outcome, fearing for the overthrow of legal positivism. Hart contended that rather than relying on courts to invalidate Nazi-made laws, it would have been preferable transitionally for the new regime to formally enact a statute that retrospectively applied to the informer's case. Fuller remarked in response that the inner morality of law had to be reckoned with and that to do so was not a problematic exercise of judicial discretion. For further discussion, see Oren Gross, 'What Both Hart and Fuller Got Wrong' (2021) 11 Wake Forest L Rev Online 54; David Dyzenhaus, 'The Hart–Fuller Debate at Fifty: The Grudge Informer Case Revisited' (2008) 83 NYU L Rev 1000.

Informers Up Close. Mark A. Drumbl and Barbora Holá, Oxford University Press.
 DOI: 10.1093/oso/9780192855138.003.0001

best, as pitiful sell-outs or pathetic wobbly souls—like Fredo Corleone in the film *The Godfather*.

Some informers, however, face a different fate. They are admired. Informers such as 'Deep Throat'—who outed US President Richard Nixon's wiretapping and thereby triggered the Watergate scandal—are generally lauded, and downright feted, as heroes.[3] These kinds of informers become perceived as whistle-blowers who valiantly expose corruption, abuse, bullying, crime, sexism, public health violations, and sleaze. This variant of informing, then, is seen as commendable rather than condemnable or contemptible. Informers, moreover, can be presented as intrepid. For example, the Soviet child informer, Pavlik Morozov, who allegedly denounced his father and grandfather to Stalinist authorities, was venerated and mythologized, only then to become derided following the fall of Communism.[4] Public reactions to informers—scorn, mostly, or adulation, sometimes—remain politically contingent.

Together with collaborators, with whom they often are lumped, informers are ubiquitous. They are everywhere. These characters pop up in all conflicts, all regimes, and all revolutions. It only took a month or two after the start of hostilities before Ukraine began to prosecute its own citizens for abetting the invading Russians.[5] Following the Second World War, thousands of Nazi acolytes were perfunctorily executed throughout Europe in the absence of coherent legal proceedings or were publicly humiliated through spontaneous forms of 'popular justice'.[6] Indeed, so goes the saying, 'snitches get stitches'. Yet all states, liberation movements, and activist causes—however iniquitous or virtuous, however lamentable or praiseworthy—need informers to survive and thrive.

Although informers are prone to sensationalist claims and vehement responses, they remain strikingly understudied in academic research.[7] This book seeks to

[3] So, too, with the US service member who outed the sexual abuse of prisoners at Abu Ghraib.

[4] Barbora Holá and Mark A Drumbl, 'Children as Informers and Denouncers' in Christelle Molima and others (eds), *Children's Fights: Commonalities and Differences Across Time, Space, and Place* (Routledge forthcoming).

[5] Lorenzo Tondo and Shaun Walker, '"A Difficult and Painful Question": Ukraine Ponders How to Punish Collaborators' *The Guardian* (London, 4 June 2022) <https://www.theguardian.com/world/2022/jun/04/ukraine-collaborators-treason-russia-war> accessed 28 August 2023 (reporting that more than 1,400 cases of treason and collaboration with the invading Russian army have been brought).

[6] Marcos Zunino, *Justice Framed: A Genealogy of Transitional Justice* (CUP 2019) 167–68 (in addition to executions, noting 'the widespread phenomenon of "shorn women" [*femmes tondues*] that targeted women accused of "horizontal collaboration" that is, having a relationship with a German soldier . . . [t]he women were taken to a public space where they would have their hair shorn').

[7] Ron Dudai, *Penality in the Underground: The IRA's Pursuit of Informers* (OUP 2022) 1. For some notable exceptions to the paucity of academic work in this area, in addition to Dudai (who considers how the Irish Republican Army (IRA) handled informers in its midst), see Barbara Miller, *The Stasi Files Unveiled: Guilt and Compliance in a Unified Germany* (Routledge 2017) (primarily relying on interviews as research method and featuring ten East German informers profiled in brief vignettes); Alison Lewis, *A State of Secrecy, Stasi Informers and the Culture of Surveillance* (Potomac Books 2021) (using Stasi files as her main source); Juan Espíndola Mata and Leigh A Payne (eds), *Collaboration in Authoritarian and Armed Conflict Settings* (OUP 2022) (addressing collaboration generally, including chapters on informers, presented in comparative format); Jacob Dlamini, *The Terrorist Album: Apartheid's Insurgents, Collaborators, and the Security Police* (Harvard University Press 2020) (discussing informers

respond to this lacuna, specifically in the case of informers in authoritarian times. Similar to many other contributors to repression, informers belie their simplistic portrayals and are multifaceted actors. Much more lurks in these characters than initially meets the eye. This book aims to excavate these complexities. It does so through a case study of secret police informers in Communist Czechoslovakia.

I. Informers: Definition and Context

It is useful to begin with definitions. Who is an informer?[8] As we have already noted, informers are often discursively jumbled with collaborators and spies. For us, however, these three words are not interchangeable synonyms despite their semantic overlaps. Each word connotes a person who assists an authority figure, in particular—but not always—a state official. While collaborators may openly assist authority figures, informing tends to be shrouded in secrecy. Moreover, collaborators may engage in a broader array of activities than informers. The spy shares the furtiveness and information-gathering function that is the hallmark of the informer. Spies, however, have become exoticized in public culture—often seen as dashing, charming, and sophisticated—and generally are recruited professionally following years of training. Informers, on the other hand, tend not to fit this pattern. As we will explore, informers largely are rank-and-file characters, often inept, and very far from James Bond even if some imagine themselves in such an aggrandized fashion. In sum, then, for us *the informer is a common citizen who gathers and then supplies information, usually clandestinely, to authorities.*

Informers operate in many contexts. Some informers collude with hostile occupying forces. Some informers surveil family, friends, neighbours, and co-workers and report their findings to authorities in repressive states. Other informers surveil family, friends, neighbours, and co-workers and report their findings to authorities in liberal democratic states—cooperating, for example, with police in investigations of problematic criminal elements or with civil servants who aim to promote salutary public policies. Informers who report to repressive authorities may become exposed should that abusive regime fall. This is when transitional justice[9]—a society's reckoning with past human rights abuses—enters the equation and informers tumble into accountability mechanisms. Some informers

and collaborators who exposed anti-apartheid activities in South Africa); Shane Darcy, *To Serve the Enemy: Informers, Collaborators, and the Laws of Armed Conflict* (OUP 2019) (deploying the lens of international humanitarian law).

[8] We use 'informer' rather than 'informant' in this book. In our view, both terms are basically interchangeable and mean the same thing, but for the sake of consistency we use 'informer'. When a quotation uses 'informant', however, then we retain that term.

[9] The term is Ruti Teitel's. Ruti G Teitel, *Transitional Justice* (OUP 2000).

may report information to leaders of non-governmental organizations, emancipation movements, and armed groups. Others may report on such activities to the states against which these groups fight.[10] Some informers may be deployed to secure political information; others may be used to obtain information about ordinary common crime. Some informers are repeat players, developing veritable careers in the information supply chain; others are one-time ad hoc denouncers who may exercise considerable initiative in coming forward with information.

II. Our Case Study

This book studies informers in the service of an authoritarian state, Czechoslovakia under Communist governance (1948–1989). In these years, the country was the common state of two national groups: the Czechs and the Slovaks. As with all other Communist states in Europe at the time,[11] the secret police played a key role in mainstreaming repression. In Czechoslovakia, the secret police were called the *Státní bezpečnost* (StB) in Czech, and the *Štátna bezpečnosť* (ŠtB) in Slovak.

This book unwinds *why* people spoke to the StB. It situates itself in detailed research about StB informers in the Czech part of Communist Czechoslovakia. We construct informing as intimacy—secret relationships between informers and their handlers—and explore the human emotions that catalysed and fuelled these interactions.

Following the fall of Communism in the wake of the 1989 Velvet Revolution, and the accompanying shift to capitalist liberal democracy, informers were

[10] See eg the 'tout' in Northern Ireland: putatively committed to the Irish Republican Army cause, but then shovelling incriminating information directly to the British occupying authorities, '[t]he tout occupies an outsize place in the Irish imagination, as a folk devil—a paragon of treachery … [b]etween 1980 and 1994, no fewer than forty people were executed by the IRA on suspicion of being touts, their bodies dumped unceremoniously'. Patrick Radden Keefe, *Say Nothing* (Doubleday 2019) 244, 270.

[11] Throughout this book, we eschew the locator term 'Eastern Europe', though it emerges frequently in the work of others about Czechoslovakia, in particular in Cold War studies and, in those specific instances, we reproduce that term. We eschew the term because of its contested nature. See eg Miroslav Vaněk and Pavel Mücke, *Velvet Revolutions: An Oral History of Czech Society* (OUP 2020) 70 ('Throughout modern Czech history, there has been a long discussion about whether the geographical space of the country is part of Western or Eastern-Europe, or whether it belongs to the symbolic intermediate area of Central Europe.'); Muriel Blaive, 'Milan Kundera and Me' *Britské listy* (Prague, 22 July 2023) <https://blisty.cz/art/114383-milan-kundera-and-me.html> accessed 23 July 2023 ('Central Europe was politically in the east, geographically in the center, and culturally in the west. Indeed … I have never used any other expression than "Central Europe" to describe East Germany, Poland, Czechoslovakia, and Hungary.') Czech novelist Jáchym Topol, through the voice of his fictional character Sara, touches this nerve:

> I was searching for the East, Eastern Europe, but, you see, going to Eastern Europe means you never stop looking for it … Slovakia was Central Europe, not Eastern. … So, I travel all the way through Siberia, thousands of kilometers on the Trans-Siberian railway, and at the end station, in Vladivostok, I climb out, all broken-boned, and the locals there tell me, East, young lady, are you crazy? Why, this is the West, the honest-to-God end of the West….

Jáchym Topol, *The Devil's Workshop* (authored 2009, Alex Zucker tr, Portobello Books 2013) 41–43.

scornfully depicted as menaces and became broadly consumed political fodder ensnared by the moralizing currents of another state-driven enterprise, namely transitional justice. Our book reflects on *how* transitional justice approached these informers, initially in post-Communist Czechoslovakia, and—following the dissolution of Czechoslovakia into two separate nation-states on 1 January 1993—in the Czech Republic (also known as Czechia).[12] We elect to use the name Czech Republic rather than Czechia. Both remain as official names pursuant to the United Nations, although Czechia as a short version (which became effective as of 17 May 2016) is now in wider circulation. We stick with the Czech Republic because for nearly three decades following Czechoslovak dissolution this was the country's sole official name.

While highlighting individual agency and idiosyncrasy, this book constructs both informing and transitional justice as interactive social practices.

The social practice of informing in Communist Czechoslovakia cannot be disentangled from the reality that the Communist regime at times benefitted from considerable levels of popular support, although its legitimacy oscillated over the years and generally waned through time as public attitudes towards it soured. Hence, the social practice of informing links with the reality that, as Václav Havel—Czechoslovakia's first post-Communist President—famously opined, 'the line between victim and oppressor ran through each person'.[13] The putative divides between state and society in Communist Czechoslovakia may be more apparent in revisionist hindsight than in the actual, lived moment.[14] On this note, informing constitutes 'evidence of the complexities of the relationship *between* state and society'.[15] Accordingly, we are drawn to constructs of life in Communist

[12] Czechoslovakia split into two states, the Czech Republic and Slovakia. We do not discuss how transitional justice in Slovakia approached informers following Czechoslovak dissolution and the emergence of Slovakia as an independent state. Nor do we discuss the ŠtB's activities in the Slovak region of Czechoslovakia. This is not to say that these are unimportant angles. Rather, it is just to say that our chosen case study is the Czech part of Communist Czechoslovakia and then the Czech Republic. This book is about the Czechs. Therefore, we primarily use the term 'Czech'. If we use Czechoslovak, we mean the former Czechoslovak state, although within that state our focus is on the Czech part of that population.

[13] James Krapfl, 'Building the Normalisation Panorama' in Kevin McDermott and Matthew Stibbe (eds), *Czechoslovakia and Eastern Europe in the Era of Normalisation 1969–1989* (Palgrave Macmillan 2022) 46 (citing Václav Havel). Tina Rosenberg, casting Communist regimes as 'conspiracies of all society', similarly notes:

> Just as almost everyone was a victim of communism by virtue of living under it, almost everyone also participated in repression. Inside a communist regime, lines of complicity ran like veins and arteries inside the human body. Even the most natural responses of self-preservation were also, in a sense, acts of collaboration.

Tina Rosenberg, 'Overcoming the Legacies of Dictatorship' (1995) 74 Foreign Affairs 134, 138.

[14] Blaive, 'Milan Kundera and Me' (n 11), who assails the state-driven rewriting of the 'history of Czechoslovak communism as a history of anticommunist heroism tamed by the Soviet domination' and which accords outsize importance on outsiders and avoids the phenomenon of wide-ranging domestic collaboration.

[15] Péter Apor, Sándor Horváth, and James Mark, 'Introduction: Collaboration, Cooperation, and Political Participation in the Communist Regimes' in Péter Apor, Sándor Horváth, and James Mark (eds), *Secret Agents and the Memory of Everyday Collaboration in Communist Eastern Europe* (Anthem

Czechoslovakia that mobilize around the twin dialectical concepts of 'participatory dictatorship'[16] and the 'engineering of human souls'.[17] These two concepts pull and push, thereby vivifying the interplay between the bottom-up agency of the individual and the top-down grip of the state. These two concepts recur as lighthouses guiding us in our work.

In light of our interest in liminal characters and social interactivity, we focus on 'everyday collaboration'[18] and the stories of 'ordinary people'.[19] We are interested in micro-histories and small-scale tales, to wit, glimpses of the quotidian. This move also helps uncork the routine structures and patterns of informing so as to recognize informing as involving the energy of varied individual dispositions within a rigidly bureaucratized frame. We concur with certain Czech oral historians that, '[w]ithout integrating the lives of ordinary people, any twentieth-century Czech history will be fragmentary and incomplete'.[20] Everyday informing could be deeply painful, implicating spouses exposing each other, parents denouncing children and children denouncing parents, as well as other forms of reporting from within families: we have come across all this poignancy in our research. We have also encountered the closeness of informer–StB officer relationships, at times bearing witness to intimacy, amiability, and trust. What is of note is that personal relationships between the informer and the informed-upons are intrinsic to the social practice of informing. Hence, betrayal—a sentiment that often proves awkward for transitional justice—festers once informers become revealed. Indeed, when an informer

Press 2017) 3 (also expressing disappointment that 'little research … discuss[es] the complexities of state–society relations embedded in stories of collaboration').

16 The term is Mary Fulbrook's from her analysis of East Germany. Mary Fulbrook, *The People's State: East German Society from Hitler to Honecker* (Yale University Press 2005) (a 'participatory dictatorship' is a regime in which, despite unquestionable political constraints and repression, many people felt they were able to lead 'perfectly normal lives', assume significant functions in social movements and statal organizations, and be critical of (and extract things from) government while attesting to their socialist *bona fides*).

17 The phrase is from Joseph Stalin, who applied it to writers: 'There are various forms of production: artillery, automobiles, lorries. You also produce "commodities", "works", "products". Such things are highly necessary. Engineering things. For people's souls. You are engineers of human souls.' Susan Ratcliffe (ed), *Oxford Essential Quotations* (6th ed, OUP 2018) (*Joseph Stalin, 'Speech to writers at home of Maxim Gorky' (26 October 1932)*, 2023) <https://www.oxfordreference.com/display/10.1093/acref/9780191866692.001.0001/q-oro-ed6-00010383> accessed 15 September 2023. Exiled Czech author Josef Škvorecký thusly, and ironically, titled one of his novels. Josef Škvorecký, *The Engineer of Human Souls* (Picador 1986). We deploy 'engineering of human souls' in the sense of top-down state control over citizens: not just their actions, but their thoughts and spirits, whether in the Communist years or in the post-Communist years, thereby echoing the track of this and other of Škvorecký's novels.

18 Apor, Horváth, and Mark (eds), *Secret Agents and the Memory of Everyday Collaboration in Communist Eastern Europe* (n 15).

19 We are influenced in this regard by Miroslav Vaněk and Pavel Mücke, who centre their work in the need to study the history of 'ordinary people' rather than 'great political moments and key players'; these scholars frame their book as centralizing 'ordinary people' instead of presenting them 'merely as onlookers to the moves of major figures on the chessboard of politics and economics'. Vaněk and Mücke, *Velvet Revolutions* (n 11) 1.

20 ibid 2.

is unmasked, the agony of Villon's deception—with which we open our book—may sear and scald: so much closeness, all that propinquity, in hindsight indeed was not 'ever what it seemed'.

The social practice of transitional justice, for its part, cannot be cleaved from Czech post-Communist political imperatives. These imperatives have largely curried public perceptions—already predisposed to disdain informers—towards scapegoating them and even ostracizing them as inimical to liberal democracy. Hence, conversations about the StB and their informers remain fraught and taut. So it has been for decades. As we were putting the final touches on this manuscript in July 2023, Milan Kundera—the celebrated author of (among other works) *The Unbearable Lightness of Being*—passed away at the age of ninety-four. A Czech national and dissident who moved to France in 1975, Kundera triggered controversy even after his death because of allegations published by a Czech magazine in 2008 that, in 1950, he had informed to the StB on a young man who fled Czechoslovakia only allegedly to return as an undercover Western spy.[21] Our book expands the discursive frame by unravelling what happened to everyday informers, not just a few high-profile media sensations such as Kundera, after Communism crumbled and was superseded by a liberal democratic successor.

The thorny and politicized nature of discourse about informers in the Czech Republic attests to the utility of a sensitive, 'up close', and granular analysis. This is what we hope to bring to the table. Indeed, we find StB informers to be a deeply heterogenous group evincing a motivational kaleidoscope: actively agentic and passively coerced, zealous and reticent, spiteful and kind. In the end, a disconnect arises between the knee-jerk viscerality of public responses to informers and the actual reality of informers as individuals.

This book is not a comparative analysis of informers among different nations, nor does it contrast informers as subjects of transitional justice modalities among different nations.[22] While we do glance towards developments in other countries, these are illustrative and supplemental. At its core, our book is a case study of one state and one of its successor regimes. It therefore fits in area studies literature. We do, however, make findings and extrapolate claims from our research. While these

[21] Harrison Smith, 'Milan Kundera, author of "The Unbearable Lightness of Being," dies at 94' *Washington Post* (Washington DC, 12 July 2023) <https://www.washingtonpost.com/obituaries/2023/07/12/milan-kundera-unbearable-ligtness-author-dead/> accessed 30 August 2023. Kundera virulently challenged the accusation. See also, during Kundera's life, discussion by Roman David, *Communists and Their Victims: The Quest for Justice in the Czech Republic* (University of Pennsylvania Press 2018) 29–30; and Petr Třešňák and Adam Hradilek, 'Milan Kundera's Denunciation' *Respekt* (Prague, 13 October 2008) <https://www.respekt.cz/respekt-in-english/milan-kundera-s-denunciation> accessed 23 July 2023.

[22] For excellent comparative work on these topics in post-Communist Europe, see Apor, Horváth, and Mark (eds), *Secret Agents and the Memory of Everyday Collaboration* (n 15); Cynthia M Horne, *Building Trust and Democracy: Transitional Justice in Post-Communist Countries* (OUP 2017); Lavinia Stan and Nadya Nedelsky (eds), *Post-Communist Transitional Justice: Lessons from Twenty-Five Years of Experience* (CUP 2015).

nest in Communist Czechoslovakia and the Czech Republic, we also believe that our findings convey broader theoretical currency. This book also gestures towards acts of informing generally, including in liberal democratic societies. We aim to offer a way of thinking about the informer—a lens, so to speak—that can be useful elsewhere.

In short, then, this book inquires why people spoke to and engaged with the StB. It thereby aims to contribute to the epistemology of informing by unwinding the aetiology of informing in Communist Czechoslovakia. It then critically reflects upon what Czech transitional justice did with informers once the *ancien régime* fell. Our principal data sources are the files in the StB archives. We moreover propose to approach StB-informer interactions through the innovative prism of emotions. We now explain, in turn, each of these moves in greater detail.

III. Secret Police Archives and File-Stories

This book is about stories. We rely on StB records to recount the stories of individual informers and surface the emotions that might have catalysed their informing. Our explorations therefore centre upon the 'past' as recorded and reproduced by the StB and as currently stored—digitally and in hard copy—in the Security Services Archive in the Czech Republic (*Archiv bezpečnostních složek* (ABS)).[23] We rely solely on one sub-category of StB files archived in the ABS, the so-called secret collaborator files, which throughout this book we refer to as 'the StB files'.[24] These are the files that the StB compiled on (and about) citizens who supplied the StB with information and which, in turn, brim to the rim with all sorts of content.

The publicly accessible ABS was established in the Czech Republic in 2007 along with the Institute for the Study of Totalitarian Regimes (*Ústav pro studium totalitních režimů* (ÚSTR)). The guiding motto of the ÚSTR and ABS, set forth in

[23] For an overview, see generally Security Services Archive, 'Home Page' (*Security Services Archive*, 2023) <https://www.abscr.cz> accessed 30 August 2023. For the digital archive, Security Services Archive, 'eBadatelna of the Security Services Archives, Prague, Czech Republic' (*Security Services Archive*, 2023) <https://www.ebadatelna.cz> accessed 30 August 2023. For more information on the creation and opening of the ABS, Chapter 3, Section IV, 'Revelations and Transparency'. Throughout the book we refer to the Security Services Archive through the acronym ABS, or the phrases 'the StB archives' or 'the archives'.

[24] The StB also compiled other files for the purposes of criminal investigation, files on enemy individuals who were subject to StB surveillance, and files concerning certain areas of interest—including church, youth, state businesses, and dissident groups. We do not peruse these files. For general discussion about the classification of the various files housed under the aegis of the ABS, see Světlana Ptáčníková, 'Aspekty odpovědnosti archivářů a badatelů při nakládání s osobními údaji v archiváliích' (2017) 2 Historie—Otázky—Problémy 24. In Czechoslovakia, informal networks also served to funnel information and reports from citizens through multiple channels to diverse authorities, such as workplace managers, school principals, and sports coaches. These networks, however, are not the focus of this book. Instead, the focus herein lies with the formal relationships between informers and the StB as evidenced in the secret collaborator files.

the preamble of the enabling legislation, affirms: 'Those who do not know their past are condemned to repeat it.'[25] Anyone over the age of eighteen can obtain access to any existing archival materials, including personal and sensitive information, stemming from StB records created before 1 January 1990.[26] In order to gain access to the files, individuals need to (i) register at the ABS by providing biographical information, (ii) affirm the purpose of their research, and (iii) present a valid identification card. Researchers also must sign a declaration that they are aware of their obligations in accessing the ABS and in dealing with sensitive or personal data. This registration is valid for one year and is renewable.

The ABS has two public reading rooms.[27] One is in Prague. The other is in Brno, a smaller city to the east. The Prague office is located on the third floor of a former residential building tucked in a side street behind the National Theatre on the bank of the Vltava River. It is barely a five-minute walk from the former StB regional headquarters. Visitors enter to face a reception and a small study room furnished with two rows of rectangular tables flanked by simple chairs (Figures 1.1 and 1.2). Here, people can sit down and sift through StB files of their interest. The room is musty. It lacks air circulation. The StB files appear in manila folders stuffed with hand- and type-written sheets, at times taking the form of tissue paper. Many of these files contain hundreds, if not thousands, of pages. Some of the StB files also are made available digitally. Microfiche and microfilm records also exist.

Throughout four decades of Communist rule, the StB meticulously collected, recorded, and archived millions of pages. These files—now stored, catalogued, and sheltered at the ABS—offer a vibrant informational treasure trove of informer 'file-stories'.[28] These file-stories comprise the backbone of our book.

Crucial introductory questions arise. What is the epistemic value of the StB files? What are their truths and accuracies? What can these files tell us about the lives of individuals, along with their joys, worries, emotions, and motivations?

[25] Zákon o Ústavu pro studium totalitních režimů a o Archivu bezpečnostních složek a o změně některých zákonů [Law on the Institute for the Study of Totalitarian Regimes and the Security Services Archive and on Change of Some Laws], Zákon č 181/2007 Sb (Czech) (adopted 8 June 2007) (hereafter Law on the Institute for the Study of Totalitarian Regimes and Security Services Archives). Chapter 3, Section VI, 'Institutes of Memory' extensively discusses the ÚSTR.

[26] Security Services Archive, 'How to Request Archival Materials' (*Security Services Archive*, 2023) <https://www.abscr.cz/en/how-to-request-archival-materials/> accessed 3 March 2023; and Zákon o archivnictví a spisové službě a o změně některých zákonů [Law on Archives and Filing Service and on Change of Some Laws] Zákon č 499/2004 Sb (Czech) para 37(11) (adopted 30 June 2004).

[27] The ABS houses about 60,000 files. Security Services Archive, 'Work of the Archive' (*Security Services Archive*, 2023) <https://www.abscr.cz/cinnosti-archivu/ > accessed 3 March 2023. See also Světlana Ptáčníková, 'Dveře Archívu Bezpečnostních Složek Dokořán' (*Lecture by ABS Director*, 27 March 2022) <https://www.youtube.com/watch?v=ovbZSJ3PdN0> accessed 16 July 2023 (remarking that, 'as of 1 January 2017, we kept 748 archival collections spanning almost 20,000 linear meters').

[28] A file-story is a narrative developed through careful interpretation of information found in secret police files. The term 'file-story' was coined by Valentina Glajar. Lewis, *A State of Secrecy* (n 7) xxix. See also Ioana Luca, 'Secret Police Files, Tangled Life Narratives: The 1.5 Generation of Communist Surveillance' (2015) 38(3) Biography 365 (observing that the files 'store individual life stories').

Figure 1.1 ABS reading room in Prague. Photograph taken by the authors (Prague, 2021).

Figure 1.2 ABS corridor in Prague. Photograph taken by the authors (Prague, 2022).

The StB files are outputs of a repressive securocratic apparatus whose overriding goal and *modus operandi* was to surveil the population and intimidate individuals. The StB's official mission was to uphold the spirit of Marxism-Leninism and to fight ostensible enemies of the state (persons suspected of anti-Communist sympathies) both external and internal and, furthermore, to prevent leakage of state secrets. This focus contoured the information the StB sought and what the StB considered worthy of recording. The StB interpreted their national security mission very capaciously, however. The StB laboured to penetrate the most personal spheres of human lives and collect any and every piece of potentially compromising evidence. Information was the StB's currency and gathering as much information as possible its *raison d'être*. Accordingly, the StB maintained a large stable of informers.

The StB's relentless recording of information (and subsequent archiving thereof) served as a control mechanism over informers as the information contained therein could have been used at any time to pressure individuals. Many informers themselves were informed upon. The files also doubled as a conduit for StB officers to demonstrate their obedience, effectiveness, and commitment to the organizational cause. Therefore, the StB archives were primarily created for the purposes of a bureaucracy of repression. The StB archives concentrated power and might.

The power relationship between StB officers and 'their' informers was therefore unequal. Yet, within this imbalance, the StB files are also outputs of interactive human dialogue. They are records of repeated conversations between an informer and an StB officer about the informer's own life and the lives of many others. The StB files document what StB officers asked, how informers replied, and the details of whatever StB officers recorded. This content reflects the exercise of some discretion, some choice, and some agency. We carefully approach agency in this frame and identify exercises of agency on the part of informers, including strategies and tactics such that there is much more, once again, to the informer–officer dyad that might be assumed or at first blush meets the eye. At alternating moments, the informer and the StB officer acted as listeners and speakers. The files diligently record in painstaking detail the daily lives of many individuals, their routines and departures from such routines, their words, and at times even their purported thoughts. Assuredly, in the StB archived files the officer-listeners adopt the authorial voice. The StB officer wrote the chronicle, thereby offering some latitude to transcend faithful stenography and advance ulterior goals.

Jacques Derrida traces the etymology of the word archive to recall that in Ancient Greece important documents were stored in the house of the *archon*, namely the ruler or chief magistrate.[29] The word 'archive' derives from an ancient Greek verb stem *arkh* which means to be first in order. Derrida posits that 'there is no political power without control of the archives'.[30] As a result, '[a]rchives act as spaces for public formations'.[31] Unsurprisingly, archival control became a central element in Czechoslovakia's transition to a liberal democratic regime. Power over archives remains a key feature of post-Communist public policy throughout Europe.[32] Indeed, '[i]f the truth of the past was contained in the gargantuan collections of Communism's bureaucracies, then a project of equal size had to be constructed in order to contain it and turn it back against itself'.[33]

The extent to which this tremendous mass of ABS archived information can be seen as truthful or accurate has been disputed. The 'truthiness' of the StB files has been intensely debated within Czech scholarship, politics, and society.

For one camp occupied by some historians, former dissidents, politicians, and individuals who considered themselves to be unjustly accused of cooperation with

[29] Jacques Derrida, *Archive Fever: A Freudian Impression* (Eric Prenowitz tr, University of Chicago Press 1996) 1–3.

[30] ibid 4. In classical Greece, archons performed public leadership functions.

[31] Shaunna Moore and Susan Pell, 'Autonomous Archives' (2010) 16 Intl J of Heritage Studies 255, 255.

[32] For general discussion of archives as means and tools of transitional justice, Julia Viebach, Dagmar Hovestädt, and Ulrike Lühe, 'Beyond Evidence: The Use of Archives in Transitional Justice' (2021) 25(3) Intl J of Human Rights 381.

[33] Apor, Horváth, and Mark, 'Introduction' (n 15) 4.

the StB,[34] the StB files are unreliable, no more than a 'a cocktail of fact and falsification',[35] and 'products of a criminal organization' that are 'full of lies'.[36] According to this sceptical camp, any quest to locate definitive truth in the files is fruitless owing to the incompleteness of the archives, the criminal character of the StB, coercive investigatory practices, the perceived sketchiness of willing informers, and a sense that the files are tainted by chronic dissembling.[37]

Other observers have, however, rebutted or contextualized some of this scepticism. It has been contended, for example, that 'StB officers were proper state officials, supervised by their superiors, by the inspection of the Ministry of the Interior, and by the military prosecution service, ... and therefore there is a very weak, very low [possibility] that there would be any untruth'.[38] Other researchers emphasize the need for sensitive analysis—confrontation, triangulation, and corroboration—when drawing inferences based on the StB files, while still acknowledging the significance and value of these files as historical sources.[39]

Moreover, despite their detail and density, the StB files do not (and cannot) say everything. Silences lurk within them. The file-stories are but partial life stories.[40] Omissions abound.

The StB files, as currently archived in and made accessible by the ABS, are frequently incomplete in that the StB destroyed many documents within the files and kept only what they considered at the time to be instrumentally valuable.[41] Many informers' reports submitted to the StB were shredded through routine operations

[34] Zdena Salivarová-Škvorecká, *Osočení: Dopisy lidí ze senamu* (Sixty-Eight Publishers 1993).

[35] Josef Škvorecký, *Two Murders in My Double Life* (Farrar, Straus & Giroux 2001) 21.

[36] Martin Kovanic, 'Institutes of Memory in Slovakia and the Czech Republic: What Kind of Memory?' in Apor, Horváth, and Mark (eds), *Secret Agents and the Memory of Everyday Collaboration in Communist Eastern Europe* (n 15) 96 (citing the Stenographic report of the 13th session of the Chamber of Deputies of the Czech Republic from 16 March 2007). One former StB officer with whom we spoke rejected the possibility of complete fabrication of information included in the StB files. According to this former officer, rampant fabrication would have been detected through the StB's internal review system, especially if it were to occur on a long-term basis. This officer acknowledged the practice of reporting hearsay or information gathered informally, such as from friends or overheard in a pub, as if an informer reported it directly, particularly when it came to reports on the 'general mood in the population'. Informal conversation with former StB officer, Brno, Czech Republic, 26 October 2021.

[37] Jan Křen, 'Dokumenty StB jako pramen poznání minulosti' (2005) 12(3–4) Soudobé Dějiny 708, 710.

[38] ibid 709 (citing Pavel Žáček). See also Ptáčníková, 'Aspekty odpovědnosti archivářů' (n 24) 32. See also generally Miller, *The Stasi Files Unveiled* (n 7) 14–15 (remarking that the contents of the Stasi files were largely 'truthful'). StB officers undoubtedly approached their job differently: Some would have been more assiduous and hence sought to corroborate more extensively, while others may simply have been more permissive, disinterested, or lazy.

[39] Prokop Tomek, 'Svazek StB jak historický pramen' (2005) 12(1) Soudobé Dějiny 208, 214.

[40] Miller, *The Stasi Files Unveiled* (n 7) 131 (writing, within the context of East Germany, that 'the histories in the files of those who worked as informers allow only a disjointed and fragmented reconstruction of past events').

[41] The StB did so for operational imperatives and out of concern over sufficient storage space. Pavel Žáček, 'Registrace, vedení a archivace svazků ve směrnicích čs. komunistické rozvědky' (2006) Paměť národa 57, 65; Pavel Žáček, 'Agenturně-operativní svazky Státní bezpečnosti a jejich registrace, 1954–1957' (2005) Paměť národa 6, 15.

during the Communist years. All the files we have seen nonetheless contain at least some, and at times fairly extensive, administrative records of cooperation describing and evaluating a particular informer (including how the cooperation began and ended) and also reams of content that informers served up to StB officers (including investigation reports on targets and potential new informers). Hence, even though some of the materials, including informers' reports, may have been destroyed, voluminous materials remain in the files with which we could work.

Additionally, immediately following the 1989 Velvet Revolution, the StB destroyed a large number of files—in particular those of active cases (ongoing operations) and documents considered sensitive—so that the new regime could not get hold of them. The precise extent to which illegal shredding or destruction of documents by the StB hurriedly occurred at the end of 1989 and the beginning of 1990 remains unconfirmed, but current estimates suggest that somewhere between 36 per cent and 44 per cent of informer files were destroyed.[42] In this respect, as well, the StB files now stored in the ABS and open to the public are incomplete and not fully representative of the population of all informers.

Scholars Péter Apor and Sándor Horváth nonetheless affirm the overall scholarly pertinence of Communist secret police archives as contributing epistemologically to what is known about informing: '[T]he stories revealed by these archives can in fact be used to demonstrate ... the everyday nature of collaboration, while also offering insights into how these regimes were able to survive for so long.'[43] Apor and Horváth add that, 'instead of examining the kinds of *truths* portrayed or revealed by the reports held in the secret police archives, we consider[] the kinds of social models and narrative modes on which the reports themselves were based.'[44] They note that their research:

> examine[s] the secret police archives not simply as storage sites of information, but also as agents in the production of knowledge and the construction of the recent past ... The files in the secret police archives, if read as dialogues between citizens and the party state ..., provide unusually intriguing insights ....[45]

We are firmly guided by Apor and Horváth's viewpoint. For us, therefore, the microscopic accuracies ('facts') matter less than what can inductively and indicatively be traced through the archived files about how individuals approached the act and process of informing in Communist Czechoslovakia. In our view, the files are not to be dismissed as irrelevant, vapid, or corroded. They provide a colourful

[42] Pavel Žáček, 'Secret Services in Murky Times' (2004) 1 The New Presence 19, 20.

[43] Péter Apor and Sándor Horváth, 'Conclusion' in Apor, Horváth, and Mark (eds), *Secret Agents and the Memory of Everyday Collaboration in Communist Eastern Europe* (n 15) 329.

[44] ibid 330.

[45] ibid 332–33.

picture of the internal workings of a murky and powerful organization. They shed light on what information the StB considered salient. They reveal the hydraulics and pneumatics of the surveillance state and recount the rawness of discursive interactions between the secret police and the public. They illuminate how the StB constructed its space within Communist society. Furthermore, the archived files offer fascinating vignettes of life as lived in Czechoslovakia during the Cold War. These files are epistemologically useful companions to official oral history projects that have been conducted to capture individual life stories as narrated by former informers, Communist Party officials, political prisoners, and persecuted individuals.[46] StB file-stories also are valuable companion sources to academic oral history projects that feature ordinary citizens' unspooling what life was like in Communist Czechoslovakia and how thirty years later Czechs feel about that life.[47] In our book, we accord considerable attention to both categories—official and academic—of oral history projects.

As researchers, while being aware of and sensitive to potential biases and distortions, we also remain committed to our position that the sources of information that we unpack add considerable value to theory, policy, and practice. As historian Anton de Baets claims, 'even from the most distorted files enough truth can be squeezed to tell us something about … the cast of mind'.[48] Alison Lewis similarly argues that East German Stasi files 'offer unprecedented insights into the secret world of informers' lives'.[49] Lewis elaborates how these files

[46] The oral history project *Paměť národa* (translated officially as Memory of Nations) is conducted by the non-governmental organization Post Bellum, in cooperation with Czech Radio and the official Institute for the Study of Totalitarian Regimes. Paměť národa, Memory of Nations, 'Witness Database' (*Memory of Nations*, 2023) <https://www.memoryofnations.eu/en/archive> accessed 22 January 2023. For a critique of such official memory projects, see Muriel Blaive, 'Sanctimony as a Distortion of the Past and a Poison of the Future' (*Dénik Referendum*, 28 July 2020) <https://denikreferendum.cz/clanek/31487-sanctimony-as-a-distortion-of-the-past-and-a-poison-of-the-future> accessed 13 July 2023 (noting in the Czech context that '[t]he more time passes, the more collective memories are reconstructed in accordance to the present political and intellectual climate').

[47] Vaněk and Mücke, *Velvet Revolutions* (n 11). Their book is 'based on the analysis and interpretation' of the responses of 'about 300' interviewees 'born roughly between 1935 and 1955'. Vaněk and Mücke, *Velvet Revolutions* (n 11) 7. The interviewed 'sources' are listed by name with a brief biography in an appendix (very few are anonymized). This otherwise compendious book barely mentions informing or the StB in any salient form, thereby further signalling the understudied place of the informer.

[48] Anton De Baets, 'The Dictator's Secret Archives: Rationales for Their Creation, Destruction, and Disclosure' in Alasdair MacDonald and Arend H Huussen Jr (eds), *Scholarly Environments: Centres of Learning and Institutional Contexts* 1600–1960 (Peeters 2004) 184. British historian Timothy Garton Ash, who bases some of his writing on his own Stasi file and his personal diaries from his time in East Germany, emphasizes the need for critical engagement with secret police files and notes 'there is a truth that can be found. Not a single, absolute Truth with a capital "T" but still a real and important one.' Timothy Garton Ash, 'Trial, Purges, and History Lessons' in Zbyněk Baladrán and Vít Havránek (eds), *Atlas of Transformation* (Tranzit 2011) <http://monumenttotransformation.org/atlas-of-transformation/html/h/history/trials-purges-and-history-lessons-timothy-garton-ash.html> accessed 16 September 2023.

[49] Lewis, *A State of Secrecy* (n 7) xxix.

> open a window onto the lives and minds of informers as well as victims we would not otherwise have. With their painful attention to details such as dates, places, addresses, and names, the files are rich sources of motivations, habitus, actions, and behaviors. They make it possible to track the changing motivation of informers and the personal impact of coercion on informants' dispositions.[50]

Our perspective aligns with that of Lewis. For us, the StB files offer insights into the informer–officer relationship, *why* and *how* people spoke to the secret police, and *what motivated* them in these iterated interactions. Microscopic facticity of the files therefore matters less to us than what can be gleaned from the files about the cadence, rhythm, provenance, and dynamic dialogic drivers of the collaborative conversation, as well as the balance between dispositional idiosyncrasies and situational constraints. Even if the reported facts might be untrue, fabricated, exaggerated, or minimized, we remain steadfast in our conviction that the ways in which the StB related to their informers, and in which informers related to the StB, can be discerned from the files.

While the StB was not particularly prone to record the feelings of their informers, the compendious, meticulous, and diaristic nature of the files lends itself to a scholarly read that reveals currents and eddies of emotion and sentiment. This is a cutting-edge aspect of our project. Assuredly, our book does not aim to be representative of each and every informer who ended up working with the StB, nor all possible or conceivable factors that might have motivated their actions. This book is not an exercise in psychotherapy or psychoanalysis. Based on what is recorded in their StB files, we infer what might have motivated informers to interact with the StB and inquire what all this might mean for transitional justice.

Initially, we chose, read, and reviewed the files of approximately 100 different informers.[51] We then mindfully selected twenty-three for extensive granular distillation. Each of these twenty-three files was read *in toto* by one of the authors and a research assistant—who are both native Czech speakers with proficiency in Slovak—and who summarized the contents (nearly all written in Czech, and on very rare occasion in Slovak) and then translated that summary from Czech to English.[52] We then selected six informers whose file-stories we narratively present in Chapter 4 of this book. The file-stories of the other seventeen informers, however, are extensively referenced in this book—thereby forming part of the dataset—and are integrally included in an accessible online educational site paired with our book.[53]

[50] ibid xxx.

[51] For further details on our methodology, Chapter 4, 'Informer File-Stories' (opening section) and Chapter 5, Section I, 'Overview'.

[52] All translations from Czech- (and on rare occasion Slovak-) language secondary sources into English have been made directly by one of the co-authors who is fluent in both Czech and English and highly proficient in Slovak.

[53] See <https://www.nscr.nl/Informers-Up-Close>.

We intentionally selected file-stories of informers active during different time periods throughout the Communist regime and embodying diverse personal backgrounds. We explicitly took the following variables into account in our case selection of the twenty-three informers: total length of time the informer cooperated with the StB (ranging from three to thirty-seven years); socio-economic status; occupation; gender; Communist Party membership (or lack thereof); family situation; foreign ties or family members abroad; professed reasons for recruitment; stipulated grounds for termination of the informer relationship; who or which groups the informer was tasked to target, if any; and whether the informer had previous entanglements with the law. Our selection was thus purposive. Our analysis also extensively draws from sources beyond the files we have distilled. We reference the contents of some files we had reviewed and ultimately decided not to select for detailed distillation. We also incorporate voluminous secondary sources, oral history projects, and informal discussions. We also weave in content from Czech fiction, literature, cinema, architecture, and museums.[54]

The StB files reflect patriarchy notwithstanding Communist visions of gender equality. Virtually all StB officers were men. Roughly 10 per cent of informers were women.[55] Hence, informers were not representatively drawn from the population as a whole. In order to surface and give voice inclusively to the experiences of women informers, we have elected to slightly overrepresent the number of profiles of women informers in our database.[56]

Gendered language tends to suffuse bits and pieces of the files. This language is reductive—men or women—with no mention of identity beyond this binary. One frequent thread is the uncritical depiction of men as 'womanizers' and 'enjoying young girls' (including sex workers). Discussion of seemingly consensual extramarital affairs pervades the files in the case of both men and women informers, yet the files also reveal concern on the part of the StB officers about adulterous conduct. The files document instances in which StB officers counselled the informer, often

[54] On this note, we are influenced by Ron Dudai, who notes in the case of his own work: 'Throughout the text, I occasionally draw illustrations of attitudes to informing in Northern Ireland from popular culture, mainly novels.... Novels can at times capture societal and political themes in transitional societies such as Northern Ireland more effectively than academic work.' Dudai, *Penality in the Underground* (n 7) 22.

[55] David, *Communists and Their Victims* (n 21) 38–39; see also Chapter 2, Section III.A, 'The StB's Work, Worth, and Network' of this book. In East Germany, Miller reports that '[f]emales were not highly represented in the Stasi's network of unofficial helpers', as 80 to 90 per cent of them were male. Miller, *The Stasi Files Unveiled* (n 7) 19. Miller posits this is because of patriarchal structures in society along with 'concern that officers [overwhelmingly male, as was also the case in the StB] might become intimately involved with the females in their charge and so run the risk of betraying confidential information'. Miller, *The Stasi Files Unveiled* (n 7) 20.

[56] For discussion of gender in the anti-Communist resistance, see Celia Donert, 'Gendering Normalisation: Citizenship in Czechoslovakia During Late Socialism' in McDermott and Stibbe (eds), *Czechoslovakia and Eastern Europe in the Era of Normalisation* (n 13) 186 (noting that 'the influence of conservative notions of masculinity and femininity in normalized Czechoslovakia were nowhere as significant as in the dissident movement associated with Charter 77').

gently, about working harder on their marriages. Homophobic references and slurs appear in the files as well. Discussions of alcoholism do not couch this as a disease but rather as a weakness or fault; threads of drunkenness and debauchery abound throughout the files. Insofar as we frequently cite directly from the archived files, gendered, sexist, and homophobic language on occasion is uploaded into the descriptive part of the book. We have decided to retain the original language of the files. On rare occasion, the files also reflect racist attitudes and anti-racist responses, notably when mention is made of immigrants arriving to Czechoslovakia from different Communist countries on various continents at that time. The files reveal criticism by StB officers of racist statements made by informers and dismissiveness towards the values of informers who made such statements.

In order not to inflict additional harm upon individuals, including mortification of family members, and to respect principles of ethical archival research,[57] we have pseudonymized our text. We have, therefore, not used the real names of individual informers but rather have opted to use their cover names. Furthermore, we use only initials or first names of other persons appearing in the files and omit any other identifying information, such as exact places (eg addresses) or personal dates (including dates of birth or marriage), and hence in these instances anonymize (unless an informer came forward and publicly discussed their cooperation with the StB in an oral history project). It is important to note, however, that all the information that we have carefully distilled and either pseudonymized or anonymized is publicly accessible in full detail in the ABS. Hence, our goal is a personal and professional ethical sensibility, namely, not to additionally harm informers or their families and to attain the highest level of integrity in scholarly research. We are also mindful of the concerns we raise in Chapter 6 regarding the cruelties that can arise when secret police files are opened up as public goods—notably in an era of online access and social media. It is our hope that our work, by pushing back against the political tendency to scapegoat and ostracize informers, might help advance more sophisticated and inclusive transitional approaches to rectify the pain that informers simultaneously endure and cause for many others.

IV. (E)motions and Human Behaviour

One final icebreaker remains. What do we mean by emotion?

The word 'emotion' stems from the Latin *movere*, meaning 'to move'.[58] In the sixteenth century, the French word '*émotion*' referred primarily to social movement,

[57] Marek Tesar, 'Ethics and Truth in Archival Research' (2015) 44(1) History of Education 101.

[58] Oxford Advanced Learner's Dictionaries, the entry 'Emotion Noun', 'Word Origin' (*Oxford Learner's Dictionaries*, 2023) <https://www.oxfordlearnersdictionaries.com/definition/english/emotion> accessed 18 July 2023.

public disturbance, and agitation. Thus, *émotion* semantically captured sentiments and movements among people, not just the inner feelings of an individual. In English, the word 'emotion' has existed since the seventeenth century (originating from French). In a similar vein, it initially denoted a physical disturbance. Only in the early 1800s did the modern concept of emotion referring to inner feelings enter common parlance. Before then, such inner states were referred to variously as 'appetites', 'passions', 'affections', or 'sentiments'.[59]

While we do not wish to rehash debates about the relationship between reason and emotion,[60] a brief stage-setting discussion might be helpful. For starters, scholars still lack consensus with regard to defining and understanding emotions.[61] For cognitivists, emotions root in judgment, perception, and thoughts: '[T]here is always cognition in emotion ... [and] ... cognitive appraisals ... cause emotions to arise.'[62] For non-cognitivists, emotions flow independently from our thoughts. In other words, emotions are taken as sensory experiences of the world and automatic body reflexes separate from reason. According to Brudholm and Lang, however:

> [the] contrast between [the] cognitivist and non-cognitivist conceptions of emotion is overdrawn. Most of the time, [both] agree that emotions (or affects) are meaningful; that they represent something beyond themselves ..., [they] affect our way of thinking and make us want to act in particular ways.[63]

In short, we adopt the following working definition:

> Emotions are a set of evaluative and motivational processes, distributed throughout the brain, that assist us in appraising and reacting to stimuli and that are formed, interpreted, and communicated in social and cultural context ... They are dynamic processes that are integral to decision making.[64]

[59] Thomas Dixon, '"Emotion": The History of a Keyword in Crisis' (2012) 4(4) Emotion Rev 338.

[60] Renata Grossi, 'Understanding Law and Emotion' (2015) 7(1) Emotion Rev 55, 55 ('While Plato saw emotions as obstructions to the attainment of our true rational selves, Aristotle believed that a true understanding of the world around us could not be achieved without reference to our emotions.'). See also David Hume, *A Treatise of Human Nature* (authored 1739–1740, Dover 2003) (contending that moral assessment hinges significantly on sentiment and feeling, not only rationality).

[61] Andrew Ortony, 'Are All "Basic Emotions" Emotions? A Problem for the (Basic) Emotions Construct' (2022) 17(1) Perspectives on Psychological Science 49.

[62] Thomas Brudholm and Johannes Lang, 'Introduction: Emotions and Mass Atrocity' in Thomas Brudholm and Johannes Lang (eds), *Emotions and Mass Atrocity: Philosophical and Theoretical Explorations* (CUP 2019) 5; see also Caroll E Izard, 'Form and Functions of Emotions: Matters of Emotion-Cognition Interactions' (2011) 3(4) Emotion Rev 371, 371.

[63] Brudholm and Lang, 'Introduction' (n 62) 6. According to Ortony, 'for a mental state to be an emotion, it must possess at least the following three features: It must be *intentional* (i.e., *about* something), it must be *valenced* (i.e., positive or negative), and it must be *conscious* (i.e., experienced)'. Ortony, 'Basic Emotions' (n 61) 51. Discussion of the differences and overlaps between emotion, mood, affect, and temperament lies beyond the scope of our book.

[64] Susan A Bandes and Jeremy A Blumenthal, 'Emotion and the Law' (2012) 8 Annual Rev of L and Social Science 161, 163–64.

We also see emotions as 'a direct product of evolutionary biology' that 'enables humans to use them as tools which, combined with logic, can assist in identifying and resolving pressing problems'.[65]

Emotions colour how humans see and experience things, including other humans. Emotions guide how individuals act and react to situations and happenings around them. Emotions are 'complex experiences of consciousness, bodily sensations and behaviour that reflect the personal significance of a thing, event, or a state of affairs'.[66] They can serve as prompts for instrumental action.[67] Emotions, despite being subjective, transcend the inner self and manifest themselves to the outside world, for instance, in facial expressions, mannerisms, and through words.[68] They play 'a key role in defining and regulating our relationships with others and, more generally, with the environment surrounding us'.[69] Emotions thereby become *(e)motions* since they propel movement and action—motion—in terms of how people act. Indeed, according to phenomenologist Maurice Merleau-Ponty, emotions are 'not psychic facts hidden at the bottom of another's consciousness: they are types of behaviour or styles of conduct which are visible from the outside'.[70] Anna Spain Bradley chimes in by unpacking how emotions contour exercises of human choice.[71]

Obviously, for the purposes of our book, we cannot peek into the minds of informers. We cannot ask them how or what they felt while informing.[72] We cannot see and assess their facial expressions and gestures. We cannot hear their words. Instead, as researchers, we avail ourselves of the secret police files to gesture towards the emotions that might have driven informers to engage (and continue—or eschew and resist—engaging) with StB officers. Because of the authorial positionality of the StB files, all we can do is infer which emotions animated informers based on how StB officers represented them in the reports and on how others described them to the StB. We therefore surmise the consciousness of emotions in informing based on what could 'be seen from the outside', based on how

[65] Jonathan Doak, 'The Therapeutic Dimension of Transitional Justice: Emotional Repair and Victim Satisfaction in "International Trials and Truth Commissions"' 11 Intl Crim L Rev 263, 267.

[66] Robert C Solomon, 'Emotions (psychology)' (*Encyclopedia Britannica*, 21 March 2023) <https://www.britannica.com/science/emotion> accessed 23 April 2023.

[67] Guido HE Gendolla, 'Comment: Do Emotions Influence Action? Of Course—They Are Hypo-Phenomena of Motivation' (2017) 9(4) Emotion Rev 348.

[68] Lisa Feldman Barrett, *How Emotions Are Made, The Secret Life of the Brain* (Pan Books 2017) 4.

[69] Claudia Marinetti and others, 'Emotions in Social Interactions: Unfolding Emotional Experience' in Paolo Petta, Catherine Pelachaud, and Roddy Cowie (eds), *Emotion-Oriented Systems: The Humaine Handbook* (Springer 2011) 31.

[70] Thomas Brudholm and Birgitte Schepelern Johansen, 'Pondering Hatred' in Brudholm and Lang (eds), *Emotions and Mass Atrocity* (n 62) 98 (quoting Maurice Merleau-Ponty, *Sense and Non-Sense* (Northwestern University Press 1964) xii–xiii).

[71] Anna Spain Bradley, *Human Choice in International Law* (CUP 2021) 33.

[72] Some informers reveal these sentiments, in retrospect, in official oral history projects, but most do not. Many informers have passed away, including already during the Communist years.

informers 'turned ... toward the world, turned toward things' in 'a relation to the world',[73] as recorded by StB officers in the secret collaborator files.

In this respect, our book is impressionistic. We note that the StB did, on occasion, record the perceived emotions of its informers. Mostly, however, the StB did not. Hence, we read the StB files as texts of social performance and extract therefrom our perceptions of the emotions, sentiments, and motivations that catalysed and fuelled informing as a social practice. We thereby 'locate [emotions] in actions, words, or situations'[74] as chronicled on hand- and type-written pages in the StB files. What is more, how StB officers acted, or did not act, upon whatever information they recorded in the file also gestures towards their own emotional reactions.

To recap, then, our goal is to identify the emotions that drive and animate behaviour, specifically, informing and talking to the secret police. This book is about how to understand why informing happens. On this note, we posit the notion of *(e)motions*, namely, emotional movement that propels human action. We deploy this notion to help elucidate the social practice of informing and why some Czechoslovaks did it. Very little work has been undertaken in this space. As Muriel Blaive noted in 2022, '[t]o date, there is no Czech historical study of collaboration as a social practice under communism'.[75] We hope to help redress this void. We read the file-stories in a way that pulls out recurrent motivations that we believe can be classed as (e)motional in nature. We present four in particular—*fear, desire, resentment*, and *devotion*—as catalysts and drivers of informing.

We aim to contribute to the aetiology of informing in Communist Czechoslovakia and, in turn, to the epistemology—namely, from where do we know what we think we know—of informing more generally. We propose an 'emotionally intelligent'[76] approach to conceptualize the dispositional, interactive, and situational dynamics that underpin why people spoke about others to the secret police. To be clear, we do not suggest that an emotions lens is the *only* or the *best* way to think about informing. We posit that it is *a* way—one that we believe has considerable potential to better 'get' informing by 'getting closer' to informers—and one that, to date, has been underdeveloped.

[73] Joel Krueger and Søren Overgaard, 'Seeing Subjectivity: Defending a Perceptual Account of Other Minds' in Sofia Miguens and Gerhard Preyer (eds), *Consciousness and Subjectivity* (De Gruyter 2012) 299 n 2 (citing Maurice Merleau-Ponty, *The Primacy of Perception, and Other Essays on Phenomenological Psychology, the Philosophy of Art, History, and Politics*, James M Edie (ed), William Cobb (tr) (Northwestern University Press 1964). See also Merleau-Ponty, *Sense and Non-Sense* (n 70) 52 ('emotion is not an ... internal fact but rather a variation in our relations with others and the world').

[74] Brudholm and Schepelern Johansen, 'Pondering Hatred' (n 70) 99.

[75] Muriel Blaive, 'An Impossible Reconciliation: National (Heroic) Memory and Individual Identity in the Czech Republic' (*Politika*, 2 April 2022) <https://www.politika.io/en/article/an-impossible-reconciliation> accessed 3 March 2023, para 40.

[76] Doak, 'The Therapeutic Dimension of Transitional Justice' (n 65) 267.

We accordingly endeavour to bring some measure of behavioural realism to why people spoke to and engaged with the StB.[77] We underscore the salience of an ontological perspective in reckoning with human behaviour; in other words, to grasp human nature and then reflect upon how institutions can respond thereto.[78] Emotions seem to be central to the entire collective dynamic of the industrialization and bureaucratization of informing in Communist Czechoslovakia. We conclude that, when it comes to informers in Communist Czechoslovakia, there is much more going on than displays of dutiful and loyal citizenship. Indeed, multiple emotions are in play at the same time and at different times among informers and within the same informer. We think this granularity, ferment, change, and messiness matter enormously. This is why we present six informer file-stories in Chapter 4 in a detailed narrative format, and why we include references to many other informers throughout the entire book. As we discuss in Chapter 6, transitional justice would do well to recognize the full panoply of diverse emotional motivations of informers and their handlers in all of their hues. Such recognition would augment the emotional quotient (EQ, so to speak) of transitional justice interventions.

V. Roadmap

Following from this introduction, this book continues with a pair of chapters that offer contextual background to situate readers who may not be well-versed in Czech and Czechoslovak history or political transition. These chapters also surface crucial dynamics.

Chapter 2 provides background on the history of the StB. This chapter focuses on StB officers as securocrats. It presents the formalities and steps in the creation and dissolution of cooperation agreements between informers and StB officers. Considerable details are proffered on the various categories of informers, methods of recruitment, and how the StB as an agency adapted to changing circumstances over time. This chapter also reassesses the post-Communist narrative of the putative dissonance between state and society in the Communist years.

Chapter 3 unveils the modalities of transitional justice that were pursued in Czechoslovakia and the Czech Republic following the Velvet Revolution in 1989 that toppled the Communist state. This chapter acknowledges that, a generation later, the outcomes of transitional justice 'are disappointing for many Czechs'.[79]

[77] Bandes and Blumenthal, 'Emotion and the Law' (n 64) 162 (noting that the study of law and emotion is an effort 'to bring a measure of behavioral realism to the legal realm').
[78] For a similar approach rooted in ontological critique, see Alan Norrie, *Criminal Justice and Moral Psychology* (forthcoming, manuscript on file with the authors).
[79] David, *Communists and Their Victims* (n 21) ix.

Transitional modalities included lustration, restitution, publication of lists of collaborators, archive opening, and memory institutes; despite investigations, very few criminal trials took place. Still, the transitional process proved rather retributive when it came to informers. Czech transitional justice cast informers as dangerous loyalists and stigmatized them instead of pursuing reconciliatory goals. Political expediency was key in this regard, notably, to bolster the legitimacy of the new regime.

Chapter 4 highlights 'up close' the file-stories of six informers: Věra, Vašek, Lily, Goldfus, Volný, and Soukup. These 'high-resolution' narratives demonstrate the complexities of the relationship between state and society in Communist Czechoslovakia. They reveal the social engineering effects of the state and the participatory role of individuals. Each file-story showcases the range of (e)motions that pulled informers towards and pushed informers away from the StB and illuminates how these sentiments changed and morphed over time. In the Czechoslovak context, this 'high-resolution' portrayal unsettles 'assumptions of the homogeneity of secret collaborators that underpin the lustration and similar laws'.[80]

Chapter 5 offers a number of key observations about the social practice of informing in Communist Czechoslovakia that came to us from our 'up close' look at actual informers when triangulated with multiple secondary sources. For us, concepts such as intimacy, power, social navigation, and exchange shape the relationship between StB officers and 'their' informers. Informing blurs the line between the political and the personal. Many informers turned to the StB to leverage their private wants and actualize their immediate needs. This chapter examines the role of emotions as catalysing and then sustaining these interactional dimensions. Four emotions in particular stand out: fear, resentment, desire, and allegiance. We address each in detail. Chapter 5 invokes the file-stories to illustrate these emotions in the life-stories of informers, while also noting that StB officers, as well, expressed sentiments such as solicitude and disappointment over the course of their engagement with 'their' informers. The emotional drivers of the contact between StB officers and informers were not static. Certain cooperative relationships between informers and the StB—perhaps initially forged in fear—lasted for decades and over time became far more reciprocal and imbued with agency on the part of the informer. In the end, informers occupy liminal spaces between being victimized—often marginal, beset with personal struggles, private and health problems, vulnerable, woeful, and chronically surveilled—and being victimizers who betray and harm others, lord power over others, and inflict considerable pain on persons about whom they funnelled information to the StB.[81]

[80] ibid 33.

[81] For general discussion of 'victims who victimize' see Mark A Drumbl, 'Victims Who Victimize' (2016) 4 London Rev Intl L 217.

Chapter 6 begins with normative takeaways for transitional justice in the Czech Republic. Following the Velvet Revolution, informers were officially vilified as dangers to the new capitalist liberal democracy. They were thusly stylized in a distorted fashion, with little justification for such an assessment based on what they actually did during the Communist years or why they did it. Heterogeneity and individuality were therefore lost: a monochrome, rather than a mosaic, was spun. This scapegoating was comforting to many Czechs. Rather than reflexively accept this comfort, Chapter 6 instead interrogates it and unpacks its problematic aspects. This comfort, moreover, became tethered to the cruelties that inhere in Czech transitional justice's opening of the StB files to the public in a largely unadulterated and at times lurid fashion. Chapter 6 then pivots from the Czech experience to the place of informers in transitional justice modalities generally. Urging circumspection in this regard, this chapter argues that the marginal and liminal place of informers offers an inflective moment to curb the increasingly retributivist tendencies that infuse transitional justice best practices. Encouraging transitional justice to embrace goals of rehabilitation, reconciliation, and reintegration in the case of everyday informers—rather than ostracism and rejection—Chapter 6 proposes a heuristic that could serve as a guidepost for transitional justice mechanisms in how to speak of and think about informers.[82] The heuristic we suggest aims to promote goals of dignity.[83] It aspires to make transitional justice more transformative.

Chapter 7 concludes by recapping and uncorking new areas for scholarly inquiry. This chapter examines motivational similarities between StB informers in repressive times and informers in so-called liberal states who assist police in ordinary criminal investigations and public authorities with regulatory compliance. This chapter introduces the concept of 'just or unjust informing theory' to ruminate upon public perceptions of individuals who help authorities in liberal states enforce laws by informing on individuals who break the law. This, then, returns the book full circle to the complexity of informing, the panoply of the various 'kinds' of informing, and the selectivity and conditionality of public derision.

VI. Conclusion

Our innovative work with the StB files, and our novel lens of (e)motions, diversifies extant scholarly work about why and how individuals spoke to the secret

[82] We concur with political scientist Roman David who, writing in the Czech context, concludes that '[w]ithout reconciliation, transitional justice is just a power game with new actors in the same role of exclusion'. Roman David, 'Transitional Justice Effects in the Czech Republic' in Stan and Nedelsky, *Post-Communist Transitional Justice* (n 22) 114.

[83] On dignity, see eg Juan Espíndola Mata, *Transitional Justice After German Reunification: Exposing Unofficial Collaborators* (CUP 2015).

police, while also complexifying other representational narratives, including those proffered by transitional justice actors and successor state officials. We believe our book makes an important contribution to a number of disciplines beyond Czech area studies. One is perpetrator and victim studies, a second is social science research on political violence generally. Both of these fields of inquiry tend to skip over informers and the harms they cause. A third domain is historical scholarship (including memory and trauma research) in which analysis dealing with everyday collaboration also is limited. Another crucial area to which we believe we meaningfully contribute is transitional justice and accountability studies. We feel that our book on informers 'up close' would bring transitional justice 'closer to' informers and, hence, augment effectiveness in particular on the reconciliatory front. Finally, we maintain that our book can be of interest to archivists, museum curators, outreach staff at international courts and national accountability modalities, as well as specialists in recording and preserving memory. Insofar as we believe our book could additionally serve as a valuable teaching tool, we have—as mentioned earlier—created a companion website (https://www.nscr.nl/Informers-Up-Close) for such purposes.

2

History of Communist Czechoslovakia and Its Secret Police

In a society of working people that has removed exploitation of one person by another, development and interests of each of its members are in accordance with development and interests of the whole society. The rights, freedoms, and duties of citizens therefore serve their free, versatile advance and the realization of their full potential and, at the same time, consolidation and development of the socialist society.

Constitution of Czechoslovak Socialist Republic,
11 July 1960, Article 19

This chapter presents a condensed survey of the history of Czechoslovakia from the 1948 Communist takeover to the 1989 Velvet Revolution. It focuses on the StB and the network of informers upon which it relied and through which it operated.

Informers and collaborators helped entrench Communist rule. That said, the Communist Party's grip over society ebbed, flowed, surged, receded, and stagnated through time.

Authoritarian regimes are neither fissiparous nor monolithic: levels of top-down repression and bottom-up engagement—along with resistance and cynicism—wax and wane. Czechoslovakia is no exception. Indeed, '[t]he [Czechoslovak] regime typically had to secure its (slender/transient/fragile) legitimacy through complex forms of negotiation and persuasion rather than relying on straightforward societal obedience toward police and governmental authority'.[1] Accordingly, the StB—one of the regime's main support pillars—operated differently amid various historical periods.

The Czechoslovak Communist Party assumed power in February 1948. In its first governance phase, sired in that frigid winter, the Party consolidated authority and promptly came to wield it like a cudgel. This phase is the Stalinist period (1948–1956). The fight against 'class enemies' and 'enemies of the state' as a necessary stage

[1] Matthew Stibbe and Kevin McDermott, 'Czechoslovakia and Eastern Europe in the Era of Normalisation' in Kevin McDermott and Matthew Stibbe (eds), *Czechoslovakia and Eastern Europe in the Era of Normalisation 1969–1989* (Palgrave Macmillan 2022) 11.

Informers Up Close. Mark A. Drumbl and Barbora Holá, Oxford University Press.
 DOI: 10.1093/oso/9780192855138.003.0002

of 'progress' towards Communist society peaked during these years. Deploying extensive repression and violence, the Party (and the StB as one of its main tools) sought to eradicate real and imagined opposition. However, repressive fierceness began to abate by the end of the 1950s as the Communist Party gradually eased its stranglehold over society.

In 1960, the 'victory of socialism' was officially declared in the Czechoslovak Constitution. Society blossomed during the so-called Golden 60s. Czechoslovaks enjoyed an increased quality of life. This relative liberalization culminated in the 'Prague Spring' of 1968. At this point, however, things went too far, too fast, and ultimately turned tragic. Aspirations for 'socialism with a human face' and all the freedoms that it had incubated were abruptly dashed in August 1968 when the armies of the Warsaw Pact invaded Czechoslovakia. Disillusion ensued. Anomie and cynicism clouded the subsequent twenty years. The Party once again ratcheted up its surveillance. Although Marxist-Leninist ideology became largely irrelevant (and even mocked), the tentacles of government endured. The regime and all it entailed simply became 'normalized'. That said, in 1989 the Communist regime crumbled and rapidly collapsed.

I. The Communist State and Its Dénouement

Czechoslovakia emerged as an independent state at the end of the First World War following the dissolution of the Austro-Hungarian Empire. The Communist Party of Czechoslovakia (*Komunistická strana Československa*, KSČ) was founded in 1921. The KSČ was quite popular: At the time, it was one of the largest Communist parties in the world, garnering nearly a million votes (13.2 per cent of the electorate) in the 1925 parliamentary election—these totals sufficed to place it second among official parliamentary representation. Pursuant to the 1938 Munich Agreement—concluded among Germany, France, the United Kingdom, and Italy in the *Führerbau* in Munich (Figure 2.1)—parts of Czechoslovakia bordering Germany (the *Sudetenland*) were annexed to the Third Reich. Here, British Prime Minister Neville Chamberlain's appeasement strategy was in full force. Czechoslovakia was essentially abandoned by the West and primed for being overrun by the Nazis.

The Nazis banned the KSČ during their occupation of the remaining Czech lands between 1939 and 1945. In these wretched years, widespread killings of Jews, Czechoslovak civilians, and resisters raged throughout the country. The brutalities of the Nazi occupation cast a long shadow over Czechoslovak history, literature, and politics.[2] The KSČ re-entered electoral life after the Soviet and US armies

[2] For literary treatment of life during the Nazi occupation of Czechoslovakia, see Bohumil Hrabal, *Closely Watched Trains* (authored 1965, Edith Pargeter tr, Penguin 2017 (a tale of sabotage and resistance with tongue-in-cheek humour); Zdeněk Jirotka, *Saturnin* (authored 1942, Mark Corner tr, Karolinum Press 2016) (unwrapping the relationship between a man and his butler and their maintaining identity

Figure 2.1 The Führerbau, where the Munich Agreement was signed on 29 September 1938, which today houses a music and theatre school. Photograph taken by the authors (Munich, 2023).

liberated Czechoslovakia in 1945. In 1946, the KSČ emerged as the largest party in the Interim National Assembly, receiving over 30 per cent of the vote. Following the Second World War, the Communists also progressively acquired control over the security apparatus, including the StB and the army, both of which proved indispensable to their future ability to govern.[3]

By the end of 1948, the KSČ—with 2 million members—was the largest Communist organization in Europe outside the USSR.[4] Exploiting both

by ignoring the Nazi occupation and enjoying nature with friends, hiking in the mountains, collecting mushrooms, wandering through pine forests, playing whist, and partaking in convivial meals); Ladislav Fuks, *The Cremator* (authored 1966, Eva M Kandler tr, Karolinum Press 2016)) (a wrenching and ghoulish tale of collaboration and shape-shifting and the extremism of a Prague doctor murdering his own family members). *Saturnin*'s popularity grew after the Second World War in that many Czechs found solace in its pages about sustaining Czechness and identity during the Communist years.

[3] Karel Kaplan, *Protistátní Bezpečnost, 1945–1948 Historie vzniku a působení StB jako mocenského nástroje KSČ* (Plus 2015).

[4] Immediately following the KSČ's assumption of power, hundreds of thousands of members of non-Communist parties reinvented themselves and joined the KSČ. For discussion on the popularity of the Communist Party in the 1940s, see Kevin McDermott, *Communist Czechoslovakia, 1945–1989* (Palgrave Macmillan 2015) 50, 90, 118.

constitutional and unconstitutional means, the KSČ seized power in 'the Victorious February' of 1948. That year, Klement Gottwald, its Secretary-General, became Prime Minister. Gottwald remained in that position until 1953.

In the aftermath of the Second World War, many Czech Germans were killed in the name of collective guilt; a further 2.4 million were expelled from the country.[5] Wide swathes of their property was confiscated. This mass deportation—coupled with the Nazi eliminationism of Czechoslovak Jews—significantly altered the ethnic and linguistic composition of the country.[6]

Czechoslovak post-war society—crushed, desensitized, and ravaged by Nazi atrocities and repression—was eager to punish not only the Germans but also any Czechoslovaks who, in one way or another, were seen as having collaborated with the Nazi regime. 'Retribution trials' dealing with Nazi officials and their Czechoslovak collaborators were zealously implemented.[7] Between 1945 and 1948, over 100,000 suspected collaborators were prosecuted. Over 30,000 individuals were convicted by hastily convened Extraordinary Peoples' Courts. Seven hundred and sixty-eight death sentences were issued, 95 per cent of which were enforced.[8] The expulsion of Germans and retribution trials were among the means used by the KSČ 'to eradicate class and ideological enemies'.[9]

Following their takeover of power in 1948, the Communists—as a single ruling party—ushered in a period of 'Stalinization' during which the country slipped even deeper into the Soviet sphere of influence. This period was by far the most repressive phase of the Communist reign, despite the fact that the Communists simultaneously benefitted from a large number of fervent ideological devotees, notably among youths, workers, and lower classes. At the time, considerable hope, optimism, and ardour for a workers' revolution fuelled the construction of an aspirationally just and fair Communist society.[10] This enthusiasm paradoxically coexisted with brutality, fear, and state intrusions into the daily lives of citizens.

Mass lustrations were implemented to eliminate 'reactionist elements' (eg individuals who failed to identify with the new Communist regime). Thousands of people were fired from their jobs because they were determined to have poor relations with the people's democracy. These purges were widespread: students were expelled from their classes and professors were barred from lecturing. Twenty-seven per cent of officers were ousted from the armed forces, particularly and poignantly those who had fought alongside the Western powers against Nazism during the

[5] ibid 44–45.

[6] McDermott provides considerable detail regarding the ethnic purification that occurred in Czechoslovakia after the Second World War—including the murder of Jews, expatriations, and the mass expulsions of Germans—and how this too helped consolidate Communism. ibid 44–47.

[7] ibid 46.

[8] Jan Rychlík, *Československo v období socialismu 1945–1989* (Vyšehrad 2020) 56.

[9] McDermott, *Communist Czechoslovakia* (n 4) 46.

[10] Rychlík, *Československo v období socialismu* (n 8) 81–82, 122–32. Of course, some Czechoslovaks rejected the system. Repression was swift and heavy-handed.

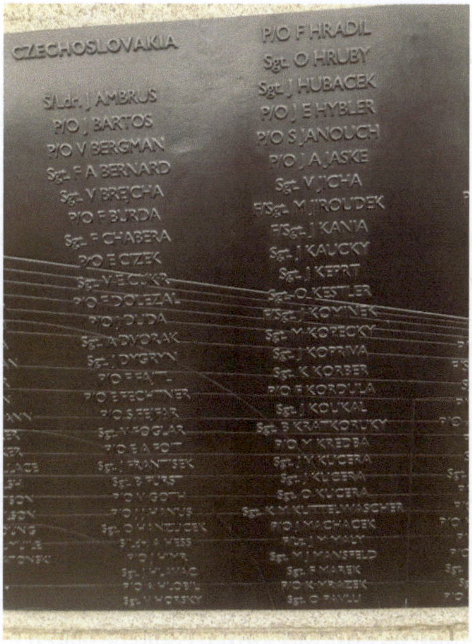

Figure 2.2 The Battle of Britain Memorial in London, listing the names of RAF pilots, including eighty-eight Czechoslovaks. Photograph taken by the authors (London, 2020).

Second World War.[11] Repatriated aviators from the Czechoslovak squadrons of the British Royal Air Force were persecuted and prosecuted. The names of some of these courageous aviators have been inscribed on the Battle of Britain Monument perched alongside the Thames River in London (Figure 2.2).

All this while, the borders to the West were shut. Citizens could not obtain a passport. They could not travel. Cultural expression was strictly regulated by the Party: only works aligning with 'social realism' were officially permitted. The elimination of private ownership and forced collectivization of commercial interests proceeded in tandem with the introduction of a planned economy. In addition to economic reforms and currency devaluation, authorities marshalled the judicial system to ensure citizen obedience with the regime.

Czechoslovak courts had been retooled in the immediate aftermath of the Communist takeover. Judges and prosecutors were removed while new 'workers cadres' became incorporated into the system. These cadres were the products of a hastily conceived institute known as the School of Law for the Workers.[12] This rebooted judicial system hosted show trials against perceived 'enemies' in the

[11] ibid, 70–71.

[12] Petr Zídek, *Příběh herečky, Dělnická prokurátorka Ludmila Brožová a její svět* (Dokořán 2010) 29.

1950s.[13] Some of these became notorious spectacles. When it came to Stalinist show trials, the Czechoslovaks delivered the harshest sentences—the highest rate of death penalties—in all Communist Europe, including the Soviet Union. By way of example, in November 1951, Rudolf Slánský, the former Secretary-General of the Communist Party (recalled as Secretary-General in September 1951), was arrested and accused of Zionism. A year later, he and ten others were prosecuted, sentenced, and executed.[14] Show trials, moreover, targeted a broad array of individuals: representatives of non-Communist political parties, people who attempted to emigrate, army officials and church representatives, anyone putatively connected to 'Western Imperialists', individuals perceived as opposed to collectivization of agriculture, religious people, farmers, intelligentsia, and even workers.[15]

Judicial persecution was buttressed by a harsh array of extra-judicial measures. The Party established special battalions, called the PTP (*pomocné technické prapory*), to re-educate unruly soldiers through hard labour. Tens of thousands of individuals were placed in forced labour camps known as *tábory nucené práce* (TNPs) which operated from 1948 to 1954.[16] TNPs were usually located near industrial complexes, mines, construction sites, or wherever extensive and cheap labour was required. Any Czechoslovak citizen could be placed in such a camp even without a condemnatory judicial verdict. Jiří Padevět notes that '[i]n the paranoid environment of Stalinist Czechoslovakia, people were sent to the camps based on suspicion that they were capable of committing a crime'.[17] KSČ functionaries and bureaucrats of the national committees, known as *národní výbory*, could decide to send an individual to a TNP.[18] Correctional labour camps, or *nápravné pracovní tábory*, functioned as a parallel punitive apparatus from 1949 to 1962. These camps held political prisoners (persons convicted of anti-state activity); 'retributive prisoners' (defined as individuals convicted of collaboration with the Nazis); and persons convicted of non-political crimes. In total, 422 camps and labour correctional

[13] See eg Barbora Holá, 'The Show Must Go On: The Trials and Tribulations of Ludmila Brožová Polednová' in Mark A Drumbl and Caroline Fournet (eds), *The Sights, Sounds, and Sensibilities of Atrocity Prosecutions* (Brill forthcoming).

[14] Prior to his demise, Slánský had ironically been a driving force behind repression in Czechoslovakia.

[15] Karel Kaplan, *Nebezpečná Bezpečnost, Historie působení StB jako mocenského nástroje KSČ 1948–1956* (Kniha Zlín 2021) 264–71. Williams discusses how, in 1951, 'most of the StB commanders, including many of its founders, were arrested and suffered the forms of torture, trial, and execution they had recently endorsed'. Kieran Williams, 'The StB in Czechoslovakia, 1945–89' in Kieran Williams and Dennis Deletant (eds), *Security Intelligence Services in New Democracies: The Czech Republic, Slovakia, and Romania* (Palgrave MacMillan 2001) 31.

[16] Barbora Holá and Thijs Bouwknegt, 'Jáchymov's Hell: Trekking in the Memoryscape of Czechoslovakia's Communist Forced Labour Camps' (2022) 22 Intl Crim L Rev 328–46; Roman David, *Communists and Their Victims: The Quest for Justice in the Czech Republic* (University of Pennsylvania Press 2018) 27.

[17] Jiří Padevět, *Komunistické lágry, Tábory nucené prace, nápravně pracovní tábory, pracovní útvary vězňů a internační místa duchovních 1948–1962* (Academia 2019) 6.

[18] These functionaries often did so to settle accounts with their political or personal rivals.

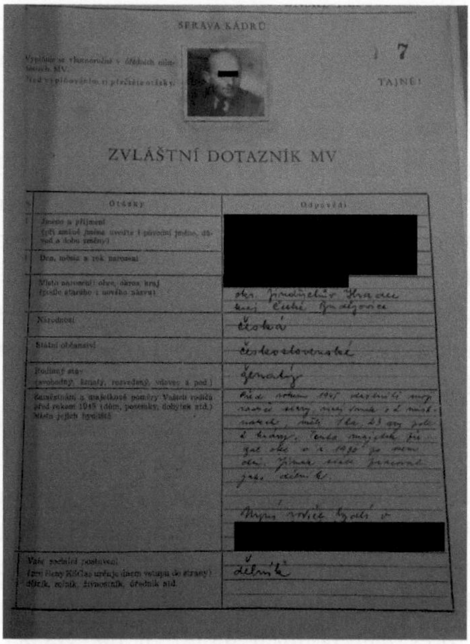

SPRÁVA KÁDRŮ

7

TAJNÉ!

ZVLÁŠTNÍ DOTAZNÍK MV

Otázky	Odpovědi
Jméno a příjmení	[redacted]
Den, měsíc a rok narození	
Místo narození: obec, okres, kraj (podle starého i nového názvu)	okr. Jindřichův Hradec kraj České Budějovice
Národnost	česká
Státní občanství	československé
Rodinný stav (svobodný, ženatý, rozvedený, vdovec a pod.)	ženatý
Zaměstnání a majetkové poměry Vašich rodičů před rokem 1945 (dům, pozemky, dobytek atd.) Místo jejich bydliště	[illegible] [redacted]
Vaše sociální postavení	dělník

Figure 2.3 Anonymized Cadre Form. ABS. File No 66075 (registration No 1348). Photograph taken by the authors (Prague, 2020).

facilities were established throughout Czechoslovakia.[19] Some of the most invidious of these facilities were uranium mines. Between 3,000[20] and 4,000[21] political prisoners perished in these camps and in other places of detention or prisons within which torture and maltreatment festered.

Communist repression also assumed more subtle forms. The state implemented a system of assessed cadre screening (*kádrování*). Citizens were scrutinized for their social fitness based on their family background, political views, statements, as well as public and private conduct.[22]

[19] Milan Hauner, 'Crime and Punishment in Communist Czechoslovakia: The Case of General Heliodor Pika and His Prosecutor Karel Vas' (2008) 8 Totalitarian Movements and Political Religions 335, 344.

[20] Williams, 'The StB in Czechoslovakia' (n 15) 25.

[21] David, *Communists and Their Victims* (n 16) 26.

[22] Marie Černá, 'Cadre Policy, Cadre Work, and Screening in Communist Czechoslovakia: Simple Ideas, Complicated Practice' (2011) 2 Acta Universitatis Carolinae Studia Territorialia 9, 10 ('[C]lassification was based on professional and ideological criteria—qualifications, class origin, political attitudes, etc.; moreover, it refer[red] to screening and placement of individuals in certain occupational positions and offices based on [specified] criteria; it also refer[red] to preventing politically undesirable individuals from holding certain jobs or positions in public life; and last but not least, it likewise refer[red] to education towards the preset ideals of appropriateness.').

An anonymized 'cadre' form is included here (Figure 2.3). At the time, since the state was generally the only employer for many vocations,[23] Czechoslovak citizens largely were obliged to complete this form so as to secure employment.[24] The cadre form—dated from 1954—was completed for the purposes of the Ministry of the Interior, which employed individuals for security services, such as the police, the StB, and prison correctional staff. Along with a person's biographical information—such as name, surname, date and place of birth, nationality, or citizenship—the sixteen-page form inquired into the applicant's property ownership and employment before the Second World War, Communist Party or correlated organization membership, education, relationship to religion, previous employment, foreign trips, knowledge of foreign languages, activities undertaken during the Nazi occupation, and participation in the Communists' February 1948 takeover. Similar inquiries were directed toward an applicant's spouse and parents.

Although the Czechoslovak Communist regime occasionally operated independently of the USSR, the fact remains that Soviets commanded considerable influence over Czechoslovak policies, practices, and governance. The iconography of Stalin, and other Soviet heroes, enshrouded—or vanished from—Prague depending on the prevalent political mood in the USSR. For example, the Czechoslovak government erected Stalin's monument in Prague on 1 May 1955 (International Workers' Day), only to have it demolished in 1962. This monument, overlooking the city, depicted Stalin followed by a retinue. Six hundred labourers worked feverishly to build it in five-and-a-half years. Measuring a length of 22 metres and scaling a height of 15.5 metres, it was the largest monument to Stalin outside of the Soviet Union at the time. It was also the largest group statue in Europe. The button on Stalin's chest, adorned with a hammer and sickle, was half a metre wide. This statue was nevertheless destroyed in 1962, albeit somewhat tardily. To be precise: in 1956, three years after his death, the 20th Congress of the USSR Communist Party had denounced the cult of Stalin, thereby triggering the de-Stalinization process, which seemingly took root more slowly in Czechoslovakia.[25] The architect responsible for creating Stalin's monument in Prague was likely to have foreseen this downfall, however, as he committed suicide the day before the statue was even unveiled.

Following Stalin's death, political and societal changes in Czechoslovakia—dubbed the gradual 'melting'—were indeed glacial, and to an extent,

[23] Cadre materials trailed individuals throughout their professional lives. Cadre screening 'involved regular professional and political evaluations, various *ad hoc* assessments accompanying any movement or change of status (e.g. a change of job or position, a new degree award, journey abroad, etc.)'. Černá, 'Cadre Policy' (n 22) 14.

[24] ibid (noting that manual workers and unskilled technical and administrative staff constituted exceptions).

[25] The de-Stalinization movement in Czechoslovakia posthumously caught Klement Gottwald in its waves. Gottwald's body was displaced from an honourific mummified place in a mausoleum to a shared, obscurely located communal grave in Prague's Olšany cemetery.

superficial, until the early 1960s.[26] The repressive practices of the preceding years still lingered—including dubious political trials—albeit at a declining rate.[27] That said, an increasing number of people began publicly to renounce the purported 'confessions' they had made during previous show trials and lambasted the coercive violence that they had endured.

In 1955, the Communist Party established the first *pro forma* committee to examine brutal and illegal practices undertaken to support the earlier political show trials. This committee was tasked to rehabilitate unfairly convicted political prisoners.[28] The first Presidential amnesty was declared that same year. Although political prisoners were not yet freed, their life sentences were reduced to twenty years and persons convicted for illegal emigration were pardoned.[29] However, the majority of political prisoners only were released through a later amnesty in 1960 with the remainder not being liberated until 1962.[30] Overall, and in contrast to the early 1950s, the judicial system—including prosecutors and judges—were no longer firmly controlled by the Party and the StB.[31]

In 1960, the new Czechoslovak constitution—whose flamboyant idealism opened this Chapter—lauded the putative attainment of socialism. Despite this virtuously proclaimed success,[32] the fact remains that the Communist Party still engaged in neo-Stalinist practices, including selective political prosecutions, extensive lustration, censorship, and compelled collectivization. It was only in 1963 that the regime meaningfully relaxed. The state—perennially yearning for legitimacy—stabilized but also reworked itself, this time from the bottom up. Repression dipped. Society became calmer, less fearful, and more open.[33] Hitherto unimaginable opportunities arose and citizens readily took advantage of them. Culture boomed.[34] For instance, the so-called New Wave of Czechoslovak cinematography offered far more colourful and engaging portrayals of the human condition and of life as lived in Czechoslovakia.[35] Intellectuals—university professors, poets,

[26] Rychlík, *Československo v období socialismu* (n 8) 135; McDermott, *Communist Czechoslovakia* (n 4) 92.

[27] Rychlík, *Československo v období socialismu* (n 8) 135.

[28] Two other rehabilitation committees were established in 1962 and in 1963. However, all of these committees were 'unsatisfactory compromise affairs designed to limit the impact of rehabilitations on the reputation of incumbent leaders'. McDermott, *Communist Czechoslovakia* (n 4) 101.

[29] Rychlík, *Československo v období socialismu* (n 8) 139.

[30] ibid 156; McDermott, *Communist Czechoslovakia* (n 4) 103.

[31] Rychlík, *Československo v období socialismu* (n 8) 156–57.

[32] This Constitution proclaimed that 'socialism was achieved' and that 'people can exercise all their basic rights' in harmony with all of society. In reality, repressive practices persisted in daily life.

[33] Rychlík, *Československo v období socialismu* (n 8) 167.

[34] See generally Jiří Petráš and Libor Svoboda, *Předjaří, Československo 1963–1967* (Ústav pro studium totalitních režimů & Jihočeské muzeum v Českých Budějovicích 2016) 9–119 (featuring a collection of historical essays on art and culture).

[35] 'New Wave' movie directors such as Jiří Menzel or Miloš Forman became internationally acclaimed. For instance, Menzel's adaptation of Bohumil Hrabal's *Closely Watched Trains* won an Oscar in 1967. A fascinating exhibit in the National Czech & Slovak Museum & Library in Cedar Rapids, Iowa presents the origin, output, and influence of Czechoslovak New Wave cinema. The authors visited this museum on 15 October 2021.

journalists, and writers—began to criticize the regime publicly.[36] The 'workers intelligentsia' endorsed these newly emergent reformist tendencies. Czechoslovakia opened up to the world. Citizens could travel, a bit at least, including to the West. Additionally, some of the new Communist elites became dissatisfied with the perceived economic stagnation of the country in contradistinction to perceptions of rapid growth in the capitalist West.[37]

Under the leadership of its reformist wing, led by Alexander Dubček, the Communist Party became more tolerant and slightly more accommodating of dissonant views and, to some extent, alternate ways of life.[38] Censorship abated. Society's engagement as stakeholders in public and political activities bloomed. An overall optimism was palpable. In April 1968, the Party adopted a so-called Action Program which envisaged a series of democratic adjustments. In the Prague Spring of 1968 exuberant liberal reforms burst onto the scene.

The USSR suspiciously eyed the reformist movements, fearing that Czechoslovakia would exit the Soviet sphere of influence. Consequently, in the overnight from 20 to 21 August 1968, the USSR—together with other armies of the Warsaw Pact—invaded Czechoslovakia and quashed the reformist ambitions of Dubček's 'socialism with a human face'.[39] This invasion crushed the restlessly festive Prague Spring. Operation Danube, as the military intervention was labelled, had as its affirmed intention to defend socialism from Dubček's counterrevolution. Dubček was captured and sent to Moscow.

Following this reassertion of Soviet influence, a period of 'normalization' ensued under Gustáv Husák, the Party's new First Secretary, who ironically himself had been imprisoned during the Stalinist purges of the 1950s. Husák reversed Dubček's policies. The KSČ was 'purified' of nearly half a million members who had tilted toward liberal reforms. Husák's government 'was harsh, orthodox, and allowed little scope for dissent'.[40] Borders once again were sealed.

1968 was a watershed in Czechoslovak history, both chronologically and metaphorically. This salience is evident in so many of the informer files we have reviewed. Indeed, 1968 was (and long remained) a touchstone and dramatic point of inflection in the lives of so many Czechoslovaks. Hopes were dashed as the reforms were quashed and the power of the state reasserted itself. This reassertion, however ideologically couched, was also profoundly devoid of ideology. A sense of resigned scepticism ensued:

[36] Rychlík, *Československo v období socialismu* (n 8) 182, 185–89; McDermott, *Communist Czechoslovakia* (n 4) 114–20.

[37] Rychlík, *Československo v období socialismu* (n 8) 172.

[38] ibid 192.

[39] Romania was the only country that openly condemned the invasion, although Albania also eschewed participation.

[40] Kieran Williams, Brigid Fowler, and Aleks Szczerbiak, 'Explaining Lustration in Central Europe: A 'Post-Communist Politics' Approach' (2005) 12(1) Democratization 22, 24.

> Before 1968, it was still possible to claim that communism was an ideal worth fighting for, even though its living present had been perverted by Stalinism. After 1968–1969, however, there could no longer be any belief in a 'purer' communism.[41]

What followed was a period known as 'normalization':

> [C]onventionally, normalization, *normalizace* in Czech, and *normalizácia* in Slovak, has been construed as the attempt by hardline pro-Soviet Czechoslovak Communists to reconstruct the *status quo ante*, a supremely retrograde undertaking designed to wipe the Dubčekite reforms of 1968 and the 'spirit of January' from . . . collective memory.[42]

Normalization involved the reinforcement of the Party's leading role in politics and society, removing reformers and oppositionists, purging officials, reimposing censorship, and returning to tightly centralized economic planning. The Communist Party moreover sought to 'ensure that the StB did not escape [its] grip and become a rogue actor',[43] and to guarantee that StB hard-liners 'did not undermine Husák's assurances to the public that there would be no return to the terror and trials of the 1950s, of which Husák himself had been a victim'.[44]

As normalization routinized things, a steady—though more *blasé*—regime emerged during the 1970s and 1980s. This is the period in which the state's grip relented and the Party molted somewhat. State interventions were less drastic, citizens had more room to manoeuvre, and official state-centred physical violence faded. That said, '[a]lthough imprisoning dissidents was less common by the 1980s, the regime could easily ruin people professionally by making them unemployable in their fields, and [by] blocking entry to universities for their "enemy" children'.[45] From 1969 to 1989, over 105,000 citizens were convicted *in absentia* for illegal emigration.[46] Apathy prevailed while any residual societal faith in Marxism-Leninism atrophied.[47] In contrast, little trinkets of joy—television, vacations,

[41] Stibbe and McDermott, 'Czechoslovakia and Eastern Europe in the Era of Normalisation' (n 1) 2–3.

[42] ibid 15.

[43] Kieran Williams, 'The Czechoslovak Security Service During Normalisation: The Appearance of Success' in McDermott and Stibbe (eds), *Czechoslovakia and Eastern Europe in the Era of Normalisation* (n 1) 122.

[44] ibid 123.

[45] Amos Chapple, 'Spy Photos from Communist Czechoslovakia' (*Radio Free Europe*, 28 October 2019) <https://www.rferl.org/a/the-communist-spy-photographers-of-czechoslovakia/30236411.html> accessed 10 March 2023.

[46] Rychlík, *Československo v období socialismu* (n 8) 280.

[47] McDermott, *Communist Czechoslovakia* (n 4) 150 (noting that 'a deep apathy towards "politics" in general appeared to envelop society by the early 1970s . . . all "isms" and master narratives became suspect as many Czechs and Slovaks retreated into their private worlds and "socialist consumerism" '); 165 (further observing that '[v]ery few, if any people genuinely identified with the goals of the regime,

jeans, sweets—trickled through society. Apartments, called *paneláky*, were built to allay housing pressures. The Prague metro was established to promote urban efficiency and connectivity. At the same time, resistance percolated in certain quarters: Václav Havel's plays, Charter 77's proclamations,[48] and the grunge songs of the Plastic People of the Universe are just some of the ways in which some social strata, albeit rather minoritarian, voiced resistance.

Normalization lingered until 1988, when students and security forces clashed near Prague's Lennon Wall. This wall, located on the west bank of the Vltava River, initially served as a spontaneous canvas for the public to post generic quotations about peace—indeed from John Lennon—along with lyrics from Beatles' songs. The content of this graffiti nonetheless became increasingly pointed and critical of the Czechoslovak Communist authorities. As a result, 'Lennonists' were denounced. The Lennon Wall is still standing, colourfully, although its tempo is far different from what it was three decades ago.[49]

Skirmishes between students and security forces in Prague sparked what came to be called the 1989 Velvet Revolution. These clashes trace to factors that had already emerged in preceding years, including the role of the Catholic community, the restlessness of environmental movements (including in regions distant from the presence of Charter 77),[50] and influences from collective uprisings elsewhere in Europe.[51] On 20 November 1989, half a million protestors filled the streets of Prague. Four days later, the leaders of the Communist Party of Czechoslovakia resigned. Democratic elections took place in the summer of 1990. Václav Havel, the celebrated playwright and formerly imprisoned dissident leader, became the first post-Communist President.

scarcely anyone—party members included—believed the hollow slogans and ritualized Marxist-Leninist teachings').

[48] Charter 77 was a civic dissident initiative. It had been named after The Charter 77, a document published in January 1977 in response to the arrest and trial of members of the music band Plastic People of the Universe. Charter 77 was signed by 242 individuals. It lambasted the government for failing to implement international human rights obligations. The regime's reaction to Charter 77 was harsh. Signatories were publicly criticized and labelled as 'anti-state', 'traitors', or 'agents of imperialism'. Some lost their jobs, their children were not allowed to study, and others were exiled or prosecuted.

[49] The Lennon Wall now exudes a distracted, emptier cadence curated for tourists, but still remains inspirational as a metaphor to express resistance: Hong Kong, for example, saw its own self-proclaimed 'Lennon Walls' emerge in 2020, dotted with colourful sticky-notes, amid its own mass protests. Jeff Hou, 'Hong Kong's Sticky-Note Revolution' (*Smithsonian Magazine*, 24 January 2020) <https://www.smithsonianmag.com/travel/hong-kongs-sticky-note-revolution-180974042/> accessed 11 July 2023.

[50] Before the Velvet Revolution, a large demonstration concerning a low-lying chemical cloud was held in a town called Teplice. Protestors beseeched the government to provide clean air. This was the biggest turnout anywhere outside of Prague for any demonstration. This protest went ahead 'without any cooperation with the dissident movement'. Miroslav Vaněk, 'Twenty Years in Shades of Grey? Everyday Life During Normalisation Based on Oral History Research' in McDermott and Stibbe (eds), *Czechoslovakia and Eastern Europe in the Era of Normalisation* (n 1) 163.

[51] The Czechs came to 'revolution' only after their neighbours in Poland, Hungary, and East Germany.

In sum, and notwithstanding the power of the Communist Party, McDermott posits that 'the 40-year communist experience in Czechoslovakia should not be seen as a foreign imposed aberration dislocating an otherwise unsullied democratic history'.[52] McDermott further suggests that the socialist dictatorship was 'a living dynamic organism in which individuals struggled to empower themselves and thereby shape and make sense of the world around them'.[53] He forcefully concludes:

> [C]ontrary to the post-1989 master paradigm which emphasizes the fundamentally alien essence of the Czechoslovak communist experience and the inherent and diffuse social resistance to the regime, I contend that popular attitudes to the socialist aims and visions of the Communist Party modulated from broadly 'supportive' in the late 1940s, to 'critical loyalty' in the 1950s and 1960s, to 'disengaged collusion' by the 1970s and 1980s.[54]

McDermott explores the interplay between outsider (Stalin, Soviet) influences and insider inputs in the life of Communist Czechoslovakia. McDermott's bottom line is that there is less of a divide between the people and the regime, and less resistance than the post-1989 story officially extols.[55] David arrives at comparable findings.[56] Similarly, Rychlík rues the disproportionate attention to resistance that has retrospectively emerged following the Velvet Revolution:

> [A]s much as the majority of people remained passive during 1939–1945 [the Nazi occupation], they remained inactive after 1948.... [During] normalization, ... the resistance was limited only to intellectual circles and was not of interest to the masses. The large part of citizens reconciled with the regime and kept on living their lives.[57]

During Communism, state and society were not irrevocably oppositional. Nor were the people and the system chronically at odds with each other. Individuals retained—and expressed—some agency.[58] It is for this reason that we are attracted

[52] McDermott, *Communist Czechoslovakia* (n 4) 16.

[53] ibid 18.

[54] ibid 20.

[55] 'It is not good enough in my opinion to view the communist regime as an alien implant with few, if any, domestic affiliations. Regardless of its allegiance to Moscow, the Communist Party was able to strike deep roots in Czech society, though to a lesser degree in Slovak, and to associate itself with certain prevailing national traditions, identities and myths, while undoubtedly rejecting others.' ibid 16.

[56] David, *Communists and Their Victims* (n 16) 22–23.

[57] Rychlík, *Československo v období socialismu* (n 8) 29.

[58] The view that Communist Czechoslovakia constituted a dyad between a resistant society and an oppressive state also suffuses Western historiography 'to the exclusion of more sophisticated understandings'. Stibbe and McDermott, 'Czechoslovakia and Eastern Europe in the Era of Normalisation' (n 1) 9.

to Mary Fulbrook's notion of participatory dictatorship.[59] The Communist Party nonetheless kept a lid on governance and aspired to be an 'engineer of human souls'.[60] This simultaneous percolation, suppression, and navigation—variably through and over time—undergird the place of informers in the overall Czechoslovak socio-political matrix.

II. The StB: Its Structure, Standard Operating Procedures, and Connection to National Security

Estimates suggest that, in Communist Czechoslovakia, somewhere between 250,000[61] and 262,500[62] individuals were found guilty of political offences between 1948 and 1989. Nearly half of these convicted individuals were judged *in absentia* for illegal emigration after fleeing the country, around 40,000 of whom were given suspended sentences.[63] Other crimes for which convictions were rendered included treason, conspiracy, and the spreading of false news. Two hundred and sixty-two people were executed for political reasons, with the vast majority of these executions occurring in the 1950s.[64] Futile border-crossing attempts resulted in 143 people shot to death, ninety-five electrocutions, and eleven drownings, with seventeen people committing suicide rather than face arrest.[65]

The State Security force, known as the *Státní bezpečnost* (StB)—or the *Štátna bezpečnosť* (ŠtB) in Slovak—constituted one of the main pillars of this repression.[66]

The StB's general mission was to 'protect the state establishment',[67] prevent leakage of state secrets, uphold the spirit of Marxism-Leninism, and fight ostensible enemies of the state (notably external and internal elements suspected of anti-Communist sympathies). However, the StB's aims, tasks, methods, and standard operating procedures changed fluidly in response to the perceived needs of the Communist Party, extant socio-political realities, and the way in which the StB defined its own relationship with the state and Party.[68] According to Czech historian Karel Kaplan, the StB was a symbol, a backbone, and an executioner of Communist power.[69]

59 See Chapter 1, 'Introduction'.
60 See Chapter 1, 'Introduction'.
61 Williams, 'The StB in Czechoslovakia' (n 15) 25.
62 David, *Communists and Their Victims* (n 16) 27.
63 Williams, 'The StB in Czechoslovakia' (n 15) 25.
64 David, *Communists and Their Victims* (n 16) 26 (noting discrepancies in the estimates, which range from 248 to 262).
65 ibid. Williams for his part reports that between 320 and 400 people were killed while trying to escape across the border. Williams, 'The StB in Czechoslovakia' (n 15) 25–26.
66 Kaplan, *Nebezpečná Bezpečnost* (n 15) 7.
67 Prokop Tomek, *Estébáckou Prahou, Průvodce po pražských sídlech Státní bezpečnosti* (2nd ed, Academia Průvodce 2020) 12.
68 Kaplan, *Nebezpečná Bezpečnost* (n 15) 4.
69 ibid 249.

Generally, the StB was akin to other political police units that had been established in various European Communist countries at the time, such as the KGB in the Soviet Union, the Stasi in East Germany, the Securitate in Romania, and the Służby Bezpieczeństwa in Poland.[70] Notwithstanding the differences among these national agencies, all were tasked with 'ideological policing'. All encouraged denunciation—the supposedly voluntary reporting of perceived wrongdoing—as patriotic duty and relied on laws that criminalized failures to report wrongdoing as levers to badger and cajole ordinary citizens into becoming informers.[71]

The StB fused intelligence gathering with criminal investigation. It had a threefold function: repression, prevention, and information.[72] The StB investigated the putatively most serious crimes against the state by harvesting evidence, questioning suspects, and assembling documentation. It then passed its findings to the prosecutor's office and the courts. It also preventatively monitored society and vacuumed information from the daily life of Czechoslovak and foreign citizens and organizations so as to uncover activities apparently hostile to the regime.[73] For

[70] Considerable literature exists on these surveillance agencies, their tactics, and how they assembled information. See generally Juan Espíndola Mata, *Transitional Justice After German Reunification* (CUP 2015); Alison Lewis, *A State of Secrecy, Stasi Informers and the Culture of Surveillance* (Potomac Books 2021); Péter Apor, Sándor Horváth, and James Mark (eds), *Secret Agents and the Memory of Everyday Collaboration in Communist Europe* (Anthem Press 2017); Barbara Miller, *The Stasi Files Unveiled: Guilt and Compliance in a Unified Germany* (Routledge 2017); Lavinia Stan and Lucian Turcescu, 'The Devil's Confessors: Priests, Communists, Spies, and Informers' (2005) 19 East Eur Politics and Society 656; James W Heinzen, 'Informers and the State Under Late Stalinism: Informer Networks and Crimes Against 'Socialist Property' 1940–1953' (2007) 8 Kritika 789.

[71] According to the Czechoslovak legal commentary of the time, a 'characteristic feature of socialist Czechoslovak law [was] the principle of increasing participation of people in the management of the state'. Oldřich Rolenc, *O socialistické spravedlnosti: (zásady našeho nového trestního práva)* (Osvěta 1952) 13. Citizens needed to 'be educated and encouraged to be alert to actively fight crime', ibid 15. In the case of selected serious crimes—such as treason, subversion of the republic, espionage, terror, or sabotage—the Czechoslovak criminal law stipulated a criminal offence of 'failure to report a crime'. The list and scope of the crimes subject to the reporting duty fluctuated over time. Additionally, some of these predicate offenses were quite vaguely defined in the law and came to be broadly interpreted in practice. Tomáš Gřivna, 'Trestní právo hmotné' in Michal Bobek, Pavel Molek, and Vojtěch Šimíček (eds), *Komunistické právo v Československu, Kapitoly z dějin bezpráví* (MuniPress 2009) 554, 564–65. The stipulated maximum sentence for a failure to report varied from one year in prison in the period 1948–1950, to five years in the period 1950–1961, to three years in the period 1961–1989. Zákon na ochranu lidově demokratické republiky [Law for the Protection of the Peoples' Democratic Republic], Zákon č 231/1948 Sb (Czech) para 35 (adopted 6 October 1948); Trestní zákoník [Criminal Code], Zákon č 86/1950 (Czech) para 165 (adopted 12 July 1950); Trestní zákoník [Criminal Code], Zákon č 140/1961(Czech) para 168 (adopted 29 November 1961). It nonetheless remains unclear just how rigorously these provisions were enforced in practice, or how many people were actually investigated and prosecuted for the crime of failure to report during Communism. That said, as discussed in Chapter 5, Section III.A, 'Fear', these putative reporting duties (along with cognate crimes such as parasitism, breach of public order, and speculation) certainly fermented fear as a driver that in turn animated individuals to engage with the StB. These dynamics recur and redound in the StB file-stories. Curiously, a crime of failure to report was retained in Czech criminal law after 1989. Trestní zákoník [Criminal Code], Zákon č 40/2009 (Czech) para 368 (adopted 9 February 2009).

[72] Tomek, *Estébáckou Prahou* (n 67) 12.

[73] Libor Bílek, 'I Undertake Voluntarily… Residents, Agents, Informers, and Others: The State Security's Secret Collaborators, 1945–1989' in Alžběta Medková (ed), *Behind the Iron Curtain: Review of the Institute for the Study of Totalitarian Regimes*, vol 4 (Ústav pro studium totalitních režimů 2016) 95 (noting that 'the assessment of what was or was not "hostile" [was] carried out by the StB according

most of its history, the StB covertly and openly surveilled society in degrees of varying intensity.[74] It served a catalytic role in stoking the climate of fear that suffused Communist Czechoslovakia.[75]

The StB comprised three cooperative components: operational, executive, and subsidiary. Civil operational forces[76] concentrated primarily on three basic counter-espionage lines: (i) defensive, to wit, checking, surveilling, and interfering with the activities of foreign intelligence services, foreigners, and foreign actions—including diplomatic, commercial, touristic, and cultural—on Czechoslovak territory; (ii) political, namely, 'fighting the enemy from within' by surveilling perceived political opponents and any non-conforming citizens; and (iii) economic, which tackled industrial espionage, protected economic secrets, and safeguarded state companies and businesses within Czechoslovakia.[77] The StB's operational sections closely cooperated with its executive parts, which investigated individuals accused of crimes against the state and prepared cases for prosecution. The subsidiary parts performed specialized tasks that deployed techniques such as intercepts, photography, or secret searches.[78]

The StB also operated a foreign espionage service, which harvested political, military and economic intelligence abroad in order to 'secure [the] stability of the Communist system and weaken outside enemies'.[79] The espionage service also actively interfered in situations abroad, spread disinformation, and—in particular in the 1950s—organized abductions, attacks, and sabotage on foreign territories.[80] Foreigners were indeed a significant area of targeted interest to the StB. Hence, gathering information on foreigners or Czechoslovaks who interacted with foreigners became an StB institutional priority. This becomes clear in our review of the StB files. Czechoslovaks who had frequent contact with foreigners—such as business people, embassy workers, socialites, artists, and members of the creative class—were dearly sought after as informers.[81]

to the judgement of its officers or Communist Party functionaries, rather than the laws then in force'). Bílek's finding implies the StB's independence from generalized legal norms.

74 Williams, 'The StB in Czechoslovakia' (n 15) 25.

75 Kaplan, *Protistátní Bezpečnost* (n 3) 11; Kaplan, *Nebezpečná Bezpečnost* (n 15) 263.

76 The StB also operated a separate military counter-espionage section that focused on the army and which remained out of reach of its civilian units.

77 Tomek, *Estébáckou Prahou* (n 67) 12. See also generally Libor Bílek, 'Agenturní centrála Státní Bezpečnosti a její vedoucí Erich Mach: Poznámky k fungování sítě tajných spolupracovníku v letech 1948 až 1950' (2014) 25(2) Securitas Imperii 132.

78 Tomek, *Estébáckou Prahou* (n 67) 12.

79 ibid.

80 ibid.

81 The StB directly recruited foreigners as informers as well. The StB archives include files on foreigners who spent a significant amount of time in Czechoslovakia and who worked closely with the StB. Some of these individuals came to Czechoslovakia to study while others came iteratively on business matters. These characters also populate some of the file-stories in our dataset. What is more, the StB also sought to recruit higher-profile foreign politicians and experts who permanently lived abroad as information sources.

Always rapaciously hungry for information, the StB deployed various means to obtain its intelligence. The first and foremost source was the StB's extensive informer network. The StB availed itself of other means, however, such as intercepts of phone conversations and correspondence, (illegal) searches of private apartments, and covert surveillance using photography and film.[82] The StB also extensively monitored its own agents, officers, and informers in a tangled web. Nearly every informer we encountered in our review of the archives was in turn informed upon by someone else.

The StB was created amid the dramatic events that followed the end of the Second World War in 1945. The StB fell under the auspices of the Ministry of the Interior which was led by a Communist Minister but was part of a national government composed of multiple political parties. At the time, the StB was not controlled solely by Communists, but the Communist Party strove to gain full authority over the security apparatus. The Communist Party rapidly and progressively succeeded in this regard. These were chaotic years in which control over the security apparatus proved to be a crucial power struggle between the Communist Party and its rivals in which the Communists decisively prevailed.

In any event, the newly constituted, largely understaffed, and inexperienced security forces were overwhelmed with their initial task, namely the search for and investigation of collaborators with the Nazi Protectorate and Slovak puppet regime.[83] Hence, an upgrade was in order. The 1947 Law on National Security Forces thusly formulated the StB's tasks as follows: 'To secure [the] Czechoslovak Republic against attacks on its sovereignty, independence, and democratic-republican form, security and defence, and further to ensure personal security of state representatives, and to defend [the Republic] against economic espionage.'[84] The 1947 Law envisaged that the StB would cease to be a separate organ of the National Security Corps once accountability processes for wartime collaborators ended.[85] However, rather than recede after addressing Nazi collaboration, the StB's footprint grew.[86] In

[82] Daniel Povolný, 'Operativní technika a StB' (2003) 10 Securitas Imperii 73. In 2008, the Institute for the Study of Totalitarian Regimes published a book entitled *Prague Through the Lens of the Secret Police*. This book displays selected photographs secretly taken by the StB during their operational work. These images capture the 'normalized street life' of Czechoslovakia in the 1970s and 1980s. This book is available for free and can be downloaded from here: https://www.ustrcr.cz/wp-content/uploads/2017/10/Praha-objektivem-tajne-policie.pdf.

[83] Kaplan, *Protistátní Bezpečnost* (n 3) 36. Until 1947, the repressive function and intelligence gathering of the security forces had been separated. The StB's mandate had been officially limited to the repressive/investigatory function while intelligence had been obtained by a separate agency named the Intelligence Agency, or (*Zpravodajská služba*), over which the Communist party had assumed control. These two functions were fused into the StB in 1947. See also František Koudelka, *Státní bezpečnost 1954–1968: Základní údaje*, vol 13 (Ústav pro soudobé dějiny AV ČR 1993) 10; Williams, 'The StB in Czechoslovakia' (n 15) 27.

[84] Zákon o národní bezpečnosti [Law on National Security], Zákon č 149/1947 Sb (Czech) para 33(1).

[85] Koudelka, *Státní bezpečnost 1954–1968* (n 83) 11.

[86] Beginning in autumn 1947, the Communists deployed the StB to populate the offices of non-Communist parties with informers who gathered compromising information on political leaders, organized provocations to upend public meetings, and circulated disinformation. See generally Kaplan, *Protistátní Bezpečnost* (n 3) 251; Williams, 'The StB in Czechoslovakia' (n 15) 28.

stark contrast to the vision of its gradual dissolution, according to the ensuing 1948 Law on National Security, the StB—by then firmly within Communist control—became cemented as a keystone of the security apparatus.[87]

In the immediate years after the full Communist takeover in 1948, the StB directed its attention towards Communist opponents both outside and within the Party. The class struggle and the fight against real and conjured 'enemies of the state' became full-blown. Under the influence of Soviet advisors who joined the StB in autumn 1949 and then essentially took charge,[88] the StB focused its attention on orchestrating large-scale political show trials. Interrogations were pitiless; forced confessions legion; drugs, including scopolamine, were injected into detainees such that they would admit even the implausible; questioning lasted for many hours; suspects were tortured, blackmailed, and broken; many ended up saying anything and everything interrogators wanted to hear.[89] The StB conjured fabricated evidence. Competitions arose among StB officers regarding who could conduct the largest number of arrests.[90] In essence, anything was allowed in 'the fight against enemies' since 'the duty to serve communism, the Party, and its regime stood above all'.[91]

Along with manufacturing political show trials, the StB compiled lists of so-called 'former people' who were considered 'enemy elements from [the] defeated bourgeoisie attempting to disturb [Communist] building efforts'.[92] The StB closely tracked selected groups of citizens, including those in touch with the West, and instantiated administrative and repressive actions against them such as forced relocation or banning them from holding certain jobs.[93] 'Operation Isolation' aimed to destroy any links Czechoslovak institutions and citizens may have had with the

[87] Koudelka, *Státní bezpečnost 1954–1968* (n 83) 12.

[88] Kaplan, *Nebezpečná Bezpečnost* (n 15) 35.

[89] ibid. See also Markéta Bártová, 'Emilie Faitová Kolářová: Spolupracovnice komunistických bezpečnostních složek i jejich obětí' (2020) 2 Paměť a dějiny 75, 75–94 (describing torture sessions organized by the StB).

[90] Kaplan, *Nebezpečná Bezpečnost* (n 15) 126.

[91] ibid 44.

[92] Tajný rozkaz ministra vnitra—Rozpracování, pozorování a evidování 'bývalých lidí' [Secret Order of the Minister of the Interior—Investigation, observation and evidence of 'former people'], Vhyl č 1/1959 Sb (Czech) Preamble (issued 3 January 1959). The Secret Order contained a list of sixteen diverse categories of 'former people' including: factory owners; businessmen and their families; *kulaks* and their relatives; representatives of international organizations or foreign companies; members of former fascist parties and Nazi organizations; high functionaries of former political parties and social organizations, such as Junák; representatives of churches and religious sects; representatives of Western organizations such as the YMCA; repatriated emigrants from capitalistic states and their relatives; individuals convicted of espionage, terror, diversion, and other anti-state activities; and other persons considered dangerous to the peoples' democratic establishment. In 1961, the list contained 97,943 individuals. Koudelka, *Státní bezpečnost 1954–1968* (n 83) 90. However, the StB soon realized that this vast array of targets was too onerous and hence untenable. In 1964, a new order was issued that focused the StB's gaze on 'enemy individuals'. Persons who were definitively suspected of enemy thinking, anti-state activities and attitudes, or those working against the socialist establishment were listed, this amounting to 5,863 individuals in total in 1964. Koudelka, *Státní bezpečnost 1954–1968* (n 83) 94–95.

[93] Kaplan, *Nebezpečná Bezpečnost* (n 15) 247.

Western world.[94] Access to Western press and publications was restricted and the sale of such media to Czechoslovak citizens prohibited. Correspondence with the West was censored. Mobility was strictly controlled. The cohort of individuals in which the StB was interested gradually expanded to include Communist cadres, functionaries from abolished non-Communist political parties, army officers, members of anti-Nazi resistance movements, national minorities, repatriated emigrants, priests, farmers, *kulaks*, administrative workers, and even factory workers who evinced a reticent attitude about their work.[95]

The expanding and increasingly exigent tasks placed upon the StB, combined with purges of StB security officers, meant that the StB required reinforcements. The Communist Party decided to bolster the StB with 'politically absolutely reliable' individuals.[96] The professional qualities of aspiring officers were considered of lesser salience. Between 1948 and 1952, the number of StB officers roughly quadrupled from 2,864 to somewhere between 10,000 and 11,000.[97] The vast majority of new StB members were of working-class origin: many of these recruits lacked 'expertise and experience in intelligence, education, general knowledge, or appropriate behaviour'.[98] The Ministry of the Interior soon became aware of this dire situation. In a secret order from 1954, it exhorted that StB officers should 'understand current international political developments and norms and tasks of building our socialist society . . . [StB officers] have to be generally educated, principled, honest, modest, and firm in character and morality'.[99] By 1956, much of the StB staff already had undertaken various professional and political courses. However, 36.5 per cent of the employees of the Ministry of the Interior and security corps had not completed basic education,[100] while 60.9 per cent of individuals who later rose in ranks and became the StB's main commanders joined the secret security forces with only a basic education.[101] The general lack of pedagogical formation and 'people skills' affected the character and quality of the StB's work, including its use of informers.[102]

Notwithstanding these staffing concerns, the StB attained the zenith of its power during the Stalinist years. It morphed into a political force distinct from

94 ibid 79.

95 ibid 263.

96 ibid 11.

97 Koudelka, *Státní bezpečnost 1954–1968* (n 83) 12.

98 Bílek, 'Agenturní centrála StB' (n 77) 8.

99 Tajný rozkaz ministra vnitra—'Rozkaz o práci s agentami' a 'Smernice o agentúrne- operatîvnej práci' [Secret Order of the Minister of the Interior—'Order Regarding Work with Agents' and 'Directive on Agency-Operational Work'] Vhyl č 72/1954 Sb (Czech) 4 (issued 20 April 1954) (hereafter Order 72/ 1954).

100 Kaplan, *Nebezpečná Bezpečnost* (n 15) 11.

101 Jan Kalous and Pavel Žáček, 'Předmluva' in Milan Bárta and others, *Biografický slovník náčelníků operativních správ Státní bezpečnosti v letech 1953–1989* (Academia 2017) 19 (compiling biographies of the main StB commanders over the forty-year span of its existence).

102 Bílek, 'I Undertake Voluntarily' (n 73) 102.

the Communist Party and was able directly and indirectly to influence the highest levels of national decision-making.[103]

Unsurprisingly, the secretive and uncontrolled actions of the StB alarmed certain leading Communists who feared becoming ensnared into its net.[104] At the end of the 1950s, the StB's muscularity resultingly became sapped. The Communist Party's wider leadership started to expose the StB's illegal and brutal practices. This leadership endeavoured to distance and insulate the Party from the terror of the early 1950s.[105] Political show trials began to be criticized; initial demands to reconsider verdicts and rehabilitate those convicted got traction.[106] The Party pointed an accusing finger at the StB, claiming that the StB had 'got[ten] out of hand'.[107] The StB's hitherto cardinal task of ginning up manufactured political show trials became deprioritized.[108] Some StB functionaries and leaders themselves were arrested and punished for their activities in the early 1950s. The StB shuddered under an existential crisis insofar as an 'atmosphere of insecurity and powerlessness' festered among its ranks.[109]

Czech historian Libor Bílek ascribes this lessening political repression to a decline in international and domestic pressures, subsiding anti-state activities, and the issuance of official Party proclamations to adhere to 'socialist legality' which essentially entailed demands from the Party that security forces more rigorously adhere to the letter of the law.[110] The StB's ability to violate existing laws grossly with impunity shrunk.[111] The number of individuals criminally prosecuted for political crime consequently plummeted in 1956 and 1957. The social and political realities no longer permitted the StB to fabricate mass show trials against Czechoslovak citizens.[112] As such, the StB responsively reoriented its gaze toward less dramatic conduct, for instance economic offences and crimes such as leaving the country or defaming the state and its representatives.[113]

In 1960, socialism was officially declared as attained in Czechoslovakia. This ringing and pealing proclamation implied that domestic enemies of the regime had largely been defeated and no longer posed any threat. Accordingly, the StB was downsized in 1964 and 1966 and was officially tasked to concentrate its efforts on external foreign enemies and their domestic helpers.[114] The StB nonetheless

[103] Kaplan, *Nebezpečná Bezpečnost* (n 15) 249–50.
[104] Kaplan, *Protistátní Bezpečnost* (n 3) 13.
[105] ibid; see also Kaplan, *Nebezpečná Bezpečnost* (n 15) 49.
[106] ibid 48–49. The Communist Party ordered a first round of reconsiderations of political trials in 1955. A second round came in 1963.
[107] Kaplan, *Protistátní Bezpečnost* (n 3) 14.
[108] Kaplan, *Nebezpečná Bezpečnost* (n 15) 49.
[109] ibid 68, 69.
[110] Bílek, 'I Undertake Voluntarily' (n 73) 106.
[111] Koudelka, *Státní bezpečnost 1954–1968* (n 83) 171.
[112] ibid.
[113] Bílek, 'I Undertake Voluntarily' (n 73) 106.
[114] ibid 107. According to the 1965 Law on National Security Corps, the StB and other security forces were to 'secure protection of the socialist social and state establishment, reveal and defuse enemy

persisted in its inward focus on Czechoslovak citizens. At the time, 75 per cent of StB officers remained constellated in units that dealt with internal hostile elements.[115] However, and consonant with the regime's overall trajectory of democratization and liberalization in the 1960s, the StB's punitive function continued to abate and the prospect of criminal prosecutions mainly became an implied threat rather than explicit reality.[116]

Amid this political moment, the StB was gradually becoming 'more of an agent of preventative control and surveillance of the entire society'.[117] Paradoxically, this meant that its bevy of informers grew substantially. In practice, the StB monitored society, gathered public opinions regarding the politics of the day, and reported on 'negative events in [the] national economy or other areas in the life of society and the state'.[118] In essence, the StB adjusted its activities and began collecting information that had little to do with self-evident matters of state security or prosecuting declared 'enemies of the state', but mainly related instead to securing the implementation of Party politics and monitoring the public's attitudes in all aspects of societal life.[119] The StB's primary interest drifted from penally punishable behaviours towards personal matters such as family and matrimonial life, affairs and squabbles, financial dealings, economic circumstances, irregular political viewpoints, iconoclastic conduct, and foreign connections.[120] As part of its putatively preventive function, the StB also was assigned to educate the population and assist in 'overcoming remnants of the past in the thinking of citizens' who, due to their 'political backwardness and class unawareness', resorted to violating 'socialist laws and norms of the socialist society'.[121]

In contrast to the extensive publicity of political trials in the early 1950s—which were public theatrical performances with a predetermined script broadcast on the radio as part of Communist Party propaganda—the StB became more reticent to reveal its activities in the 1960s. In a sense, it became even more secretive.[122] The public was to fear the StB not because of its brutal methods but for its omniscience and its perceived superior knowledge of all that was going on.[123] Indeed, this

activities directed against the Czechoslovak Socialist Republic, and protect [Czechoslovak] citizens against such enemy activities'. Zákon o Sboru národní bezpečnosti [Law on National Security Corps], Zákon č 70/1965 Sb (Czech) art 3(1)(a).

115 Bílek, 'I Undertake Voluntarily' (n 73) 107.
116 Koudelka, *Státní bezpečnost 1954–1968* (n 83) 172.
117 Bílek, 'I Undertake Voluntarily' (n 73) 107. See also Koudelka, *Státní bezpečnost 1954–1968* (n 83) 172–73.
118 Koudelka, *Státní bezpečnost 1954–1968* (n 83) 131.
119 ibid 142.
120 Mirek Vodrážka, 'Svazek jako pohádkový pramen?' (2015) 4 Paměť a dějiny 74 (citing Milan Churaň, *Encyklopedie špionáže: Ze zákulisí tajných služeb, zejména Státní bezpečnosti* (Libri 1993) 30).
121 Koudelka, *Státní bezpečnost 1954–1968* (n 83) 123.
122 ibid 128.
123 ibid 129.

thread of genuflection before the StB's superior knowledge weaves its way into a number of the file-stories we have reviewed.

In order to obtain a clearer sense of how the StB operated, it is helpful briefly to mention some figures and numbers. According to Koudelka, from 1951 to 1968 the StB investigated and documented the potential 'anti-state activities' of 125,000 individuals.[124] Between 1955 and 1968, 7,169 (or 9.53 per cent) of these cases ended with a proposal to a public prosecutor to conduct a criminal investigation.[125] Most cases were closed for lack of evidence. In 1964, only 4.7 per cent of all informers actively engaged with foreign enemies, despite the fact that problematic foreign elements were declared to be the StB's core preoccupation at the time.[126] According to Williams, the StB archives 'tell a story of chronic dissatisfaction with the product of informers' prying ... [and] operational preoccupation with grumbling workers and former members of political parties, and ignorance of real enemies' whereabouts'.[127] Furthermore, Williams notes that the StB was not particularly efficient during the period of normalization: '[L]ike the economy, the StB remained 'extensive' in its reliance on low-productivity labour and wasteful use of resources relative to results.'[128]

The StB consistently maintained a malleable and capacious understanding of 'national security' to cover all information of any sort and to justify the extractive marshalling of informer human capital. On the one hand, this led to trivial, gossipy, and scurrilous information being vacuumed and recorded in the name of national security, despite this information having no tangible bearing on actual or potential threats to the state. While seemingly ludicrous or absurd,[129] the StB's broad definition permitted it to act invasively and thereby lord substantial power over individuals which concomitantly anchored its authority and that of the Communist state. To be sure, our review of the StB files indicates that the StB considered its informers of lower value when they failed to provide any information related to what a conventional understanding of national security might prioritize, including, for example, uncovering an act of sabotage, a resistance political rally, printing *samizdat*, meeting foreigners, planning public order crimes, or obtaining goods in violation of legal restrictions. That said, the sheer breadth of the working definition of national security still meant that the StB considered virtually any content worthy of transcription and documentation. This optic pervades the StB files. Indeed, the

[124] ibid 78.

[125] ibid 79.

[126] ibid 55.

[127] Williams, 'The StB in Czechoslovakia' (n 15) 35.

[128] Williams, 'The Czechoslovak Security Service During Normalisation' (n 43) 137. Although this research is focused on the normalization years, the inefficiency of the StB remained chronic.

[129] See also Miller, *The Stasi Files Unveiled* (n 70) 4, 54 (noting that 'Stasi informers were primarily engaged in the amassing of vast amounts of often seemingly trivial pieces of information' and that 'many of the reports on specific individuals to be found in the Stasi files are concerned with apparently trivial information').

creation of systemic informer networks transcends the collection of information and also serves the controllingly manipulative social function of generating pervasive anxiety.

In 1968, a downsizing of the StB was envisaged. The StB was to be renamed 'the Czechoslovak Counterespionage Service'. Its focus was to be limited exclusively to activities against foreign intelligence. According to Order 39 of the Ministry of the Interior from August 1968, all criminal offences unrelated to 'foreign powers or foreign representatives' were to be transferred to the ordinary police—the *Veřejná bezpečnost* (VB)—and any StB units tasked with internal political issues were to be merged with those units dealing with economic matters.[130] However, these development plans were halted by Operation Danube in 1968 and ultimately voided by the ensuing reversal of any liberal reforms by the 'normalized' Party.[131] Indeed, '[d]uring the week after 20 August 1968, the StB was torn apart, with one faction collaborating with the invading forces, another trying to thwart them and still another adopting a "wait and see" stance'.[132]

The StB nevertheless 'rose from the ashes' in the aftermath of Operation Danube.[133] This apparent resurrection cannot be shorn from Soviet pressure or Moscow's ensuing support of the normalization regime. Due to their problematic attitudes, over 2,000 members of the national security forces were purged from the corps after having been assessed as unreliable,[134] and a significant number of StB officers went so far as to request their own dismissal.[135] By 1972, 73 per cent of StB commanders had been replaced.[136] Over time, however, StB ranks stabilized and then in fact grew. To be specific: 'Having numbered around 10,000 employees in spring 1968, by the start of the 1980s the StB had recovered its losses and grown to more than 12,000.'[137]

Constitutional reform in 1969 also affected the StB. After 1 January 1969, a move toward devolution occurred as Czechoslovakia transitioned 'from a unitary into a federal state' with more autonomy drifting to Czech and Slovak authorities.[138] Williams notes that

[130] Koudelka, *Státní bezpečnost 1954–1968* (n 83) 36.

[131] Jerguš Sivoš, 'Kontrarozvědka' in Bárta and others, *Biografický slovník* (n 101) 105.

[132] Williams, 'The Czechoslovak Security Service During Normalisation' (n 43) 122. This constitutes another form of collaboration in Czech history, namely among individuals who abetted the invading Soviets against the Czechoslovak leadership of the time.

[133] Pavel Žáček, 'Ostrá zbraň Státní bezpečnosti: Spolupracovníci StB ve směrnicích pro agenturně operativní práci 1947–1989' (republished from Petr Blažek (ed), *Opozice a odpor proti komunistickému režimu v Československu 1968–1989* (Dokořán 2005)) <https://www.ustrcr.cz/data/pdf/clanky/ostra-zbran-stb.pdf> accessed 10 March 2023, 25.

[134] Sivoš, 'Kontrarozvědka' (n 131) 107.

[135] Pavel Žáček, 'Secret Services in Murky Times' (2004) 1 The New Presence 19, 19.

[136] Williams, 'The StB in Czechoslovakia' (n 15) 32. See also Williams, 'The Czechoslovak Security Service During Normalisation' (n 43) 124.

[137] Williams, 'The Czechoslovak Security Service During Normalisation' (n 43) 124.

[138] ibid.

> [s]ecurity was not an exclusively federal matter, so separate Czech and Slovak interior ministries were created, and with them Main Directorates (coordinating and analytical staffs) for the StB in the respective republics ... [t]his change disrupted what had historically been a unified military-style hierarchy....[139]

In 1970, some recentralization occurred, which also allowed the federal government to abolish the Czech Main Directorate 'which had become a bastion of petulant hard-liners'.[140] Slovaks were afforded some asymmetric recognition. On a broader note, 'responsibility for the StB was concentrated in the federal interior ministry but divided among several deputy ministers, so that no individual could use it as a long-term power base, and probably also to dilute the StB's sense of a distinct corporate entity'.[141]

The 1970s and the first half of the 1980s were more or less dull years, as the majority of Czechoslovaks retreated to lull in their private spaces of home, hearth, and cottage. The last two decades of Communist rule are characterized by selective political repression of a milder nature. The StB again refocused on the enemy within—the so-called ideological diversion[142]—and on capitalist enemy influences.[143] The StB barely engaged with foreign foes. Although criminal prosecutions of high-level dissidents and other non-conformist individuals certainly occurred,[144] incarceration and state violence were not commonplace. Rather, the populace complied with regime norms due to resigned apathy or were kept in check by means of administrative harassment, including calling people in for repeated interrogations,

139 ibid. Overall, this change meant that '[t]he two parts of the country became more isolated and their interaction continuously declined, which caused alienation at the level of elites and the general public'. Adam Hudek, 'An Uncommon Course: Normalisation in Slovakia' in McDermott and Stibbe (eds), *Czechoslovakia and Eastern Europe in the Era of Normalisation* (n 1) 114.

140 Williams, 'The Czechoslovak Security Service During Normalisation' (n 43) 124.

141 ibid.

142 The concept of 'ideological diversion' was developed within the StB in the first half of the 1960s. This concept germinated within the idea that foreign intelligence services sought to foment subversion 'from within' by spreading propaganda and inciting conflict among Czechoslovak citizens. Foreign agents accordingly recruited 'ideologically unsteady and volatile' individuals from broader social groups in Czechoslovakia. Bílek, 'I Undertake Voluntarily' (n 73) 108.

143 Petr Zeman, 'XI. správa SNB (1974–1988): Stručný nástin vývoje a činnosti Správy kontrarozvědky pro ochranu ekonomiky' (2010) 7 Sborník Archivu bezpečnostních složek 277, 280.

144 Between 1969 and 1989, 4,758 individuals were convicted of political offences. This number does not include persons convicted of illegal emigration. However, in many cases, regime opponents were charged with non-political crimes such as attacks on state organs, parasitism, or public disturbance. Rychlík, *Československo v období socialismu* (n 8) 292, 293. See also Prokop Tomek, 'Špionáž v normalizačním Československu' (2008) 3 Paměť a dějiny 5, 8 (documenting instances of highly repressive persecution and prosecution of espionage). According to Tomek, the dire consequences of charges of alleged espionage, the pervasive manipulation of facts and evidence, and the protracted use of illegal means in these prosecutions during normalization resembled the StB tactics in the 1950s. The largest group of individuals affected by these practices were citizens who had emigrated from Czechoslovakia after 1968, and returned in the wake of the amnesty of 1969. Rozhodnutí prezidenta republiky o amnestii [Decision of the President of the Republic on Amnesty] Rozhodnutí č 52/1969 Sb (Czech) (adopted 27 May 1969).

banning individuals from certain jobs, selectively doling out benefits, or confiscating documents such as driving licences.[145]

Yet, much like it did in the 1960s, the StB actively harvested information on attitudes, predilections, and movements in society. Charter 77 and other more vocal dissident activities presented a challenge for the Communist Party at the time. The StB was preoccupied with monitoring and quashing such activism, as well as manipulating events.[146] For instance, because of 'Operation Asanace', hundreds of Charter 77 signatories and other regime opponents were compelled to emigrate through sustained blackmail, harassment, and even physical violence.[147] In response to mounting discontent within Czechoslovak society, the StB again created lists of supposedly hostile persons and also of groups that potentially involved 'antisocialist elements'.[148]

The Communist Party was cognizant of the StB's role in maintaining its power monopoly and consequently suppressed any potential criticism of the StB within its circles. In turn, the StB 'displayed total loyalty to the Communist Party and deliberately forewent any interventions into the higher echelons of the state administration or among party functionaries—the directives expressly forbade the enlisting of informers from top Party milieus'.[149] After 1985, and a leadership change at the Ministry of the Interior, the StB began to modify some of its 'obsolete work methods'.[150] Owing to economic pressures and gradual political changes throughout Communist Europe, the Party was forced to reorganize and downsize its security apparatus.[151] However, the Velvet Revolution had already begun before the envisaged large-scale reform agreed upon in 1988 could be implemented.[152] The StB fell into disarray. Its main preoccupation at the end of 1989 was how and where it could destroy its extensive archive and operational files. Perhaps symbolically, the StB's final large-scale covert operation consisted of annihilating any records of its past activities. On this note, current estimates suggest that somewhere between 36 per cent and 44 per cent of informer files were destroyed.[153]

The StB was dismantled in mid-February 1990. Its members and informers were banned from returning to positions of power and influence. The StB's former regional headquarters on Bartolomějská 4, a street named after the Church of Saint

[145] Rychlík, *Československo v období socialismu* (n 8) 292.

[146] Žáček, 'Secret Services in Murky Times' (n 135) 19, 20.

[147] Tomáš Bursík and Jaroslav Pažout, 'Odbojové, opoziční a nonkonformní aktivity v komunistickém Československu a jejich trestněprávní postihy: Základní charakteristika' in Tomáš Bursík and Jaroslav Pažout (eds), *Třídní nespravedlnost, Proměny politicky motivované perzekuce v Československu 1948–1989* (Ústav pro studium totalitních režimů 2020) 34.

[148] Žáček, 'Secret Services in Murky Times' (n 135) 20.

[149] Bílek, 'I Undertake Voluntarily' (n 73) 108.

[150] Žáček, 'Secret Services in Murky Times' (n 135) 20.

[151] ibid.

[152] Pavel Žáček, 'Iluze a realita: Poslední pokus o reformu Státní bezpečnosti' (1996) 3 Securitas Imperii 7.

[153] Žáček, 'Secret Services in Murky Times' (n 135) 20.

Bartholomew in Prague, were repurposed as the city's ordinary police headquarters. The StB had commandeered these buildings from their former use as a convent and had relocated the nuns to a detention camp. Convent cells became StB prison and interrogation chambers.[154] The street is lovely, with a gentle curve, belying the terrors that occurred within these architecturally pleasing structures. Today, other than Number 4 and some other adjacent buildings, the property has been restituted to the nuns.[155]

III. The StB and Its Informers

Facilitated by its capacious interpretation of what constituted 'national security', the StB largely relied on its reputation for omnipresence to fragment Czechoslovak society and endemically sow mistrust, particularly after Stalinism.[156] The StB usually employed around 9,000 people out of a population of 15 million.[157] Much like its counterparts in the other states of the Soviet bloc, the StB relied on wide agglomerations of 'secret collaborators' (*tajní spolupracovníci*)[158] to function effectively and sustain its reputation of ubiquity. The numbers of informers oscillated in light of structural factors such as varying levels of statal repression and surveillance. The Communist regime endeavoured to mobilize Czechoslovaks to participate actively in the fight against enemies by invoking propaganda. The media repeatedly issued calls for 'vigilance' and 'alertness',[159] and Communists created an atmosphere of fear and insecurity in which citizens were urged to keep their eyes open and report perceived wrongdoers.[160]

StB members and their informers infiltrated all parts of society from embassies to offices, schools, and sports clubs.[161] The StB crafted a dense surveillance network and thereby curried betrayal, mistrust,[162] fear, phlegmatism, and cynicism

[154] Tomek, *Estébáckou Prahou* (n 67) 37–38.

[155] ibid 50.

[156] Williams, 'The StB in Czechoslovakia' (n 15) 32.

[157] ibid.

[158] The direct translation of *tajní spolupracovníci* is 'secret collaborators'. However, in this book we use the overarching term 'informer'. We do so to distinguish informing from collaboration and spying, as mentioned in Chapter 1, Section I, 'Informers: Definition and Context'. Hence, we deploy the term 'informer' to refer to all categories of StB secret collaborators. The typology of informers and its development in StB internal guidelines is extensively discussed in Chapter 2, Section III.B. 'Categories of Informers'.

[159] Milan Bárta, 'Úvod' in Milan Bárta (ed), *Člověk v soukolí StB* (Ústav pro studium totalitních režimů 2020) 9.

[160] To be sure, in a theme which we explore in Chapter 7, 'Informers Here, Informers There, Informers Everywhere', the notion of citizens' reporting on troubling things is a constant among police work anytime and anywhere. Indeed, in the current language of the British Transport Police: 'See it. Say it. Sorted' (*British Transport Police*, 2023) <https://www.btp.police.uk/police-forces/british-transport-police/areas/campaigns/see-it-say-it-sorted/> accessed 12 August 2023.

[161] Kaplan, *Nebezpečná Bezpečnost* (n 15) 115.

[162] Incubating mistrust was a common practice of state security forces throughout Communist Europe. Herta Müller's book *The Land of Green Plums* offers a gripping account of the lives of four

throughout society; the StB was simultaneously 'nowhere and everywhere'.[163] It stewed and brewed unease by turning citizens against citizens; loyalties frayed and individuals pettily looked out for themselves.

The StB regarded its network of informers as 'the main weapon in its fight against enemies'.[164] An StB officer 'without a well built, organized, and directed network of agents is merely an office bureaucrat unable to uncover and defuse enemies'.[165] Informers were considered the main tool of StB activities and the most important component of the StB's operational outreach.[166]

A. The StB's Work, Worth, and Network

The intensity, forms, and methods of StB 'agency work' with informers fluctuated amid Communism's different phases.[167] StB professional practices were often officially revised. These methods were modified according to how Party leadership or top StB officers viewed the international situation, as well as perceptions of the regime's internal stability at the time.[168] The Ministry of the Interior repeatedly issued directives and orders to govern operational work with informers.[169]

young people who are members of a German-speaking minority in Ceauşescu's Communist Romania. The main character laments: 'My distrust caused everything close to me to slide away.' Herta Műller, *The Land of Green Plums* (Picador 1993) 131.

[163] Tomek, *Estébáckou Prahou* (n 67) 9.

[164] Order 72/1954 (n 99) 4. See also Tajný rozkaz ministra národní bezpečnosti—'Práce s agenty' [Secret Order of the Minister of National Security—'Work with Agents'], Vhyl č 36/1951 Sb (Czech) (issued 10 December 1951) 132 (identifying informers as the 'primary' tool in this regard) (hereafter Order 36/1951).

[165] Order 72/1954 (n 99) 4; Order 36/1951 (n 164) 132.

[166] Koudelka, *Státní bezpečnost 1954–1968* (n 83) 45.

[167] Agency work refers to the ways in which the StB operated with its informers, including recruitment and management.

[168] Bílek, 'I Undertake Voluntarily' (n 73) 95.

[169] The Minister of the Interior promulgated confidential orders and directives to regulate the recruitment of secret informers, work methods, and informer classification. Such regulations were frequently issued and updated. See eg Ministerstvo vnitra—'Pomůcka administrativně—operační pro krajská velitelství Státní bezpečnosti' [Ministry of the Interior—'Administrative-Operational Aid for Regional Headquarters of the State Security'], Vhyl č 30640/022-48 Sb (Czech) (issued 15 December 1948) (hereafter 1948 Administrative-Operational Aid); Ministerstvo vnitra—'Pomůcka administrativně—operační pro skupinu BA a' [Ministry of the Interior—'Administrative-Operational Aid for the Group BA a'], Vhyl č 30641/022-48 Sb (Czech) (issued 17 January 1949) (hereafter 1949 Administrative-Operational Aid); Order 36/1951 (n 163); Order 72/1954 (n 99); Rozkaz ministra vnitra—'Směrnice pro agenturně operativní práci Státní bezpečnosti' [Order of the Minister of the Interior—'Directive for Agency-Operational Work of State Security'], Vhyl č 13/1962 Sb (Czech) (issued 16 May 1962) (hereafter Order 13/1962); Rozkaz ministra vnitra—'Směrnice pro práci s tajnými spolupracovníky československé kontrarozvědky' [Order of the Minister of the Interior—'Directive for Work with Secret Collaborators of the Czechoslovak Counter-Intelligence'], Vhyl č 8/1972 Sb (Czech) (issued 16 February 1972) (hereafter Order 8/1972); Rozkaz ministra vnitra—'Směrnice pro práci se spolupracovníky kontrarozvědky (A-oper-I-3)' [Order of the Minister of the Interior—'Directive for Work with Collaborators of the Counter-Intelligence A-oper-I-3'], Vhyl č 3/1978 Sb (Czech) (issued 25 January 1978) (hereafter Order 3/1978).

Nonetheless, the StB's work with informers was characterized by 'a longstanding lack of legal norms governing at least in outline not only the use of secret collaborators but the work of the secret police in general, as well as StB officers' continued unwillingness to adhere to the laws that did exist'.[170]

The StB 'essentially did not use informers' between 1945 and 1948, instead 'focusing its energies in that period primarily on the investigation of cases of retribution'.[171] It was only after the intelligence service was formally incorporated into the StB in 1947 that the StB's work with informers began to develop in earnest. At the time, the Communist Party was preparing for its takeover of power and was therefore eager to harvest compromising information on members of other political parties. The Communist Party recruited informers from the ranks of other political parties.[172] However, Bílek notes that in these early years the StB's intelligence work was not particularly effective. The inexperienced StB officers

> lacked higher education, a broader perspective, social skills and the ability to deal with people from different classes. Though they carried out their work with enthusiasm and total dedication, the[se] shortcomings ... necessarily impacted the quality of their agency network.[173]

While zealous, StB officers 'had no idea what to ask of their collaborators'.[174] Moreover, in these tumultuous early days, many informers were recruited among friends and lovers of the officers or they were sketchy characters who were only willing to cooperate for money.[175]

The post-1948 'intensification of class struggle' was reflected in the progressive standardization and growing emphasis placed on the development of methods and best practices to work effectively with informers. However, recruiting useful and suitable informers proved a daunting challenge. According to Bílek, the informers' network was still dominated by overt proponents of the regime or members of the Communist Party who in both cases simply could not obtain and deliver relevant information from hostile circles.[176] Informers enlisted from the opposition and hostile groups moreover tended to sabotage their cooperation and did not really provide the StB what it sought.[177]

Although the StB demonstrated some capacity to build an extensive agency network, the quality of informers and the harvested information remained subpar.

170 Bílek, 'I Undertake Voluntarily' (n 73) 95.
171 ibid 103.
172 Kaplan, *Protistátní Bezpečnost* (n 3).
173 Bílek, 'I Undertake Voluntarily' (n 73) 104.
174 ibid.
175 ibid; Bílek, 'Agenturní centrála StB' (n 77) 9.
176 ibid 9, 21.
177 ibid.

From 1948 to 1951, coordinating the StB informers' network took the form of 'continuous improvisation and a rather chaotic alternation of different conceptions'.[178] The challenges of earlier times largely persisted. Recruitment was random and opportunistic. StB officers seemingly did not pay attention to whether an informer was useful or capable of obtaining the desired information; the StB appeared to simply take its chances with willing individuals.[179] Blackmail remained a predominant recruitment tool. In certain instances, StB officers did not shy away from deliberately conjuring fake materials, such as pornographic pictures, to compromise selected individuals.[180]

The StB leadership soon realized that informing under coercive blackmail did not lead to steady cooperation nor particularly reliable information.[181] In short, these methods were unproductive. Furthermore, scandals arose. For instance, in Prague certain StB officers maintained intimate relations with their female informers or with arrested individuals.[182] In other instances, excessive and inappropriate drinking sessions among StB officers and informers came to light. Professionalism was lacking.

In 1951, an audit of StB agency work identified serious flaws in prevailing practices, such as inappropriate selection and governing of informers and the use of blackmail or physical violence.[183] Soviet advisors, moreover, began to push for enhanced standardization. In 1954, a new directive governing interactions with informers lauded the results achieved while simultaneously identifying 'important shortcomings' that hindered the fight against the enemies.[184] Rather than 'recruiting agents with access [to enemy circles]', StB officers squandered 'most of their time on meetings with confidants' who, as noted in this same directive, tended to be workers and functionaries already congenial with the Communist establishment.[185] In the 1950s, the burgeoning prison population and number of forced labourers in TNPs enabled the StB to make use of political prisoners who were either intimidated into cooperation or came forward with the expectation of preferable treatment amid their desperate circumstances. These individuals informed on fellow inmates. A number of the informer files we reviewed reveal such StB recruitment methods; in some cases, the recruited informer nonetheless developed a decades-long relationship with the StB after being released from prison. At times, the StB provided these informers with information the StB wanted to

178 Bílek, 'I Undertake Voluntarily' (n 73) 105.
179 ibid.
180 ibid.
181 ibid.
182 Bílek, 'Agenturní centrála StB' (n 77) 28.
183 Žáček, 'Ostrá zbraň Státní bezpečnosti' (n 133) 7.
184 Order 72/1954 (n 99) 4.
185 ibid. See also Žáček, 'Ostrá zbraň Státní bezpečnosti' (n 133) 11.

hear: informers simply repeated what the StB had told them to 'report' or in a similar vein just signed reports that were preprepared by StB officers.[186]

Changing times nevertheless necessitated new practices. Political trials, where one or two informers sufficed to uncover close-knit enemy groups, dwindled in number during the second half of the 1950s. The StB gradually refocused on blanket surveillance of society and its agency work became 'far more systematic and long-term'.[187] The number of informers rose from 30,000 registered individuals in 1954 to 41,859 in 1959.[188] To be clear: these figures reflect the total number of informers, not the number of new informers recruited in that particular year.

In 1955, the Ministry of the Interior promulgated a rule that each StB officer working in operational units should manage eight to ten informers, which induced some StB officers to compete over who could secure more informers.[189] However, in the 1960s, the dynamics of liberalization and the attenuation of the Party's paranoia created a situation in which the numbers of informers steadily declined each year. According to Bílek, this was a period in which the StB's agency work stagnated.[190] For example, in 1968, the StB registered merely 11,337 informers.[191]

Moreover, many individuals rejected collaboration in the wake of the Soviet-led 1968 invasion. In 1969, the StB recorded a 'bleak' total number of 5,693 informers.[192] According to Bílek, 'after losses in 1968 and 1969, the network of agents consolidated again in quantitative terms at the start of 1970s, and the number of collaborators started growing again [until 1982 at least]'.[193] In 1976, a total of 10,038 informers officially collaborated with the StB.[194] Bílek states that 'the StB maintained the standard that it had reached in preceding periods in this area and continued to consolidate it'.[195] Williams generally corroborates these findings:

> Before 1968, the StB had relied in an average year on more than 17,000 citizens to spy on family, friends, neighbours and colleagues, but this number had been falling steadily as agents ending their collaboration outstripped those being

[186] Martin Tichý, '"Vše je vymyšleno, vylháno a zkombinováno mnou ..." Konfrontace výpovědi agenta StB ve vězení a vzpomínek pamětníka: Několik otázek nad příběhem jména B' (2011) 9 Sborník ABS 125.

[187] Bílek, 'I Undertake Voluntarily' (n 73) 106. See also Kaplan, *Nebezpečná Bezpečnost* (n 15) 114.

[188] Koudelka, *Státní bezpečnost 1954–1968* (n 83) 52. It is worth noting that the reliability and credibility of such numbers obtained from internal StB documents and sources remains partially questioned by historians. ibid and also detailed discussion in Chapter 1, Section III, 'Secret Police Archives and File-Stories'.

[189] Koudelka, *Státní bezpečnost 1954–1968* (n 83) 53.

[190] Bílek, 'I Undertake Voluntarily' (n 73) 107–08.

[191] Koudelka, *Státní bezpečnost 1954–1968* (n 83) 52.

[192] Sivoš, 'Kontrarozvědka' (n 131) 106.

[193] Bílek, 'I Undertake Voluntarily' (n 73) 109.

[194] Pavel Žáček, 'Obnova agenturní sítě kontrarozvědky na počátku normalizace' in Jiří Petráš and Libor Svoboda (eds), *Bezčasí: Československo v letech 1972–1977* (Ústav pro studium totalitních režimů & Jihočeské muzeum v Českých Budějovicích 2018) 264.

[195] Bílek, 'I Undertake Voluntarily' (n 73) 108.

> recruited. With the suspension of most domestic operations in spring 1968, the number on the books plunged by 41 per cent. In all of 1969, only 144 new informers were added. There was some growth in 1970 and 1971, but then in 1972 Minister Kaska ordered a review that thinned the ranks again. After reaching a nadir at the end of 1972, the number of informers almost doubled in 1973 and by the end of 1976 had swelled to 10,038. As before 1968, turnover also remained high, so even in 1980, the estimated total stood at 12,566, still well below pre-1968 levels.[196]

In 1990, the StB and its remaining stable of informers were abruptly abolished. Nevertheless, the presence of the informer did not evaporate from Czech discursive spaces. Quite the contrary: following the Velvet Revolution, the shadow of the informer seared the public imagination and polarized political discussion on dealing with the Communist past. We elaborate upon the political, legal, and transitional aspects of this reckoning in Chapter 3.

Estimates of the aggregate number of StB informers throughout its forty-year existence vary. Indeed, data are a bit fuzzy. Koudelka states that already by the end of 1968, 153,000 individuals had passed through the ranks of informers.[197] Moran, for his part, identifies 18,000 full-time StB workers and 140,000 informers.[198] Other reports put the StB informer figure as hovering between 150,000 and 160,000.[199] In comparison, Moran concludes the East German Stasi had 86,000 full-time workers and 2 million informers.[200] Hence, according to Moran, 'while the ratio of security to non-security people in the GDR was 1:8, in Czechoslovakia it was 1:100'.[201] Moran also effects a comparison with Bulgaria, where the ratio of security

196 Williams, 'The Czechoslovak Security Service During Normalisation' (n 43) 124–25.

197 Koudelka, *Státní bezpečnost 1954–1968* (n 83) 62. Unfortunately, we are not aware of work as detailed and meticulous as Koudelka's that presents a statistical overview of the basic numbers and figures related to the StB beyond 1968. In short, to our knowledge, there is no academic research presenting StB developments and work in rigorous quantified fashion for the full period of Communist rule (1948–1989). That said, it is possible to cobble together an overview from a variety of partial sources.

198 John P Moran, 'The Communist Torturers of Eastern Europe: Prosecute and Punish or Forgive and Forget?' (1994) 27(1) Communist and Post-Communist Studies 95, 104.

199 Hauner, 'Crime and Punishment in Communist Czechoslovakia' (n 19) 346.

200 Moran, 'The Communist Torturers of Eastern Europe' (n 198) 104. Espíndola Mata provides different figures for the DDR. He finds that nearly 600,000 citizens were informers. Espíndola Mata, *Transitional Justice After German Reunification* (n 70) 2. One of the challenges in the German Democratic Republic (East Germany, DDR), and perhaps in other former Communist regimes throughout Europe, is precisely estimating the number of informers. For example, evidence is emerging that the actual number of DDR informers substantially increases if informal informer networks, rather than only official Stasi networks, are included in the totals. Peter Wensierski, 'East German Snitching Went Far Beyond the Stasi' *Spiegel International* (Berlin 10 July 2015) <https://www.spiegel.de/international/germany/east-german-domestic-surveillance-went-far-beyond-the-stasi-a-1042883.html> accessed July 13, 2023 (noting *inter alia* how every apartment building maintained a superintendent [*Hausbuchbeauftragter*] who kept notes on who visited whom and when; that the ordinary police benefited from voluntary helpers; and that schools, factories, and many social organizations were bursting with informers). Such inclusions might help explain the differences between the figures cited by Moran and Espíndola Mata when it comes to total estimates of the number of informers in East Germany.

201 Moran, 'The Communist Torturers of Eastern Europe' (n 198) 104.

to non-security associated people stood at 1:33.[202] Yuri Druzhnikov estimates that one in every eighteen Soviet citizens was a KGB informer.[203] Regardless of exact totals and ratios, which are always difficult to discern precisely and do not necessarily quantify informal reporting, the bottom line is that the informer network in Czechoslovakia was less dense than in other Warsaw Pact countries.

Only a minority of StB informers was recruited from the Communist Party and this number decreased over time. Compared to 38.6 per cent of informers registered as Party members in 1955,[204] from 1964 to 1967, Party members accounted for between 7 and 10 per cent of informers, thereby mirroring the proportion of Party membership in the Czechoslovak population.[205] That said, Party members regularly provided information without any formal agreement with the StB, this being another dynamic that affects the total number of informers as well as the pervasiveness of a culture of informing.[206]

As the StB focused most of its attention on social groups whose members were perceived as openly or secretly hostile to, critical of, or at a minimum indifferent to the regime, recruiting collaborators from the ranks of such groups was not straightforward.[207] However, Williams notes that the majority of informers were not coerced into signing up.[208] Nevertheless, blackmail was not uncommon, and compromising material was leveraged by the StB, particularly in the early years before it realized that informers recruited in this way could not be dependably harnessed.[209] On this note, Koudelka reports that in 1962, 30 per cent of agents were bullied into cooperation when confronted with evidence of their own criminal activity, their collaboration with the enemy during the Second World War, or their sexual indiscretions.[210]

Additionally, David notes an apparent gender imbalance among informers. David reports that his estimates reveal that 85.8 per cent of informers were men, and 10.2 per cent were women.[211] Women and men were recruited in similar ways, but the StB considered women to be particularly susceptible to threats

[202] ibid 107.

[203] Yuri Druzhnikov, *Informer 101* (Routledge 1997) 179.

[204] Koudelka, *Státní bezpečnost 1954–1968* (n 83) 58. The Ministry of the Interior considered the large proportion of KSČ members among informers to be a problem. Accordingly, the StB was urged to ratchet down the proportion of Communist Party adherents among the informer population.

[205] Williams, 'The StB in Czechoslovakia' (n 15) 34 (relying on Koudelka, *Státní bezpečnost 1954–1968* (n 83) 59).

[206] ibid.

[207] Bílek, 'I Undertake Voluntarily' (n 73) 96.

[208] Williams, 'The StB in Czechoslovakia' (n 15) 34.

[209] Jiří Urban, 'Pedagog, Agronom a Úředník Mlékárny: Agenti Státní bezpečnosti proti odpůrcům kolektivizace' in Bárta (ed), *Člověk v soukolí StB* (n 159) 195.

[210] Koudelka, *Státní bezpečnost 1954–1968* (n 83) 57–58 (noting also percentages of 4.4 per cent for residents and of 18.6 per cent for the specific StB category of informers).

[211] David, *Communists and Their Victims* (n 16) 38–39 (noting that in the remaining 4 per cent of cases it was not possible to determine gender).

and blackmail.[212] The StB noted women's 'gender-specific' intelligence capabilities, which included 'their ability to induce compassion and solidarity (woman to woman), their art of capturing [the] interest of men and gain their trust', and thereby being able to infiltrate very private spheres.[213]

Although not without exception, informers were typically over the age of eighteen at the time of their recruitment.[214]

B. Categories of Informers

In a classificatory sense, the StB differentiated among informers based *inter alia* on the characteristics of their relationship with the StB and their intelligence potential.

In the immediate heyday following 1948, the StB adopted a rather sloppy heuristic when it came to classing informers,[215] and these categories were tightened in ensuing years. Despite longitudinal variations, as well as some categories becoming obsolete over time, it is possible to identify six recurring categories of informers. The first four—agents, residents, informers, and owners of conspirational flats—were officially considered 'secret collaborators', meaning that their relationship with the StB was routinely formalized by their written pledge to collaborate; these individuals were also seen as part of the StB agency network. Secret collaborators were conceptualized as the main tool in the fight against subversion, and they helped StB officers to 'disclose, elaborate on, prevent, and document anti-state criminal activities'.[216] The two remaining categories, confidants and candidates, played more auxiliary roles: their cooperation assumed an ad hoc character and they were meant to 'assist [the StB in] fulfilling partial tasks of state security character'.[217] Any one individual could move from one category to another and thus could be, in a sense, promoted or demoted. Indeed, such movement was not at all uncommon. In fact, it radiates through many of the file-stories in our dataset.

[212] Markéta Doležalová, 'Věra Hložková: Žena, Přítelkyně Ministrů, Agentka StB' in Bárta (ed), *Člověk v soukolí StB* (n 159) 198.

[213] ibid.

[214] In the 1980s, the StB also used teenagers, aged fifteen to eighteen years, in its counter-intelligence activities, but did so only sparingly. Matúš Burčík, 'Child Agents of the ŠtB Escaped Even Historians' (*SME*, 20 November 2011) <https://domov.sme.sk/c/6147564/detski-agenti-stb-unikli-aj-historikom.html> accessed 22 February 2023 (interviewing Milan Bárta). See also 'File no 745498 MV', registration no 33360 (Ivana). Ivana's file describes a girl who began her informing career at the age of seventeen. She supplied the StB with information about her peers who were unable to graduate high school as a result of her informing. Ivana's story also features in Jiří Plachý, 'Operace Kněz a Zahradník, Dvojitý úspěch Mělnické StB v boji s vnitřním nepřítelem' (2003) 10 Securitas Imperii 59. For a more granular discussion of Ivana, Barbora Holá and Mark A Drumbl, 'Children as Informers and Denouncers' in Christelle Molima and others (eds), *Children's Fights: Commonalities and Differences Across Time, Space and Place* (Routledge forthcoming).

[215] See eg Žáček, 'Ostrá zbraň Státní bezpečnosti' (n 133); Marián Gula, 'Vývoj typů spolupracovníků kontrarozvědky StB ve směrnicích pro agenturní práci' (1994) 1 Securitas Imperii 6– 17.

[216] Order 3/1978 (n 169) art 5.

[217] ibid art 17.

We list here the six official categories of informers, together with the dates when this classificatory nomenclature was operative. Just as a reminder to readers, we generically use the term 'informer' to describe a person who fits into any one of these six categories. Because the StB used the term 'informer' as only one of the six categories until 1972, confusion may arise: just to be clear, then, throughout this book our definition of informer is broader and covers all six categories.[218]

Agent [in Czech: Agent]. 1948–1989. Agents were conceived as 'the highest rank' or most capable informers. They were individuals with the capacity to infiltrate foreign and domestic opposition circles and work on individual cases germane to state security. They were considered trustworthy and reliable.

Informer [in Czech: Informátor]. 1948–1972. Informers were individuals who could not fully earn the confidence of 'enemies' but could still collect valuable information. Similar to agents, informers regularly stayed in touch with the StB, and they proffered more general information from hostile environments. However, criteria for their recruitment became increasingly restrictive over time. By the early 1970s existing informers were either to become agents or removed from the StB agency network.[219]

Resident [in Czech: Rezident]. 1948–1989. Residents were tasked by the StB to manage a group of agents and mediate between them and the StB. Residents were mainly used in cases where circumstances impaired regular contact between StB officers and agents, such as in foreign states or in military counter-intelligence.[220]

Owner of a conspirational or loaned flat [in Czech: Držitel konspiračního/propůjčeného bytu]. 1954–1989. Owners of conspirational flats allowed the StB to use their residences to meet with informers. This category also included persons who agreed to permit their names to be listed as a proxies for premises actually owned by the StB.

Confidant [in Czech: Důvěrník; Důvěrný pramen].[221] 1950–1989. Confidants were individuals who did not enter into formal relationships with the StB. They furnished information on an irregular basis. Much of the information they supplied was anecdotal. They did not routinely submit reports, and the StB considered them to be outside the formal bureaucratic agency network. Anyone who provided an StB officer with any banal information could have

218 As an aside, our review of the StB files involves individuals from each of these six categories. We mention the StB category or categories (if there was movement) of each informer in each of the file-story summaries we have prepared.

219 Žáček, 'Ostrá zbraň Státní bezpečnosti' (n 133) 26.

220 Bílek, 'I Undertake Voluntarily' (n 73) 96.

221 To make matters even more complex, it should be noted that, in the 1948 Administrative-Operational Aid, the term 'confidant' was used for the category subsequently named 'agent'. 1948 Administrative-Operational Aid (n 169). The StB at that time considered the label 'agent' to be 'opprobrious'. Žáček, 'Ostrá zbraň Státní bezpečnosti' (n 133) 2.

theoretically been considered a confidant. According to Bílek, when pressures existed for StB officers to expand their agency network, '[i]t was child's play for an adroit intelligence officer to pass a confidant off as an informer'.[222] In some instances, confidants and candidates for secret collaboration (the last of the StB's categories) were unaware that the StB had opened a file on them or that the information they shared with the StB was being diligently recorded in all its detail.

Candidate for secret collaboration [in Czech: Kandidát tajné spolupráce]. Candidates were individuals with whom the StB entered into preliminary contact. Basically, the StB considered them as potential recruits. However, in practice, as our review of the files indicates, some candidates met with the StB on a regular and long-term basis, and their 'candidacy' could have lasted for years without their status ever being modified. The opening of the StB archives may have been startling to those confidants and candidates who may have been ignorant of the import of the conversations they were having. Still, some confidants and candidates knowingly supplied reams of information to the StB that the StB may well have acted upon.

Looking at all the categories, there was no discernibly direct relationship between the 'type' of informer and the content of the information supplied or the StB's response to that information. Moreover, based on our review of the files as we discuss in Chapters 4 and 5, there does not seem to be much motivational congruence clustered within the category in which the StB placed an informer. In other words, these classifications do not reveal different drivers as to why individuals spoke with the StB in the first place.

C. The Informing Relationship

The informing relationship between StB officers and their informers was idiosyncratic: it hinged upon context (historical, socio-political, and situational) and the dispositions of the implicated individuals.

Although the recruitment process was initially unregulated, 'Ministerial administrative aids' elucidated the first brief instructions in 1948 and 1949.[223] StB officers were asked to screen prospective candidates, collect all actual information, and draft a recruitment proposal to be approved by their superior. A similar practice was maintained in subsequent years, particularly for comprehensive screening and approval. Shortly after recruitment, it became customary for an informer to sign a pledge to collaborate. After that, it was often the case that no further instructions

222 Bílek, 'I Undertake Voluntarily' (n 73) 97.
223 1948 Administrative-Operational Aid (n 169); 1949 Administrative-Operational Aid (n 169).

were provided, although later directives became somewhat more specific. That said, Bílek notes that *de facto*, especially in the early years, many StB officers did not punctiliously adhere to prescribed procedures.[224] StB officers at times acted whimsically, even cruelly fabricating compromising material with which recruits were strong-armed into cooperation,[225] and even going so far as to deploy physical violence to compel people into signing pledges.[226]

The 1954 directive formalized three bases for recruitment: (i) compromising material, meaning information of a person's criminal activities; (ii) patriotic reasons and sympathies for the official peoples' democratic establishment; and (iii) material advantages, monetary or otherwise.[227] The most reliable informers were to be considered those recruited on the basis of patriotic reasons. Indeed, the 1962 directive stipulated that 'agents are to be recruited primarily voluntarily, based on patriotic reasons, in particular from groups of honest and politically conscious citizens who are willing to help state security and socialist consciousness'.[228] StB officers were still permitted to leverage compromising materials, such as minor criminal offences or violations of principles of socialist cohabitation. However, these materials were always to be 'properly established and supported by documents'.[229] The goal herein was to temper the use of blackmail, which became methodologically disfavoured insofar as it tended to yield subpar informational results.

Reflecting the new political situation following August of 1968, the 1972 and 1978 directives 'rehabilitated'[230] enlistment based on compromising materials. In fact, these directives pronounced all three bases of recruitment, ideological, material, or compromising as effective and scrapped ordinality as among them. Article 50 of the 1972 Directive and Article 38 of the 1978 Directive specified that ideological reasons relate to

> personal persuasion of a candidate of the necessity of the fight against internal and external enem[ies] stemming from the Marxist-Leninist worldview, socialist patriotism, [and] aversion to imperialism and imperialist wars, hate toward imperialist espionage, aversion to internal enemies, in particular after the experience of 1968.

Material advantages could entail 'regular salary, material care for the family of a secret collaborator, depositing in advance agreed amounts to [their] saving account, targeted bonuses, and other forms of material rewards'.[231] StB officers were

224 Bílek, 'I Undertake Voluntarily' (n 73) 100.
225 Order 72/1954 (n 99) (identifying this as one of the flaws of the previous recruitment practices).
226 Bílek, 'I Undertake Voluntarily' (n 73) 100.
227 Order 72/1954 (n 99) 13.
228 Order 13/1962 (n 169) art 4.
229 ibid art 5.
230 Bílek, 'I Undertake Voluntarily' (n 73) 108.
231 Order 8/1972 (n 169) art 51; Order 3/1978 (n 169) art 38.

instructed to avail themselves of compromising material only in reasoned or justified cases. Such material could include information relating to a person's reputation in public life, at work, or in private, as well as any information that could otherwise lead to criminal prosecution for misdemeanours.[232] The StB's search for compromising materials incited its interest in all sorts of gossip and scandal—including in intimate matters of personal life—the details of which fill many of the archived files. Although this scurrilous information appears irrelevant to the existential security of the state, the process of culling and harvesting all these tidbits fulfilled longer-term goals of reeling in new persons of interest and thereby further embedding authoritarianism.

StB officers were asked to record the reasons for recruitment in each case of an informer they successfully enlisted. Overwhelmingly, a 'patriotic/ideological' motivation was reported to the higher-ups and dutifully recorded in each informer file. Our read of the actual files and the dynamics they evince, however, suggests that this putative motivational reason does not seem to genuinely bear out, in actuality, for the vast majority of informers when it comes to identifying the drivers of their informing relationships. This discursive misalignment, in turn, then becomes a concern when former informers, after regime change, face calls for accountability, reckoning, and transitional justice.

According to the directives, prospective informers were to be selected based on personal characteristics (including their intellectual, psychological, and physical dispositions) along with their perceived abilities to infiltrate enemy and émigré circles.[233] All candidates were subjected to background checks and had to be approved by StB superior officers. Potential informers were to decide on their own volition whether to collaborate: voluntariness was emphasized as an integral pillar of recruitment.[234]

After initial recruitment, the modalities of contact and modes of collaboration differed in each individual case despite the fact that the directives did stipulate overarching guidelines. That said, similar to recruitment policies, best practices for the 'management' of informers grew increasingly stringent (and regularized) over time. Officers had to prepare properly for each meeting and carefully listen to and record what informers said while simultaneously resolving any residual ambiguities.[235] Routine meetings with informers were conducted in public spaces, such as cafés and restaurants, or in conspirational flats. Sometimes informers were involved in ongoing StB operations and were solicited to undertake particular tasks, while at other times they were dispatched to merely proffer general observations from their social circles.

[232] Order 8/1972 (n 169) arts 52–56; Order 3/1978 (n 169) arts 40–41.
[233] Order 8/1972 (n 169) arts 40–41; Order 3/1978 (n 169) arts 27–29.
[234] Order 8/1972 (n 169) art 49; Order 3/1978 (n 169) art 37.
[235] Bílek, 'I Undertake Voluntarily' (n 73) 101.

It is again important to underscore that the StB was still figuring out how to work productively with prospective collaborators in the initial phase after the Communist takeover. At that time, the StB approached informers as 'an essentially useful but also instrumental and often *ad hoc* tool'.[236] The largely inexperienced StB officers became either too close to and intimate with their cooperatives, or they remained too distant and disinterested. Either way, the informer's utility was not maximized. Indeed, striking the functionally optimal balance between intimacy and formality in the frame of StB agency work proved a challenge. The push and pull between proximity and intensity, on the one hand, and distance and reticence, on the other, surfaces in so many of the files that we have reviewed.

As early as 1948, StB officers were instructed to avoid behaviour that could give the impression of blackmail. Rather, they were to act more connivingly, even in situations of intimidation. They were to create a friendly atmosphere in which 'the recruit realizes that [the StB officer] helped him out of complicated situation'.[237] StB officers were to generate 'respect and a certain level of affection' during recruitment.[238] However, in 1951, a directive warned of excessive intimacy: '[I]n no case it is acceptable to admit any familiarity ... StB officers [were] prohibited from accepting any gifts, meals etc.'[239] Informers were to be educated by StB officers to 'realize that [they] work for the state' and not for the benefit of the individual StB officers.[240] Still, the connection between informer and StB officer remained a key predictive ingredient of the quality and regularity of the information supply. This, too, became immediately clear to us from our read of the files.

In 1954, the Ministry of the Interior still lamented the bimodality of excessively warm ('undesirable familiarity') or unduly frigid ('austere, superior, and disinterested') relationships between officers and their informers as one of the main defects of agency work.[241] Overall, the StB higher-ups seemed to fret more about those relationships that were too warm and consequently a balanced middle-ground was seen in StB officers' being instructed to conduct themselves as 'an authority'.[242] The StB top brass sought to discourage StB officers from 'enter[ing] into familiar relationships [with their collaborators], go[ing] on drinking sessions, [or] accept[ing] gifts or favours ... It [is] unacceptable to bring [informers] into officers' families, as well as to maintain relation with [informers]' famil[ies].'[243] We nonetheless located

236 Bárta, 'Úvod' (n 159) 9.

237 1948 Administrative-Operational Aid (n 169) art IV(1)(A)(c); 1949 Administrative-Operational Aid (n 169) art IV(1)(A)(c).

238 1948 Administrative-Operational Aid (n 169) art IV(2); 1949 Administrative-Operational Aid (n 169) art IV(3).

239 Order 36/1951 (n 164) art IV.

240 ibid.

241 Order 72/1954 (n 99) 6–7.

242 ibid 24.

243 ibid.

numerous instances in the archived files of such amities, particularly with family members, notably celebrating occasions together along with personal gift-giving.

In the 1950s a tweak in the relational model occurred, to wit, that the nurturing of a 'teacher–pupil relationship'[244] was considered ideal. Officers were to be 'examples of politically mature, devoted, modest and decent individuals with [proper] Communist morality'.[245] According to Bílek, '[m]utual trust and an "amicable" atmosphere (so that the collaborator would willingly share information gathered) was to be obtained ... [and] officer[s] w[ere] to cultivate this by taking an interest in the collaborator's personal and work life'.[246] This atmosphere was also to be sustained by 'systematic, individual, and concrete' education of informers.[247] StB officers should foster devotion to the regime, amelioration of intelligence and counter-intelligence skills, honesty, truthfulness, seriousness, moral firmness, and dedication among their informers.[248] Additionally, informers could be rewarded for their good services tangibly with money and gifts or symbolically with praise.[249] These policies are evident in the archived files, and we can readily see how they sculpted conversations, interactions, and expectations over decades.

Here, what emerges is a companionship of sorts between informer and officer—an emotional interactivity. The connective nature of the relationship between informers and 'their' StB officers can be palpable, especially when that relationship continues for years. We discern threads of this bonding, friendship, caring, and solicitude throughout the files.[250] Keefe identifies similar dynamics in Northern Ireland, where he notes that informing is 'lonely' so informers come to rely emotionally on their recruiters. Moreover, the relationship is not one way. Keefe notes that the police officer 'is the only person who knew [the informer's] secret ... as such [becoming] doctor, social worker, and priest'.[251] In the end, '[t]he tout's [note: Irish lingo for an informer] problems became his problems: repairs to the house, Christmas presents for the kids'.[252]

How did the informer-StB relationship end? This was generally by formal termination paperwork. Why did these relationships draw to a close? Multiple reasons surface. At times the ending was undramatic: the relationship just faded away in the sense that the informer lost relevant leads to supply pertinent information by getting a new job or moving to a different town. In other cases, informers

244 Bílek, 'I Undertake Voluntarily' (n 73) 101.
245 Order 13/1962 (n 169) art 34.
246 Bílek, 'I Undertake Voluntarily' (n 73) 101.
247 Order 72/1954 (n 99) 23; Order 13/1962 (n 169) art 32; Order 8/1972 (n 169) art 70; Order 3/1978 (n 169) art 55.
248 Order 72/1954 (n 99) 23; Order 13/1962 (n 169) art 32.
249 Order 72/1954 (n 99) arts 27–28; Order 13/1962 (n 169) art 36; Order 8/1972 (n 169) arts 108–113; Order 3/1978 (n 169) arts 86–88.
250 For detailed discussion, see Chapter 5, Section II, 'Informing as Intimacy and Conversation' and Chapter 5, Section V, 'Solicitude And Disappointment'.
251 Patrick Radden Keefe, *Say Nothing* (Anchor 2020) 248.
252 ibid.

gradually wilted owing to mental or physical health struggles or substance abuse. In such situations the StB no longer considered them sufficiently safe and terminated the collaboration. At other times, the ending was brusque. Some informers committed the StB's deadly sin of deconspiration, meaning that they revealed their contact with the StB, and hence their status as an informer, to somebody else. The informer–StB agent relationship was after all based on a strict commitment of secrecy. Occasionally, collaboration was also terminated because an informer's file was transferred to the ordinary police with a proposal for investigation.[253] Koudelka also reveals that in a surprisingly high number of cases an informer simply refused to continue to collaborate.[254] On infrequent occasion, collaboration was terminated because an informer 'misinformed' the StB.[255] Finally, collaboration obviously would end by virtue of the death of an informer, or if that informer fled the country or emigrated. We encountered each of these grounds for termination in our review of the archived files.

IV. Conclusion

Gazing beyond the *who* and *how* of informing, we wrote this book to help discern *why* people engaged with the StB and informed on others, including their families, neighbours, coworkers, and colleagues. This chapter serves as a starting point for this discussion.

Persons who lived under the Communist regime had to work through officially available political and professional structures—these could be coterminously coercive from the top down and navigable from the bottom up. Acts of collaboration with the StB can be seen as one way of tactically and strategically scaling possibilities and seizing the limited opportunities on tap in Czechoslovak Communist society. Similar to informers in neighbouring states, informers in Czechoslovakia had variable—sometimes very mundane—reasons to enter the web of the StB and continue engaging therein.[256]

Assuredly, as Bílek observes, the particular motivation of each informer was specific to that individual and also profoundly situational.[257] Bílek adds that a 'majority of people were "asked" to [inform] (albeit perhaps covertly or ambiguously,

[253] Koudelka, *Státní bezpečnost 1954–1968* (n 83) 63 (surveying the documented reasons as to why StB collaboration was terminated in the years 1954 to 1968).

[254] ibid.

[255] ibid.

[256] Krisztina Slachta, 'Unofficial Collaborators in the Tourism Sector: GDR and Hungary' in Apor, Horváth, and Mark (eds), *Secret Agents and the Memory of Everyday* (n 70) 310 (discussing a case study of two collaborators from DDR and Hungary).

[257] Bílek, 'I Undertake Voluntarily' (n 73) 100; Koudelka, *Státní bezpečnost 1954–1968* (n 83) 64; Milan Bárta, 'Snahy Státní bezpečnosti získat tajné spolupracovníky mezi bývalými příslušníky ministerstva vnitra' in Bárta (ed), *Člověk v soukolí StB* (n 159) 283.

as officers acted in such a way as to get the committed person to make the actual proposal) and rejecting such an "offer" was ... very difficult and in some cases virtually impossible.'[258] Our granular review of the StB files—further elucidated in Chapters 4 and 5 of this book—confirms Bílek's observations and nonetheless further indicates that many informers ignited the engine of their collaboration with their own ambition, career aspirations, or—more desperately—their willingness to fulfil the demands that the StB placed on them in order to retain their jobs, social status, or way of living.[259] Some informers even rejected the StB's offers, resolutely cabined the scope of their informing, and routinely found ways to rebuff or circumvent the StB's entreaties. Others began with little choice, as Bílek notes, but over time transcended this choicelessness and indeed came to exercise discernible agency and autonomy in their interactions with the StB along acquisitional lines.

It is important to emphasize that the history of Communist Czechoslovakia was not bleakly monotone. Seasons changed as did the ways in which the Party, the StB, and ordinary people interacted. The regime was exclusionary and participatory at the same time, and was laced with interactive pathways.

This effervescence interfaces queasily with the widely projected romanticist resistance narrative of Charter 77, the Prague Spring, and the Velvet Revolution. This resistance narrative bifurcates state (Communist authorities) from society. These bifurcations are somewhat artificial insofar as for decades the Communist Party of Czechoslovakia was sturdily buttressed by informers and a vast number of sycophants, connivers, believers, opportunists, supplicants, bystanders, passive acquiescers, side-standers, and along-goers. The regime was not imposed only from above, or from afar, or from outside. Historian Muriel Blaive trenchantly concludes:

> [T]he more distant the 1989 Velvet Revolution, the more the Czech state has been rewriting the history of Czechoslovak communism as a history of anticommunist heroism tamed by the Soviet domination. Since the woes of communism and therefore of post-communism are now conveniently blamed on the Russians and their Czechoslovak communist agents, historical research on the collaboration of ordinary Czechs with the communist regime is not only unwelcome, it is almost illegal. The law creating the Institute for the Study of Totalitarian Regimes in 2007 listed the themes of research this national institute of memory was to pursue: resistance and repression—*not* collaboration as a social practice.[260]

[258] Bílek, 'I Undertake Voluntarily' (n 73) 100.
[259] ibid. To be clear: Bílek also acknowledges these various different motivations.
[260] Muriel Blaive, 'Milan Kundera and Me' (*britskélisty*, 22 July 2023) <https://blisty.cz/art/114383-milan-kundera-and-me.html> accessed 23 July 2023.

The broadly circulated post-Velvet Revolution response to 'what did you do back then?' is somewhat reductionist.[261] Resistance was not as pervasive as the post-Communist political narrative intones.[262] Yet this narrative has become a powerful force in contemporary Czech life, spawned as part of Czech transitional justice. Thirty years after the Velvet Revolution, a 2019 exhibition of its anniversary at the National Museum in Prague featured (in a side room) around ten video interviews with individual Czechs of today, each of whom share strikingly similar stories, to wit, recounting acts of resistance in the past. Yet, in a sense anything and everything can retrospectively count as resistance:

> [I]t is tempting to evince 'resistance' not only in brazen acts of anti-government violence, but also in common practices such as low labour productivity, listening to jazz or the ubiquitous political joke. But the implication that all those workers who operated a 'go-slow' or flitted from job to job or engaged in anti-Gottwald banter in the pub were putative 'resisters' is surely problematic. While remaining at all times sensitive to the barbarous nature of the Stalinist system, we should not, I think, posit an undifferentiated oppositional Czech society locked in some unequal 'heroic' confrontation with an inorganic illegitimate state.[263]

Indeed, without conjuring *faux* nostalgia for halcyon days that never were, the fact remains that life under Communism was about much more than depressingly and passively following the state. Czech historian Miroslav Vaněk contests the extensive use of the colour grey to depict the Communist years.[264] He traces this penchant to many sources, including Havel's likening of normalization to a grey picture. Vaněk notes that, '[o]n account of his profession, interests and attitudes, the normalisation period was indeed a stagnant grey time for Havel'.[265] However, Vaněk hastens to add that Havel:

> [E]mployed a different frame of reference than most of the population. The majority had different needs which, on the basis of the 'social contract', they could more or less fulfil in their private lives.... It is ... unsatisfactory and misleading

[261] Muriel Blaive, 'Sanctimony as a Distortion of the Past and a Poison of the Future' (*Dénik Referendum*, 28 July 2020) <https://denikreferendum.cz/clanek/31487-sanctimony-as-a-distortion-of-the-past-and-a-poison-of-the-future> accessed 13 July 2023 (noting that 'people ... resented the post-communist attempt to present them as nothing but victims and heroes ... The painful historical truth [is] that the country massively collaborated with the communist regime, be it through the secret police, the communist party, or simply through having to survive in a dictatorship. This is not a value judgment; it's a fact...').

[262] David, *Communists and Their Victims* (n 16) 24 ('The proponents of the leading opposition movement, Charter 77, initially gathered 241 signatures and fewer than 2,000 in total by the end of the regime, again in contrast to the mass Solidarity Union movement in Poland.').

[263] McDermott, *Communist Czechoslovakia* (n 4) 84.

[264] Vaněk, 'Twenty Years in Shades of Grey?' (n 50) 145.

[265] ibid 148.

> to use [Havel's] experience, or the experiences of other persecuted dissidents, to characterize and label in retrospect an entire historical era.[266]

It is this intersectionality of informing with the navigation of diverse ordinary human needs, wants, desires, frailties, and resentments that beguiles us as researchers. The bottom line is that many tens of thousands of informers facilitated Communist governance. For a whole host of reasons, they brought at times even the most embarrassing private information forward to security forces. These security forces, in turn, could make use of that information in ways they considered fit and, thus, blight if not downright ruin people's lives. Sometimes tragic, at other times bullying, StB informers were hurt and they hurt others. This 'in between' space constituted a major challenge for transitional justice and dealing with the Communist past following the 1989 Velvet Revolution.

In Chapter 3, we will illustrate how post-Communist transitional justice viewed, dealt with, and stylized informers. Czech transitional justice did not pick up this challenge of finessing the subtle 'in between' when it came to informers. We will show that transitional justice moralized a construction of history in which Czechs were divided into categories of heroes, victims, and traitors, which came to serve political ends for the new regime.[267] Informers were largely consigned to the dustbin of traitors. Czech transitional justice was rather more retributive than it was restorative.[268] In the newly formed democracy, much nuance was lost. The figure of the dangerous informer, however much a caricature, instrumentally emerged as one of the symbols of the former Communist regime, its criminality, and all its depravities.

[266] ibid 148.

[267] Muriel Blaive, 'An Impossible Reconciliation: National (Heroic) Memory and Individual Identity in the Czech Republic' (*Politika*, 2 April 2022) <https://www.politika.io/en/article/an-impossible-reconciliation> accessed 3 March 2023, para 8.

[268] ibid para 11.

3
Reckoning with Informers and the Communist Past

We are all in this together—those who directly, to a greater or lesser degree, created this regime, those who accepted it in silence, and also all of us who subconsciously became accustomed to it.[1]

Václav Havel, 1993

We are not like them![2]

Among the chants of the Velvet Revolution, 1989

Political transition is not new to Czechs. Indeed, as political scientist Roman David notes: 'The Czechs are experts in regime change ... [t]he years 1918, 1938, 1945, 1948, 1968, and 1989 are years in which fundamental changes took place in the country's political structure.'[3] Secret police and informers were present in and embedded throughout many of these regimes. This observation is important, for it reveals informing as cyclically recurrent: a method of navigation, a modality of muddling through life, and an intrinsic strand of governance.[4]

I. Velvet Transition(s)

The 1989 Velvet Revolution was peaceful, reasoned, and modulated by apparent moderation.[5] The Velvet Revolution retained certain structural elements from

1 Adam Michnik and Václav Havel, 'Confronting the Past: Justice or Revenge?' (1993) 4(1) J of Democracy 20, 21 (in dialogue).

2 In Czech: '*Nejsme jako oni!*'

3 Roman David, *Communists and Their Victims: The Quest for Justice in the Czech Republic* (University of Pennsylvania Press 2018) 52.

4 See also Ron Dudai, *Penality in the Underground: The IRA's Pursuit of Informers* (OUP 2022) 34, 63 (describing the normalization of informing, namely, that it can become a routine aspect of life or, in other words, a given, and asserting that '[t]he use of informers has been an integral part of authorities' efforts to maintain law and order 'from the dawn of history') (citing Gary T. Marx, 'Thoughts on a Neglected Category of Social Movement Participant: The Agent Provocateur and the Informer' (1974) 80(2) American J of Sociology 402 (invoking a police manual)).

5 According to Czech lawyer and philosopher Jiří Kozák, 'an amicable take-over of power [in 1989] predetermined a moderate character of legal reaction to the past'. Jiří Kozák, *Právo na pomezí diktatury a demokracie* (Auditorium 2014) 98.

Informers Up Close. Mark A. Drumbl and Barbora Holá, Oxford University Press.
 DOI: 10.1093/oso/9780192855138.003.0003

the past.[6] That said, these retentions necessitated public repudiation of other past parts. The informer became thrust into this politicized place and therein assumed the role of foil. The case of Czechoslovakia is no exception to Ron Dudai's general observations that '[i]nformers are typically viewed with disdain by society',[7] and that, in moments of political transition, 'the informer seems to always be the least popular actor'.[8]

Indeed, after the Velvet Revolution, the construct of the informer served to ventilate some of these negative and destructive sentiments. Informers were doused in contempt. They became flotsam and jetsam to be cast aside. The 'collaboration question' was one of the more pugnacious dimensions in assessing and recasting the Communist past.[9] The StB informer was hoisted in public imagination and political discourse into traitorous status. As Timothy Garton Ash observes, since the Stalinist period Czechoslovak 'society was kept down by millions of Lilliputian threads of everyday mendacity, conformity, and compromise'.[10] Accordingly, blaming informers could assuage or obscure these endemic complicities. Havel's claim, that then and now 'we are all in this together' did not sit well with the popular motto—'we are not like them'—vociferated to advance the Velvet Revolution. This popular motto signifies separateness, cleanliness, and generational differentiation.

Conveniently, most StB collaborators were ostracized. They were blamed and shamed and excluded from public functions.[11] They were purged as deviants and menaces, outcast from what was held to be proper and well-mannered society. They were not the future; rather they were to be excised as part of rotten yesteryears. Informers were stylized as ideological degenerates. Paradoxically, other (at times fervent) supporters of and participants in the *ancien régime*—albeit not in informing capacities—who were deemed operationally useful to the new regime

[6] For instance, although Law No 480/1991 proclaimed that 'the Communist regime was violating human rights and its own laws', it also declared that all the laws adopted during Communism remain valid unless explicitly revoked. Zákon o době nesvobody [Law on the Time of Unfreedom], Zákon č 480/1991 Sb (Czech) paras 1–2 (adopted 13 November 1991). This law thereby provided continuity with the majority of existing laws. See also Zákon o protiprávnosti komunistického režimu a o odporu proti němu [Law on the Illegality of the Communist Regime and on the Resistance Against It], Zákon č 198/1993 Sb (Czech) (adopted 30 July 1993) (designating the Communist regime as 'illegal and criminal' while accepting the continuity of all laws and treaties from the Communist period unless explicitly abrogated) (hereafter Law on the Illegality of the Communist Regime). Nor was the Communist Party banned, dissolved, or prohibited; indeed, it remained in Parliament and entertained considerable voter support until the 2021 Parliamentary elections. The 2021 election marked the first time since the Velvet Revolution when the Communist Party failed to attain the threshold of 5 per cent of the vote to secure representation in the Chamber of Deputies.

[7] Dudai, *Penality in the Underground* (n 4) 37.

[8] ibid 8.

[9] Francoise Mayer, *Češi a Jejich Komunismus: Paměť a Politická Identita* (Helena Beguivinová tr, Argo 2009) 192–216.

[10] Timothy Garton Ash, 'Trials, Purges, and History Lessons' (*Atlas of Transformation*, 2011) <http://monumenttotransformation.org/atlas-of-transformation/html/h/history/trials-purges-and-history-lessons-timothy-garton-ash.html> accessed 23 July 2022.

[11] Martin Tichý, 'Tři rozdílné osudy' in Milan Bárta (ed), *Člověk v soukolí StB* (Ústav pro studium totalitních režimů 2020) 46.

could be presented as well-meaning deluded dupes capable of being reborn (in a sense vaccinated) through re-education—or simply out of necessity— into the new ideology of capitalist neo-liberalism.[12]

In the Czech Republic, transitional justice emerged as a mechanism to channel the viscerality of these public sentiments, lance the boil, purify society, rehabilitate victims, and reconstruct the *polis* from the 'time of non-freedom' into a putatively transparent, democratic, and liberal state. Transitional justice made the validation of the new regime official and ostensibly dissuaded vigilantism as well as ad hoc private shaming. Similar to other countries of the former Communist bloc, new Czech elites employed 'anti-Communism to distance themselves from their predecessors, to bring legitimacy to their new leadership, and to advance their political and economic agendas'.[13] Anti-Communism, in conjunction with the need to break decisively from the past, rhetorically animated policy choices, contoured perceptions of legitimacy, and directly sculpted transitional legislation and institution building.[14]

In this chapter, we briefly describe transitional justice laws and practices enacted and implemented in Czechoslovakia after the fall of the Communist regime, as well as in the Czech Republic in the wake of Czechoslovakia's dissolution at the start of 1993. Examples of such practices include proclamations, criminal trials, lustration, the opening of StB archives, rehabilitation, property restitution, and edification of memory institutes. We also touch upon architectural transitions and repurposing, namely, the 'look' of cities, towns, and villages. Although these methods, taken as a whole, were not *prima facie* retributive—for example, there were hardly any criminal trials—they were still starkly condemnatory. We concur with Muriel Blaive's insight that these methods favoured punishment, exclusion, and scapegoating over reconciliation.[15] What is more, regime change always creates new opportunities, and transitional justice served to regulate access thereto. We nod in the direction of Roman David's observation that '[w]ithout reconciliation, transitional justice is just a power game with new actors in the same role of exclusion'.[16]

Assuredly, Czech transitional justice mechanisms were never static. They underwent numerous changes and were recurrently contested. Critics popped up in many places from all spaces along the political spectrum. As we illustrate throughout this chapter, some critics asserted that the chosen transitional justice

[12] For example, local functionaries.

[13] Hillary Appel, 'Anti-Communist Justice and Founding the Post-Communist Order: Lustration and Restitution in Central Europe' (2005) 19(3) East Eur Politics and Societies 379, 379. See also Adam Czarnota, 'Lustration, Decommunisation, and the Rule of Law' (2009) 1 Hague J on the Rule of L 307.

[14] Appel, 'Anti-Communist Justice' (n 13).

[15] Muriel Blaive, 'An Impossible Reconciliation' (*Politika*, 2 April 2022) <https://www.politika.io/en/article/an-impossible-reconciliation> accessed 12 March 2023 para 4.

[16] Roman David, 'Transitional Justice Effects in the Czech Republic' in Lavinia Stan and Nadya Nedelsky (eds), *Post-Communist Transitional Justice: Lessons from Twenty-Five Years of Experience* (CUP 2015) 114.

modalities were insufficiently individuated and thereby stoked collective guilt. Others insisted they were overly retributive or were instrumentalized for ulterior political purposes. Some observers opined that transitional justice tediously trapped the country in the past, rather than let bygones be bygones. The Czech transitional path cannot be disentangled from the trajectories pursued by other former Warsaw Pact countries; nor can it be shorn from emergent transitional justice best practices that have gelled over recent decades and to which the Czech experience itself has contributed.[17]

Given our focus, we accord greater attention to laws and measures that directly addressed informers and the retrospective assessment of acts of informing. We observe that the specifics of an individual's path to informing, and the motivations and emotions that catalysed and sustained this path, did not seem to matter much to the machinery of transitional justice. Czech transitional justice lacked granular assessment or inquiry beyond determining whether the informing was knowing or unknowing. This machinery tended to cast informers as ideologically motivated dangers. While this move is perhaps politically understandable as a matter of pragmatics, we believe that digging deeper into the muck of why ordinary Czechs spoke to the StB is a worthwhile endeavour.

II. Proclamations and Prosecutions

In 1993, the Czech Parliament adopted a law that defined the Communist regime as 'criminal, illegitimate, and condemnable'.[18] Despite its predominantly declaratory character,[19] this law triggered some tangible legal consequences. For instance, the law suspended the statute of limitations for crimes committed during Communism which it defined as the period of time between 25 February 1948 and 17 November 1989.[20] Simply stated, the law declared that the four decades of

[17] Following the fall of Communism and the lifting of the Iron Curtain, affected states pursued similar yet divergent transitional justice trajectories. See eg Monika Nalepa, *Skeletons in the Closet, Transitional Justice in Post-Communist Europe* (CUP 2010); Lavinia Stan (ed), *Transitional Justice in Eastern Europe and the Former Soviet Union, Reckoning with the Communist Past* (Routledge 2009). Accordingly, although this chapter is a case study of the Czech Republic, abridged reference is occasionally made to experiences in other jurisdictions.

[18] Law on the Illegality of the Communist Regime (n 6) para 2(1).

[19] This law acquired considerable symbolic purchase for former political prisoners. It became their manifesto and was displayed in their offices and on their websites. Roman David and Susanne Choi Yuk-Ping, 'Victims on Transitional Justice: Lessons from the Reparation of Human Rights Abuses in the Czech Republic' (2005) 27(2) Human Rights Q 392, 400.

[20] Law on the Illegality of the Communist Regime (n 6) para 5. In its 1999 amendment of the Criminal Code, the Czech Parliament went one step further and legislated that certain crimes committed between 1948 and 1989 were forever excluded from any statute of limitation. Zákon, kterým se mění zákon č 140/1961 Sb., trestní zákon [Law which Amends the Law 140/1961 Sb., Criminal Code], Zákon č 327/1999 Sb (Czech) (adopted 9 December 1999). Similar laws were enacted in other nearby states. For example, in 1991, Hungary passed the Zétényi–Takács Act 'which retroactively suspended prescription of crimes committed in the period between 21 December 1944 and 2 May 1990 if they were not punished due to political reasons'. Martin Faix and Ondřej Svaček, 'Dealing with the Past: Prosecution

Communism did not count for any statute of limitation purposes. Moreover, in January 1995, a new Office for the Documentation and Prosecution of Communist Crimes (*Úřad dokumentace a vyšetřování zločinů komunismu*, ÚDV) was established under the auspices of the Ministry of the Interior; in 2002, the ÚDV became part of the regular police.[21] The ÚDV investigates crimes committed between 25 February 1948 and 29 December 1989 which, owing to political reasons, had historically been left unsanctioned. The ÚDV also documents Communist repression.

Despite all this bustle, only a very limited number of criminal cases have materialized. In contrast to the post-Second World War reckoning with Nazis and their local collaborators, retributive justice in the form of criminal prosecutions did not dominate the post-Communist transitional landscape. Between 1995 and October 2022, 43 individuals received conditional sentences, twelve were sent to prison and two were fined (in 137 cases, prosecution was suspended because authorities could not identify a perpetrator, and in 189 cases prosecution was terminated because a suspect had died).[22] The ÚDV concentrated its investigative efforts on 'the most conspicuous cases of the communist party and security nomenclature offences',[23] such as activities following the 1968 Soviet-led invasion, 'Operation Asanace' implemented by the StB against Charter 77 signatories, shootings at state borders, torture, the involvement of judicial and police officials in show trials against political prisoners in the 1950s, and excessive measures adopted against demonstrators in 1989.[24]

The record of prosecuting Communist crimes has therefore been meagre.[25] The lack of criminal prosecutions can be accounted for in part by: (i) policy

and Punishment of Communist Crimes in Central and Eastern Europe' (2015) 16(3) Espaço Jurídico J of L 31, 42, 44, 46 (noting also that in 1993, the Hungarian Parliament and Constitutional Court enabled prosecution of crimes committed during the 1956 Soviet invasion under international law, notably, as war crimes and crimes against humanity).

[21] Michal Kopeček, 'Czech Republic: From the Politics of History to Memory as Political Language' (*Cultures of History Forum*, 2 December 2013) <https://digital.herder-institut.de/publications/frontdoor/deliver/index/docId/39/file/Kopecek_Czech_Republic_From_the_Politic.pdf> accessed 12 March 2023.

[22] Official Correspondence C.j. UDV-1105-2/ČJ-2022-260011-OBČ from the ÚDV to authors (11 October 2022) (noting additionally that two other individuals were acquitted).

[23] Michal Kopeček, 'The Czech Republic: From Democracy Legitimization to the Politics of Memory' (2010) 8(2) J of Modern Eur History (Timothy D. Snyder (ed), Forum on Politics of History in Eastern Europe) 141, 146. In its publications, the ÚDV details human rights violations committed by the Communist regime. Some of the ÚDV's publications are available on its website: <https://www.policie.cz/clanek/publikace-udv.aspx> accessed 18 January 2024.

[24] See eg Barbora Holá, 'The Show Must Go On: The Trials and Tribulations of Ludmila Brožová Polednová' in Mark Drumbl and Caroline Fournet (eds), *The Sights, Sounds, and Sensibilities of Atrocity Prosecutions* (Brill forthcoming) (describing the case of a former people's prosecutor who was tried for her participation in a political trial in the 1950s and subsequently convicted of judicial murder).

[25] On a general note, retrospective criminal prosecutions were not particularly favoured as transitional justice mechanisms throughout the former Warsaw Pact nations though there were exceptions. For example, over 20,000 trials were held in East Germany. The 'border guard trials' were high profile. Some East German Communist leaders were also convicted, including Erich Mielke, the former head of the Stasi. At the age of eighty-five, Mielke was sentenced to six years in prison on murder charges. Gary Bruce, 'East Germany' in Stan (ed), *Transitional Justice in Eastern Europe* (n 17) 25–27. In 2016,

determinations;[26] (ii) a politicized environment as well as the legally complex nature of the cases; (iii) technical realities, including the death or infirmity of implicated state officials and the loss or destruction of probative evidence;[27] and (iv) personnel continuity with the past, to wit, the fact that some individuals appointed to judicial posts during the Communist period remained in place after the Velvet Revolution.[28] Owing to the fact that criminal prosecutions never garnered sufficient political, judicial, or public traction, the nascent democratic government turned to other measures to deal with the Communist past.

III. Exclusions and Lustrations

Lustration constituted the core transitional justice mechanism adopted after 1989 to deal with StB collaborators and other individuals linked to the Communist regime. Operationally speaking, lustration—from the Latin word *lustratio*, meaning 'purification by sacrifice'[29]— meant 'the systematic vetting of public officials for [their] link to the communist era security services'[30] and connections to the higher echelons of the erstwhile regime. Lustration was not new to the Czechoslovak political context. In 1948 and 1969, the Communist government had issued orders

two Romanian courts convicted Alexandru Visinescu, an abusive prison commander, and Ion Ficior, a labour colony commander, separately on charges of crimes against humanity. Lavinia Stan, 'Romania' in Stan (ed), *Transitional Justice in Eastern Europe* (n 17) 140–46.

26 Law on the Illegality of the Communist Regime (n 6) extended the statute of limitations only with respect to 'crimes' committed according to Communist laws but which were never actually prosecuted. Only actions which were criminal pursuant to Communist law in force at the time could be prosecuted.

27 Milan Hauner, 'Crime and Punishment in Communist Czechoslovakia: The Case of General Heliodor Píka and His Prosecutor Karel Vaš' (2008) 9(2–3) Totalitarian Movements and Political Religions 335, 347; Prokop Tomek, 'One Past, Two Paths' (2006) 1 The New Presence 38; Nadya Nedelsky, 'Czechoslovakia and the Czech and Slovak Republics' in Stan (ed), *Transitional Justice in Eastern Europe* (n 17) 59–60.

28 David, *Communists and Their Victims* (n 3) 59. On this note, even in August 2023 these (dis) continuities still generate tension. For instance, Robert Fremr, a Czech judge who served as Vice-President of the International Criminal Court, stepped down from his proposed appointment as a Czech Constitutional Court judge following fierce criticism related to his involvement in a controversial trial in 1988, in which he had sentenced three young men to imprisonment in proceedings rigged by the StB. See eg Radio Prague International, 'Fremr turns down constitutional judge nomination' (*Domestic Affairs*, 15 August 2023) available at <https://english.radio.cz/fremr-turns-down-constitutional-judge-nomination-8791518> accessed 19 August 2023.

29 Roman David, 'Lustration and Transitional Justice' in George Ritzer (ed), *The Blackwell Encyclopedia of Sociology* (John Wiley & Sons Ltd 2016). See also Vojtěch Cepl and Mark Gillis, 'Making Amends After Communism' (1996) 7(4) J of Democracy 118, 120; Roman Boed, 'An Evaluation of the Legality and Efficacy of Lustration as a Tool of Transitional Justice' (1999) 37(2) Columbia J of Transnational L 357, 365–66. For a discussion of lustration in Poland, Magdalena Kaj and Megan Metzger, 'Justice or Revenge? The Human Rights Implications of Lustration in Poland (*Humanity in Action*, January 2008) <https://humanityinaction.org/knowledge_detail/justice-or-revenge-the-human-rights-implications-of-lustration-in-poland/> accessed 24 March 2023.

30 Kieran Williams, Brigid Fowler, and Aleks Szczerbiak, 'Explaining Lustration in Central Europe: A "Post-Communist Politics" Approach' 12(1) Democratization 22, 23.

that aimed to get rid of politically unreliable elements and prevent tainted individuals from acceding to important posts. Additionally, the StB itself deployed lustrative screening as standard operating procedure to target two categories of persons: those considered hostile to the regime and those recruited as informers (these individuals were pervasively surveilled).[31] Therefore, lustrations, screenings, and exclusions regularly occur and recur throughout modern Czech(oslovak) history. As times and sensibilities change, lustrators may ironically become lustrated.

After the Velvet Revolution, lustration was considered to be a crucial step in the process of 'decommunization', to wit, a strenuous effort to cleanse the 'remnants of Communism'[32] and related 'sins'[33] from public life and state organizations. Lustration institutionalized the political defenestration of selected groups of people, including former informers, based on their affiliation with the repressive state apparatus.[34] Lustration 'combined elements of both vetting and exclusion from certain public offices for secret service functionaries and Communist Party officials'.[35] The assumption was that these individuals would undermine collective transition towards democracy and free markets.[36] Therefore, lustration would neutralize the influence of 'yesterday's heroes' by scouring these former influencers from public functions and casting them as 'today's villains'.[37] In the case of StB informers, the exclusion was akin to an excision, where the informer was perceived as malignant, and also as an excommunication, where the informer was perceived as devilish.

A period of 'wild lustrations' began as early as the spring of 1990. In this initial phase, the new Ministry of the Interior instituted spontaneous and unregulated screenings of potential members of Parliament and other public officials regarding any antecedent StB affiliations. These screenings triggered calls for the resignation of certain individuals allegedly affiliated with the StB.[38] However, due to numerous public scandals—as well as accusations and counter-accusations among political rivals[39]—some former dissidents started exhorting a more rule-based approach

[31] David, 'Lustration and Transitional Justice' (n 29) 1.
[32] Czarnota, 'Lustration, Decommunisation, and the Rule of Law' (n 13) 311.
[33] Boed, 'An Evaluation of the Legality and Efficacy of Lustration' (n 29) 358.
[34] David, 'Lustration and Transitional Justice' (n 29) 1–2.
[35] Williams, Fowler, and Szczerbiak, 'Explaining Lustration in Central Europe' (n 30) 24.
[36] Boed, 'An Evaluation of the Legality and Efficacy of Lustration' (n 29) 359.
[37] David, 'Lustration and Transitional Justice' (n 29) 1.
[38] Kopeček, 'Czech Republic' (n 21) 2. According to Kopeček, the aims of 'unofficial' lustrations were primarily to 'prevent the possibility of blackmailing members of the new political elite, whose past record was not untainted'. However, the motivations of lustration laws shifted with the drift of public sentiments from 'an increasingly obsessive agentomania' in the second half of 1990 to 'ridding public life of the supposedly malicious influence of the "old structures"'. See also Jan Kavan, *Spravedlnost s Náhubkem* (Doplněk 1999). Czech scholar Pavel Žáček claimed that lustrations 'enabled a fundamental discontinuity in [the] personnel composition of state government'; Pavel Žáček, 'Lustrační zákon po dvaceti letech' (2011) 4 Paměť a dějiny 127, 127.
[39] Kozák, *Právo na pomezí diktatury a demokracie* (n 5) 102.

that focused on 'publication of the names of all collaborators listed in the StB registers and the public exposure of any elected to the new legislature'.[40]

Heated parliamentary and public debates ensued.[41] Proponents of lustration did not present the threatened exclusion of groups of individuals from public service per se as a matter of transitional justice for past wrongs but instead presented it as a matter of securing the nation's fragile democracy.[42] According to these proponents, lustrations were necessary: (i) to stymie any covert continuation of influential networks nestled in the remnants of the former regime; (ii) to prevent blackmail of erstwhile informers by their former StB officers who could have access to their files and threaten them with publicizing their links to the StB, thus ruining their lives; and (iii) to render state institutions open and transparent to the public and thereby cultivate public confidence and enhance the credibility of the new political order.[43]

Lustration certainly had its opponents, some of whom went so far as to call the policies 'draconian'.[44] President Havel notably castigated the lustration bills as 'harsh and unjust'.[45] Other sceptics contended that lustration was based on a presumption of guilt and affronted the principle of equality before the law.[46] Lustration laws were additionally reprimanded in principle by the International Labor Organization, the Council of Europe, and the European Parliament.[47] Moreover, in the specific cases of informers, the fact that StB files and registers constituted proof undergirding lustrative determinations problematized the process from a microscopic evidentiary perspective.[48] A whiff of hypocrisy arose across post-Communist jurisdictions throughout Europe insofar as lustration advocates relied on the very StB files they had ridiculed as risible, such that they came to

[40] Williams, Fowler, and Szczerbiak, 'Explaining Lustration in Central Europe' (n 30) 32.

[41] Vojtěch Cepl, 'Ritual Sacrifices' (1992) 1 East Eur Constitutional Rev 24.

[42] Williams, Fowler, and Szczerbiak, 'Explaining Lustration in Central Europe' (n 30) 27.

[43] Williams, Fowler, and Szczerbiak, 'Explaining Lustration in Central Europe' (n 30) 28. See also Roman David, 'Lustration Laws in Action: The Motives and Evaluation of Lustration Policy in the Czech Republic and Poland (1989–2001)' (2003) 28(2) L and Social Inquiry 387, 392.

[44] Timothy Garton Ash, 'The Truth About Dictatorships' (*The New York Review*, 19 February 1998) <https://www-nybooks-com.proxy-ub.rug.nl/articles/1998/02/19/the-truth-about-dictatorship/> accessed 14 July 2023, 6.

[45] Michnik and Havel, 'Confronting the Past' (n 1) 23. Havel had a vacillating and erratic relationship with a number of transitional justice mechanisms. Ultimately, he supported these initiatives while also seeking to rein them in. See eg John P Moran, 'The Communist Torturers of Eastern Europe: Prosecute and Punish, or Forgive and Forget?' (1994) 27(1) Communist and Post-Communist Studies 95, 103; Williams, Fowler, and Szczerbiak, 'Explaining Lustration in Central Europe' (n 30) 38; Hauner, 'Crime and Punishment in Communist Czechoslovakia' (n 27) 346.

[46] David Kosař, 'Lustration and Lapse of Time: "Dealing with the Past" in the Czech Republic' (2008) 4 Eur Constitutional L Rev 460, 470.

[47] The European Parliament 'objected to the treatment of individuals based on their past associations *per se* with insufficient regards to mitigating circumstances and present activity'. Williams, Fowler, and Szczerbiak, 'Explaining Lustration in Central Europe' (n 30) 38.

[48] Michnik and Havel, 'Confronting the Past: Justice or Revenge?' (n 1) 23. See also Moran, 'The Communist Torturers of Eastern Europe (n 45) 103; Appel, 'Anti-Communist Justice' (n 13) 329; Petr Blažek, 'O lustračních zákonech koluje řada mýtů, tvrdí historik Blažek' (*iDNES.cz*, 7 December 2013) <https://www.idnes.cz/zpravy/domaci/historik-blazek-o-lustracnich-zakonech-a-spolupraci-s-stb.A131206_165129_domaci_jav> accessed 13 July 2022.

effectively 'validat[e] the history of these systems as written by the now distrusted members of the security apparatus'.[49]

The lustration legislation[50] was nonetheless passed by the Federal Assembly in October 1991, and President Havel grudgingly signed it into law. Notwithstanding that more than thirty years have since passed, the lustration laws still remain in force in the Czech Republic.[51]

Czech lustration laws are more comprehensive and sweeping than those of other former Soviet bloc countries.[52] These laws exclude certain groups of individuals from access to public positions (so-called protected positions) based solely on their membership in various organizations or by dint of the listing of their names on StB registries as knowing collaborators (so-called suspect positions).[53] Lustration targets 'former secret policemen and their agents, former communist officials from the district level up, members of the Peoples' Militia, and members of the National Front Action [and verification] committees [established after 1948 and 1968]'.[54] These individuals thereby become

[49] Matt Killingsworth, 'Lustration After Totalitarianism: Poland's Attempt to Reconcile with Its Communist Past' (2010) 43 Communist and Post-Communist Studies 275, 281 (discussing practices generally, not just those specific to the Czech Republic).

[50] Zákon, kterým se stanoví některé další předpoklady pro výkon některých funkcí ve státních orgánech a organizacích České a Slovenské Federativní Republiky, České republiky a Slovenské republiky [Law Setting Further Requirements for the Execution of Functions in State Organs and Organizations of Czech and Slovak Federative Republic, Czech Republic and Slovak Republic], Zákon č 451/1991 Sb (Czech) (adopted 4 October 1991) (hereafter Lustration Law); Zákon České národní rady o některých dalších předpokladech pro výkon některých funkcí obsazovaných ustanovením nebo jmenováním příslušníků Policie České republiky a příslušníků Sboru nápravné výchovy České republiky [Law of the Czech National Council Setting Further Requirements for Execution of Functions Filled by Appointment of Members of Police of the Czech Republic and Members of Prison Service of the Czech Republic] Zákon č 279/1992 Sb (Czech) (adopted 28 April 1992). The dissolution of Czechoslovakia into the Czech Republic and Slovakia in 1993 meant that the initial lustration laws adopted by the Czechoslovak Parliament entered the domestic regulatory framework of these two successor states. Each addressed their lustration policies differently. Lustration was more robust in the Czech Republic where the Lustration Law has since been amended fourteen times, with the most recent amendment occurring in 2021.

[51] In 1995 and 2000, the Czech Parliament overrode two presidential vetoes to indefinitely extend the validity of these laws beyond the formerly prescribed five-year period. Zákon č 254/1995 Sb (Czech); Zákon č 422/2000 Sb (Czech).

[52] Czarnota, 'Lustration, Decommunisation, and the Rule of Law' (n 13) 319. See also Killingsworth, 'Lustration After Totalitarianism' (n 49) 278 (depicting Czech lustration laws as broad in nature, in contrast to Poland where lustration was 'light' and prompted less sanction). In Poland, for instance, the 1997 lustration law required public officials to declare whether they had been involved with state security services either as employees or as informers. Individuals were banned from public office only if their declaration was proven to be false by the Institute of National Remembrance. Bulgaria and Romania had contentious lustration processes with some public disclosure of evidence. In Slovakia, the 1991 Czechoslovak lustration law was never seriously enforced; this law in fact lapsed in 1996. Lavinia Stan, 'Introduction: Post-Communist Transition, Justice, and Transitional Justice' in Stan (ed), *Transitional Justice in Eastern Europe* (n 17) 8.

[53] Veronika Bílková, 'Lustration: The Experience of Czechoslovakia/The Czech Republic' (Past and Present-Day Lustrations: Similarities, Differences, Applicable Standards Conference, Prague, September 2015) 4; Kosař, 'Lustration and Lapse of Time' (n 46) 463.

[54] Moran, 'The Communist Torturers of Eastern Europe' (n 45) 103.

> barred … from holding jobs in high-level governmental [and] administrative posts, the military, the intelligence services, the police corps, state radio and television organizations, news agencies, state-owned enterprises …, railways, banks, high academic positions, the judicial bench, and other positions connected with the courts.[55]

Members of the chamber of deputies, senators, elected municipal authorities, or governmental ministers do not fall within these protected positions.[56] In addition, all persons born after 1 December 1971[57] and individuals who held Communist Party positions from January 1968 until April 1969 are excluded from lustration.[58] These two exclusions, based on chronology and elected office rather than individual experience, blunt the scope of lustration. In many European post-Communist countries, coerced informing—meaning informing based on duress—did not trigger actionable lustration.[59] The only experiential difference acknowledged in the Czech Republic, however, is between 'knowing collaboration' and 'unknowing collaboration'.[60]

Despite the forward-looking discourse on protecting the nascent democracy which suffuses the enactment of lustration,[61] David lumps lustration into the box of retributive justice mechanisms.[62] Blaive finds that the lustration laws are far from reconciliatory.[63] Similarly, Moran observes how, in the early days of

[55] ibid.

[56] The reasoning behind this exemption is that since these are elected positions, the public can vote these individuals into and out of office, whereas individuals bureaucratically appointed in the Communist years could have remained in place for indefinite periods of time. In 2023, the scope of the lustration laws was again raised in the Czech Parliament. The governing coalition proposed to expand the categories of protected positions to include those of the prime minister and governmental ministers. See eg 'Lustrační zákon je stále téma, tvrdí Letocha ze STAN. "Společnost už nezajímá," říká Feranec z ANO' (*iROZHLAS*, 28 February 2023) <https://www.irozhlas.cz/zpravy-domov/lustracni-zakon-svazky-stb-petikoalice_2302281126_elev> accessed 24 March 2023.

[57] This establishes a generational divide clustering at the age of eighteen.

[58] According to David, this exemption exists because, 'since the selection of Alexander Dubček as the secretary general, the [Communist Party] tried to launch social and political reforms of the totalitarian system, which might have led to the abandonment of authoritarian ways of governance and to the building of "socialism with a human face"'. David, 'Lustration Laws in Action' (n 43) 410. Therefore, those who held high ranking Communist Party positions in the year 1968—to wit, the year when the regime was being humanized and democratized—were presumably considered less inimical to the nascent post-1989 democracy.

[59] Cynthia Horne, 'Roundtable' Washington and Lee University, February 2022 (commenting on duress and lustration, notes on file with the authors).

[60] According to the Federal Constitutional Court, which reviewed the lustration laws in 1992, confidants and candidates for secret collaboration should not be assumed to have cooperated knowingly and therefore fall outside of the scope of lustrations. Nález Ústavního soudu České a Slovenské Federativní Republiky (pléna) ze dne 26 listopadu 1992 (ÚS) [Decision of the Constitutional Court of the Czech and Slovak Federal Republic of 26 November 1992], sp zn Pl ÚS 1/92 (Czech) (hereafter 1992 Constitutional Court Decision).

[61] Kieran Williams, 'Lustration as the Securitization of Democracy in Czechoslovakia and the Czech Republic' (2003) 19(4) J of Communist Studies and Transition Politics 1, 2.

[62] David, *Communists and Their Victims* (n 3) 56–63.

[63] Blaive, 'An Impossible Reconciliation' (n 15).

post-Communist transition in Czechoslovakia, 'calls for punishment ... overwhelmed those for forgiveness'.[64] Indeed, lustration served to condemn individuals and endeavour to expiate the anger of those who had been wronged, especially political prisoners, torture victims, and others who had suffered immensely from Communist persecution. The Czech pursuit of lustration has been branded as 'radical' in its systematicity.[65] Lustration activists succeeded in implementing this policy even though the 'urge to purge ... could easily be deplored as retribution for bygones'[66] and was indeed instrumentalized and exploited as a political weapon at times.[67] Lustration laws aimed to remove those whose 'morals, values, and commitments to the new democracy [might have been] compromised by [such individuals'] previous beliefs, affiliations, and actions'.[68] In other words, lustration

> excludes from governmental power those whose actions have manifested hostility to democratic principles. It also gives democracy a breathing space, a kind of grace period during which it can put down roots without the fear that enemies in high places will try to undermine it. Fundamental change in a society requires replacement of its elite. Members of the old communist elite ... have questionable values and loyalties.[69]

Therefore, lustration is not solely about individual accountability. It also gives voice to moral cleansing and institutional change.[70] Exempting certain categories of citizens from lustration also serves declaratory functions. As such, lustrations double as expressive measures aimed at 'restoring the social order' and 'transforming the moral culture of citizens'.[71] Lustration also symbolically frames certain categories of individuals, including informers, as derelict and deficient. Informing is

64 Moran, 'The Communist Torturers of Eastern Europe' (n 45) 101.

65 Lavinia Stan, 'Vigilante Justice in Post-Communist Europe' (2011) 44 Communist and Post-Communist Studies 319, 321.

66 Williams, Fowler, and Szczerbiak, 'Explaining Lustration in Central Europe' (n 30) 27, 38.

67 Appel, 'Anti-Communist Justice' (n 13) 399. 'In the Czech Republic, a survey conducted in July 1991 (three months before the lustration law was enacted) found that 54 per cent of respondents concurred that lustration was necessary for the development of a democracy, and a full 80 per cent welcomed the prospect of a public sector rid of StB collaborators. Equally noteworthy, however, was that two-thirds of respondents felt lustration to be a means of political competition between parties and a distraction from more pressing matters.' Williams, Fowler, and Szczerbiak, 'Explaining Lustration in Central Europe' (n 30) 34. However, according to the Public Opinion Research Center (CVVM), in 2014, 40 per cent of Czechs considered lustration necessary at the time but not in 2014 anymore, while 14 per cent opined that lustrations have always been of low utility. Jan Červenka, 'Postoje veřejnosti k lustracím: říjen 2014' (Sociologický ústav AV ČR, *Centrum pro výzkum veřejného mínění (CVVM)*, 11 November 2014) <https://cvvm.soc.cas.cz/cz/tiskove-zpravy/politicke/politicke-ostatni/1799-postoje-verejnosti-k-lustracim-rijen-2014> accessed 13 July 2022.

68 Cynthia M Horne, 'The Impact of Lustrations on Democratization in Post-Communist Countries' (2014) 8 Intl J of Transitional Justice 496, 503.

69 Cepl and Gillis, 'Making Amends After Communism' (n 29) 122.

70 Horne, 'The Impact of Lustrations on Democratization' (n 68) 501.

71 Vojtěch Cepl, 'The Transformation of Hearts and Minds in Eastern Europe' (1997) 17 Cato J 229, 231.

retrospectively cast as deviant and wrong. Informers are stylized as suspect characters when it comes to credibly serving the public in a healthy capitalist democracy.

Both the Constitutional Court of the Czech and Slovak Federal Republic and the Czech Constitutional Court reviewed the lustration laws, the former in 1992 and the latter in 2001.[72] In 1992, the Federal Court identified the goals of these laws as protecting and promoting democracy, securing the political loyalty of individual public and bureaucratic officials to democratic principles, and shoring up citizen faith in the government.[73] The Court observed that 'a tight affiliation with a totalitarian regime and its repressive organs ... can cast doubts on ... political loyalty and [can] harm [the] trustworthiness of [the] public services of a democratic state and eventually threaten such [a] state'.[74] Secret collaborators were too 'risky' and 'dangerous' for democracy. In the specific words of the Court, '[t]aking into account [the] interests of a democratic state, certain behavior and/or position of an individual in a totalitarian regime is generally regarded as a risk for [the] impartiality and trustworthiness of his [or] her public service',[75] and:

> It cannot be assumed that [democratic values and principles] would be without reservations put into practice by members of former power structures, or by those who worked or cooperated with the StB and who were appointed to important state, social, and economic positions on the basis of contradictory values and principles, only to serve as representatives of [the] previously prevailing ideology to maintain the monopoly of power of the ruling bureaucratic apparatus.[76]

In this space, collaboration and informing become tethered to 'political loyalty', which intimates an ideological inclination. Informers are associated with Communist beliefs and practices, assumed to be averse to democracy, unable to

[72] 1992 Constitutional Court Decision (n 60); Nález Ústavního soudu České Republiky (pléna) ze dne 5 prosinec 2001 (ÚS) [Decision of the Constitutional Court of the Czech Republic of 5 December 2001], sp zn Pl ÚS 9/01 (Czech) (hereafter 2001 Constitutional Court Decision).

[73] The same reasoning was adopted by the Czech Constitutional Court in 2001. In both instances, use was made of the doctrine of 'militant democracy', or 'democracy capable of defending itself', which permits derogation or limitation of certain fundamental human rights in situations when respect for those rights would threaten democracy or its basic principles. Therefore, democracy must be capable of defending itself against its enemies or enemy ideologies, which might require curtailment of the rights and freedoms of those propagating such ideologies. See also Štěpán Výborný, 'Koncept bránící se demokracie v judikatuře Ústavního soudu ČR' (2012) 2 Časopis pro právní vědu a praxi 157, 158.

[74] 1992 Constitutional Court Decision (n 60). This reasoning was reiterated in 2001 by the Czech Constitutional Court, which acknowledged that with the passing of time the relevance of an individual's past affiliations and past attitudes correspondingly diminishes. The Court still considered the lustration laws to be 'necessary for a democratic society'—meaning proportionate to attain a legitimate goal at the time—because they pertain to 'a limited scope of significant public functions' and do not restrict access to the majority of positions in public administration and public services. 2001 Constitutional Court Decision (n 72) s X.

[75] 2001 Constitutional Court Decision (n 72) s IX.

[76] 1992 Constitutional Court Decision (n 60). See also 2001 Constitutional Court Decision (n 72) s IX (reiterating the logic from the 1992 Constitutional Court Decision).

function amid capitalist liberalism, and even to pose a revanchist threat to modernity. All of this belies the vexing question whether informers actually spoke to the StB *because* of their ideological allegiance to Communism or their overt approval of Communist practices, or whether they even cared about Communism or democracy. Perhaps informers were simply navigating the system, which would imply that they could fare rather well in the *nouveau régime* due to their political agnosticism. We read the files to shed some light on these motivational drivers. Our review of archived informer file-stories unsettles the confident certainty of the Court's premise.

The Court also suggests that former collaborators are biased, untrustworthy, and incapable of properly fulfilling democratic public service. This is somewhat ironic as in some cases informers spoke to the StB—grudgingly, perhaps even in disgust—on account of feeling that once they had been officially approached by the state informing was a fulfilment or embodiment of the notion of public service. In other words, they were doing what the state had asked of them. Many other everyday ordinary citizens informed to get ahead personally or to get even.

Over 40,000 'protected' official positions required an individual to show a negative lustration certificate to prove that he or she did not hold any of the 'suspected positions'.[77] David estimates that official lustration implicated over 23,000 StB members who were under the age of sixty-five and not retired in 1989.[78] Other categories included 165,000 'verification committee' members that facilitated purges after the Soviet invasion in 1968, and about 100,000 members of the People's Militia.[79] The attempted scale of lustration in Czechoslovakia—initially, at least—was unprecedented as compared to other post-Communist countries.[80] According to the Czech Ministry of the Interior, by 1 March 2023 a total of 506,449 lustration certificates had been issued, of which 10,836, or 2.1 per cent, were positive, meaning that it was found that the individual had held a suspected position or was registered as an StB collaborator under one of the law's categories.[81] As of July 2022, 1,057 of these decisions were contested in court. In about 80 per cent of these contested cases, courts found that the StB's registration of the person was unjustified.[82] Similarly, the validity of some negative lustration certificates has

77 Appel, 'Anti-Communist Justice' (n 13) 386.

78 David, *Communists and Their Victims* (n 3) 60.

79 ibid.

80 Nedelsky, 'Czechoslovakia and the Czech and Slovak Republics' (n 27) 49–50. As of 2005, the Czech Ministry of the Interior issued 451,000 lustration certificates.

81 Ministerstvo vnitra České republiky, 'Statistika provedených lustrací' (*Ministerstvo vnitra České republiky*, 2023) <https://www.mvcr.cz/clanek/lustrace-29644.aspx?q=Y2hudW09MTg%3d> accessed 24 March 2023.

82 Email from the Czech Ministry of the Interior to the authors (12 July 2022). '[A] major reason for the high verdict turnover rate is that the courts accept only original paper evidence, not records transferred to microfiche (which was done with much StB documentation) as signatures then cannot be verified. Because many paper records have been destroyed or have gone missing, and because the Ministry of Interior has the burden of proof, this rule works overwhelmingly to the advantage of those

been challenged.[83] Either way, the StB files can serve evidentiary purposes. To be sure, whether these legal proceedings can fully exonerate—discursively, not only legally—an individual from the taint of a collaborative accusation remains uncertain.[84] Conversations about erstwhile Communist collaborators remain lightning rods in the contemporary Czech Republic.[85] While many individuals associated with the Communist regime have become marginalized, notably everyday informers, other former functionaries have managed to survive and thrive, and even successfully strive, within market capitalism.

IV. Revelations and Transparency

Various clarity measures exposed the identities, conduct, and information shared by informers. We introduced these in Chapter 1 of this book. It was estimated that the StB had files on approximately 600,000 people, be it as potential or actual informers or simply as subjects of surveillance.[86] That said, even before post-Communist state authorities publicly and officially opened all the extant secret files the StB had maintained on its informers and their targets, informers had become subject to the vicissitudes of popular justice and public shaming. StB files and registers also yielded considerable information that connected to formal lustration initiatives.

While many secret agent files were destroyed in late 1989 and early 1990, the unofficial, unauthorized, and supposedly complete lists of StB collaborators were leaked to the public in 1992. These so-called Cibulka's lists, which included approximately 160,000 names,[87] were published for everyone to see in the widely read 'Uncensored Newspaper: *Rudé krávo*'.[88] Petr Cibulka, a former dissident variously

challenging the verdict.' Nedelsky, 'Czechoslovakia and the Czech and Slovak Republics' (n 27) 49–50 (quoting Pavel Brunnhofer, assistant director of the Czech Ministry of Interior archives).

[83] Nedelsky, 'Czechoslovakia and the Czech and Slovak Republics' (n 27) 50.

[84] See discussion in Chapter 6, Section I.B, 'Cruelty' on scandalization.

[85] Czech newspapers today continue to report on the 'StB past' of police agents and officers. Jan Horák, 'Inspektoři pražské městské policie: Dva byli u StB, další studoval pod KGB v Moskvě' (*Aktuálně.cz*, 17 November 2019) <https://zpravy.aktualne.cz/domaci/vlivni-muzi-prazske-mestske-policie-jeden-byl-u-stb-dalsi-st/r~b6b7fdbe078c11eaac60ac1f6b220ee8/> accessed 20 November 2019. One of the former Prime Ministers of the Czech Republic, Andrej Babiš, had been registered as an StB collaborator. Babiš challenged this listing in court, claiming that he had never knowingly collaborated with the StB. Thus far, courts have dismissed his appeals based on procedural justifications.

[86] Nedelsky, 'Czechoslovakia and the Czech and Slovak Republics' (n 27) 50.

[87] Hauner, 'Crime and Punishment in Communist Czechoslovakia' (n 27) 346. Some authors cite slightly different numbers. Nedelsky, 'Czechoslovakia and the Czech and Slovak Republics' (n 27) 51 (reporting that Cibulka published names of 'roughly 200,000 alleged StB officers and collaborators'). Similar developments occurred in Poland, where the Wildstein List, which is named after a journalist, appeared on the Internet in 2005 without providing any safeguards for the listed parties.

[88] 'Rudé krávo' (meaning loosely in Czech 'red cow') is a word play on the name of the main Communist newspaper which was called 'Rudé právo', meaning 'red law' or 'red right'.

branded as 'a fanatical anticommunist' and an 'unbalanced crackpot',[89] received an extensive list of names, dates of birth, and codenames of purported StB informers from a panoply of obscure sources. Cibulka brazenly published these lists, 'claiming that a Bolshevik conspiracy [with Havel at its top] was lurking around the corner'.[90] Havel responded by calling the publication of these lists 'one of the biggest victories of the former state security'.[91]

Cibulka's lists indeed 'provoked public scandal, rocked the ... political scene, and curdled a hostile reaction to those named ... which culminated in a witch-hunt against informers'.[92] Many individuals whose names were listed and published contested the validity of these 'wild' lists and responsively asserted that they had been unfairly included.[93] Tensions ran high. In 1993, some of the stories of these aggrieved complainants were collected in an edited volume entitled 'Condemned: Letters by the Persons from the Lists'. Certain of these individuals recounted how they were tricked into signing a pledge of cooperation with the StB, while others stated that they were forced, intimidated, or blackmailed. Many equated the post-transition public listing of their names to erstwhile StB practices.[94] Since accusations of collusion tend to stick publicly once levelled,[95] these aggrieved complainants lamented the lack of nuance or context, along with the foreclosure of any opportunity to retort, explain, or exonerate themselves in the eyes of the public. Despite—or perhaps due to—heated debates and controversies surrounding the lists, Cibulka continued to publish the names of StB collaborators until 1996: in 1999 he furthermore listed an additional 15,000 purported StB informers.[96]

[89] Hauner, 'Crime and Punishment in Communist Czechoslovakia' (n 27) 346.

[90] ibid.

[91] Kopeček, 'From Democracy Legitimization to the Politics of Memory' (n 23) 146.

[92] Stan, 'Vigilante Justice in Post-Communist Europe' (n 65) 321.

[93] See generally Mayer, *Češi a Jejich Komunismus* (n 9) 192–206.

[94] Zdena Salivarová-Škvorecká, *Osočení: Dopisy lidí ze seznamu* (Sixty-Eight Publishers 1993).

[95] See eg Ron Dudai, 'Informers and the Transition in Northern Ireland' (2012) 52 British J of Criminology 32, 43, 44 (noting that '[n]ot unlike witchcraft accusations, once someone is alleged to be an informer, it is almost impossible to shake off the accusation and any action could be interpreted as "confirming" suspicion').

[96] Stan, 'Vigilante Justice in Post-Communist Europe' (n 65) 321, 325. In 2009, yet another unofficial list of StB 'persons of interest' emerged. This list was published online by former dissident Stanislav Penc, who claimed 'to have received the database from the former head of the Slovak National Memory Institute, Jan Langos'. Stan, 'Vigilante Justice in Post-Communist Europe' (n 65) 325 (the next two quotations in this footnote derive from this same source). Lagos was subsequently killed in a car accident and was allegedly 'frustrated with failures to lift the secrecy' of StB records. Penc criticized the government for monopolizing 'the interpretation of history' and for only releasing 'data on cases, it is for sure will not upset a majority of population' or 'big name cases'. This list differs from Cibulka's both in format and content: it is broader and includes approximately 770,000 persons of interest to the StB, including victims, informers, and the names of individuals reviewed by the StB for important posts within the regime. A website linked to this list claims that the database is 'a reaction to state authorities' lax attitude toward revealing the truth about the recent past'. For the website, see Stanislav Penc, 'Vyhledávání v databázi' (*Svazky.cz*, 2022) <https://www.svazky.cz> accessed 9 September 2022.

In contrast to lustration, the Czechoslovak state initially was somewhat less forthcoming with publishing official lists of former collaborators, opening the StB files, and rendering the archives publicly accessible. Following the heated political debates triggered by publication of Cibulka's lists in 1992, however, 'the situation eventually made it necessary to open the files because it would not be just to have [only] the names of people with no background information'.[97] Beginning in 1993, various versions of the law governing the opening of the StB archives were debated in Parliament. Many citizens, including President Havel, expressed grave misgivings. Havel argued that 'children will be ashamed of their parents, families will break up, people will treat those who they find were informers [like] poison'.[98] According to Havel:

> [O]ne should not leave the door open to unlawful revenge and hunt people down, because that would be only another version of what we had gotten rid of. This kind of approach also has a broad tradition in our country. I can remember all those postwar avengers after the Second World War—usually the most energetic ones were themselves the most guilty.... [A] call to reveal the names of all those who in some way were in contact with the police—no matter when or why—is very dangerous. It is a bomb that could go off at any moment and ruin the social climate. It could reintroduce elements of fanaticism, lawlessness, and injustice.... It is enough that people were afraid of the secret police for 40 years. They should not be afraid that someone may reveal something about them in 15 years' time.[99]

Notwithstanding these objections, Law 140/1996[100]—allowing individuals to inspect their personal files and requiring the redaction of any third-party names therein—passed the Czech Parliament and was thereafter signed into effect by the President. In subsequent years, politicians continued to debate the virtues of opening up the archives. These discussions were polarized. The arguments against publicly uncorking access to all archived materials revolved around issues of privacy and claims that the StB files are full of lies, scurrilous accusations made by neighbours, and fabrications.[101] Nevertheless, in 2002, Law 107/2002 broadened access beyond a person's own personal file to all files in the StB archives.[102] Private

[97] Nedelsky, 'Czechoslovakia and the Czech and Slovak Republics' (n 27) 51 (quoting Jiří Pehe, a former Havel advisor).

[98] ibid (quoting Havel).

[99] Michnik and Havel, 'Confronting the Past: Justice or Revenge?' (n 1) 22.

[100] Zákon o zpřístupnění svazků vzniklých činností bývalé Státní bezpečnosti [Law on Disclosure of Files Created by Activities of the Former State Security], Zákon č 140/1996 Sb (Czech) (adopted 26 April 1996).

[101] Nedelsky, 'Czechoslovakia and the Czech and Slovak Republics' (n 27) 52.

[102] Access was limited to persons over the age of eighteen. Zákon, kterým se mění zákon č. 140/1996 Sb., o zpřístupnění svazků vzniklých činností bývalé Státní bezpečnosti, a některé další zákony [Law amending the Law 140/1996 Sb. on Disclosure of Files Created by Activities of the Former State Security, and Some Other Laws], Zákon č 107/2002 Sb (Czech) (adopted 8 March 2002).

sensitive information regarding third parties, including dates of birth, places of residence, details on private and family life, past criminal activities, health, and wealth was to be redacted from requested files.

In 2003, the Czech Ministry of the Interior posted a list of over 75,000 StB informers on the Internet.[103] In contrast to Cibulka's list—but more similarly to the lustration laws—this database was limited to those who, according to the Ministry, had 'knowingly collaborated'. A year later, and for the purpose of enabling a 'comprehensive dealing with the past and discovery of the ways [that] the Communist regime systematically violated human rights', the Czech Parliament pushed the transparency measures one step further through Law 499/2004.[104] This law stipulated that protection of personal, sensitive data does not apply to documents created by the StB prior to 1 January 1990. As such, this law unveiled the StB archives, unredacted and virtually without limitation, to anyone keen to take a look.[105]

The files can be seen and read in the publicly accessible Security Services Archive (ABS) which, as detailed in Chapter 1 of this book, was established in 2007.[106] The ABS attracts over 2,000 visitors annually who on average access files pertaining to approximately 6,500 individuals.[107] In 2016, owing to modern technological advances, the ABS launched an e-application that permits registered individuals to access digitized archival content remotely.[108] Now, anyone can browse through the StB's 'intelligence' and the life stories of the informers and informed-upons detailed therein.

After overcoming their initial hesitation to publicize StB secrets, Czech authorities ended up pursuing one of the more liberal approaches in post-Communist Europe as regards clarity measures.[109] Informers' dealings with the StB, including

[103] Stan, 'Vigilante Justice in Post-Communist Europe' (n 65) 322.

[104] Zákon o archivnictví a spisové službě a o změně některých zákonů [Law on Archives and Filing Service and on Change of Some Laws] Zákon č 499/2004 Sb (Czech) (adopted 30 June 2004).

[105] Světlana Ptáčníková, 'Aspekty odpovědnosti archivářů a badatelů při nakládání s osobními údaji v archiváliích' (2017) 9(2) Historie, Otázky, Problémy 24, 26.

[106] Zákon o Ústavu pro studium totalitních režimů a o Archivu bezpečnostních složek a o změně některých zákonů [Law on the Institute for the Study of Totalitarian Regimes and the Security Services Archive and on Change of Some Laws], Zákon č 181/2007 Sb (Czech) paras 12–17 (adopted 8 June 2007) (hereafter Law on the Institute for the Study of Totalitarian Regimes and Security Services Archives). See also Archiv bezpečnostních složek, 'Činnosti Archivu' (Archiv bezpečnostních složek, undated) <https://www.abscr.cz/cinnosti-archivu/> accessed 21 July 2022.

[107] Archiv bezpečnostních složek, 'Činnosti Archivu' (n 106).

[108] Ptáčníková, 'Aspekty odpovědnosti archivářů a badatelů při nakládání s osobními údaji v archiváliích' (n 105) 24.

[109] Kopeček, 'From Democracy Legitimization to the Politics of Memory' (n 23) 147. To be clear, many former Communist countries opened their archives and permitted, to varying degrees, public access thereto. Divergences arose when it came to the question how all this information ought to be operationalized. Should it be up to the subject of the file—in other words, the informed-upon individuals—to determine what to do with the physical file? Should the files be digitalized? Should they serve as a basis for criminal prosecutions? Should access be totally open to all members of the public? Even to foreigners? In 1999, Romania enacted a law to 'manage the files from the Romanian secret police, provide file access, disclose former agents and collaborators, and expose the repressive actions of the former Communist system'. Cynthia M Horne, 'Silent Lustration: Public Disclosures as Informal Lustration Mechanisms in Bulgaria and Romania' (2015) 62(3) Problems of Post-Communism 131, 135. Hungary had more limited file access and the contents thereof were redacted to ensure maximal

very intimate and private details of their lives, as well as the lives of persons upon whom they reported, have been made public for use and potential abuse.[110]

Unsurprisingly, this transparency has jolted dissonance. For example, in 2017, a certain Mr V.H.—who fervently disagreed with the broadcast of his StB story for a television documentary—commenced litigation concerning the use of his personal information gained from an StB file. After a rather lengthy courtroom saga, the Czech Constitutional Court was tasked with assessing the interface of generous access to the StB archives with the right to privacy.[111] The Court considered unbridled access to the archives justified by the social significance of authentic discovery of the past, the education of citizens, and the furtherance of objective historical research. However, the Court also noted that access to private information does not automatically include the right to its publication without the consent of the concerned individuals or their surviving relatives, insofar as unauthorized reproduction can potentially lead to violations of personal dignity and rights to privacy, along with denigration of good reputation.[112] This differentiation adopted by the Court between 'access' and 'publication' limits the extent to which the public can theoretically abuse the information meticulously collected and maintained by the StB.[113] However, the Court's ruling does not preclude children unearthing secret indiscretions of their parents, friends and partners discovering 'skeletons in the closet', or business associates tracking down minutiae about their colleagues.[114]

V. Rehabilitation and Restitution

Penal prosecutions, extensive lustration, and generous access to StB files each targeted 'the oppressors', namely individuals considered to be linked to Communist repression and perceived in the public and political imagination as responsible for historical wrongs. That said, the first measures to deal with the Communist past

privacy. In Germany, access to Stasi files was also circumscribed by privacy concerns. In Poland, it was emphasized that only files of individuals performing the highest state functions may be disclosed, and that sensitive data may not be revealed without the consent of the parties involved.

[110] Blaive, 'An Impossible Reconciliation' (n 15) para 10 ('The list of secret police collaborators was not used to the prospect of reconciliation but as a "proxy for justice"; the exposure of former informers became a means of shaming and socially isolating them, not of understanding the past. The historical evidence contained in secret police archives was mobilized in the same retributive manner....').

[111] Ptáčníková, 'Aspekty odpovědnosti archivářů' (n 105) 29.

[112] Nález Ústavního soudu České Republiky (pléna) ze dne 20 prosince 2016 (ÚS) [Decision of the Constitutional Court of the Czech Republic of 20 December 2016], sp zn Pl ÚS 3/14 (Czech) (hereafter 2016 Constitutional Court Decision).

[113] In accordance with ethical concerns and the Court's ruling, we pseudonymized any and all information that could potentially lead to identification of the informers whose file-stories we present in this book. On this note, we have been more protective than other published historical work related to the StB files. cf Milan Bárta (ed), *Člověk v soukolí StB* (Ústav pro studium totalitních režimů 2020).

[114] See generally Nedelsky, 'Czechoslovakia and the Czech and Slovak Republics' (n 27) 53.

implemented immediately after the Velvet Revolution focused on 'the oppressed', namely those individuals who had been wronged. These modalities assumed the form of rehabilitation and restitution.[115]

Immediately before the first democratic elections in June 1990, the Czechoslovak Federal Parliament enacted laws rehabilitating persons who had suffered political prosecution between 1948 and 1989.[116] The 1990 Law on Judicial Rehabilitation was intended to clear the names of and partially redress the harm that had been done to approximately 260,000 political prisoners.[117] The law annulled (or allowed the judicial re-examination of) criminal sanctions that had been imposed on individuals who simply exercised their fundamental rights and freedoms but were nonetheless punished for doing so by Communist authorities. Accordingly, this law aimed to socially rehabilitate individuals who had been unlawfully convicted, in addition to granting them proportional material reparation.[118] Compensation to cover legal fees, loss of income during detention, judicial fines, and any damage to health was offered to those rehabilitated.[119] An award of 100,000 Kčs was paid to surviving relatives of those who had been executed or died in detention.[120] Former political prisoners were also provided with other material supports, including free public transport, special medical treatment, and state subsidies.[121] The group of people entitled to compensation was gradually expanded to include inmates detained in forced labour camps, individuals abducted to the USSR, and

[115] These mechanisms were certainly not unique to Czechoslovakia or the Czech Republic. They were commonplace throughout all post-Communist Europe. For example, Bulgaria's 1992 Restitution Act established property rights related to tobacco, oil, alcohol, mining, and other industries regulated by Communist laws; if the state had instituted a legal 'taking' and there was evidence of ownership, then the property owner was entitled to restitution. Leland Rhett Miller, 'Land Restitution in Post-Communist Bulgaria' (2003) 15(1) Post-Communist Economies 75, 78.

[116] Zákon o soudní rehabilitaci [Law on Judicial Rehabilitation], Zákon č 119/1990 Sb (Czech) (adopted 23 April 1990) (hereafter Law on Judicial Rehabilitation). Rehabilitation of political prisoners was a very long and winding process. It began in the late 1950s, post Stalinism, and continued in the 1960s. For instance, Law No 82/1968 on judicial rehabilitation has been described as

> a humane step, rare in history, and unique in the Communist world, to restore justice to the victims of illegalities of an entire historical period. It was proposed to re-examine the cases of up to 100,000 individuals unjustly sentenced in the years 1948 to 1965, to offer financial compensation to *bona fide* victims to a maximum of 20,000 Kcs *per annum*, and to permit, in certain instances, the criminal punishment of those guilty of illegal actions in the security and judicial services and in the relevant ministries. For the first time, judicial and social rehabilitation was to be extended to tens of thousands of non-Communists, not just leading Communists.

Kevin McDermott and Klára Pinerová, 'The Rehabilitation Process in Czechoslovakia: Party and Popular Responses' in Kevin McDermott and Matthew Stibbe (eds), *De-Stalinising Eastern Europe: The Rehabilitation of Stalin's Victims After 1953* (Palgrave Macmillan 2015) 109–31, 118.

[117] Hauner, 'Crime and Punishment in Communist Czechoslovakia' (n 27) 345; Appel, 'Anti-Communist Justice' (n 13) 382; David, *Communists and Their Victims* (n 3) 64.

[118] Law on Judicial Rehabilitation (n 116) para 1(1).

[119] ibid paras 23, 25. A loss of retirement pension due to a period of detention was also to be compensated. Additional financial compensation was provided by the Law on the Illegality of the Communist Regime (n 6).

[120] Law on Judicial Rehabilitation (n 116) para 27.

[121] David, *Communists and Their Victims* (n 3) 65.

university students who had been politically precluded from completing their studies. Communist-era orders expelling students or dismissing employees for political reasons were also repealed.[122]

In the first two years following the enactment of the Law on Judicial Rehabilitation, at least 257,864 individuals indeed were judicially rehabilitated.[123] However, some political prisoners chided the law because 'former secret police had received greater compensation payouts at the time of their forced retirement than many political prisoners received'.[124]

The initial rehabilitation laws construed political prisoners as victims of Communism. However, and rather interestingly, a shift occurred in how the historical role and significance of political prisoners was understood over the years. Despite initial perceptions of former political prisoners as victims, their public and self-image subsequently shifted to that of anti-Communist fighters and resisters. According to McDermott and Pinerová, 'this politicization of history and search for "heroes" who opposed the "totalitarian" behemoth'[125] is also visible in a 2011 law stipulating additional one-off compensation of 100,000 Kčs to persons determined to have actively resisted Communism'.[126] Interestingly, the 2011 law explicitly excluded as beneficiaries individuals deemed to have engaged in past collaboration with the StB.[127] That said, many informers who, after 1989, were predominantly cast as villains and acolytes of the oppressor also were victims of Communist persecution. These intricacies, dualities, and vulnerabilities surface from our review of the files. For example, many informers were cajoled into informing because of the fact they had been convicted of trumped up political offences. Others became informers because the alternative was to leave their jobs or abandon their studies. Regardless of how their informing journey was initially ignited, however, some informers became habituated to informing and remained active in the StB services for decades afterwards—often demonstrating tangible agency and autonomy.

[122] Zákon o mimosoudních rehabilitacích [Law on Extrajudicial Rehabilitations], Zákon č 87/1991 Sb (Czech) paras 18(3), 21 (adopted 21 February 1991) (hereafter Law on Extrajudicial Rehabilitations).

[123] František Koudelka and others, *Soudní Perzekuce Politické Povahy v Československu 1948–1989: Statistický přehled* (Ústav pro soudobé dějiny AV ČR 1993) 57–68.

[124] David and Choi, 'Victims on Transitional Justice' (n 19) 399. See also Mayer, *Češi a Jejich Komunismus* (n 9) 167.

[125] McDermott and Pinerová, 'The Rehabilitation Process in Czechoslovakia' (n 116) 118. See also Kopeček, 'Czech Republic' (n 21) 10.

[126] Zákon o účastnících odboje a odporu proti komunismu [Law on the Participants in Anti-Communist Opposition and Resistance], Zákon č 262/2011 Sb (Czech) (adopted 20 July 2011) (hereafter Law on Anti-Communist Opposition and Resistance).

[127] ibid para 4(1)(b) ('A citizen is not recognized as a participant in anti-Communist opposition and resistance if he or she, during the time of non-freedom … was on record in the documents of security forces as their collaborator or secret collaborator, and/or was a member of the Assistant Guards of the Police, an assistant of the Border Guards, or an informer to the intelligence apparatus of the Communist Party of Czechoslovakia, and/or otherwise collaborated with the security forces or the Communist Party of Czechoslovakia in a similar manner.').

This in-between positionality of informers illustrates yet another challenge inherent in transitional justice's application of clearly reductive oppositional categories—such as good versus bad, or perpetrator versus victim—into social conditions that are far from crisply binary. Dudai's observation from Northern Ireland that 'informers rarely feature as victims' is applicable to the Czech context.[128]

In addition to rehabilitation, restitution aimed to repair injustices related to acts of unlawful appropriation of property undertaken by the Communist regime. David states that, during Communism, '[v]irtually all private property, as well as 88 percent of agricultural land in Czechoslovakia, was nationalized'.[129] Accordingly, property confiscated between 1948 and 1989 was to be returned, or the monetary equivalent compensated, to former owners or their heirs. David notes that property restitution was 'mainly based on a belief in the liberal notion of justice ... coupled with the need to delegitimize the previous regime'.[130] Moreover, restitution formed part of the privatization process and served as a stepping-stone towards a market economy. Appel maintains that returning property to past owners was done to 'create a constituency supportive of capitalist reforms, spark entrepreneurship, and capital formation'.[131] That said, while property nationalized by the Communists between 1948 and 1989 was restituted, the vast amounts of property brusquely appropriated from the *Sudeten* Germans (who were expelled wholescale from Czechoslovakia after the Second World War) was ignored and title thereover was never challenged. Indeed, whoever held title immediately prior to the Communist takeover in 1948 (however that title had been acquired) was determined to be the legitimate title holder.[132] The European Court of Human Rights has adjudicated certain challenges to the restitution laws brought by good faith owners.[133]

The first restitution laws were enacted in 1990. These laws most frequently concerned residential houses and small businesses such as restaurants, hotels, and shops.[134] Subsequent measures dealt with other property that had been nationalized or seized by the Communist state, property that had been acquired under blatantly disadvantageous conditions,[135] agricultural

[128] Dudai, *Penality in the Underground* (n 4) 168.

[129] David, *Communists and Their Victims* (n 3) 21.

[130] ibid 66.

[131] Appel, 'Anti-Communist Justice' (n 13) 395. See also Kozák, *Právo na pomezí diktatury a demokracie* (n 5) 123.

[132] Marcos Zunino, *Justice Framed: A Genealogy of Transitional Justice* (CUP 2019) 88; Vojtěch Cepl, 'A Note on the Restitution of Property in Post-Communist Czechoslovakia' (1991) 7 J Communist Studies 367, 368.

[133] See eg European Court of Human Rights, Application No 36548/97, 5 November 2002, *Pincová and Pinc* (permitting those who had acquired lands confiscated by Communist authorities some rights of recompense when that land was decreed by law to return to the original owner on record at the time of confiscation).

[134] David, *Communists and Their Victims* (n 3) 60.

[135] Law on Extrajudicial Rehabilitations (n 122).

land,[136] and estates originally owned by churches.[137] In sum, the scale of property restitution was significant.

Restitution unsurprisingly proved controversial and triggered considerable litigation that is ongoing to this day. Assuredly, the process of restitution was made more complex by the fact that people lived in these nationalized properties, that tenants had rights and were accustomed to a rent price that was unsustainable under a free market, and that the law precluded claims by *émigrés*.[138] Insofar as many informers came from social groups that were targeted by nationalization, such as wealthy farmers and businessmen, their status as an informer did not per se block them from benefitting from restitution of their lost properties. As with rehabilitation, the duality of restitution nonetheless proved prickly and uncomfortable. Informers were not cast jointly as liminal victims and victimizers—as our granular read of the file-stories routinely suggests—but were instead parsimoniously reduced to the category of ineligible traitors.

VI. Institutes of Memory

As an integral part of dealing with the past, and similarly to many other transitional regimes,[139] the post-Communist Czech government adopted measures and established official institutions to construct national memory and naturalize a particular way to recollect the Communist past.[140] In the early 2000s, some influential politicians became increasingly preoccupied with the fact that the Communist Party was still thriving within the Czech political system. This was taken as 'proof

[136] Zákon o úpravě vlastnických vztahů k půdě a jinému zemědělskému majetku [Law Regulating Ownership of Plots and of Other Agricultural Property], Zákon č 229/1991 Sb (Czech) (adopted 21 May 1991).

[137] Zákon o majetkovém vyrovnání s církvemi a náboženskými společnostmi [Law on Material Settlement with Churches and Other Religious Communities], Zákon č 428/2012 Sb (Czech) (adopted 8 November 2012).

[138] The requirement of the permanent residency of claimants in the Czech Republic was quashed by the Constitutional Court in 1994. The claimants, however, were required to have Czech citizenship, which has also led to extensive litigation. Nález Ústavního soudu České Republiky (pléna) ze dne 12 července 1994 (ÚS) [Decision of the Constitutional Court of the Czech Republic of 12 July 1994], sp zn Pl ÚS 3/94 (Czech). See generally Kozák, *Právo na pomezí diktatury a demokracie* (n 5) 124.

[139] Similar institutes had previously been established in neighbouring states. For example, in Poland, the Institute of National Remembrance—in Polish, *Instytut Pamięci Narodowe*—was established in 1998. Its role was to address the history and operation of Poland's Communist-era secret police, as well as the paths taken by its secret collaborators. See generally Dariusz Stola, 'Poland's Institute of National Remembrance: A Ministry of Memory?' in Alexei Miller and Maria Lipman (eds), *The Convulsions of Historical Politics* (Ingram 2012) 45 (discussing also the controversies that this institute triggered). In Slovakia, the Nation's Memory Institute was created in 2002. In Romania, Law 95—enacted in 1997—established the Sighet Memorial, which includes a museum collection of testimony and documents relating to Communist repression as an official site of memory. On Romania, see Monica Ciobanu, 'Criminalising the Past and Reconstructing Collective Memory: The Romanian Truth Commission'(2009) 61 Europe-Asia Studies 313.

[140] Statutes designated certain days as official memorial days. For example, 27 June is the 'Day of Remembrance of Victims of Communism'.

that society had not dealt radically enough with its communist past'.[141] The solution to this perceived problem was to implement 'an uncompromising politics of memory that strove to re-educate the nation about the 'totalitarian past'[142] and concomitantly to reinforce the anti-Communist paradigm by promoting or producing 'anticommunist collective memory'.[143]

Accordingly, in 2007 the Czech Parliament established the Institute for the Study of Totalitarian Regimes (*Ústav pro studium totalitních režimů* (ÚSTR)).[144] The preamble of the ÚSTR's enabling legislation pithily affirms: 'The ones who do not know their past are condemned to repeat it.'[145] The ÚSTR is an official publicly financed memory institute that researches, analyses, and disseminates the history of 'the time of unfreedom [defined as the time period from the Munich Agreement in September 1938 until the end of the Second World War in May 1945] and the Communist totalitarian power'.[146] Despite its mandate to study the past objectively and impartially and accordingly to (re)educate Czech citizens, the name of the ÚSTR and its mission already predetermines the extent of its objectivity and impartiality: The Communist regime is *a priori* labelled as consistently 'totalitarian', regardless of its changing character and the ebbs and flows of repression and societal (dis)engagement over the four decades of its rule, and is essentially put on par with the Nazi occupation.[147] Kopeček concludes that the ÚSTR has:

> from a dissident emancipation tool ... become a state-supported civic education project that stresses the voices of the victims of and resisters to communist rule. Their testimonies were ascribed the highest authenticity in contrast to those supposedly 'tainted' by the former regime mentality.[148]

In sum, the official Czech politics of memory have been suffused with potent anti-Communist sentiments. As Kovanic observes, transitional justice in the Czech Republic thereby 'proceeded within an anti-Communism paradigm, including a

141 Kopeček, 'Czech Republic' (n 21) 9.

142 ibid.

143 Martin Kovanic, 'Institutes of Memory in Slovakia and the Czech Republic: What Kind of Memory?' in Peter Apor, Sandor Horvath, and James Mark (eds), *Secret Agents and the Memory of Everyday Collaboration in Communist Eastern Europe* (Anthem Press 2017) 82.

144 Kovanic illustrates how the establishment of the Institute and its work has not only been motivated by a genuine moral attempt to deal with the past but also by political aims (including discrediting opponents) and ideological inclinations (such as presenting Czechs more heroically as victims and far less supportive of or collusive with the Communist state). Kovanic also points to what he calls 'memory entrepreneurs' who at various points ran and worked for the ÚSTR and 'were members of, or had strong connections with, right-wing political parties'. Kovanic, 'Institutes of Memory in Slovakia and the Czech Republic' (n 143) 98 (providing considerable detail on the myriad of controversies swirling around the Institute's work). See also Kopeček, 'Czech Republic' (n 21) 9–11.

145 Law on the Institute for the Study of Totalitarian Regimes and Security Services Archives (n 106).

146 ibid para 4(a).

147 See also Kovanic, 'Institutes of Memory in Slovakia and the Czech Republic' (n 143) 97.

148 Kopeček, 'Czech Republic' (n 21) 9.

complete condemnation of communist ideology and its practices, as well as the majority of its proponents'.[149] This paradigm generated political gain and, as Blaive aptly puts it, awarded 'substantial professional capital' to its proponents.[150]

VII. Architectural Renovation, Refurbishment, and Overgrowth

Dealing with the past in the Czech Republic has also implicated sites, memorials, and plinths. Indeed, these are among the most seen visibilities and visualities of political transition following the Velvet Revolution and, interestingly, were among the most seen indicia of movements among the various internal phases of the Communist regime itself.[151]

Mihaela Mihai deftly unwraps the linkages between architecture and transitional justice. For Mihai, the moniker 'architectural transitional justice' encapsulates the myriad of ways that 'architectural scabs and scars' become repurposed in post-conflict times.[152] Mihai specifically addresses the 'reinvention' of Nazi 'flak towers'—anti-aircraft shooting sites constructed by slave labour—in Vienna and Hamburg in the aftermath of the Second World War. Her geography of violence involves structures explicitly used in a war effort. In this regard, we add to Mihai's framework in two ways.

First, we discuss sites that Mihai engages with, namely 'torture centres, forced labour or internment camps, or military installations [that] constitute the armature of political violence'.[153] Indeed, such grievous *lieux* of former human rights abuses are scattered throughout the Czech Republic. Here, we think of the StB's headquarters and offices in Prague—some of which were housed in a former convent—that currently serve as the regular police headquarters. Additionally, we think of atrocity sites where forced labour and correctional camps (TNPs) were located in the 1950s, including in the Jáchymov area at the eastern borders of the Czech Republic. In the early 1960s, the Communist regime attempted to eradicate any physical remnants of these camps. Some structural artefacts from TNP camps were destroyed, while some were repurposed; others languished in nature's hands to slowly disappear through the weathering effects of time. However, after 1989,

[149] Kovanic, 'Institutes of Memory in Slovakia and the Czech Republic' (n 143) 82.

[150] Blaive, 'An Impossible Reconciliation' (n 15) para 4. Concerns over the work of so-called memory institutes are certainly not limited to the Czech Republic. See eg Robert Traba, *The Past in the Present: The Construction of Polish History* (Peter Lang Edition 2015) 36, 43 (noting that the Polish Institute promotes the 'national politics of memory' and thereby poses the danger of Polish history being grossly over-simplified to fit a political narrative).

[151] See discussion in Chapter 2, Section I, 'The Communist State and Its Dénouemment' on the destruction of Prague's Stalin monument.

[152] Mihaela Mihai, 'Architectural Transitional Justice? Political Renewal Within the Scars of a Violent Past' (2018) 12 Intl J of Transitional Justice 515, 515–17.

[153] ibid 525.

Figure 3.1 Remnants of the former correctional labour camp close to Horní Slavkov. Photograph taken by the authors (Horní Slavkov, 2020).

some of these forgotten places were made visible again including for the purposes of tourism. For instance, the Jáchymov Hell trek was publicized, so as to 'remind [people] of the atrocities of labour camps'.[154] Other TNPs were forgotten and are now overgrown with thick weeds; others have become repurposed for other aims, such as residential areas or children's playgrounds; and others have devolved into dumping grounds for rubbish and waste, such as the site of the former correctional labour camp close to Horní Slavkov (Figure 3.1).[155]

Second, we hope to contribute to Mihai's frame of architectural transitional justice by wondering about other sites of life, events, and quotidian movements in the Communist years. These sites are stylistically aligned with the aesthetics and sensibilities of social realism and hence are culturally congruent with Communism, thereby demonstrating Mihai's observation that 'architecture has often been instrumentalized for political and social engineering'.[156] Many of these sites are benign: hotels, the subway, apartment blocks. They are just things that

[154] Političtí vězni.cz, 'Naučná stezka Jáchymovské peklo' (Političtí vězni.cz, undated) <https://www.politictivezni.cz/cz/naucna-stezka-jachymovske-peklo.html> accessed 12 March 2023 (providing a touristic description of the trek).

[155] Barbora Holá and Thijs Bouwknegt, 'Jáchymov's Hell: Trekking in the Memoryscape of Czechoslovakia's Communist Forced Labour Camps' (2022) 22(1–2) Intl Crim L Rev 328.

[156] Mihai, 'Architectural Transitional Justice?' (n 152) 519.

were built then and remain. At times, they were indeed sites of violence, but they were not intentionally built or run for violent purposes. Mostly they were just sites of quotidian life. What became of these places? Did they also transition?

Hotel International (Figure 3.2) was initially named Hotel Družba, meaning collective or friendship. It is the largest Stalinist-style building in Prague. It was built between 1952 and 1954 as a miniature copy of the Seven Sisters skyscrapers in Moscow (it also resembles the Polish Palace of Culture in Warsaw and the Latvian Academy of Sciences in Riga). The building was initially constructed to host high-ranking military staff for the Department of Defense. Notwithstanding this intention, it never fulfilled this function and was instead inaugurated as a luxury hotel. After the Velvet Revolution, Hotel Družba molted. It was bought by a series of private international hotel chains, including Crown Plaza, Holiday Inn, and the Mozart Hotel Group. Hotel Družba's transitional justice 'moment' involved a paint job on the star that adorns its central tower: the Holiday Inn franchise converted it from statist red to commercial green. The hotel is currently operative. Its exterior walls still retain friezes of hammers, sickles, and other typical examples of Communist iconography. Paintings and murals steeped in socialist realism adorn the interior. Some of this artwork finds itself adjacent to a massage therapy salon that pampers hotel guests. The sixteen-floor building is located just north of Prague's city centre and is easily reachable by an uphill tram ride. Similarly to

Figure 3.2 Hotel International in the neighbourhood of Dejvice, Prague. Photograph taken by the authors (Prague, 2019).

lustration, 'architectural transitional justice' implicates choice over which bits and pieces of Communist cultural property, so to speak, to retain, remove, or refurbish,[157] and—much like archival clarity—implicates choice over which architectural stories to open and which to submerge.

Paneláky apartment buildings are among the sturdiest living remnants of the Communist years. Initially inspired by French architect Le Corbusier, who fancied classless pods of residential harmony in efficiently self-contained mini-cities, *paneláky* are constructed from large prefabricated concrete slabs and panels (this is from where the name *paneláky* derives). They are scattered among the Prague suburbs, many to the south-east. *Paneláky* once were toweringly grey.[158] Their façades, while structurally retained, have since been brightly painted over in their own post-Communist transitional repurposing, such as *paneláky* in Kamýk which is one of Prague's suburbs (Figure 3.3). While certainly superficial and undoubtedly cosmetic, the colourful paint jobs nonetheless buoy the mood. *Paneláky* are full of children, stores, and beer bars. The green grass and surrounding trees soften their boxy angularity. Park benches dot the communal sidewalks, each hosting stories of lives led regularly or irregularly, moments of tranquillity, passion, amity, quarrels, sunbathing, sitting together, and solitude. It was here, in the *paneláky*, that many informers listened through thin walls and reported on others, while others met with their handlers in conspirational flats. Curiously, and on a transitional note of a different kind, because *paneláky* were entirely state owned during the Communist years, these apartments were provided to families and individuals by the state, yet with the fall of the *ancien régime* these formerly state-owned apartments became privatized. Some of the people who lived there bought the flats at modest prices. As real estate rose in value, so too did the fortunes of these early capitalist purchasers.

The Prague metro opened in 1974 and has since been significantly expanded. At first, many of the metro stations were named in ideological fashion, no different than other place names in other Communist countries. However, after 1989 these

[157] For discussion of cultural property, including Communist cultural property, such as statutes and busts of Marx and Lenin, see Mark A Drumbl, 'From Timbuktu to The Hague and Beyond: The War Crime of Intentionally Attacking Cultural Property' (2019) 17(1) J of Intl Crim Justice 77. One very inspiring place on the theme of ornamentation from the Communist years is the Neon Museum in Warsaw, Poland. This museum displays neon lights that Communist authorities had installed throughout Warsaw to brighten things. However, these public works projects were extinguished in the energy and power crises that engulfed Poland during the awakening of the Solidarity Movement and then under the responsive Martial Law. After the fall of Communism, many of these elegant signs were removed and unceremoniously dumped.

[158] While the buildings themselves were grey, Vaněk chides the use of the term 'grey' as a metaphor to describe life within these buildings. Vaněk notes that they served important housing purposes to respond to excessive demand; he adds that 'those who had experience of prefabricated housing were most often the least harsh in their judgment' and that such interlocutors often had positive memories of their modern amenities. Miroslav Vaněk, 'Twenty Years in Shades of Grey? Everyday Life During Normalisation Based on Oral History Research' in Kevin McDermott and Matthew Stibbe (eds), *Czechoslovakia and Eastern Europe in the Era of Normalisation 1969-1989* (Palgrave Macmillan 2022) 156–57.

Figure 3.3 *Paneláky* at Kamýk, Prague. Photograph taken by the authors (Prague, 2019).

names reshifted in furtherance of transitional policies. For example, 'Anděl', a stop on Prague's B line, meaning 'Angel' in English, was formerly known as Moskevská or 'Moscow's'; 'Dejvická', on the A line, which is currently named after a part of Prague, was formerly known as 'Leninova', meaning 'Lenin's'. 'Háje', on the C line, meaning 'Groves', was formerly known as 'Kosmonautů', meaning 'Cosmonaut's', after a sculpture dedicated to the Cold War space race located near its entrance. 'Opatov', on the C line, is also named after a part of Prague, but was formerly called 'Družby', meaning 'Of Friendship'; 'Chodov', also on the C Line, is now named after a part of Prague, although it was formerly 'Budovatelů', meaning 'Builders'; Vyšehrad station, on the C line, is named after a medieval castle but was once named Gottwaldova to honour Czechoslovakia's first Communist President. And so on, examples abound. One station is particularly noteworthy, however. This is Florenc, again located on the C line, and which was formerly known as 'Sokolovská'. This station has a mosaic-like mural on an underpass between two perpendicular metro lines that harmonizes with the station's original namesake. This mural—rough to the touch—depicts the 1943 Battle of Sokolovo in Ukraine, where the Red Army joined Czechoslovak troops to fight against the Germans for the first time.

While some of Prague's socialist realism still persists thirty years later, much has been shuffled out, covered up, replaced, and supplanted. Today, a red kinetic

Figure 3.4 The Metronom at Letná, Prague. Photograph taken by the authors (Prague, 2019).

metronome—installed in 1991—sits where Stalin and his gigantic retinue had once lorded over the city (Figure 3.4). The metronome is 23 meters high and occupies the same plinth as the Stalin statue had until that gargantuan colossus was blown up in 1962. The metronome tick-tocks away. It tells time as it elapses from the end of Communism and foretells the click-clock of the journey into the future. Mostly, however, this space belongs to skateboarders and graffiti artists who seem to enjoy the concrete jungle. The site does attract some discards of its own, namely empty beer cans left by carousers.

Pivoting back to Mihai, such new and repurposed structures indicate how 'architecture can support—though not ensure—political renewal'.[159] In the end, metamorphoses within these sites reveal their own forms of transitional movement and present a balance between continuity and discontinuity. At times, the changes are cosmetic—a paint job or a renaming—yet cosmetics may nevertheless be rather meaningful. The Swedish language has a word for cosmetics, *smink*. The Czech word, *šminky*, also meaning cosmetics, is very similar. When uploaded to the English language, a play on words arises. This is 'smink' as the fusion of 'to

[159] Mihai, 'Architectural Transitional Justice?' (n 152) 515.

Figure 3.5 Memorial to the victims of Communism in Petřín, Prague. Photograph taken by the authors (Prague, 2019).

smile' and 'to wink', or 'to smoke' and 'to drink'. Some of these structures stand with one foot in the past and the other in the present. They can be seen to be *sminking* at onlookers and in-livers. These buildings become transitioners.

Art, architecture, and sculpture can also newly emerge to commemorate transition and grieve the past. The starting point for Prague's contemporary post-Communist transitional justice commemorative tourism is the Memorial to the Victims of Communism at Petřín Hill (Figure 3.5). Completed in 2002, this memorial gives visual force to Primo Levi's delineation of what it means to demolish a man—although the site has been chided for only featuring men.[160] An engraved bronze strip, which runs down its centre, affirms the generally accepted estimates of the number of people whose lives were gutted by the Communist Party of Czechoslovakia. The disintegration of the emaciated figures, who ascend a slight gradient in reverse, strikingly depicts the progressive erasure of humanity during the Communist repression which Havel unfurled in his essays.[161]

[160] Primo Levi, *If This Is a Man* (authored 1947, Orion Press 1959).

[161] Václav Havel, 'Power of the Powerless' in Václav Havel, *Open Letters* (Alfred A. Knopf 1991) 125–214.

VIII. Conclusion

This chapter summarizes the core transitional justice mechanisms implemented in the Czech Republic to reckon with the past and bump the state into liberal capitalist democracy. These involved a balance between mechanisms focused on deemed 'wrongdoers', such as lustration, criminal prosecutions, and clarity laws, and mechanisms focused on deemed 'victims', namely rehabilitation and restitution. In addition, landscapes changed, remodellings occurred, and artworks popped up while others tumbled down. All of these measures proclaimed justice outcomes while also promoting broader political goals of delegitimizing the former Communist regime and simultaneously uplifting the new liberal capitalist state.

Transitional justice, as implemented in Czechoslovakia after 1989, and then in the Czech Republic after 1993, has been politicized and infused with an anti-Communist paradigm. The Czech historical reckoning has been emotional and polarizing. Indeed, '[m]arketing a national heroic past has worked wonders for those who have built their careers on an alleged anti-Communism, even when their own past does not have much in common with heroism'.[162] Reconciliation was not a goal. Unsurprisingly, the Czechs did not create a truth and reconciliation commission.

Transitional elites seized the figure of the informer as a cudgel and scapegoat. The names of alleged informers were revealed, their StB files were opened to public, and they were excluded from public service functions through lustration. The informer was largely constructed as a distrustful threat to society, as loyal to a failed and ugly ideology, as a menace to the new enlightened order, and scornfully dumped—'we are not like them'—from the remainder of society. With this in mind, this book now begins to explore whether the assumption of the ideologically committed informer as a toxic danger meshes with what we learned about informers based on the StB files. We conclude that totalizing informers as ideological and condemning them as inimical to the new regime departs from what our research actually suggests drove informers to engage with the StB. The historical record, in short, has become distorted.

[162] Muriel Blaive, 'Sanctimony as a Distortion of the Past and a Poison of the Future' (*Denik Referendum*, 2020) <https://denikreferendum.cz/clanek/31487-sanctimony-as-a-distortion-of-the-past-and-a-poison-of-the-future> accessed 12 March 2023.

4
Informer File-Stories

This chapter narratively presents the file-stories of six informers we selected from the StB files we have reviewed.[1] These file-stories are rich and chock-full of detail. They offer a kaleidoscope of lives lived across different periods of the Cold War Communist regime. As these file-stories demonstrate, informer motivations and the (e)motions that drove informer engagement with—and withdrawal from—the StB were idiosyncratic, dynamic, and complex.

Because these files are voluminous—at times bursting with nearly 1,000 out-of-order pages—we significantly distilled them into file-stories. Certainly, we could have made the file-stories shorter or even tightened them down to their bare bones. But we decided not to. We wanted to keep them rich, and vivid, yet not excessive. Hence, while we condensed the content, we were mindful not to over-condense. This is because the wealth of 'high-resolution' granularity greatly matters to us. Tipping our hat to this detail tags the StB's ability (and propensity) to record: StB ears were always listening, pens always writing, and typewriters continually clacking.

We present the contents of the individual files largely in chronological order, beginning with the informer's childhood and ending with the conclusion of the informer's collaboration with the StB (as a result of death, sickness, termination, or refusal). These detailed narratives paint a moving picture of how life changed in the various decades of Communist rule, as well as how individual lives situationally connected to political overtones and embedded themselves within the home and workplace. Ultimately, these files unwrap the balance between collective structure and individual agency central to life in a participatory dictatorship.

Chapter 5 then places these six file-stories in a dialogic synthesis with seventeen additional profiles featured in an online appendix,[2] along with considerable content from a plethora of secondary sources, so as to showcase what we find 'jumps out' at us when informers are looked at 'up close'.

[1] For discussion of our methodology, see Chapter 1, Section III, 'Secret Police Archives and File-Stories'. The quotations presented in the file-stories are drawn directly from the StB files and translated into English from either Czech or Slovak—on rare occasion, some documents were written in Slovak—by one of the co-authors and a research assistant. Every photograph in this chapter has also been sourced directly from the StB's files; we added the bar over the eyes.

[2] See http://www.nscr.nl/Informers-Up-Close.

Informers Up Close. Mark A. Drumbl and Barbora Holá, Oxford University Press.
 DOI: 10.1093/oso/9780192855138.003.0004

I. 'Věra'

Věra was born in Prague in 1928.[3] Her father was a construction and agricultural labourer. Her mother worked in a fruit packaging factory and thereafter became a homemaker. Both of Věra's parents passed away when she was in her early thirties. Throughout her life, Věra held different manual labour and administrative jobs; as a result of financial constraints she occasionally worked two jobs simultaneously. Věra never pursued higher education.

Věra's life was tumultuous. One of the first reports in her StB file describes how she was detained by the Nazis in 1944 for missing her appointment at a labour office. As a result, she was sent to a correctional camp for two months. This was her first conviction. Věra would later be imprisoned for property-related crimes at least two other times. Her file details how she had been repeatedly convicted for multiple offences including fraud in 1959 and 1975; embezzlement in 1970; and parasitism in 1970 and 1973.[4]

Věra frequently broke social convention and legal norms, especially as a young adult. She liked hanging out in pubs and drinking, she had extramarital affairs, and she befriended individuals regarded as enemies of the regime. Indeed, Věra's photo in her StB file depicts her with a subtle smile (Figure 4.1). Ultimately, her carefree lifestyle proved to be one of the reasons the StB took interest in her. Indeed, her putatively inappropriate behaviour provided sufficient fodder to blackmail her into collaboration. Her defective social circles—namely, the trust she received from her problematic friends and acquaintances—promised a clear pathway to the type of information fancied by the StB.

Věra did not fare well politically. In 1948, she joined the Communist Party, but was expelled two years later because 'she was utterly disinterested' in Party matters and 'did not fulfill even the basic obligations of Party members'. In the early 1950s, Věra reportedly 'disagreed with the current people's democratic establishment' to which she was 'absolutely indifferent'. She 'did not join [in] the process of building socialism … and want[ed] to gain money only effortlessly, not through honest work'. Later StB reports indicate that Věra's indifferent and passive political attitude towards the regime stayed with her for the rest of her life.

In 1945, Věra's family moved to a small village near Liberec in northern Bohemia. There, Věra assisted her parents with the family farm. In 1948,[5] Věra married a man named Alois. He was the head of a small shop in another village

[3] Positions: Confidant. Agent. Candidate for secret collaboration.
File No: 15534, 92098.
Registration No: 16236, 2762.
File created: 1952.
File archived: 1989.
Page count: 370 pages.

[4] For definition of the crime of parasitism, see Glossary.

[5] Some later reports say that she got married in 1952.

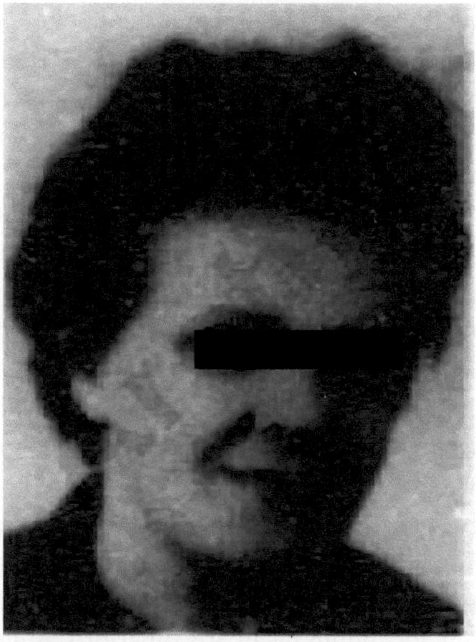

Figure 4.1 A photograph of Věra (source StB file No 15534, 92098, ABS archive).

close to Liberec. The young couple settled there after their wedding and had two children, a daughter and a son.[6] Věra's marriage was turbulent from the outset. Soon after their wedding, Alois was sentenced to seven months in prison. He had been convicted because—as the head of his business—he was deemed responsible for the unsanctioned disappearance of 30,000 Kčs from the shop's balance sheet.[7] However, before his period of incarceration could even begin, the couple moved to Karlovy Vary—a spa town located in western Czechoslovakia—where Věra began working as an administrative assistant at the Jáchymov Mines, these being ones of the most brutal forced labour camps of the time.

Věra had multiple affairs while her husband was in prison, primarily with men assessed as having 'a negative attitude toward the current establishment'. Věra was described as deceitful, even towards her own family; as very social and talkative; as someone who liked drinking alcohol and going out; as a contrarian and libertarian;

[6] The son tragically passed away in a car accident when he was thirty years old.

[7] Czechoslovakia joined the International Monetary fund on 18 December 1946. At that time, the exchange rate between the Kčs and the $US was set at 50:1. On 1 June 1953, further monetary reform was initiated in which the exchange rate was set at 7.2 Kčs to $US 1.00. At this point a controlled rationing system of foreign exchange funds was introduced. This remained in place until the end of 1990. For more discussion of Czechoslovak currency on international markets during Communism, see Acronyms in the front matter herein. See also 'Stručná historie české měny a jejího kursu' (*Hospodářské noviny*, 11 April 1996) <https://archiv.hn.cz/c1-873861-strucna-historie-ceske-meny-a-jejiho-kursu> accessed 3 September 2023.

and as someone who relished money, although she 'could not treasure her fancy due to her expensive lifestyle'. She did not have any noteworthy hobbies.

In 1951, Věra moved back to the Liberec area and found a job as an assistant worker in a sawmill company. At that time, the StB were not only intrigued by her private affairs but also by the fact that she allegedly committed petty crimes. Specifically, she befriended individuals considered delinquent by the regime and associated with persons who smuggled goods, such as watches, across borders—she would then supposedly sell these smuggled goods for profit. Věra was also aware that her friends facilitated illicit emigrations by arranging the necessary paperwork, or by physically assisting people in covert border crossings. As if this were not enough, Věra and her friends also allegedly listened to jammed foreign radio broadcasts from the West. In July 1952, these allegations prompted the StB to interrogate Věra. During this interrogation, Věra reportedly confessed to 'all her criminal activities' and signed 'an interim pledge to cooperate with the StB'. A recruitment proposal from 25 August 1952 reveals that the StB considered this interrogation to be the first step in Věra's recruitment. Interestingly, the proposal also contains a handwritten addendum by an StB superior stating 'compromise [her] also with her infidelities'.

The StB afforded Věra, by virtue of her recruitment, an opportunity to redress her deviant behaviour. Věra knew the majority of people in her village and the surrounding towns. Insofar as this region was close to the borders, the StB saw Věra's value as a prospective informer. Věra moreover 'enjoy[ed] the full trust of the class enemy because her husband was imprisoned for 7 months', and her village friends and acquaintances were mostly 'reactionar[ies] oriented against the current establishment'. Thus, her social standing was well suited to attain the StB's goals.

Věra's recruitment meeting took place on 5 September 1952. She was taken to the StB regional headquarters in Liberec, where she had previously been interrogated. Věra was again questioned on her criminal activity after 1950, which prompted her to admit some previously undisclosed dubious conduct. The StB officers seized the moment to repeatedly condemn her infidelity to her husband, and she 'seemed to have been embarrassed' about this conversational line. According to a report on the meeting, Věra was initially subdued, but then started crying and confessed to all of her 'errors'. In response, the StB 'emphasized the seriousness of [her] criminal activities' and noted Věra's 'bad attitude toward ... the people's democratic establishment'. Věra 'knew that some persons had been illegally taken across borders [,] and that there would be others ... [this alone] [was] very criminal because she did not report [these illegal border crossings] to security organs. [Věra's failure to disclose] sufficed for a [major] conviction.'

The StB saw 'potential for [Věra's] rectification ... through conscientious and diligent cooperation with [the StB] to reveal and defuse our class enemies'. According to the meeting report, Věra agreed to cooperate. An StB officer read her collaboration pledge out loud, and then passed it to her for careful review.

He subsequently asked her to read it out loud while 'facing a portrait of comrade Klement Gottwald',[8] and then sign it.

Věra's signed, typewritten pledge includes the requisite performative language, such as a voluntary commitment to collaborate, the fulfilment of all tasks in the name of peace, and the 'build[ing] [of] a better, socialist order throughout the world'. Furthermore, a promise of confidentiality is embedded in her pledge.

After Věra performed the signing ritual, the StB officer said that she had already conveyed valuable information—even prior to formalizing her collaboration. He elaborated that her disclosures demonstrated her willingness and preparedness to cooperate and her resolve to continue 'revealing the enemies of our people's democratic republic'. Věra was then free to leave the building. According to the report, she left smiling and visibly happy.

An evaluation report from October 1954 portrayed Věra as an eager and engaged informer who delivered 'very good results' such that 'on the basis of her reports, several persons were realized'.[9] In 1954, Věra worked with military counter-intelligence on Operation ÚLET. This operation endeavoured to expose military pilots assisting in the illegal flight—can also be translated as *úlet* in Czech—of individuals who 'hated ... the establishment'. The evaluation report indicates that Věra was committed to Operation ÚLET: She submitted '25 truthful reports, which revealed the intentions of [the] persons' planning these escapes abroad. She worked 'honestly, diligently, and even sacrificed her private life' to the extent that the StB elected not to use the rest of its compromising material against her because she 'worked very well'. For her effort, Věra was rewarded with two terry towels valued at 84 Kčs. The evaluation report states that, in addition to material rewards like these, Věra relished 'minor financial awards ... [s]he [also] liked dressing up and attending "high-society" parties'.

Around 1954, Věra made plans to move to Teplice, a town in the north-west of Bohemia, and her file was accordingly transferred to a local StB office. The StB told Věra that she would be contacted by another 'comrade, who [would] again start further cooperation [with her]'. While she was planning her move, she asked her acting StB officer to help her find a flat in one of the newly constructed high-rise buildings in Teplice. Věra must have thought that the StB would help her out due to her prior good service. However, instead of assisting in the property search, Věra's StB officer simply referred her to her future contact at the StB, as 'for sure comrades in Teplice [would] try to advise and help her'. Ultimately, the StB did not intervene. An evaluation report from February 1955 noted that Věra found neither a job nor an apartment in Teplice.

[8] Klement Gottwald led the Communist Party from 1929 until his death in 1953. He became President of Czechoslovakia in June 1948.

[9] In other words, these other persons were arrested.

By April 1956, Věra had moved again—this time to Prague. Because her file is scattered and incomplete, it is not possible to reconstruct exactly what prompted her relocation to Prague. Things get a bit cryptic. Indeed, in that same month, the StB drafted a proposal to archive Věra's file. At the time, Věra submitted reports that primarily concerned Prague residents and their criminal activities. Accordingly, the StB and the VB (ordinary police) agreed that Věra would be transferred from the StB to the VB in the capacity of surveilling ordinary criminal conduct as opposed to state security.

In May 1960, Věra was convicted for fraud and embezzlement and sentenced to two years in a correctional labour camp. Her fellow inmates, along with the officials running the camp, were of interest to the StB. Thus, in February 1961, an StB officer employed at the labour camp drafted a proposal to renew Věra's collaboration. According to the proposal, the StB contacted Věra immediately upon her arrival in prison. She agreed to work with the StB. Within a relatively short period of time, Věra had in fact 'submitted several written and oral reports relating to [the] general situation in the camp, as well as about certain individuals'. Since all of her reports were verified and turned out to be accurate, an StB officer drafted a request to formally renew her collaboration.

According to an evaluation report from September 1961, Věra submitted a total of twenty-four written reports regarding either the general situation among the convicts at the labour camp or the particular 'deficiencies at the workplace' with respect to both the convicts and their supervisors. Moreover, the StB specifically directed Věra's attention towards 'former persons' who allegedly undermined assigned work. Based on Věra's reports, 'various [disciplinary] measures' were deployed by the prison authorities. For instance, certain convicts were 'punished while unaware that the information [spurring their punishment] came from [Věra]'. The StB praised Věra's social qualities and the fact that she could easily talk to anyone to gain their confidences. She was regarded as a 'good cooperative even when imprisoned'. For example, Věra informed on a fellow prisoner who corresponded in German and endeavoured to smuggle letters in her shoes; allegedly, these letters contained complaints about prison officials.

Věra was released from prison in August 1962; ironically, her release suspended her collaboration. Her evaluation report from September 1962 states that, at the time of her release, she had submitted more than fifty reports of 'average quality'. She was said to have satisfied appointed tasks well and there were 'no major deficiencies in her discipline or work ethic'. Indeed, she was released eight days earlier as 'a reward for her collaboration and good work morale'. There is almost no information in the file as to what occurred for nearly two decades after Věra's release from prison. Documents in her file reveal that she divorced Alois in 1966. Moreover, an official transcript from her criminal records in 1987 shows that she was reconvicted and reincarcerated throughout the 1970s.

In 1981, Věra's daughter emigrated to Switzerland. This appeared to be the impetus for rekindled interest on the part of the StB in Věra. Thus, almost twenty years after the termination of her second stint as an informer, Věra began to inform once again. Despite this considerable passage of time, she remained a determined operative. She was living in Prague at the time of her re-recruitment.

Věra was officially re-recruited as an agent in 1983, although she had been in touch with the StB as early as 1981 due to StB interest in her extensive contacts with Czechoslovak emigrants. Accordingly, the StB demanded that Věra 'signal any preparations for emigrations'. Documents in her file reveal that she began meeting with the StB on a more consistent basis in May and June 1982. She was questioned on the following two subjects: various acquaintances of hers who had emigrated (or were supposedly planning to do so) and her daughter. By November 1982, Věra had submitted 'more than 30 reports'. Indeed, 'six persons [as a result] were barred from emigration'.

It is reasonable to assume that Věra was at least partially motivated to inform because it gave her the opportunity to travel abroad to visit her daughter, who had in the intervening years become a Swiss permanent resident. Indeed, over the next few years Věra travelled to Switzerland at least twice a year for several weeks, usually during the summer and Christmas. She forged close relationships with many Czechoslovak emigrants while she travelled, some of whom were still believed by the StB to be 'actively hostile against our socialist establishment'.

Much like her previous cooperation, Věra was willing to locate and report any information the StB requested of her. There are no extant copies of the reports Věra herself submitted, but from reviewing evaluation reports and various meeting reports contained in her file it becomes evident that she endeavoured to gather information while she travelled. For example, she informed on a Czechoslovak family in Switzerland who ran a 'Czech Restaurant' in Schaffhausen that served as a gathering place for Czechoslovak residents and tourists. Allegedly, the owner of this restaurant 'was persuading Czechoslovak tourists to emigrate, praised the [Swiss] establishment, and promised them [the Czechoslovaks] work'. Some of these other emigrants openly published anti-regime books or worked for institutions such as Radio Free Europe, and Věra was reportedly able to provide 'very detailed and precise' information about them.

When Věra was back in Prague, she primarily kept herself busy by working two jobs. She frequently picked up extra shifts from her colleagues. Initially, she was a shop assistant in a large mall in the city; later, she worked at a local train station. Věra even continued working after her official retirement. According to a report from February 1983, Věra was a 'closed, quiet person, who avoid[ed] contacts with her surroundings'—a stark contrast to how she had been depicted in her youth. It is possible that Věra changed her ways, yet equally possible is that her latest StB handler simply saw things differently than his predecessors did. Věra allegedly had a 'very good relationship' with her StB officer, answered all questions 'without reserve, and [even] confided her private problems [to her StB officer]'.

As we have noted, the StB decided to formally re-recruit Věra in June 1983. During the re-recruitment meeting on 23 June 1983, Věra once again signed a typewritten pledge to cooperate. In the spirit of the normalization era, and in stark contrast to her recruitment in the 1950s, there was no ritual, no oath-taking in front of any Communist functionaries, and the text of the pledge itself was comparatively sparse: it did not refer to world peace or spreading socialism, but instead affirmed that cooperation was 'in the interest of the defense of the Czechoslovak Socialist Republic'.

Thereafter, Věra regularly supplied the StB with information she amassed during visits with her daughter. Thus, her file contains numerous travel proposals paired with detailed, albeit largely reiterative, performance expectations for her time abroad which she frequently signed in her code name. The StB occasionally instructed Věra to monitor certain individuals, to verify their addresses, and to observe their activities or political opinions. Although Věra's file does not contain any of her reports or observations, the StB's evaluation reports indicate that she continued to be an 'able', 'serious', and 'active' cooperative who 'fulfilled required tasks, even beyond their scope'. For instance, Věra provided information that was used 'to bar the emigration of three persons' and a married couple, as well as to stymie the planned emigration of other individuals. She even alerted the StB to individuals she recommended as prospective informers. On her fifty-fifth birthday, the StB gave Věra a financial reward of 500 Kčs, with one report describing this gift as 'a boost for successful cooperation'.

Despite her frequent travels, the StB trusted Věra not to emigrate. This trust was rooted in the fact that she 'had a nicely furnished apartment, was financially very well off, and had possibilities to regularly travel to visit her daughter'. The StB also had other informers check in on her to quell their lingering doubts, none of whom found 'any signs of preparing emigration'. However, Věra's file does contain a rather dubious anecdote. In December 1984, while on her way to Switzerland, Věra crossed into West Germany. Upon a routine luggage inspection at the border, Czechoslovak officials found her son's death certificate; this prompted these officials to question whether Věra did indeed have the intention to emigrate. However, during a subsequent interview, Věra reassured them that the certificate was a sort of 'memory token', and that she always carried it with her because she liked to reminisce about the life of her son. The border officials nonetheless seized the document. Věra was compelled to travel without it.

Notwithstanding Věra's commendable performance and the trustworthiness she had seemingly engendered by her disinterested attitude towards emigration, the StB nevertheless routinely surveilled her. Their methods included using other informers, monitoring her phone calls after her return from Switzerland, and general reviews of her correspondence. In fact, Věra's file contains several reports about her from a secret cooperative, PETA, who was probably a colleague from work. Because these surveillance tactics did not reveal any inkling of her desire to emigrate, the loop of trust cemented. Ultimately, however, the StB's efforts did cause other rather unattractive tidbits to rise to the surface.

One such tidbit is that Věra had an alleged affair with a married man who resided in the same apartment building as she did. Following a lovers' quarrel, she gossiped about him to the other residents. Věra's lover was described as an unsavoury character—he had reportedly exposed himself to a resident and spied on others by listening behind their doors at night. Another tidbit from one of PETA's reports in 1987 recounted how Věra regularly brought 'shortage goods' from Switzerland. She then reportedly sold these goods for profit or gave them to her work superiors as 'gifts'.

In January 1989, the StB terminated Věra's collaboration because of her 'advanced age and frequent illnesses'. The proposal to terminate notes that, during the final stage of her cooperation in the 1980s, 112 meetings took place and 163 'agency records' (*agenturní záznamy*) were written using information she supplied. No-one was arrested during this phase of her informing. That said, some of the information Věra provided was reportedly used by the criminal police, played a part in various StB security checks, and barred people from emigrating. In retrospect Věra overall had a 'positive attitude toward cooperation, upheld principles of conspiration [ie secrecy], [and] fulfilled her tasks well'. Indeed, the StB had recognized the positive contributions she made during collaboration, as she had been rewarded with gifts whose total value was 5,900 Kčs. The StB believed that her 'results corresponded to her possibilities, acquired education, and social standing'.

In sum, Věra was a marginal and vulnerable youth. She was initially blackmailed into cooperation. She agreed to the StB's somewhat baleful offer to collaborate likely out of fear of ruining her and her family's lives otherwise. Nevertheless, over the course of her lengthy career as an informer, Věra proved to be a committed and assiduous operative. Individuals were arrested, precluded from emigrating, or disciplinarily punished as a direct consequence of her informing.

Věra lived an unsettled life. She moved a lot, frequently changed jobs, and often transgressed law and social convention. Although it seems that Věra did not approach the StB on her own initiative, she appears to have done everything that was asked of her and did it well. She was recurrently amenable to the StB's overtures when they flipped the switch from off to on. Perhaps Věra felt that cooperation with the StB could blunt the potential harmful consequences of her lifestyle and even provide her with some sort of cover. Informing did partially shield her from prosecution and, in conjunction with her 'good behaviour', afforded her an early release from prison. Moreover, after her daughter emigrated to Switzerland, Věra took advantage of the opportunity that informing gave her to visit her daughter abroad.

Overall, Věra's active engagement with the StB was seemingly spurred by a mix of fear and greed, as well as a predilection for the benefits it provided. At times, she was financially insecure. Her cooperation with the StB took the edge off this precarity, although, as she got older, she appeared to become more economically stable. Věra aged in partnership with the StB, leaving her youthful prison days behind to settle into greater comfort and steadiness.

II. 'Vašek'

Vašek was born in Prague in 1932.[10] His father worked in an administrative capacity. His mother was a homemaker until 1955, when she began employment at an unspecified research and military facility where she was not permitted to discuss the content of her job. Vašek's father was a proactive Communist who organized Party activities at their place of residence. He was seen as 'a good and conscientious Party member who was politically fully trusted'. Vašek's mother was not affiliated with any political party; however, she was 'a progressive woman' with 'a positive attitude toward the people's democratic regime'. The whole family benefitted from its positive social standing. As such, Vašek never experienced 'any shortages'.

In 1952, Vašek graduated from a *gymnasium*—an institution of learning that is roughly equivalent to a secondary school. Thereafter, he began working at a state shipping company called *Čechofracht*. During his time with *Čechofracht*, Vašek—with the permission of the Ministry of Foreign Trade—spent nearly one year engaged on a ship operating under the Polish flag. He travelled the world as a sailor. When he returned to Czechoslovakia, his employer sent him to study at the University of Economics. In 1957, Vašek married one of his peers, Dagmar, and together they had two sons. Vašek graduated with distinction in 1958, having obtained a degree in economics with a specialization in foreign trade.

Overall, Vašek had quite a successful career. He ably mined the possibilities for personal and professional growth offered by the Communist regime. Like Věra, he would go on to inform for over thirty years. However, in stark contrast to Věra, who often lived on the margins of society, Vašek prospered throughout his entire life in various public functions. For his active involvement in building socialist society, and for his work with the country's youth, he was awarded a state prize. Vašek

[10] Positions: Agent. Candidate for secret collaboration. Agent.
File No: 616005.
Registration No: 8852.
File created: 1956.
File archived: 1988.
Page count: 388 pages.
Vašek's file does not contain a photograph of him.

did not hail from an outcast group or begin as a disenfranchised individual. By all appearances, he was a consistently successful member of socialist society.

A multiplicity of reports in his StB file describe Vašek as having a positive attitude towards the Communist regime. When he was in gymnasium, he was a leading figure for the local branch of the Party youth union—known as the *Československý svaz mládeže* (ČSM)—and he was a volunteer at several Party-run youth projects and events. His file reveals that he was a 'responsible' citizen who always 'oriented his political opinions toward building [a] people's democracy'. Vašek became a candidate for membership in the Communist Party at the age of nineteen. After a two-year trial period, he fully joined the Party. Vašek was seen to be 'a good member' of the Party and 'a mature Comrade' who was fully trusted. Unlike many others, his membership withstood the tumultuous events of 1968.

Vašek's file describes him as polite, intelligent, and 'a direct, honest young man with no inclinations [towards an] extravagant or abnormal way of life'. In university, he enjoyed playing football and hanging out with his wife, Dagmar. Subsequent reports characterized his professional demeanour as 'hard working and devoted'. However, other informers who surveilled him had a less favourable view of his professional behaviour, describing him as 'self-confident', 'haughty', 'calculating', and 'utilitarian'. These latter two traits apparently, according to these sources, manifested in Vašek's desire for friendships with 'individuals from whom he could benefit' and high-ranking Party and governmental officials. According to the StB, Vašek had the ability to 'always correctly assess any situation and adopt suitable opinions'. He was a very good public speaker, and addressed public gatherings and even spoke on television. Interestingly, later reports stated that he also owned a gun.

The StB attempted to formally recruit Vašek while he was a student at the University of Economics. Thus, in April 1957, an StB officer publicly approached him.[11] Such a public gesture was rather extraordinary in light of the StB's obsession with secrecy and confidentiality. The officer agreed to meet Vašek at the Stalin statue at Letná in Prague. At this meeting, the officer inquired about Vašek's language skills and future aspirations. The officer then asked Vašek whether he would be interested in working 'with the security'. Vašek declined, allegedly explaining that he would rather work for the Ministry of Foreign Trade and that he would like to travel abroad again. In response, the StB officer emphasized that working with the StB would enable Vašek to travel abroad. This statement reportedly piqued Vašek's interest, and he subsequently inquired whether he could 'travel as a diplomat'. Because the officer responded in the negative to this query, Vašek quickly lost interest, as he preferred to travel abroad 'either as a diplomat or as a tradesman'.

[11] In that report, Vašek is referred to as 'Lodník' (in English: Sailor), meaning that he had already been given a cover name. This implies that Vašek likely had had some sort of previous interaction with the StB or that the StB had been keeping a file on him because he was a person of interest to them.

The officer then 'explained the political importance of [StB] work', to which Vašek replied that he understood but that he would like more time to think about it. Accordingly, a follow-up meeting was set. A handwritten note from a report on this follow-up meeting indicates that it was not very successful for the StB: 'At the meeting on April 17, 1957, [Vašek] mentioned that he was not keen to work with us, that he would rather go to MZO [ie the Ministry of Foreign Trade]. After a short discussion I ended the meeting.' Thus, Vašek initially declined StB entreaties. He did not do so for ideological or dissident reasons but rather because he contemplated a different career for himself.

Regardless of this initial hiccup, just over a year later—on 2 July 1958—the StB drafted a proposal to recruit Vašek. It is unclear whether the StB remained in touch with him or surveilled him from afar in this interim year, but it certainly seems that Vašek's interest in working with the StB accelerated during this time. The recruitment proposal notes that Vašek had 'enhanced abilities for social contacts with foreigners', and therefore would be 'a good cooperative' for 'the issue of visa foreigners' coming to Czechoslovakia. The StB also envisaged that Vašek would travel and work for them abroad.

In the recruitment proposal, Vašek was characterized as 'bright, intelligent, able to control himself, disciplined, capable of taking initiative', and also evidenced the ability to 'react quickly and adjust to complex situations'. The StB also noted that, 'due to his appearance and slightly extravagant clothing [,] he could earn the trust of individuals from capitalist states'. According to the proposal, Vašek had 'a very good attitude toward the … establishment and [was] thought of as a mature member of the Party'. He was also clearly 'interested in cooperating with the Ministry of the Interior' as he considered it to be his 'Party and patriotic duty'. Moreover, Vašek reportedly perceived his cooperation to be a sign of the regime's considerable trust in him. The proposal further noted that Vašek 'indirectly offered cooperation himself', and it commended his ability to remain silent—a skill he had learned at home due to his mother's secretive job. For all these reasons, the StB concluded that Vašek would be a devoted and reliable informer.

Thus, Vašek was formally recruited on 17 July 1958. Compared to the StB's first recruitment attempt—which took place in public—this time StB officers invited him to an isolated room at their headquarters. Vašek reportedly offered his cooperation without the need for nudges or inducements. He stated that he would most likely have ample opportunities to meet foreigners and therefore could be useful to the StB. He also reiterated that he considered collaboration to be 'his Party duty'. Vašek handwrote his pledge to cooperate that very day:

> I commit, on the basis of my Party membership and conscious of consequent responsibilities, to cooperate with the organs of the Ministry of the Interior. I also commit to never disclose my cooperation to any acquaintance, not even to closest

> family members, I will also hold in absolute secrecy all things, which I will find out about and which relate to the cooperation with the Ministry of the Interior....

Vašek's file stipulates that he agreed to cooperate with the StB for patriotic and ideological reasons.

Vašek was initially instructed to focus on the 'French basis' within 'visa foreigners' in Czechoslovakia. That said, Vašek's first report on 24 July 1958 was about a fellow university student and Czechoslovak, Štefan. Vašek commented on Štefan's political opinions and expressions. Although Štefan did not share his political opinions with large groups, Vašek noted that when Štefan partook in smaller groups in a dormitory he was a very active debater who did not always evince 'correct opinions'. Vašek also disclosed that Štefan spent a lot of time on his hobbies, including 'sport, dancing, girls, dressing up and passionate reading of newspapers'.

According to evaluation reports from 1960 and 1961, StB officers were satisfied with Vašek. He was an 'effective', responsible, and interested informer with a 'good attitude toward his tasks'. He could create 'very good situations to extract information'. Politically, the StB saw him as 'absolutely reliable and devoted'. The only downside was that, due to his professional responsibilities and frequent travels abroad, Vašek's cooperation was on the less intensive side.

That said, as an aside, in 1960 the StB received an anonymous letter alleging that, in 1952, Vašek had stolen a chocolate bar from a supermarket in Antwerp, Belgium (he stayed there while he was working on the Polish ship). When caught, he allegedly claimed that he was a Czechoslovak refugee, an anti-Communist fighter, and that he was stealing because he was hungry. This letter affirmed that, due to these proclamations, the Belgians did not pursue the matter. Such claims, if proven to be true, could have cast doubts on Vašek's purported devotion to the Party and Communist regime. However, this 'chocolate affair' ultimately turned out to be a misunderstanding: Vašek, in his own words, was purportedly unfamiliar with the supermarket's payment system and, as a result, he overlooked the cashiers and inadvertently walked past them. After he was stopped by a supermarket employee, Vašek clarified the situation and promptly paid for his purchase. Vašek's file also contains a handwritten account from July 1960 where he explained what happened and how. Perhaps in a quest to protect his reputation, Vašek concluded this document by stating: 'I declare, given my Party consciousness and honor, that I had never proclaimed anything about the fact that I pretended to be an emigrant, and that all details which I hereby describe are absolutely true.' It seems that the StB went with Vašek's version of the story.

In 1961, Vašek and his family moved to Romania upon relocation by his employer at the time, namely, the Czechoslovak Ocean Shipping Company (*Československá námořní plavba*). Pursuant to his later reports, he had been posted to Romania *inter alia* to organize weapons exports to Vietnam, Iraq, and Syria. The foreign relocation interrupted Vašek's engagement with the StB.

Nevertheless, the StB contemplated occasionally meeting with him during his holidays or upon his business trips to Czechoslovakia. It is not evident whether such meetings indeed occurred. In May 1964, the StB received a troubling report from a Czechoslovak citizen who, during his own business trip to Romania, was alerted to Vašek's 'shortcomings in work and behaviour'. Vašek was allegedly behaving 'arrogantly', being disrespectful towards his business partners and colleagues, lagging in his organization of political activities, and stealing food—'especially sausages'—from ships that fell under his professional purview. Furthermore, when his wife left Romania for around five months, Vašek reportedly had an affair with a Romanian citizen. However, much like the 'chocolate affair', the StB overlooked these allegations. An evaluation report from July 1964 indeed emphatically notes that Vašek 'was experiencing a severe family crisis, which manifested at his workplace and in fulfilling tasks stemming from his cooperation [with the StB]'.

However, after Vašek's return to Czechoslovakia in 1964, his informing output failed fully to satisfy the StB's expectations. Because Vašek had been elected chairman of the Party committee at his company in 1966, the StB however ascribed this poor performance to his very active engagement with workplace Party activities. Ultimately, the StB concluded that his 'possibilities as a cooperative ... are minimal and a further collaboration due to these circumstances [is] not suitable'. Thus, in 1967, the StB terminated the collaboration without rancour, once again demonstrating the relative ease with which Vašek was able to navigate various spaces and places.

Vašek was not lustrated from the Communist Party following Operation Danube in 1968. As he would later tell the StB, he had spent the first half of the year abroad 'at the sea' in Morocco and Iraq dealing with weapon exports for the Czechoslovak Ocean Shipping Company. In August 1968, when 'the armies entered the Czechoslovak territory', Vašek was, in his own words, 'on a ship heading to Yugoslavia and Iraq'. He revealed that in Yugoslavia he tried 'persuading Czechoslovak citizens/ sailors /to return to Czechoslovakia and not to attempt to emigrate'.[12]

The events of 1968 and immediately thereafter seemingly launched Vašek's career with top-Party politics. His file contains numerous reports and cadre assessments in which his behaviour during the 'crisis years' was most positively evaluated. He always 'expressed himself according to the current Party politics' and was a 'devoted, tenacious, honest and fair communist'. For these reasons, and because of his 'rich theoretical and practical experience', Vašek was chosen to execute various leading functions in the state administration after 1968. In 1969, he became the head of the youth department at the Ministry of Youth and Physical Education.

[12] In their typewritten reports, StB officers sometimes used slashes as breaks in their transcription. When applicable, we retain these slashes to remain true to our sources.

In addition to holding this position, Vašek was also active in many other youth-related Party organizations.

Despite such overwhelmingly favourable evaluations of Vašek's political and civic engagement, one stain appeared in his cadre profile. In 1968, he had actively engaged in the Junák organization—a Czech branch of the Scouts and a frequent target of StB suspicion. Various reports in Vašek's file reveal that he participated in Junák 'to enforce its socialist character'. This assumption seemed to protect him. In November 1968, Vašek was elected vice-chairman of Junák's board, where he 'purposefully enforced the politics of the Party'.

The StB nevertheless remained wary of Vašek's engagement with Junák: the organization had been disbanded by the regime in 1948 and only fleetingly re-emerged in the liberalizing year of 1968. Thus, the StB's interest in Vašek reignited, partially because of his activities in Junák—which were reportedly not as harmless as they seemed—and partially because Vašek was allegedly of 'rightist inclinations'. That said, in October 1970, the Federal Ministry of the Interior issued an order re-banning Junák. So this matter closed.

Nonetheless, the StB remained eager to scour information from Vašek regarding his new job in government. Thus, in 1975, the StB began meeting with him again. As cause to renew the collaboration, the StB referenced Vašek's 'absolutely reliable' intelligence from earlier years, and affirmed that he 'took initiative and [was] able to fulfill all his tasks'. Moreover, documents in the file indicate that Vašek had, yet again, indirectly offered to cooperate without pursuing any personal benefits because Vašek understood cooperation to be his 'Party and patriotic duty'. The StB recalled these points as further indication of Vašek's dependability as an informer. Due to his previous relationship with the StB, Vašek was not required to sign a renewed pledge to collaborate.

In April 1975, the StB interviewed Vašek after he had returned to Czechoslovakia from a business trip in England. During that interview, the StB probed into Vašek's membership with Junák several years prior. Vašek stated that his membership was motivated by a desire to promote Communist ideals within Junák. Vašek divulged that, as a member of Junák's directing body, he had been asked to adopt a stance on 'the entering of armies of the Warsaw Pact to the territory of Czechoslovakia'. Because he did not call it an 'occupation', he was allegedly rebuked as 'a Russian swine' and 'a collaborator'. He also revealed that he had experienced 'certain troubles' after Junák's dissolution in 1970. However, Vašek staunchly maintained that 'if he had any political "flaws" from 1968–69, he would not have been allowed to work at the Office of the Government'. The StB then asked Vašek whether he 'would be willing to convey information of interest [to the StB]'. He agreed.

From that point on, Vašek began meeting with the StB on a regular basis. In these encounters, he shared that 'he was quite busy, however, he considered it natural and right to convey necessary information to [the StB]'. On another note, he confided to StB officers that his marriage was not going well and that he and his wife were probably going to divorce. Indeed, multiple informers' reports described how Vašek had been having an affair since 1973 with a divorced woman. Both of them worked in the same office building.

In 1976, the StB started referring to Vašek as a candidate for secret collaboration. He was asked about his colleagues at work, the general mood at his workplace, and any organizational changes that may have eventuated there. The StB was particularly curious about individuals whose Party membership had been terminated after 1968, and Vašek shared some—albeit mostly complimentary—information about them. During one of his meetings with the StB, Vašek reportedly said that 'he did not see anything wrong with informing to the Ministry of the Interior', and that he did not consider it to be 'snitching' because he was aware that such information was needed by the Ministry. He considered it to be 'a great honor that the Ministry trusted him'.

Indeed, Vašek proved, yet again, to be a determined and proactive secret cooperative. He continued to inform and submit written reports on his colleagues[13] and on former members of Junák. He specifically named the 'quite reactionary' members and, in contrast, those of 'socialist inclinations who could potentially be counted on to provide information'. He also described observations he had gleaned from his travels abroad. For instance, unbeknownst to his wife, Vašek gave the StB a letter that she had received from a Yugoslav national who was also a person of interest to them.

Outwardly, Vašek appeared to be successfully striving. He worked in the state administration and was directly engaged with Czechoslovak youth. He co-organized a youth club in Prague. He participated in summer camps assembled by the Party youth organization '*Pionýr*' ('Pioneer'). Despite these outward appearances of success, Vašek's personal life was deteriorating. Dagmar had allegedly been expelled from her workplace for her pro-reformist opinions. Unlike Vašek, her membership in the Communist party had not been renewed in 1970. According to other informers, both spouses had other partners. Their marriage ultimately ended in divorce. Vašek later remarried and moved in with his new wife and their newborn son.

Reports from this tranche of Vašek's StB collaboration predominantly contain information from other informers on Vašek himself. For example, some informers reported that Vašek had been lanced from leading positions in the Pioneer youth movement in Prague because 'there was a danger of influencing Pioneers [through] Junák ideology or Junák practices'. Another informer mentioned how he thought that, back in 1968, it was not the Party that had sent Vašek to Junák, but rather that 'former representatives of Junák / given their character and tactics / used [Vašek] as a member of the Party to disguise their true interests'. This same informer also

[13] Although these reports are not included in Vašek's file, StB officers mention their existence multiple times in records from their meetings with him.

accused Vašek of benefitting from nepotism, and subsequently assumed that, in all likelihood, Vašek was backed by someone very influential in the Party, 'as how could it be possible that [Vašek], as a former high representative of Junák, and its vice-chairman, could still occupy such important functions in the area of youth'. Another informer characterized Vašek as a 'spineless' individual who

> [n]ever acted directly. At meetings of the Pioneer [,] [Vašek] always talked as a devoted Pioneer [,] and at Junák's meetings he propagated Junák's thoughts, quite ... uncompromisingly. At joint meetings [of both organizations] [,] he spoke only in generalities....

Other informers, on the other hand, were more favourably inclined towards Vašek. One such informer stated that Vašek was very active in public and political life, held multiple functions in the Party and its youth organizations, and had close contact to leading Party functionaries. According to this informer, Vašek led an ascetic life: '[Vašek] was very strict ..., did not smoke, did not drink, not even coffee and alcohol—only very occasionally in negligible quantities. He was very focused on being in good physical condition.'

Notwithstanding these swirling rumours and divergent ruminations, the StB remained satisfied with Vašek's performance. An evaluation report from February 1977 noted that he was 'conscientious, took initiative [,] [that] he could create necessary conditions for getting information', and that his relationship to the StB was 'very good'. In 1977, Vašek was financially rewarded for the year's collaboration in the amount of 135 Kčs.

In 1978, Vašek received a promotion at work. An informer's report stated that he had accepted this appointment because of the extraordinary benefits it provided, including a higher salary, a company car, and numerous opportunities to travel abroad. Moreover, and despite the reported opposition of some of his coworkers, Vašek continued to receive such promotions due to his cosy relationship with top Party brass. Interestingly, Vašek's file is bereft of self-submitted reports or of any records from his meetings with the StB in the wake of this promotion, yet evaluation reports from the early 1980s laud his performance as an informer and commend his 'very good relationship' with his StB officer. Specifically, Vašek 'provided ... interesting information from the area of physical education and top sport'. All of his reports apparently turned out to be 'fully true' and 'objective'. In 1984, Vašek received another reward—this time in the amount of 200 Kčs—for his 'good results'. An evaluation report in the file notes that in May 1984 Vašek told the StB about his plans to join the diplomatic services.

Indeed, in 1985, Vašek left his job at the Office of the Federal Government and moved to the Ministry for Foreign Trade. As of 1986, his file contains reports relating to his upcoming travels to *inter alia* Colombia, Finland, Cyprus, Spain, Bulgaria, Australia, the USSR, Kuwait, Poland, France, and Algeria. Vašek began to travel the world again, this time not as a sailor, but as a diplomatic representative of the Czechoslovak government. This is the realization of Vašek's expressed goals at his very first meeting with the StB in 1957, where he had rejected the offer to collaborate in favour of becoming a diplomat or trader. Vašek's youthful ambitions had fully materialized.

Vašek kept in touch with the StB notwithstanding his frequent travels abroad. An evaluation report from 1987 describes how, every month, the StB and Vašek would meet in a conspirational flat. As expected, Vašek was noticeably (and commendably) punctual: 'For the whole time of his collaboration' he was 'precise, objective, and conscientious'. His relationship with his StB officer was one of 'comradery and friendship', and it was noted that his reports were 'well worked out'.

However, in 1988, the StB terminated Vašek's cooperation due to his diminishing potential for supplying relevant information. The proposal to end collaboration unsurprisingly notes that Vašek had always fulfilled his tasks 'responsibly and on time', and that his reports were 'serious and truthful'. Vašek was rewarded 'twelve times with material gifts amounting to 1,893 Kčs' throughout the entirety of his cooperation. According to the termination proposal, Vašek and the StB met a total of 129 times over twelve years of cooperation (since 1976, the latest tranche), resulting in '261 [pieces of] information', although his file does not mention a single person as having been 'realized' as the result of his informing.

Vašek's collaboration with the StB was terminated in a calm, appreciative, and professional manner. There were no personal crises, no downfalls, no mental breakdowns, no health issues, and no articulated disappointments. Nor were there evident grudges, regrets, or recriminations. It was as if two friends said farewell, appreciated their convivial common past, and maturely let go of each other. Indeed, similar characteristics—calm, respectful, and professional—can also be used to characterize Vašek's overall relationship with authorities. He excelled within the interstices of the Communist regime and built himself a good career.

Vašek seemed to have treated his relationship with the StB like a side gig. Nevertheless, he played this gig with relative fervour and determination, at least during certain periods of his life. He did not appear to need the StB as he already held a comfortable position in the Party. He nonetheless engaged with the StB and gave them the impression that he was providing them with interesting intelligence, despite the fact that his disclosures did not result in any arrests or detentions (in as much as can be gleaned from his StB file). Collaterally, informing might have been Vašek's attempt to bleach the stain of his involvement with Junák (together with other minor irregularities), though he did not seem to need the StB to rescue him from professional obliteration or to remedy inappropriate conduct. In sum, of the files we have reviewed, Vašek was one of the apparently more proper, adjusted, professional, successful, and untroubled informers. He was also the informer who *prima facie* was the most motivated by his devotion to Communist ideology. From a virtue ethics perspective, whether Vašek's devotion was genuine, or whether he was an adroit social navigator who skilfully pretended to be a Communist devotee, is far more difficult to discern.

III. 'Lily'

Lily was born in 1908.[14] At the time of her birth, her parents were well-off. They owned a large house in Prague and up until 1948 her father was a successful businessman in paper wholesale. Lily was an only child. She always had a fascination with the Western world and foreign countries and languages. She studied at a *gymnasium* in Prague and, in her final year, transferred to a French school. She then spent a year in France training to be a teacher and mastering the French language. After returning to Prague in 1924, Lily attended a college and learned English. She subsequently passed the state exam for both languages.

In 1927, Lily married a Yugoslav man named Djord. She subsequently moved to Yugoslavia with him and became a Yugoslav citizen. As a result, she had to renounce her Czechoslovak citizenship. Because her husband was a well-established and wealthy doctor, Lily's social status in Yugoslavia was quite elevated. A report in her file notes that she 'lived very well'; she had two maids, a cook, and a private driver. Lily gave birth to a son who later studied medicine at the Charles University in Prague. However, his studies in Prague did not fully materialize as local authorities refused to let him stay in the country after diplomatic relations between Czechoslovakia and Yugoslavia deteriorated following the fallout between Stalin and Tito (the then-leader of Yugoslavia). Therefore, in 1948 Lily's son was forced to return to his father's home in Yugoslavia.[15]

In 1936, Lily divorced Djord and came back to Czechoslovakia, alone, to live with her parents. Her file reveals that the couple divorced because of Djord's excessive jealousy and financial stinginess. Notwithstanding their divorce, Lily and Djord stayed in touch through letters. She also visited him and their son in Yugoslavia. Djord came to Prague on several occasions. In 1938, Lily started working as a translator for the Prague branch of the French Havas, a news agency. Her file, preoccupied as it is with such matters, noted that her social status declined upon her

[14] Position: Agent.
File No: 357023.
Registration No: 312.
File created: 1949.
File archived: 1957.
Page count: 244 pages.
Lily's file is even more scattered than other files we have reviewed. Many of the reports and letters therein are undated, unsigned, and some were poorly scanned, although essentially all the documents are readable. Lily's file does not contain a photograph of her.

[15] Interestingly, Lily's file refers to her husband as 'a Tito-ist' rather than as a 'Yugoslav.' Beginning in the 1950s, tensions between the USSR and Tito's regime in Yugoslavia led to the creation of this term to designate Tito supporters.

divorce and return to Czechoslovakia as she had no significant personal property. During the Nazi occupation, Lily spent most of her time in Czechoslovakia apart from some brief trips to visit her son in Yugoslavia in 1940 and 1941.

Lily's file describes her as 'bourgeois', 'vain', and accustomed to living in so-called higher society. According to one of the first reports in her file, Lily was a very social character and fancied being treated 'like a lady'. She was keen on fashion and was always tastefully dressed. As mentioned previously, she lived with her parents and she took care of them in their advanced age. Politically, she was passive.

In 1945, Lily found employment at the Embassy of Yugoslavia. She was seemingly unhappy there, and she allegedly caused tension by refusing to call other employees 'Comrade' (*soudruh*, in Czech). Moreover, she resisted socialist etiquette. Her file does not however suggest that her dissident behaviour was politically motivated. Rather, it is likely that Lily simply did not value such discourse and social practice, or perhaps she just wanted to act provocatively. Regardless, in 1949, diplomatic relations between Czechoslovakia and Yugoslavia eroded and, accordingly, Lily's contract at that embassy expired. She subsequently joined the diplomatic service of the Kingdom of Belgium in Prague in an administrative capacity.

At that time, Lily was also an active member of francophone society in Prague. She travelled to France on several occasions. She joined the Czechoslovak-French society of health workers and began to assist them with minor administrative matters including translations and correspondence. Although this society was dissolved in 1948, it played a catalytic role in Lily's life. It was through this society that she became involved with the military attaché of France in Prague, Captain Vincent, and his wife. They all reportedly had extensive discussions on the political and economic situation in Czechoslovakia. Vincent was particularly interested in the upcoming Czechoslovak election, as well as the position of the Communist party in Czechoslovak society. Upon his request, Lily began seeking out information on these issues and on at least one occasion put Vincent in touch with another supposed informer. Unfortunately, the person she had approached immediately alerted the StB. As it turned out, Lily was unlucky—terribly so, in fact.

An anonymous, typewritten letter in Lily's file recounts how, in January 1948, Lily had allegedly approached the author of this anonymous letter directly and asked him to cooperate with French military intelligence, most notably with Vincent.[16] The letter author was confused and thought that this offer was a provocation orchestrated by Lily—or whoever he thought she was working for—to compromise him. He refused to answer, asked Lily to return in a week, and immediately alerted the StB because he found 'the whole affair very suspicious'. The letter also asserted that Lily 'was as an intelligence cooperative of the French Embassy

[16] A review of Lily's interrogation from the 1950s reveals that the author of this letter was a board member of the Czechoslovak Press Agency located in the same building as the Havas Agency where Lily had previously worked.

and worked for Captain Vincent'. The author of this fateful letter suggested that the StB follow up on Lily's offer and deploy a third person to play the intelligence game with Lily and Vincent. A follow-up did indeed occur, as another report in the file describes a meeting between an unidentified person, Lily, and Vincent. At this meeting, Vincent set out the initial tasks and inquiries he requested of this ostensible informer, who happened to be an employee of the Czechoslovak Press Agency. In return, Lily gave this informer 1,000 Kčs from Vincent as a reward.

Unbeknownst to Vincent and Lily, this informer was planted and under the command of the StB. Thus, this double agent delivered the requested information to Lily and simultaneously informed the StB of the whole operation in detail. In one of the many interrogations that Lily became subjected to later in life, she firmly denied that she procured any other information, or secured informers on behalf of Vincent, or ever received any financial incentives from him.

Ultimately, this series of events became known to the StB as the 'French Affair'. This imbroglio went on to play a pivotal role in Lily's recruitment as an StB informer, as well as in her eventual criminal conviction. Rather unfortunately, Lily did not realize that the StB saw her as a dangerous foreign spy. Her subsequent encounters with the StB were framed by blackmail, as the StB threatened her with criminal prosecution and serial threats to terminate her Czechoslovak residence permit (Lily was no longer a Czechoslovak citizen, hence her residence in the country was contingent). Nevertheless, Lily was not an easy nut to crack. She consistently defied and avoided the StB.

Following his role in the French Affair in the late 1940s, Vincent was obliged to leave Czechoslovakia as *persona non grata*. Lily, for her part, was arrested and interrogated. In 1948, she was recruited into collaboration with military counterintelligence. The main grounds for her recruitment were her 'alleged criminal activities' connected to the French Affair. On 3 May 1948, a blackmailed Lily signed a seemingly euphemistic typewritten 'Commitment':

> I declare that I want to collaborate with the Czechoslovak Intelligence service voluntarily[,] and I commit to fulfill all the tasks given to me honestly and conscientiously in the interest of building [the defense of] the People's Democratic Republic .... I am aware of serious consequences, which would ensue in case of violating this commitment.

In less than a decade after she 'voluntarily' signed the pledge, Lily herself came to experience these serious consequences first-hand insofar as she was arrested and convicted in the late 1950s.

Initially, Lily's cooperation was not fruitful for the StB: She was avoidant, reluctant, and clearly maintained only superficial, irregular, and minimally necessary contacts. According to evaluation reports included in her file, Lily made it crystal clear that 'she would rather endure punishment than work against the

West'. Perhaps this was due to her ideological persuasion, affection for the Western lifestyle, or fond acquaintances from the West—indeed, in prior interrogations, Lily had admitted that her actions were inspired by helping out a friend, thereby evincing her interpersonal loyalty and fidelity.

The StB wanted Lily to bring information related to her work in the Belgian embassy. However, a 1950 report noted that Lily continued to evince a defiant attitude: 'She reject[ed] [cooperation] and request[ed] conviction.' The report—reflecting the *Zeitgeist* of 1950s Stalinist Czechoslovakia—intoned how Lily 'most probably assume[d] there would be a new war and [she] would be liberated by a Western army as a martyr'. Lily 'openly and cynically expresse[d] her wild hostility to [Czechoslovakia]', and during her interactions with the StB her behaviour was 'impudent' and 'hostile'. This report noted a long-standing suspicion that Lily had been 'working against Czechoslovakia'. Moreover, this report stated that Lily was a 'fascist of the wors[t] kind, absolutely condoning the racist discrimination of Blacks' because 'they smell terrible'. The report ends with a proposal to criminally prosecute Lily—a recommendation that would come to fruition years later.

Instead of immediately subjecting Lily to prosecution, the StB terminated her cooperation in January 1951 because 'she did not want to deliver written reports. When [the StB officer] partially pressured her, [she] responded: "So imprison me."' At the time, the dissolution of her collaboration did not trigger any additional negative consequences for her. Two years later, however, these repercussions trickled in when the StB began to harass Lily regarding the contingency of her residence permit in Czechoslovakia and her need to take care of her parents.

In 1953, Lily—a then-citizen of Yugoslavia residing in Prague—applied for a permanent residence permit in Czechoslovakia. The StB used this application to badger her back into cooperation. Lily's re-recruitment proposal describes how the StB planned to intercept her on her way home from work and interrogate her at their headquarters on Bartolomějská Street regarding her personal life, updates from the Belgian Embassy, and details regarding individuals working at the Embassy. To elicit a participatory response, the StB intended to use her residence permit request and to remind her of the 'enemy activities of Western embassies' and 'the expulsion of two Belgian military attachés'. If these tactics proved to be insufficient, the StB would leverage 'the question of her espionage [for Vincent]' and 'her relations to Germans during the occupation'.[17] The re-recruitment proposal notes that if she resisted collaboration, 'her residence [request would] not be allowed' and 'her parents [would] be moved out of Prague[,] as Prague is meant for active builders of socialism'. The StB also threatened to expose her collaboration with the StB to their Yugoslav counterparts. In sum, the StB assumed that

[17] A report in Lily's file cryptically intones that her ability to travel to and from Czechoslovakia during the Nazi Protectorate was suspicious, but fails to furnish any further details or explanations.

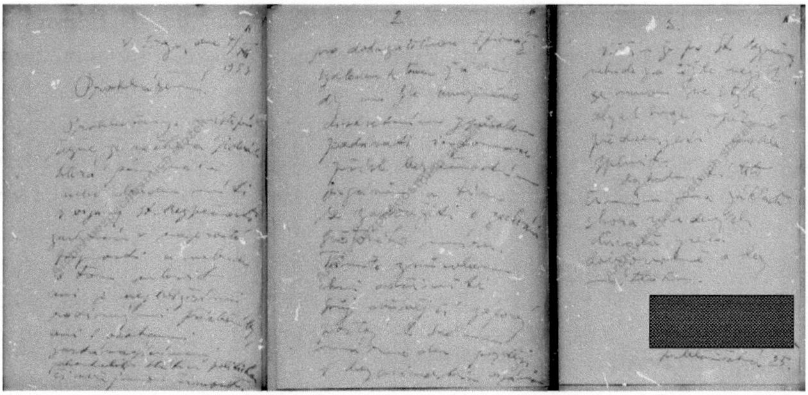

Figure 4.2 A photograph of Lily's handwritten declaration from 4 December 1953 (source StB file No 357023, ABS archive).

all these menacing threats would compel Lily to 'adopt a correct attitude toward cooperation'.

The StB was justified in its assumption. On 4 December 1953, after a three-hour interrogation, Lily handwrote a 'Declaration' (Figure 4.2) containing a pledge to collaborate, that was dictated to her verbatim by the StB officers present:

> I solemnly declare that I will keep each and every meeting I have had or will have with organs of the StB in absolute confidentiality [,] and I will not talk of it even with the closest relatives nor persons executing whichever political or public activities.... Due to the fact that previously it was permitted to me to discretely convey information to representatives of security organs and by doing that contribute to maintaining world peace. By this means I want to redress my previous negative attitude toward my nation and later also toward security organs. I believe that for the StB it will not be difficult to enter into contact with me so that I can fulfill my honest resolution. I am making this decision on the basis of the above stated reasons absolutely voluntarily and without any pressure.

Lily's handwriting looks contorted and unsettled, which gives rise to the question of what exactly went on behind the scenes of this interrogation. Lily was asked to monitor the schedule and activities of high-ranking employees of the Belgian embassy (and their visitors) and to provide information related to their business agendas. She agreed. Nevertheless, Lily's cooperation seemingly languished once again, as her file is bereft of any of her submitted reports or reports summarizing her meetings with the StB. Lily's file nevertheless evinces the extent to which the StB was displeased with Lily after she had written her purportedly 'voluntary' pledge to collaborate.

In 1954, Lily's residence permit was denied. The StB played a key role in this refusal. The StB had intervened in the proceedings arguing that she should not be allowed to remain in Czechoslovakia. The StB letter recounted how Lily had avoided the StB in the past, only informed on 'insignificant' issues, and had potentially de-conspired herself by revealing her contacts with the StB to a third-party despite strict instructions not to do so. Moreover, when the StB told Lily that her collaboration was mediocre, she reportedly said that she would not betray her employer. Thus, the StB concluded that she was of 'enemy disposition toward the current establishment', should not be allowed to remain in Czechoslovakia, and would be required to leave forthwith and forever. This meant that Lily would be forced to part with her parents and friends.

In response, Lily wrote an appeal letter to the Czechoslovak authorities—a bold act given the political and social climate of the time. In her appeal, Lily insisted that the decision to reject her application was devoid of reasoning, except for a vague justification that she was purportedly 'a threat to public interest'. Lily argued that she was not aware of any 'action or omission [of her own] that would have in any way whatsoever threatened the public interest'. She recounted how she had forsaken her Czechoslovak citizenship after getting married, but emphasized that, following her divorce, she had consistently lived and worked in Czechoslovakia. Moreover, Lily highlighted her willingness to support her parents until their deaths. She ended her letter with an emotional plea to the authorities, describing how painful it would be for her if she could never return to her homeland. She stated: 'I request you kindly to consider if reasons of humanity do not overtake reasons of public interest.' Reportedly, Lily also asked her employer, the Belgian Embassy, to support her request to stay, but there is no information as to whether the Embassy actually did so. Ultimately, and perhaps surprisingly, Lily's entreaties to Czechoslovak authorities worked: her residence document was in fact granted and she was allowed to stay in Czechoslovakia. Her file does not provide any explanation for this decision.

Lily did not fall into regulatory compliance, however. In a flagrant violation of StB protocol, Lily revealed her cooperation to her colleague Eva, who also worked at the Belgian Embassy. Ironically, Eva had also signed a cooperation agreement with the StB,[18] and both Lily and Eva revealed their contacts with the StB to the Embassy head. Lily reportedly offered to resign thereafter to avoid damaging the Embassy and its employees, but the Embassy head refused her resignation because, in his opinion, '[o]ther people do it [cooperate with the StB] here, why should you not'.

[18] Eva's own StB file is under registration number 357032. It only has thirty-four pages. The StB recruited Eva in 1951 following her employment with the Belgian Embassy. Unlike Lily, Eva supposedly funnelled important information to the StB and was a conscientious informer. Notwithstanding this good performance, Eva, like Lily, was sentenced to ten years in prison in 1957 for revealing the cooperation and for espionage.

Lily disclosed her StB recruitment to two additional employees who also happened to be involved with the StB. This group of employees then shared and compared their respective recruitment experiences with each other, ruminating about who had asked them about what, how often they had met (or would meet), and other tidbits pertaining to the informing and social praxis of the time. One of these employees, Mr T., allegedly asked Lily and other informers for details regarding their meetings at the Ministry of the Interior. Apparently, Mr T. was also in touch with the StB; he became visibly agitated after one of his meetings with the StB, which prompted Lily to inform the StB that Mr T. admitted to Lily that 'it was terrible for him not to know what they [the StB] know'.

Lily's tepid cooperation with the StB ended brutally. The StB eventually found out about Lily's admission of her cooperation to her colleagues and to the Belgian ambassador. Lily was arrested in September 1956 and, along with a number of her colleagues, charged with treason and espionage against Czechoslovakia. Espionage was a vastly more serious matter than de-conspiration.

Protocols from Lily's investigation and summaries of her interrogations comprise roughly half of the documents in her file. The interrogation transcripts however seem to be incomplete. According to available records, each interrogation was quite lengthy, ranging from three to seven hours. In contrast, the written records are strikingly brief: the documents span only a couple of pages and contain very short questions and perfunctory answers. The abridged nature of the records begs the question as to what actually transpired behind the closed doors of the interrogation rooms. In any event, Lily seemed to have been quite a courageous woman.

Lily was accused of being the initiator of the offences. Elsewhere, phraseology such as 'the organizer' and 'the seduced (to crime)' is also used. During interrogations, Lily was asked about her colleagues, daily life at the Belgian Embassy, and about Czechoslovaks who were in touch with either Belgian or Czechoslovak employees—some of them had, in the opinion of the StB, illegally emigrated.

Lily confessed that she had exposed her cooperation to the Embassy head, explaining that 'I considered it right [to tell him], because they should know who their employees are, and because I knew that [Eva] told them [about the co-operation]'. Notwithstanding this admission, Lily defended herself against other accusations—such as failing to report other alleged crimes—by claiming that she was not aware of them or that she prioritized the loyalty she had to her friends. The interrogations were lengthy. This gave the StB questioners the opportunity to harp on inconsistencies in Lily's testimony and to confront her with things she had not previously revealed. As a justification for her reluctance towards utter honesty and complete transparency, Lily again evoked the concept of friendship: she did not want to 'burden' nor 'harm' her friends or acquaintances through her disclosures to the authorities. Similarly, when asked about her motivation for engaging in putative 'espionage' on behalf of Captain Vincent in the late 1940s, Lily referred to the relationship she had with his family. Lily cherished her social life. A transcript from one of her interrogations echoes this sentiment:

> I was not gathering the information because of some specific hostile motivations against Czechoslovakia. I was doing this out of social connections that I maintained with his family, so I wanted to satisfy his wish. Soon I realized the seriousness of these activities and decided not to go on ... but I had not enough courage to report it to the relevant organs [of the Ministry of the Interior].[19]

In 1957, Lily was sentenced to ten years in prison for her offences. Three of her colleagues were also convicted on espionage charges and sentenced to ten to twenty years' imprisonment.[20] Lily's file does not contain any information on her years in prison or her life thereafter.

In sum, Lily may have been viewed as an unproductive, ad hoc informer for the French and Belgians, and a longer-lasting—yet nevertheless unproductive—informer for the StB. The StB tried to leverage her through various threats, including prosecution, expatriation, and the compelled relocation of her parents. Lily was a strong person. She was unphased by this blackmail. Lily never warmed up to—nor feared—the StB. Lily was a risk-taker who acted out of affection, fealty, love, and devotion for her friends, acquaintances, and her fancied way of life. After Lily de-conspired herself, the totality of her conduct was boot-strapped into a harsh conviction for treason at a particularly brutal period in Communist Czechoslovak history. Lily's seeming allegiance to anti-Communism, her steadfastness, her dreams of a cosmopolitan life in the West—and her emotional loyalty and affection for those with whom she shared the allure of those dreams—tragically and defiantly led her to a prison cell.

IV. 'Goldfus'

Goldfus was born in 1919 to a Czech mother and a German father.[21] His parents were unmarried. Goldfus' mother later married another man who would become

[19] Indeed, the social connection must have been very friendly as Lily reportedly helped Vincent's wife buy clothing and toys for their children.

[20] The convictions and sentences were reported in 'Hlas Domova', an exile newspaper whose title can be translated to mean 'voice from home'. J.K., 'ŠPIONI, PROCESY, ROZSUDKY' (*Hlas domova*, Melbourne, 18 February 1957) <http://scriptum.cz/soubory/scriptum/%5Bnode%5D/hlas-domova_1957-04_ocr.pdf> accessed 3 September 2023 3.

[21] Position: Confidant. Agent.
File No: 652225.
Registration No: 10780/548.
File created: 1952.
File archived: 1986.
Page count: Volume I, 984 pages. Volume II, 100 pages. Volume II is a surveillance file the StB maintained on Goldfus.

Goldfus' stepfather. In 1937, Goldfus' biological father left Czechoslovakia and moved to Germany for work. Goldfus' biological father was a long-standing member of the German Nazi party. In 1938, while Goldfus was visiting him in Munich, he asked Goldfus to declare himself an ethnic German and then introduced him to a local branch of the Gestapo. The Nazis wanted Goldfus to furnish them with information about the political situation in Czechoslovakia, especially regarding far-right parties or fascists. Goldfus reportedly refused and returned to Pilsen, a city in the southern part of Bohemia.

In 1939, Goldfus graduated from high school and continued his education in trade and economics. After the Nazi occupation had begun that same year, the Pilsen branch of the Gestapo contacted Goldfus and demanded his cooperation. Goldfus' StB file states that he agreed to cooperate, albeit reluctantly, and was tasked with informing on far-right units, including organizations like The Flag (*Vlajka*, in Czech).[22] Goldfus later moved to Prague and made contact with the Prague branch of the Gestapo. During his collaboration with the Nazis, Goldfus met a member of a Yugoslav secret fascist organization, assisted one of its members in Prague, and then attempted to leave for Yugoslavia. He was arrested following this foiled escape plan and subsequently sent to numerous concentration camps, including Dachau and Sachsenhausen. Goldfus remained imprisoned until the end of the war.

In 1947, Goldfus again was arrested, this time by Czechoslovak authorities. He was imprisoned for his erstwhile collaboration with the Nazi regime. Goldfus served five years for his crimes—partially in prison and partially in a correctional labour camp in Jáchymov—and was deprived of his civil and political rights for ten years. He was released in April 1951. Goldfus subsequently found employment as a manual and administrative worker in Prague. He also began working as an independent journalist, thereby giving voice to his interest in politics and social life.

Goldfus' relationship with the StB began in 1952 and was subject to many turbulent twists and turns. On 27 March 1952, Goldfus approached the StB and offered to cooperate. He affirmed a desire to remedy his previous 'mistake', namely his collaboration with the Nazis. Nonetheless, the causality of motivation might be muddy: there is extrinsic evidence that the StB blackmailed Goldfus into collaboration.[23] In any event, Goldfus was officially recruited by the StB on 18 April 1952,

[22] *Vlajka* was a Czech nationalist anti-Semitic organization that abetted the Nazis during the Second World War. In 1943, the organization ceased to exist after various interventions by the Nazis and the Protectorate government, although many of its former members continued to collaborate with the Gestapo.

[23] Czech historian Tomáš Malínek—who researched the StB Operation 'Obora' that focused on West German diplomats in the years 1968 to 1989—tangentially mentions that Goldfus was blackmailed into cooperation in 1952. Tomáš Malínek, '"Dub" v "Oboře"—Západoněmečtí velvyslanci v hledáčku Státní bezpečnosti v letech 1968–1989' (2017) 30 Securitas Imperii 176, 181. Goldfus' StB file repeatedly states that he offered to cooperate with the StB out of his own volition. However, in the 1970s, one of Goldfus' many letters to the StB recounts how he had been blackmailed into cooperation—not because of his prior engagement with the Gestapo, but due to threats of criminal prosecution based on his 'critical remarks towards the regime'. Goldfus also wrote that he had only started cooperating 'really voluntarily' in 1955 after his second release from prison.

and initially assigned the code name 'OPAVSKÝ'. His handwritten letter to the StB in Prague states that

> [d]ue to the wrongdoing which I committed during occupation and for which I was convicted, and due to the international situation, which clearly shows a necessity to choose sides between the two camps, either the capitalist or socialist, I have decided to voluntarily cooperate with the organs of the StB and contribute to the building and strengthening of socialist establishment in our state.

The StB considered Goldfus to be a politically and socially astute individual who revelled in various aspects of public life, politics, and international relations. Goldfus' picture in his StB file shows a man in formal attire wearing a tie, earnestly gazing at the photographer (Figure 4.3). The StB also recognized that his vocation as a journalist gave him a unique opportunity to establish many potentially valuable contacts. Thus, the StB decided to make use of Goldfus.

That said, over the arc of time, collaboration with Goldfus did not unfold as the StB would have anticipated. Indeed, Goldfus proved to be a double-edged sword for Czechoslovak authorities. For example, in 1953 Goldfus reportedly helped several people illegally escape abroad. He was arrested and sentenced to 2.5 years' imprisonment for this crime, but he only served 1.5 years in prison due to an amnesty. After his release in 1955, he approached the StB and offered further cooperation. The StB agreed. In accordance with StB instructions, Goldfus began working as a

Figure 4.3 A photograph of Goldfus (source StB file No 65225, ABS archive).

tour guide for foreigners at the Czechoslovak Travel and Transport Agency, known as ČEDOK (*Československá cestovní a dopravní kancelář*).

During this time, the StB effusively praised Goldfus for his achievements in Operation 'JACYN', which required Goldfus to extract valuable intelligence from an alleged American diplomat-spy whom he had befriended during one of the tours he led for ČEDOK. For the purposes of Operation JACYN, Goldfus pretended to be an American cooperative who gave US authorities information on Czechoslovakia. The StB later tried and failed to recruit this US diplomat. Assuredly, this attempted recruitment left Goldfus and the StB in a vulnerable position insofar as this failure could have exposed Goldfus' engagement with the StB to the Americans.

Therefore, so as to obscure any trace of his involvement with the StB, Goldfus was demonstratively 'arrested [by the StB] for espionage for the US'. As part of the cover up, and to dilute any American suspicion, the StB sent Goldfus to Ostrava, a provincial town in the north of Moravia. The StB found Goldfus a job as an administrative employee and encouraged him to change his name. Goldfus did not like working in Ostrava, however, as he believed it to be a remote and boring town. He complained to the StB about these unsatisfactory working conditions which were the opposite of what had been promised to him upon the success of Operation JACYN.

In 1959, a slightly embittered and disappointed Goldfus returned to Prague, where the StB helped him locate provisional housing and a job as a gatekeeper at the Cambodian Embassy. Goldfus was displeased with this employment, as he endeavoured to advance his career in journalism and 'did not like manual labor'. To further his professional ambition, Goldfus seized every opportunity to read foreign magazines in the library at the US Embassy in Prague and he simultaneously began contributing to various newspapers and magazines. Over time, Goldfus befriended some of the embassy employees who the StB believed to be committing 'ideological diversion' in Czechoslovakia. Reportedly, Goldfus began spreading rumours to his foreign contacts and other journalists that he was working for the Ministry of Foreign Affairs. Perhaps he did so to create a veneer of increased stature and importance or to hide his involvement with the StB. The StB directed Goldfus towards German-speaking foreigners, and although this subset of individuals was neither his primary field of familiarity nor of personal interest to him, he reportedly performed well.

A September 1962 report described Goldfus as an agent with 'good prospects' and a 'good perspective' whose work produced satisfactory results. Goldfus delivered worthwhile intelligence from the Americans. He was rewarded for his 'good cooperation' on more than one occasion. However, the StB also believed that he required strict supervision, as he often engaged in undesirable actions out of his own volition and sought personal profit.

Notwithstanding his favourable results and relevant contacts, the StB terminated Goldfus' cooperation in 1963. His StB officer informed him that the relationship was terminated for two reasons: (i) because Goldfus had de-conspired himself; and (ii) in light of this de-conspiration, the StB was leery of the potential for trouble with the Americans following Operation JACYN. Thus, the StB subsequently required Goldfus to cease contact with the US Embassy.

A report from Goldfus' file recounts his devastation at the truncation of his collaboration. This report details how Goldfus beseeched the StB to stay in touch because informing conveyed an 'existential' dimension for Goldfus. The StB rebuffed his plea and instead instructed Goldfus to 'make use of his personal resources' to resolve his issues. Interestingly, an StB superior added a handwritten note to the termination proposal which stated that 'there [was] no reason to cease seeing [Goldfus]', but that Goldfus was not to be deployed at the US Embassy or any embassy whatsoever for that matter.

Goldfus appeared to be addicted to informing. Despite his termination, he allegedly continued to see his former StB officers and US contacts, including higher-ranking embassy officials that 'began to value him [more]' over time. These dynamics concerned the StB, as StB officers were unable to decipher whether the Americans truly trusted Goldfus, were simply using him as a pawn, or whether they were aware of Goldfus' involvement in Operation JACYN. The StB suspected that Goldfus had disclosed his involvement to the Americans in order to game them against the StB.

Goldfus' array of foreign contacts and his simultaneous allegiance to different authorities, feigned or otherwise, further heightened the StB's suspicion of him. From 1967 to 1971, Goldfus frequently travelled to West Germany. There he encountered many important, high-ranking politicians and trade representatives. In 1968, Goldfus' US Embassy contacts introduced him to a West German diplomat in Prague who subsequently organized Goldfus' future trips to West Germany. That same year, the StB discovered that Goldfus had allegedly relayed incomplete information to his StB handlers that he had obtained from the Americans. The StB also noticed a surge in his already brazen confidence, exemplified by his intentional neglect of StB instructions in favour of his own private agenda during one of his many visits to West Germany. Furthermore, since the beginning of 1968, Goldfus had 'been an ardent advocate of so-called progressive politics, admiring and advocating [for] the revisionist politics of the rightist political forces in Czechoslovakia and later adopting counter-revolutionary positions'. This advocacy prompted the StB to conclude that Goldfus had allowed himself to be voluntarily recruited by foreign intelligence services. Thus, the StB seemingly perceived 1968 to be 'the breaking point' for Goldfus—indeed, as well as for many others.

In the early 1970s, the StB finally came to the conclusion that Goldfus had been playing a devious game: He was feeding relevant and useful information to the US and West German representatives rather than supplying the StB with probative content. Indeed, a follow-up investigation revealed that Goldfus had garnered monthly emoluments of 800 to 1,000 *Deutschmarks* (DM) from the West Germans, for a total value of 28,000 DM. At the time, this was a considerable sum of money. US intelligence reportedly had not paid Goldfus in cash for his informing but offered him a study stipend in the US instead.[24]

A 1972 internal report from the StB states that

> the 'hostile activities' were conducted by [Goldfus] after the events of August 1968 and during 1969–1970. [Goldfus] was reportedly passing to the US and West Germany information regarding national politics within Czechoslovakia, detailed descriptions of its economic and military standing, etc. Some of the information reportedly contained state secrets too.

Initially, the StB considered 'turn[ing] him back' to their side and deploying him against the US and West German intelligence services; however, this recalibration never occurred. In 1970, Goldfus was arrested and sentenced to ten years in prison for treason, espionage, and *inter alia* leaking state secrets.[25] Thus, on the one hand, Goldfus was somewhat loyal to the StB, as he continued to engage intensively with them but, on the other hand, he was routinely castigated and harshly punished for his betrayal and collusion with outsider enemies of the state, even though it is unclear whether he provided them with any valuable information.

Goldfus routinely contacted the StB and other state authorities both while he was in prison as well as after his release. Goldfus offered them his services, asked for help, and baited their responses by offering information on his fellow (political) prisoners and close family members such as his wife and daughter. At the time, the StB classified Goldfus as a confidant. His file contains extensive and often extremely personal information from this period. For example, Goldfus wrote numerous lengthy letters to his StB officers that read as if they had been written to a very close companion. Some of Goldfus' letters—those addressed to 'My Friend'—are also included in his file. The letters reveal a self-reflective introspection as regards Goldfus' way of being and doing. More specifically, these letters reveal intimate family issues. They contain pleas for attention, comfort, and help with scheduling meetings or with finding someone to listen to him. Goldfus frequently asked his supervisor 'just to meet and talk because he [felt] so down'. On a few occasions, Goldfus asked for money. Goldfus also wrote poetry. His file contains one of his poems, entitled 'Sigh' (Figure 4.4).

Goldfus also pestered the StB for 'work' while he was in prison. He outlined his potential future 'strategies and possibilities' as an informer. The StB was responsive

[24] The StB also noted that US intelligence supplied Goldfus with luxurious alcoholic beverages. He later offered these beverages to his sources in exchange for information.

[25] Malínek, '"Dub" v "Oboře"' (n 23) 181.

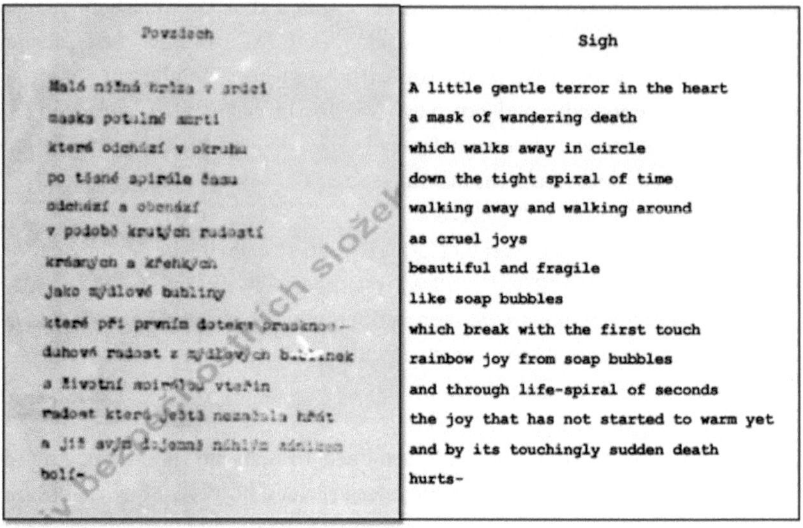
Povzdech

Sigh

A little gentle terror in the heart
a mask of wandering death
which walks away in circle
down the tight spiral of time
walking away and walking around
as cruel joys
beautiful and fragile
like soap bubbles
which break with the first touch
rainbow joy from soap bubbles
and through life-spiral of seconds
the joy that has not started to warm yet
and by its touchingly sudden death
hurts-

Figure 4.4 A photograph of Goldfus' poem, 'Sigh' (source StB file No 65225, ABS archive).

and asked Goldfus to inform on other inmates—mostly those known as 'far-right opportunists'—and later praised him for having produced very favourable results.

On 4 June 1976, Goldfus received a pardon. He was released under the explicit condition that he not commit any criminal offences in the next five years and under the implicit condition that he continue to collaborate with the StB. After his release, Goldfus yearned to work as a journalist again; however, because of his past, no publishing house was willing to employ or compensate him fairly. Goldfus eventually ended up in various administrative and accounting positions with multiple different enterprises in Prague. Thereafter, he worked as an interpreter.

Despite the belief that Goldfus 'would betray [the StB] again' if given the opportunity, the StB decided to send him to the West German Embassy, as the StB felt that his most recent imprisonment would induce the West Germans to have faith in his loyalty. Goldfus asked the West German Embassy for a job as a translator or consultant, but another individual had reportedly informed Embassy officers about Goldfus' ongoing cooperation with the StB, thereby collapsing the entire plan. Goldfus later suggested that the StB could make use of his old contacts who were employed at the Chinese Embassy; it is unlikely that this plan ever materialized and Goldfus' file contains no additional information about this proposal.

In 1979, Goldfus became eligible for retirement, but he opted out of this opportunity—despite his advanced age—and instead chose to share his opinions with the public through his continuous contributions to the media. The remainder of Goldfus' cooperation, as well as his relationship with the StB more generally, exuded one dominant characteristic: a passionate desire on Goldfus' part to continue informing. Goldfus routinely requested more tasks. He desperately pleaded for more attention and personal contact. He was hungry to inform. Goldfus seemingly wanted to feel important and beneficial to someone that could appreciate his skills. Yet, despite his extensive efforts, the StB considered his reports to be of only middling importance. Goldfus nevertheless received frequent financial rewards from the StB for his contributions.

Goldfus died in 1985. His file was archived in 1986. It reveals a 'hard working' and 'very intelligent' man evidently hooked on 'reporting'—be it to authorities or to the public as a journalist—who also yearned for validation and recognition. Indeed, Goldfus was a very active informer: he interacted intimately and personally with his StB officers and he was repeatedly rewarded for his collaboration.

Goldfus wore many hats throughout his life. He changed jobs many times. He informed for and against many sides. He was like a chameleon that alters colours to blend in with the prevailing climate. Goldfus reported to and collaborated with many authorities and was imprisoned for collaborating with the 'wrong side' after the fact. Despite repeated punishment, Goldfus always slipped back into his ways. It seemed intrinsic to Goldfus' nature to inform, as if he could not help it.

Goldfus' devotion was not to Communist (or any) ideology nor the socialist (or any) establishment. Rather, he craved adventure, attention, acknowledgement, and perhaps the thrill of spying and leading a secret double life. As an informer, he allegedly fed information to US and West German authorities. The StB summed Goldfus up as

> [an] initiative-taking, willing, and devoted collaborator, who without StB contact cannot even live anymore. He needs to be moderated in his creativity. Collaboration and intelligence gathering [are] his hobby and great personal interests, to which he subsumes everything.

V. 'Volný'

Volný was born in Prague in 1921 to highly educated parents.[26] His father lectured on Latin and foreign languages at a secondary school and his mother was a medical doctor. Prior to 1948, both of Volný's parents had been members of the National

[26] Position: Agent. Informer. Confidant.
File No: 115712, his file from the 1950s. 780065b, his file from the 1970s.
Registration No: 504, his file from the 1950s. 29543, his file from the 1970s.
File created: 1952.
File archived: 1986.
Page count: 346 pages.

Socialist Party,[27] but shortly after the Communists took power in February 1948, they joined the Communist Party. In 1951, both parents were expelled from the Party for reasons unknown.

Volný thrived in his studies. In 1949, he graduated from the School of Medicine at Charles University in Prague with 'exceptionally excellent' grades. After graduation, he began working at the National Health Institute, where he would later become the head of one of its labs and also practice medicine.

In 1949, Volný married a fellow medical student named Jarmila. Immediately after the wedding, the couple moved in with Volný's parents; however, this arrangement was ultimately untenable due to tension that simmered between Volný's mother and Jarmila. As a consequence, Jarmila moved out of the home to live with her sister. Even though the couple lived in separate households, according to Volný's file they got along well with each other and did not quarrel. After Jarmila graduated from medical school, she worked as an internist at a hospital in Prague. According to a nurse who worked with her, Jarmila had a hostile attitude towards the establishment.

Volný's file describes him as a reclusive, introverted person with only a handful of friends. He 'appeared as fearful', 'very frightened', and 'indecisive', such that 'everyone g[ot] from him whatever they ask[ed] for'. Volný's picture in his StB file somehow reflects these characteristics insofar as he appears timid, shy, and even withdrawn (Figure 4.5). Volný was said to be easily persuaded and swayed by others. The StB noted that he found it difficult to say no. Volný spent his free time studying and reading. He was very proud of his university degree and his doctor title.

Politically, Volný was not a member of any party. The StB began recruiting him in the early 1950s. Back then the StB determined that Volný's 'behavior and opinions were clearly bourgeois and hostile toward the ... state establishment'. Volný's 'life goal [was] to have a bar with two damsels and no work', and he allegedly confided in a colleague that he was waiting for the 'US occupation'. Volný's friends and closest colleagues, such as his boss, similarly espoused an 'absolutely negative attitude towards ... the state establishment and opposed the USSR'. Volný's boss was 'a fanatical supporter of the National Socialist Party ... a person without character, an opportunist [,] and a careerist'. Naturally, the StB was intrigued by and interested in these alleged enemies of the state.

Volný met many people as a general medical practitioner. On the one hand, it is anomalous that the StB chose Volný for recruitment—shyness, introversion, and indecisiveness after all are typically not the characteristics of a successful and

[27] The National Socialist Party—not to be confused with its German namesake—was an important and influential left-wing political party in Czechoslovakia before the Second World War. It initially advocated for class struggle and collectivization but over time became a moderate party that endorsed social democratic principles and actively participated in the government of the pre-war Republic. One of its members, Edvard Beneš, was elected as the second President of Czechoslovakia in 1935.

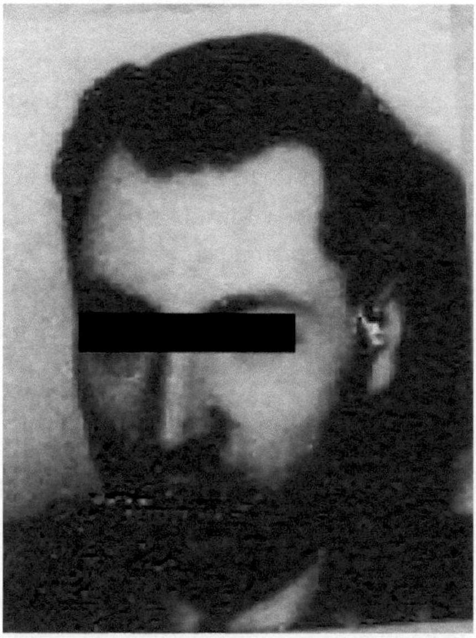

Figure 4.5 A photograph of Volný (source StB file No 115712, ABS archive).

effective informer. On the other hand, perhaps the StB knew that Volný would not resist recruitment. Indeed, by manipulating his fears, taking advantage of his submissive nature, and weaponizing his anti-state remarks, the StB groomed him into collaboration.

Due to his character traits and allegedly hostile attitude towards the regime, Volný's recruitment process also involved subterfuge. The StB had a female informer 'run into' him in 'a deserted street' and ask him whether he would be 'willing to share information about the … Institute'. She pretended to have the recommendation of a doctor who had purportedly worked at one of Prague's major hospitals prior to emigrating to the West. Volný's file describes his leeriness towards the situation: in response to this informer's inquiry, Volný stated that 'he did not know her and could not share the information'. He also announced that he 'would not report her to the security organs' and asked her to leave. This statement ultimately proved to be problematic for Volný as it ran afoul of the legal duty to report criminal behaviour.

Volný's recruitment proposal describes how he then went home and spoke of the encounter with his father who became alarmed and told him that this was 'a serious matter'. His father told him to report the occurrence to a security officer at the Institute. Volný followed this advice and, in so doing, walked right into his first 'open' encounter with the StB. During the interrogation that followed, Volný 'confessed that he committed a crime by not reporting the matter immediately [,] and by providing the person a possibility to escape arrest'.

The StB proceeded to use this fabricated crime as leverage to blackmail Volný into collaboration, although the StB also capitalized on other misdeeds as well. For example, the StB accused Volný of committing 'fraudulent machinations with expensive medications' by prescribing imported drugs to his colleagues without conducting any prior examination. The StB also accused him of acting irresponsibly as the head of a review committee on medical hygiene and sanitation. This committee had identified some concerns regarding drinking water in the region. Volný, however, failed to provide timely notice to relevant authorities as to these findings. Volný's StB file notes that this delayed disclosure led to typhoid outbreaks.

Volný reportedly acknowledged to his misdeeds and 'wrote down a request for collaboration with security organs to partially make up for things he had done'. His file contains his handwritten letter addressed to the 'Headquarters of the [StB]' from 15 May 1952. This letter reads:

> Due to the fact that I committed a crime against the people's democratic establishment, I request to be allowed to cooperate with the security organs to obtain peace in the whole world. I will execute the required tasks to fulfil this commitment. I promise I will execute the tasks given to me by the security organs. I will not talk about this with anyone, except authorized persons (including my closest family members irrespective of their function).

In addition to pressuring Volný into collaborating, the StB also secretly listened to his phone calls and checked his mail for two months to make sure he was towing the line. The StB did not find anything suspicious.

Volný's formal recruitment took place at the end of May 1952. The StB called and asked to meet with him. He agreed, although he arrived fifteen minutes late to the meeting and 'apologiz[ed] a lot as he could not come earlier because he was lecturing at the Czechoslovak Red Cross'. He was then taken to the StB office where he had previously been interrogated. The StB officer who drafted the report from the recruitment meeting noted that, 'due to his fearful character, [Volný] was visibly pale and nervous'. Volný immediately promised 'to share the whole truth and not to hide anything' and reportedly said that 'he [had] thought … hard, day and night' and realized that he had 'made mistakes'. He even told the StB about other 'incidents' at work where he did not 'play according to the books'. Volný also confessed to telling his wife and father about how he had been interrogated by the StB, but he immediately emphasized that he did not reveal any details of the interrogation. Volný also admitted to discussing this 'interview' with another friend of his. All of these kinds of disclosures trip into problematic 'de-conspirations'.

The StB officer predictably responded that 'by sharing this information, you [Volný], committed a new crime by revealing state secrets to an unauthorized person'. Volný said that he was fully aware of what he had done, and he further admitted that he 'had made various mistakes at his workplace[,] did not act responsibly as the head of his laboratory, or as a general practitioner [at the Institute]'. The meeting report describes Volný as 'highly distressed', and recounts how he had 'promised to do anything that [the StB] requested'. This report remarks how Volný only 'calmed down' after he was told that 'his offer for cooperation was accepted' and was reassured that he would not be imprisoned or face other charges. Volný was then invited to sign a typewritten pledge to cooperate, and 'he did so without any pressure'. The pledge affirmed both his voluntary decision to cooperate and his resolve to fulfil all requisitioned tasks 'precisely, conscientiously, [and] with discipline, care, [and] prudence'.

Volný's file does not contain any additional materials from this time, but his narrative can nevertheless be reconstructed from fragments of subsequent evaluation reports. Despite his best efforts, Volný seemingly failed to meet the StB's expectations in full. A 1965 decision from an StB committee that reviewed archived materials states that Volný 'willingly conveyed informative reports on ... his colleagues and general work-related issues', but he could not 'gain the trust of the defective persons' and hence was unable to satisfy his primary objective. Another report recounts how Volný's results were 'minimal' at the time, despite his 'showing efforts to fulfill the tasks'. Volný's collaboration was suspended in 1955 due to 'loss of possibilities'. His file was archived.

In November 1957, the StB however renewed Volný's cooperation just as he began working as an academic at the School of Medicine and Hygiene. The StB was generally curious about foreign scientists, experts, and general health matters in Czechoslovakia, but StB officers were especially intrigued by Volný's new workplace and the contacts and connections that his colleagues and students had abroad.

An evaluation report from 1962 notes that Volný's StB officer assessed this stage of his cooperation 'very positively'. The StB and Volný 'met 129 times during which [he] submitted 85 reports'. He was reportedly a proactive and forthcoming cooperative who produced 'truthful reports'. Despite his favourable performance, the StB classified him only as an informer—in the StB's taxonomy of the term—as 'he was not being focused on hostile activities'.

In 1965, Volný underwent a series of personal tribulations that 'significantly interfered with his cooperation', and in July 1965 his collaboration was terminated for a second time. His StB officer stated that, 'due to very poor family relations [note: the file does not specify what these were] [Volný] became mentally disordered'. He was 'delusional, which was reflected in his reports', derelict in his tasks, missed meetings, and 'turned out to be a fearful and shy individual'. Moreover, the StB was concerned that he was rather vulnerable to the overtures of foreign special services and believed that there was 'no guarantee that he would not agree to offers from Western intelligence out of fear'. Accordingly, Volný's StB officer considered it 'unbearable to keep [him] in the network of informers'. Thus, for the second time, his collaboration was terminated and his file archived; nevertheless, Volný's story continued.

The StB approached Volný twelve years later, and this time the relationship lasted until his retirement. In October 1977, the StB contacted Volný 'in his official capacity' as an associate professor at his faculty, and in April 1978 he was formally re-recruited as a confidant due to 'his results and the [high] level of the meetings'. Even though Volný 'was conveying interesting intelligence' at this time, the StB was aware that he was an anxious character, 'a weak individual, indecisive[,] and easily swayed'. That, however, also meant that Volný assumed that 'the organs of the Ministry of Interior knew everything about him' and he therefore 'confided the smallest details to us [the StB]'.

Compared to the scant number of extant records from the two prior phases of Volný's interaction with the StB, his file contains numerous reports and meeting summaries from his post-1978 cooperation. For example, Volný informed on the general office behaviour of his co-workers. Specifically, he provided information on persons working with him on a secret, government-commissioned research project. Unsurprisingly, the StB was keen to know whether any of his colleagues would have an interest in leaking any secret information because of their ties to capitalist states or because they had been expelled from the Party after the 1968 watershed. Thus, Volný kept an eye out for any such hostile elements. Volný also endeavoured to identify potentially valuable recruits for the StB, and he consequently evaluated his colleagues' 'political reliability'. For instance, he told the StB how some of his fellow academics had publicly displayed poems with 'socially defective content'. He also informed on former colleagues who had been discharged from their jobs after 1968 due to their 'negative attitudes in crisis years'. Volný disclosed that these individuals would occasionally come to his workplace to encourage other lab employees 'not to work, [and] to reject fulfilling state research tasks'. Volný also noted that even though some of his coworkers outlasted post-1968 purges, they remained 'hostile toward the socialist establishment'.

Volný's reports were not limited to his colleagues' political stances and policy inclinations. He provided commentary on workplace gossip and broader debates and discussions at his faculty. For example, Volný revealed that two of his colleagues were in an intimate relationship with each other, that another co-worker was found 'with a naked student' in his office, and that another colleague had drug problems. Volný also described how his co-workers criticized a new law on higher education that allegedly imperilled academic culture at universities and compromised scholarly research. Volný frequently decried instances of workplace nepotism and his colleagues' allegedly unprofessional behaviour, such as bribery and violations of internal directives. He also accused one of his colleagues of committing fraud and of 'stealing socialist property'. Ultimately, this individual was fired and disciplined, but Volný believed that these measures 'did not reflect the social dangerousness' of the impugned acts.

Volný frequently mentioned a woman named Mrs B in his reports. Like Volný, Mrs B was also a doctor, but—unlike Volný—she worked as a specialist in toxicology. Mrs B was particularly relevant to the StB owing to her extensive international network and 'questionable political inclinations'.[28] Volný revealed that she had been part of a 'circle of people who became very active in 1968–69 and [she] still maintain[ed] contacts with [those people]'. Mrs B's political attitudes were hardcore 'national socialistic'— decidedly not Communist—and she often 'led openly antisocially oriented discussions'. Volný supposedly knew Mrs B from his studies and they were 'on friendly terms'. However, their friendly relationship did not stop him from believing that she was 'hostile' to the regime, nor did it stop his detailed reporting on her deeds and misdeeds. Volný informed on Mrs B's private affairs, wealth, family (apparently her husband was a distant relative of the late pre-war Czechoslovak President), and her extensive travels abroad.[29] He also reported her legally questionable activities, including machinations with drugs and medicines.

Over the years, Volný attended various scientific conferences and took numerous business trips abroad. For example, he went to an expert meeting in Denmark and a conference in Algeria. He wrote detailed reports on these travels. He complained about how poorly state employees organized foreign travel. Specifically, Volný lamented how his connecting flights to Algeria had not been prearranged. As a result, he had gotten stuck in Paris and found himself in 'a hopeless situation' where he was 'dependent on random help'. He reminded the StB that 'a Czechoslovak citizen who ends up in such a situation could under certain circumstances succumb to offers of hostile centers or be manipulated into undesirable situations'.

Furthermore, Volný would occasionally share his personal assessment and expert opinion on issues of food and hygiene. For instance, in October 1985 he told his StB officer that he had attended a symposium on macrobiotics. He explained that macrobiotics putatively were '[a] term also for vegetarians who refuse to eat any meat products, cheese, or proteins. Their diet consists of plants, which, however, grow at their place of residence. They must not consume any other food.' Volný opined that 'this [macrobiotic] movement ha[d] strong religious underpinnings'.

One of the largest so-called international affairs in Volný's reports pertained to a business deal with Finland for the delivery of animal fodder. Czechoslovak authorities wanted to revoke the already signed contract, so they asked Volný to author an expert opinion on the unhealthy composition of the animal fodder product to facilitate revocation. The Finnish authorities allegedly pressured Volný to write a positive evaluation of their product, and they threatened to 'destroy his international professional reputation' if he refused to do so. Volný stated that the Finns

[28] She was a person of interest for the StB and targeted in Operation 'FARMAKOLOG'.

[29] These travels were officially undertaken on behalf of various medicine-related bodies in Czechoslovakia.

tried to bribe everyone even remotely involved in the deal, including himself: he had been offered —but allegedly rejected— 'a full bag of alcohol and a free trip to Finland' in exchange for drafting a more favourable written assessment. Volný's file does not reveal how the deal was ultimately resolved, though Volný did affirm that the deal 'was absolutely not beneficial for Czechoslovakia'.

In November 1986, the StB ended its cooperation with Volný in rather uneventful fashion: Volný retired, left the faculty, and lost his relevant contacts thereby wilting his value as an informer. His file was subsequently archived and he was let go. The StB's termination proposal notes that Volný had 'brought many valuable insights [to the StB], which were used in some operations'. Ultimately, despite a shaky start, Volný served the security apparatus well.

In sum, Volný was a fearful, anxious individual. He was initially blackmailed into informing for his failure to report wrongdoing. The *début* of his relationship with the StB did not go well. At the outset, he failed to meet the StB's expectations, either because of an inability or an unwillingness to do so. However, upon further renewal of his cooperation two decades later, this disappointment faded. Volný seemingly did not receive rewards or advantages for his collaboration, and his relationship with the StB did not appear to benefit his career in any way. He was not much of a political person. Volný was quite forthcoming with the StB: he frequently exposed his colleagues by name, implicated them in mischief and misdemeanours, and occasionally held personal grudges against them such that he informed out of resentment. However, Volný's impulse to inform mostly stemmed from the StB's commissioning him to keep an eye on certain individuals. Perhaps he was motivated by fear and his submissive personality and simply 'could not say no' to whatever the StB demanded of him. Volný was compliant and a pleaser, but despite his appreciable performance in the last stage of his collaboration, he was never promoted to the rank of agent.

VI. 'Soukup'

Soukup was born in 1949 in Prague.[30] His father was head waiter in a hotel in Jíloviště, a small village just outside of the city. An unspecified, property-related offence forced Soukup's father to leave this position and become a forest worker. Soukup's father died when Soukup was only nine years old. Soukup's mother worked primarily as a homemaker, though she occasionally performed jobs as a

[30] Positions: Candidate for secret collaboration. Agent.
File No: 790363.
Registration No: 22940.
File created: 1982.
File archived: 1987.
Page count: 390 pages.

seamstress. She too passed away relatively early in Soukup's life—he was only in his early twenties when she died in 1972.

After completing his basic education, Soukup followed in his father's footsteps and entered vocational training to become a cook or waiter. Soukup never was politically active. A report in his StB file describes him as disinterested in public life. Soukup is portrayed as someone who minded his own business and equally as enjoying money and getting things even if doing so meant bending rules or breaking laws. Much like his father, Soukup's financial machinations routinely got him in trouble with law enforcement. In short, Soukup was a schemer.

Soukup was both an informer and an informed-upon. This, duality—a common thread among informers—pervades the arc of his time with the StB.

An StB report from 1975 recounts how Soukup's neighbours described him as 'arrogant in his public demeanor with no interest [in making] friends or chat[ting]'. The neighbours noted that he was always well-dressed, and it was 'clear from his overall behavior that he like[d] to draw attention to himself'. The report also notes that Soukup appeared 'cheerful and social' around his acquaintances. In fact, 'he frequently [hosted] loud parties', much to the dismay of some of his neighbours. Another informer stated that Soukup was 'a typical waiter' who knew how to behave, had very good social skills, could promptly 'read' situations and people (including their character and financial means), and always used the right 'tactics' to make money from customers. Indeed, Soukup 'like[d] money' and 'was willing to take risks to get it'. Perhaps unsurprisingly, he enjoyed chess and gambling. Soukup's picture in his StB file radiates confidence and a sense of irreverence (Figure 4.6).

After graduating from vocational training in 1968, nineteen-year-old Soukup travelled to Yugoslavia on an approved trip. This approval meant that Czechoslovak authorities expected him to return to Czechoslovakia at the end of his voyage. Soukup, however, had no intention of fulfilling this expectation. On his trip back, he attempted to cross the Italian border several times and ultimately succeeded. Soukup ended up in a refugee camp in Italy. He later escaped this camp and illegally entered West Germany via Austria. Soukup then applied for political asylum at a different refugee camp known as Zirndorf. Soukup should have been granted asylum on 11 November 1968, but by that time he had already returned to Czechoslovakia—for unspecified reasons—with the intervention of the Czechoslovak Embassy in West Germany.

Soukup's file is unclear as to why he exerted such strenuous emigration efforts as a young adult and why he abruptly returned to Czechoslovakia after only staying abroad for a couple of months. Whatever the cause, this push and pull—fleeing and returning—recurred throughout his whole life.

Soukup did temporarily adopt a more stable lifestyle in 1968 when he returned to Prague. In December of that year, he began working as a waiter at Jalta, a luxury hotel in Prague, where he also met his first wife, Anna, a fellow hotel employee.

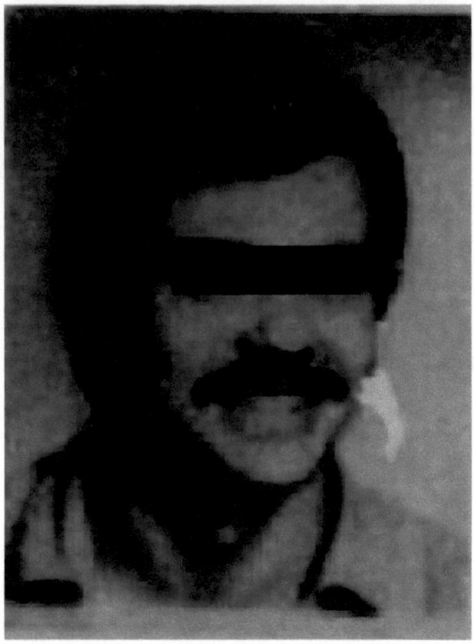

Figure 4.6 A photograph of Soukup (source StB file No 790363, ABS archive).

The couple married in 1969 and had two children together: a son and a daughter. Soukup was said to be a devoted father who loved his children dearly.

Soukup also found himself in trouble with law enforcement. Indeed, his StB file begins with numerous documents and reports that label him as the target of Operation TOMÁŠ. While Soukup was working as a waiter at Jalta in the beginning of 1974, the StB was informed of his alleged involvement in shady business dealing with foreign currencies and foreign nationals who frequented the hotel. Various informers reported that Soukup, a group of his colleagues, and some foreign guests had been engaging in '*veksl*' since 1970, this being the illegal purchase and resale of foreign currencies.[31] Accordingly, the StB suspected Soukup of committing the criminal offence of speculation.

One informer let the StB know that Soukup was 'very predatory—he [did] not waste any opportunity to exchange foreign currencies'. This source added that Soukup was quite confident: He believed that '[Soukup] [had] good connections,

[31] Trade in foreign and especially Western currencies was strictly regulated and restricted in Communist Czechoslovakia. Oral historians Miroslav Vaněk and Pavel Mücke remark that moneychangers were popularly seen as high-status individuals who pumped hard currency into the economy with their lucrative, secret jobs. These scholars also note that moneychangers got a jump start in the new economy of liberal capitalism: '[M]any moneychangers accumulated great wealth, which gave these "pioneers of capitalism" . . . an excellent starting position after the 1989 revolution. They had useful contacts in all social circles, and they also had access to free capital which they invested as soon as they could.' Miroslav Vaněk and Pavel Mücke, *Velvet Revolutions: An Oral History of Czech Society* (OUP 2020) 124. This was not the case for Soukup, insofar as he passed away in 1987.

so he [was] not afraid of any punishment because he bribe[d] everything away'. Yet another informer stated that Soukup was the most active member of the group engaging in *veksl* at Jalta. The StB also suspected that Soukup was involved in the illicit sale of foreign drugs and medicines, and that he had amassed significant personal wealth in so doing. According to his StB file, Soukup had used these illegally obtained profits to build an expensive house for his family in Jíloviště.

Consequently, the StB investigated Soukup. The goals were either to criminally prosecute him—'depending on the extent of [his] criminal activities'—or otherwise 'use these activities as compromising material to recruit [him as an informer]'. Apparently, at this juncture the StB pursued the former track. The StB transferred Soukup's file to the VB's department of economic criminality in September 1975. A later report in his file notes that Soukup was ultimately convicted of fraud.

It is unclear how Soukup's illegal activities and criminal conviction contributed to the breakdown of his first marriage or his subsequent attempts to leave Czechoslovakia. Nonetheless, following his divorce in 1977, Soukup sought to emigrate. Although his applications to leave the country were routinely rejected by the authorities, Soukup was not deterred. In August 1980, he married his second wife, Monika, a citizen of West Germany. The couple met during Monika's first visit to Czechoslovakia in 1979. They married when she visited Czechoslovakia for the second time. Soukup later told the StB that this was a sham marriage arranged so that he could leave and go to the West. Indeed, immediately after the wedding, Soukup filed a request to exit the country for family reasons. In January 1981, with the approval of the Czechoslovak authorities, Soukup legally moved to West Germany. That said, he was permitted to retain his Czechoslovak citizenship and he returned to his homeland for one to ten days nearly every month.

Soukup's frequent cross-border travels stoked the suspicions of both the StB and of West German security services. Apparently, Soukup's wife rarely accompanied him on these trips and, when she actually did, she stayed at a different hotel. The StB also suspected that Soukup had committed other petty property-related offences in Czechoslovakia. Accordingly, the StB monitored him closely. An informer's report from January 1981 notes that the StB was also concerned that Soukup was being targeted by West German security services. A report from 1982 concluded that there was proof that Soukup was indeed 'a person of interest of West German special services', and that 'it [was] not excluded that he [was] in contact with them'. That said, whatever encounters Soukup had with West German security agencies never were confirmed as being of an informer nature. While Soukup was undoubtedly an StB informer, and was of interest to West German counterparts, there is no indication in the StB file of his being a double agent.

In 1982, the StB obtained further information about Soukup's life in West Germany. A letter in his file describes how he and his wife had opened a small Czech jewellery and antique shop at a tourist resort south of Koblenz. Apparently, most of the items for sale had been illegally or semi-legally exported from Czechoslovakia.

Soukup was quite diffident in sharing this information with the reporting source, stating that if such information were leaked, he 'would be in trouble not only in West Germany/ "they would destroy my shop" / but also in Czechoslovakia / "they would have me for a snitch"'.

The StB launched Operation REGÁL to discern whether Soukup '[did] not abuse his arrivals to [Czechoslovakia] for committing criminal offences against the country'. The StB again vetted its two options: recruit Soukup for collaboration or criminally prosecute him. This time around things turned out differently.

Further investigation revealed that the accusations against Soukup for his fraudulent activities in Czechoslovakia were false—one of his former co-workers from Jalta was evidently trying to cover up his own criminal offenses by blaming Soukup. When the truth emerged, Soukup reportedly expressed his gratitude and willingness to maintain cordial relations with law enforcement. An StB evaluation report in Soukup's file describes how, after release from investigative detention, Soukup 'attempted to prove his gratitude by declaring his willingness to help security organs, in case they were interested'. In addition, Soukup repeatedly emphasized his interest in visiting his children and in regularly returning to Czechoslovakia. Reports that described Soukup's recruitment as an informer repeatedly mention this gratitude. Specifically, the proposal to initiate personal contact with Soukup stated that the StB would leverage his 'gratitude [to authorities] for dispersing the suspicion for property offences and [Soukup's] personal ties with the StB officer, who up [until] then acted as a member … of the regular criminal police'.

Soukup's recruitment process began on 29 June 1982. His eventual StB officer continued to pose as a normal police officer throughout the recruitment and he talked to Soukup about life in West Germany and the false accusations brought against him by his former colleague from Jalta. In response, Soukup told the officer about his interview with the employees of a 'certain *Geheimdienst* [ie secret service]' after his arrival to West Germany in 1981, and that he was asked if he had collaborated with Czechoslovak security services.

Soukup was reportedly 'spontaneous and willing' to share personal details. He repeatedly expressed his thankfulness and commitment to maintain good relations with the Czechoslovak security apparatus. He placed particular emphasis on the importance of regularly visiting his children. He wanted 'to prove his good relationship to Czechoslovakia by [keeping his] Czechoslovak citizenship, even though he had troubles because of it in West Germany' because it hindered his ability to get a business permit on a timely basis. The StB concluded that Soukup's behaviour suggested 'that he [was] still willing to be in touch with the security services'. Indeed, 'his only request was that the contacts remain confidential' in Czechoslovakia as well as in West Germany. Thus, in June 1982, Soukup handwrote 'a statement of confidentiality':

> I declare that I will keep silent about my meetings with a representative of the Ministry of the Interior, and about circumstances which I got acquainted with during these meetings. At the same time, I request that similar silence will be kept from the representative of [the Ministry].

Soukup met with the StB whenever he was in Czechoslovakia. He talked in detail about his encounters with West German law enforcement after his regular returns from Czechoslovakia—the West Germans were suspicious of his frequent travels to Czechoslovakia and wanted to know the reason for his border crossings. Because he had been permitted to move out of Czechoslovakia, the West Germans were also curious whether he had started collaborating with Czechoslovak security services. Soukup explained that these border officers issued very subtle threats. Soukup reportedly denied any form of cooperation with Czechoslovak authorities.

West German security organs were not interested in Soukup solely because of his border crossings. In November 1981, West German customs police searched Soukup's store after he had allegedly been accused of importing goods without proper paperwork. Soukup stated that the investigation rendered these claims baseless but that the police had nevertheless confiscated his book containing his contacts and customers in West Germany and Czechoslovakia. This book subsequently re-emerged in Soukup's file on multiple occasions.

Soukup told the StB that he and his wife had tried to get this precious book back from the West Germans, but that this task proved quite challenging. On one occasion, Soukup's wife had travelled to the '*Zollfandung* [ie customs investigation]' office in Nuremberg to ask for it. When she returned, she refused to tell Soukup what had transpired at the customs investigation office, what had been discussed, or why she was unable to retrieve the contact book. She only mentioned that she had been 'very well welcomed' and cryptically warned Soukup that he should also be expecting an invitation. She recommended that he 'be forward with the gentlemen, ... in the interest of the whole family and him personally'.

Soukup subsequently asked the StB for guidance on what to do if he were summoned by West German authorities. Soukup doubted that the situation had been orchestrated by the customs police, as 'he was not a little boy anymore and had read some spy novels', and he was worried that his wife would try to persuade him to work for the West Germans. On the one hand, Soukup did not want to compromise his shop and residence permit in West Germany. On the other hand, he did not want to lose his opportunity for regular travel to Czechoslovakia. Ultimately, he decided to express these concerns to his StB officer. The StB appreciated his openness and further reminded him that he had signed a declaration of confidentiality with them. The StB instructed him to act according to his conscience and to stay out of trouble in West Germany. In 1983, after he had already been officially recruited by the StB, Soukup was directed by his handlers to engage with West German security agencies and inform them of his findings.

As a candidate for collaboration, Soukup provided the StB with information on his encounters with West German authorities and about his acquaintances in Czechoslovakia, such as Radomír. Soukup told the StB that Radomír had previously been involved in currency machinations, and that he was in the process of marrying a West German citizen because 'that was the only way to legally move out'. Soukup divulged that Radomír was curious about Soukup's departure from Czechoslovakia and was particularly interested in whether Soukup had been recruited by any security services. Soukup reportedly replied to this inquiry in the negative. Later, Soukup also told the StB that Soukup's former wife was having an affair with an unidentified West German citizen.

In September 1982, Soukup reported to the StB about one of his former associates at Jalta, Mr J., who had emigrated to West Germany in 1972, but returned to Czechoslovakia after his stay in West Germany proved unsuccessful. That said, things did not work out for Mr J. in Czechoslovakia either. As a result, in 1980 Mr J. entered a fake marriage with a West German citizen and returned to West Germany. In August 1982, Soukup and Mr J. allegedly met at the *U Švejka* pub in Frankfurt, where Mr J. loudly admonished Soukup in German, stating that he must be 'a snitch' and 'collaborated with the Czechs as he did not have any problems with moving out and was allowed to regularly visit'. Soukup always seemed to be surrounded by a cloud of suspicion, yet this always seemed to disperse when it mattered most.

Soukup was generally forthcoming with StB officers, who in turn seemed content with his performance. StB officers always gave him space to contact them whenever he was in Czechoslovakia, and he always did. Soukup supplied information on his West German wife's family, including their political opinions, and internal developments in that country. On a different note, Soukup had also offered to take photographs or sketch different towns and various border crossing posts in West Germany, but the StB refused his offer noting the 'dangerousness of taking pictures, especially of police buildings'.

The StB was still somewhat concerned about Soukup's past, together with his questionable activities, to wit, his machinations with foreign currencies and his export of goods under dubious conditions. However, Soukup told the StB that his second wife forced him to cease all illegal or semi-illegal activities immediately after they had gotten married. Nonetheless, certain reports in Soukup's file indicate that he might not have been as virtuous as he seemed. For example, an informer told the StB about how Soukup wagered large sums of money when gambling, that he had once gambled away a Mercedes, and that gambling was the main reason for his frequent returns to Czechoslovakia. Indeed, Soukup himself would occasionally reveal how he bent rules for profit. For instance, he had once promised his friend from Jalta that Soukup would give him a ride to West Germany, but only if his friend signed a fake declaration stating that he had gifted Soukup an antique clock that he was now transporting to

West Germany. This false declaration form allowed Soukup to pay lower customs fees.

Despite any residual or lingering misgivings, Soukup's cooperation with the StB proceeded smoothly until October 1982, when he missed a scheduled meeting because he was at '*záchytka*'—a Czech word for the English colloquialism 'drunk tank' or 'detox cell'. Soukup called his StB officer to apologize for the incident, explaining that he had wanted 'to find a woman for an evening program' but got very drunk. He claimed that the woman must have drugged him and that two men had attacked him and stole his watch and jewellery. He said that when he tried to report the incident, the police patrol simply brought him to the *záchytka*. Even though he had apologized, his StB officer reprimanded him. The StB officer told Soukup that such reckless behaviour was unacceptable for an informer. He also reproached Soukup for calling him directly from a public phone, as this could have led to de-conspiration.

Because this incident was considered an anomaly in Soukup's rapport with the StB, in January 1983 the StB drafted a formal proposal for his official recruitment. The proposal stated that Soukup would be tasked with 'acquir[ing] knowledge on interests of the adversary on the territory of Czechoslovakia' and 'fulfill[ing] tasks at the territory of West Germany … including on Czechoslovak emigrants'. The StB wanted to use the fact that Soukup was 'a person of interest to German special services' to their advantage. The StB planned to recruit Soukup on the basis of his 'ideological motives', as the StB believed that he had a very good relationship with Czechoslovakia and considered himself to be a Czechoslovak citizen. The StB report specifically noted that his 'ideological motivation was reinforced by his dependency on his kids [ie two underage children still in Czechoslovakia] … and his inclination for adventures'.

Soukup's formal recruitment took place on 23 February 1983. After a brief conversation including cursory mention of his former criminal offenses, Soukup was invited to sign a pledge to collaborate. According to the report from the recruitment meeting, Soukup signed the pledge without hesitation:

> From patriotic reasons I commit to voluntary cooperation. I will be fulfilling given tasks according to my best possibilities, abilities and conscientiously, abroad but also at the territory of Czechoslovakia, a citizen of which I will always consider myself, even if I gain West German citizenship.

Soukup's first assignment was to ask West German authorities about his confiscated contact book. The StB planned to 'deliver' him to the West German security services, let him inform on their putative inner workings, and spread disinformation—although that ambition was never fulfilled. The StB provided Soukup with detailed instructions on how to use his contact book to get in touch with the authorities and on what to do thereafter. The StB also tutored him on the information that he could openly share —such as his 1978 conviction for fraud and the dismissal of another allegation of fraud against him in 1983—and on which information to keep secret. Under no circumstances was he to admit to his contacts with the StB. To ensure Soukup's compliance, the StB planned to wiretap his former wife's telephone. In April 1983, Soukup confirmed that he had accomplished this mission, complied with the StB's instructions, and had been in touch with West German authorities about his contact book. He also told the StB that he had been followed by two men in a strange car after he crossed the border on one of his trips to West Germany. The StB awarded Soukup 1,000 Kčs for having been so active, open, and forthcoming, and also reimbursed his expenses in the amount of 100 DM.

Initially, Soukup produced good results. However, he began to produce fewer and fewer reports over time, although the information he did bring was still considered to be worthwhile. For instance, the StB evaluation report from January 1984 notes that he delivered 'valuable knowledge regarding the situation in [West Germany], Czechoslovak emigrants ... and activities [of West German enforcement] related to him'. The StB also strove to 'deepen [his] personal bond with [his] StB officer' and 'consistently lead him away from engaging in property crime in relation to his arrivals to Czechoslovakia'.

Later, Soukup's cooperation started to flag, mainly due to what his file noted as 'the significant deterioration of his mental health'. Soukup appeared unable to handle the constant state of liminality between two countries, with two different security services, and secreting multiple truths, in addition to being beset with financial woes. His constant involvement with law enforcement, be it in Czechoslovakia or in West Germany, must have surely worn him down.

In 1984, Soukup had allegedly begun working at a hotel as a waiter to earn extra money for his family but this additional work further exhausted him. In May 1984, he visited a representative for the Czechoslovak trade agency in Köln to inquire 'if Czechoslovakia [could] provide him [with healthcare] in case of [a] breakdown'. Another informer's report on this meeting notes that Soukup appeared 'nervous' and told the trade agency that he was 'very much overworked' and 'felt clueless'. Soukup also revealed that he had personal problems with his boss at work and was consequently forced to quit his job at the hotel. Soukup stated that he did not have any money and that he feared that West German authorities were going to discover that he committed tax-related offences while running the shop he and his wife had in West Germany.

In July 1984, Soukup confided in his StB officer that he 'had had psychological troubles' and had decided to undergo treatment in West Germany. Soukup revealed how, at the time, he had been very afraid that he was being followed by the West German police. In response, the StB asked Soukup whether he wanted to suspend their collaboration but he declined. The StB was never able to shed their reservations about Soukup: At the end of this report, the StB starkly notes that it 'did not want to exclude the possibility that [Soukup] [was being] used by enemy special services'.

Meanwhile, the StB discovered that Soukup was again committing minor criminal offenses in Czechoslovakia so as to acquire more money. Soukup admitted to these mischiefs but justified them on the grounds that he was unemployed and that his wife earned very little money. Around that time, Soukup also repeatedly badgered the StB for money, and a meeting report from August 1984 notes that 'he [was] willing to do anything for [the StB] for money'. During that meeting, Soukup repeatedly emphasized that the StB 'should ask what [they] want [of him] but have to pay him'. Soukup's StB officer also observed that Soukup was 'absentminded' and unable to provide clear answers to questions. According to the report, Soukup lamented that 'the most terrible [was] the loneliness and each morning, he felt that someone [was] suspecting him of enemy activities against Germany'. The StB reiterated that they '[could] not exclude the possibility that [Soukup] [had gotten] in touch with the German security services', was working for them, and was keeping it secret from the StB.

Despite many concerns and warning signs –as well as demonstrable psychological turmoil–the StB did not give up on Soukup, who continued to deliver some valuable information. According to an evaluation report from January 1985, Soukup relayed intelligence on two hotels in West Germany that the StB had asked him about. Things seemed to have improved for a while. In June 1985, Soukup told the StB that he was feeling 'absolutely healthy', that his situation in West Germany had calmed, and that he had started working in a restaurant again. He also informed the StB that he had been approached by a man named Mr Köhler, who he suspected was from the West German security services. Soukup led him on by telling him that he would be happy to provide information on Czechoslovakia, but only for a financial reward. Mr Köhler allegedly visited Soukup again and was curious whether he 'knew anyone from the StB'. Soukup reportedly joked and said that he 'knew ... the head of the passport department in ... Prague, and when [Soukup's] kids wanted to visit him in Germany, for a bottle [of alcohol], [that person] [could] issue the travel permits in short time'.

Despite these stable periods, Soukup's life progressively was unravelling. In March 1986, he allegedly appeared in Czechoslovakia in dismay—he had reportedly obtained a disability pension for his mental health issues and was contemplating a divorce. Receipt of a disability payment made him ineligible to legally work at his private business. Aware of his past inclinations and familiar with his avarice, the StB warned Soukup that if he re-engaged in property criminality he would be prosecuted and that this time the StB would not intervene on his behalf. Soukup responded that he had no plans to partake in any future illegal activities. In July 1986, an informer's report describes how Soukup arrived in Czechoslovakia in a red Porsche and was allegedly spending some time at a prostitute's apartment. This informer also said that Soukup was 'not psychologically healthy, judging from his behavior and manner of speaking'. Moreover, Soukup had reportedly told this informer that he was being prosecuted for tax evasion in West Germany.

In January 1987, the StB contemplated ending its relationship with Soukup as a result of his repeated erratic behaviour. Soukup however passed away before a final decision was made. Prior to his death, Soukup had failed to contact the StB for over five months and in March 1987 his StB officer began to worry about him. Subsequent inquiries revealed that Soukup had suddenly died at a 'random acquaintance's' apartment during what proved to be his final stay in Czechoslovakia. The StB's official proposal to end collaboration with Soukup was drafted in December 1987—well after the StB became aware of his death. The termination proposal noted that as of the start of his collaboration in 1983 the StB had held thirty-four meetings with Soukup and had given him a total of 6,500 Kčs and 200 DM—partially as reimbursements for his expenses and partially as awards.

In conclusion, Soukup was a petty criminal. Throughout his life, he drifted in and out of illicit activities. He openly liked money and did whatever it took to get as much as he could. His relationship with the StB evolved from his being a target of their investigation to his being a relatively willing participant in their targeting of others. At the beginning of his trajectory as an informer, Soukup was very grateful to the StB for having freed him from a property-related criminal investigation. His desire to pursue other business interests and to maintain regular contact with his children after emigrating to West Germany encouraged him to collaborate with the StB. Initially, Soukup was quite forthcoming and open: He took initiative and fulfilled all his tasks. However, despite this commendable performance, the StB could not shake the suspicion that he was a delinquent. As such, the StB fixated on his illicit businesses, developed a concern that he was not being straight with them, and wondered whether he was simultaneously collaborating with enemy West German security services.

Soukup oscillated between being trusted and doubted. Much like many other informers whose files we reviewed, Soukup's personal situation deteriorated and his cooperation with the StB dissolved over time. He kept losing jobs, he broke down emotionally, he got divorced. Things simply fell apart for him. Soukup was a marginal character on the edges of society, a scammer and a schemer, an informer who was chronically informed upon, yet all the while a father who dearly loved his children. StB officers appeared to have developed some amities towards Soukup, however. They appeared to care about his psychological struggles, whether genuinely or for ulterior purposes. Soukup was no patriot. He lived in contempt of both the capitalist and Communist state and the laws and rules of either. Although he presented no danger to the public, he was certainly not a devoted citizen. There is no suggestion that among the plethora of words Soukup exchanged with the StB—and among all the praise, care and criticism he received—that anything that implicated national security or conveyed strategic significance ever passed from his lips to StB ears.

5
What Jumps Out
Informing as Intimacy and Emotions as Drivers

The StB files, up close, reveal the engineering effects of authoritarianism on the human soul[1] and the participatory nature of the individual amid dictatorship.[2] The archived files brim with nattering and expiation, betrayal and conniving, cunning and candour, dominance and subservience, as well as illness and health. File-stories are detailed and biographic, so much so that their length, comprehensiveness, and diaristic hues are remarkable. They read like epics. We have been somewhat bushwhacked by the volume of miscellaneous, personal, and gossipy content that the files surface: reports about work conduct, grades from school, revelations of affairs, minutiae about intimate relationships, consumption patterns of alcoholic drinks, carousing, scheming, cavorting, and whether the person is popular (or not) and fits in (or not).

In short, the archived files illuminate individual lives while also illustrating the 'complexities of the relationship *between* state and society'.[3] File-stories cast light upon the personal connections between informers and StB officers. Acts of collaboration with the StB can be seen as one way of negotiating possibilities, tactically navigating, and socially manoeuvring the lean opportunities offered within Communist society.[4] Similar to informers in other European Communist regimes, informers in Czechoslovakia had variable—sometimes prosaically plain, at times rivetingly poignant—reasons to collude with the StB.

[1] Josef Škvorecký, *The Engineer of Human Souls* (Picador 1986).

[2] Mary Fulbrook, *The People's State: East German Society from Hitler to Honecker* (Yale University Press 2005). Péter Apor, Sándor Horváth, and James Mark assert that Fulbrook's term participatory dictatorship 'captures the paradoxes of socialist citizenship'. Péter Apor, Sándor Horváth, and James Mark, 'Introduction: Collaboration, Cooperation, and Political Participation in the Communist Regimes' in Péter Apor, Sándor Horváth, and James Mark (eds), *Secret Agents and the Memory of Everyday Collaboration in Communist Eastern Europe* (Anthem Press 2017) 16, n 32.

[3] Apor, Horváth, and Mark, 'Introduction' (n 2) 2–3, 10 (noting also that '[t]hose living under socialist regimes who [sought] social improvement or economic change had to work through official party-political or professional structures … [p]arty membership or cooperation with the state security forces could provide a sense of active political participation').

[4] Miroslav Vaněk and Pavel Mücke, *Velvet Revolutions: An Oral History of Czech Society* (OUP 2020) 3 ('Within such networks, the state and its citizens renegotiated a social consensus daily.').

Informers Up Close. Mark A. Drumbl and Barbora Holá, Oxford University Press.
 DOI: 10.1093/oso/9780192855138.003.0005

I. Overview

The informers presented in the StB files that we reviewed constitute a diverse group. These informers vary widely in terms of age, social status, and occupation (including office administration, petty criminality, health sector, arts, business, academia, hospitality industry, sex work, science, translation, and diplomacy). Nearly all were married at some point (often re-married); nearly all had children. Their lives nonetheless took starkly different tacks: some aged happily, others melancholically. Of the twenty-three files we reviewed in depth, the length of the informing relationship ranged from thirty-seven years to three years (with the mean and median both around eighteen years). One informer was recruited in the 1940s, ten in the 1950s, three in the 1960s, five in the 1970s, and four in the 1980s. Their relationships with the StB were definitively terminated due to varying reasons: imprisonment (one informer); mental or physical health/old age/retirement (seven); death (two); the informer did not wish to be transferred to another StB officer (one); deconspiration (one); criticism of the Communist Party (one); meagre results (eight); change of workplace (one); and emigration from Czechoslovakia (one).[5] Twenty of these informers were definitively terminated in the 1980s, with one in each of the 1950s, 1960s, and 1970s. In twelve cases, collaboration had been ended only to be subsequently renewed, hence our use of the phrase 'definitively terminated' to indicate the final end of cooperation.

The informers in our sample hailed from almost all categories that the StB had created for informers, as listed in Chapter 2, Section III.B ('Categories of Informers'), but many shifted from 'candidate for secret cooperation' to the status of 'agent'. We did not note any correlation between being an informer and being a member of the Communist Party: of the twenty-three informers whose files we explored in detail, eight were members of the Communist Party (with disparate degrees of involvement). Seventeen informers were explicitly noted as having received financial or material rewards. Twenty had travelled internationally. Fourteen had meaningful family, personal, or professional contacts outside Czechoslovakia.[6] Indeed, some—like Soukup and Goldfus—inhabited a zone of push-and-pull as double informers or as bouncing between Czechoslovakia and foreign countries. This interstitiality must have become exhausting as time passed. Indeed, it seems that, for Soukup juggling demands from two sides—the StB and West German authorities—ultimately shattered his mental health and contributed to his alcoholism as well as the sorrowful note on which his file reports his life concluded. For Lily, too, it remains unclear whether, subjectively, she considered

[5] The numbers in parentheses indicate the numbers of informers in our sample whose informing relationships ended for the stipulated reason.

[6] Two were foreign citizens, albeit temporarily or intermittently residing in Czechoslovakia.

herself a Czech or a foreigner. Lily sought meaning in a cosmopolitan space that, at the time, she constructed for herself in her own 'in-between'.

Although considerable diversity arises as among individual trajectories and experiences (a granularity that we believe to be crucially important), the files themselves share certain stenographic and substantive similarities. Common themes routinely appear: familial backstories; political views; socio-economic standing; the methods that the StB used to encourage or secure collaboration; how the StB and the informer leaned into (and at times leaned out of) the collaborative dynamic, surveillance of the informer; and profound concern with de-conspiration or double agenting.

In this chapter, we impressionistically tease out some observations about what jumps out at us from the archived StB files we have reviewed in detail. While detailed distillations of six informer files appear in Chapter 4, seventeen others are similarly condensed in an online appendix:[7] We reference all of these in this chapter. We furthermore invoke our research into the files of those informers we have considered but then elected not to include in the appendix or book. While the archived StB file-stories constitute the epistemological foundation of this book, we additionally incorporate extensive content and perspectives from a robust array of secondary sources: accounts in the *Paměť národa* (Memory of Nations),[8] general academic literature, newspaper articles, informal discussions we have conducted, and literary works (including fiction).

In addition to Mary Fulbrook's notion of 'participatory dictatorship' and Josef Škvorecký's optic of governmental 'engineering', our work is conceptually guided by scholars who unspool the webbed relationships between individuals, society, and the state in Communist Czechoslovakia. On this note, Matěj Spurný, Jakub Jareš, and Katka Volná conclude:

> People in any modern political and social system find themselves in difficult situations connected to politics and ideology. They have to solve dilemmas, such as whether to accept compromises forced upon them and whether to vet their colleagues or, in contrast, be vetted by them. The fact that in dictatorships these dilemmas are of another, perhaps more ominous, nature than in liberal democracies does not mean that in authoritarian systems one does not come across people who make decisions or search, if possible, for the most dignified solution

[7] See https://www.nscr.nl/Informers-Up-Close. For detailed discussion of our methodology, Chapter 1, Section III, 'Secret Police Archives and File-Stories'.

[8] *Paměť národa*, Memory of Nations, 'Witness Database' (*Memory of Nations*, 2023) <https://www.memoryofnations.eu/en/archive> accessed 22 January 2023; see also Chapter 1, Section III, ' Secret Police Archives and File-Stories' n 46. While we pseudonymized the informers in their file-stories, and anonymized other individuals mentioned in their StB files (in other words, in both cases redacted personally identifying information) in order to protect their privacy and dignity interests, we retained the names of individuals who volunteered to publicly share their stories with *Paměť národa* and therefore are accessible on its website.

> to various problems in their lives and for ways of making personal profit that, whatever advantages they may enjoy, nonetheless allow them to maintain their sense of personal integrity. It is impossible therefore to reduce the lives of individuals, even in dictatorships, to merely mechanical parts of a large totalitarian machine. Not even in dictatorships is human behavior merely the fulfillment of assigned tasks.[9]

This chapter distils and interprets. We present our impressions as to what the files indicate, to us, about why and how people spoke to the StB. We advance several propositions in this chapter. The first one is that informing dynamically takes shape as an intimate and relational act of social navigation. Second, and centrally, the archived files reveal the (e)motions of the informing process, with multiple sentiments—including fear, resentment, desire, and devotion—percolating and simmering throughout. We construct these emotions as initially *catalysing* why people collaborated with the StB and then *fuelling* the kinetics of that collaboration, namely how it evolves, stalls, or intensifies over and through time. Third, crocheted to the notion of time, we underscore how informing has a longitudinal dimension to it—an ebb and flow—which suggests some level of interactive agency among informers and StB officers. Fourth, the files reveal that StB officers occasionally expressed sentiments of concern or solicitude towards 'their' informers. And, fifth, our reading of the archived files indicates the variability of situational power and individual positioning: we note the liminality and at times woefulness of informers. Some informers may be victims who in turn may victimize; some are dispositionally meek and weak but wreak havoc in the lives of others; other informers do not present as vulnerable or marginal; some informers may not really victimize anyone, as they appear adept at engaging the StB and, while garrulous, manage to dissemble and stall so as to promote their own interests while minimally imperilling others.

II. Informing as Intimacy and Conversation

How does the informer–StB dynamic commence? The general path is for an StB officer, after eyeballing or getting word of a possible source (including from existing informers), to approach that individual. That individual then falls into the category of a candidate for secret collaboration. The files indicate that candidates could be in touch with an StB officer-handler for protracted periods of time—years even—and

[9] Matěj Spurný, Jakub Jareš, and Katka Volná, 'Intellectuals between Collaboration and Independence in Late Socialism: Politics and Everyday Life at the Faculty of Arts, Charles University, Prague' in Apor, Horváth, and Mark (eds), *Secret Agents and the Memory of Everyday Collaboration* (n 2) 171–72 (where the authors discuss the professional lives of two academics during normalization).

proffer considerable information before any proposal to formally start collaboration is made. In other instances, the eventual informer directly approaches the StB with a complaint, denunciation, or concern. Therefore, although many informers were initially contacted by the StB, others came forward on their own initiative. In some cases, however, clear-cut identification of the initial lead (the officer or the informer) can be difficult to pinpoint.

In most instances, the ongoing informer relationship becomes official with the issuance of the signed (and sworn) 'pledge' to cooperate. That said, not all informing relationships are formalized with a signed pledge, and certain of these unformalized relationships nonetheless remained very active. Indeed, in certain instances the StB found it unnecessary to request a written commitment.[10]

Nearly all pledges affirm that the informer cooperated for ideological motives to further Communism or patriotic motives to protect Czechoslovakia. We have a number of reactions to these affirmations. For starters, the putative primordiality of ideological motivations is belied by the documented conversations between informer and StB handler. This deeper analysis renders it somewhat otiose to ascribe definitiveness on the motivational declarations in the pledge. During the Communist years, public language of patriotism and fealty to Marxism-Leninism was pervasive and constituted a basis to anchor any and all sorts of conduct, thereby offering cover to mask mundane or opportunistic private motivations.[11] Furthermore, these pledges depart from the recruitment proposals initially drafted by the StB. Based upon our review, these recruitment proposals tended to present more kaleidoscopic motivations. For example, in Soukup's case, the recruitment proposal noted Soukup's 'ideological motivation', but also how he loved his children and hence wanted to visit Czechoslovakia frequently; this proposal also noted his inclination for adventure. Time also matters. Pledges conducted in the 1950s seemed heartier than the drier bureaucratic recitations that eventuated in the 1980s. Věra's two pledges, in the separate chronological phases of her cooperation, display these differences. The first pledge, during which Věra solemnly faced a portrait of then President Gottwald, contrasts with the second pledge—expedited and seemingly vacuous—in the 1980s. Some informers appear reluctant such that they concertedly avoided contact with their handlers or provided cryptic, scattered information. Lily, for her part, was brazenly defiant and paid the price. Others—such as Věra and Goldfus—were eager and creatively developed ways to gather more and more information. The interactive dynamics between informer and secret police officer evolved (or devolved, at times dissolved) through time. The social bond between the two individuals, then, was fluid and pliable, rather than static. It

[10] See eg File No 752665, registration No 2664 (Rolf). Rolf's file is not included among our twenty-three summarized informers.

[11] Michal Pullmann, 'The Ideological Face of Normalisation: Socialist Modernity and the "Quiet Life"' in Kevin McDermott and Matthew Stibbe (eds), *Czechoslovakia and Eastern Europe in the Era of Normalisation 1969-1989* (Palgrave Macmillan 2022) 65.

waxed and waned. Indeed, one recurrent factor we identify in an informer's willingness to speak was the identity of the specific StB officer with whom the informer engaged.[12] If StB higher-ups switched an informer's handler, this led in some instances to more informing while in other cases the informing dipped because the informer might not have felt comfortable with the new officer (no trust, no chemistry) or simply missed the old one. Informers could go from hot to cold depending on whether 'their' StB officer was present as an interlocutor or audience. All this suggests the salience of individual interpersonal connection amid the structural bureaucratic machine. Organizationally, the StB was not an implacable monolith. Officers came and went. Some were replaced, some were purged, some persisted, some disagreed with each other, and some paternalistically ministered to their informers while others were more dismissive.

A form of 'relational contracting' therefore seems to arise. Relational contracting is a theory developed by US private law scholar Ian Macneil to conceptualize bargains made among individuals.[13] Whereas many contracts are short-term one-shot moments (eg buying a hammer), others are long-term, variable, and often less formalized. Within these longer-term relationships, power as between the two parties shifts with market and personal conditions, thereby embodying give-and-take and a fluctuating emotional and personal connection. Examples include franchising agreements, rental arrangements, employment and service commitments, and requirements contracts (to supply goods to a retailer, for instance croissants to a café) that extend for decades. We believe that StB pledges made by informers resemble these relational contracts while the provision of the information approximates what contract lawyers call 'consideration', namely the content of the bargain, in this case information in exchange for receipt of some benefits (eg some money) or as relief from state-sponsored harm.

To be sure, Macneil was not writing within the context of a command-and-control Communist dictatorship whose entire surveillance apparatus created an ominous climate of fear and suspicion exacerbated by legal duties to disclose. As Volný's file-story demonstrates, the StB could gin up fateful entrapment encounters in which

[12] See eg File No 3492, 564136, registration No 7216 (Luděk). Luděk began his cooperation during his military service in the 1950s. His cooperation was terminated in March 1963 when an StB officer (presumably of higher rank) disagreed with the favourable assessment that Luděk's then supervising StB officer had made of Luděk's cooperation. According to Luděk's StB file, the dissatisfied StB officer felt that Luděk's abilities were 'overrated', that the positive recommendation that Luděk had been assigned was 'inconsistent with the results of [his] work', and that Luděk was 'selfish'. That said, Luděk continued to meet with the StB, although taxonomically in the capacity of a confidant and not an agent, and continued to supply additional information. This suggests that the informer–StB relationship was, on the one hand, bound by official categories yet, on the other, also was fluid and amorphous.

[13] Ian R Macneil, 'The Many Futures of Contract' (1974) 47 Southern California L Rev 691; Ian R Macneil, 'Contracts: Adjustment of Long-Term Economic Relations under Classical, Neoclassical, and Relational Contract Law' (1978) 72(6) Northwestern University L Rev. 854. See also generally Stewart Macaulay, 'Elegant Models, Empirical Pictures, and the Complexities of Contract' (1977) 11 L and Society Rev 507.

potential informers could incriminate themselves. No Czechoslovak citizen could ever know what the StB would choose to do with whatever information—however petty—accumulated in its remit. The StB could easily dash someone's life. The power differential between StB handler and individual informer was significant, far greater than that between employer and employed in a market economy. We are well aware of these profound power differentials. That said, we believe these private law contracting analogies serve as apertures to help discern the agency, constrained action, and bargains struck between informer and StB officer. Despite the power gaps, informers retained capacity and leeway.[14] Informers could refuse to cooperate with the StB and could vow not to divulge certain things. Informers ceased cooperating at times without proffering any stated reasons or facing any evident recrimination. The StB–informer relationship was a two-way road—action and reaction—with both sides iteratively shaping the trajectory: while stacked in favour of StB officials, the energy has some mutuality and reciprocity. The tempo of these interactional bargains, moreover, hinged on the national politics of the time. Such relational contracts were much different in Lily's time in the 1950s than they were in the 1980s. The arc of long-term informing in Soukup's and Věra's files reveals how broad political forces tinctured the individual micro-rhythms amid various historical phases of Communist Czechoslovakia.

The content of the bargain—in private law parlance the consideration (the *causa*) for the contract—was, as we alluded to earlier, information. And 'information' was most broadly conceived. Much of the information contained in many of the files we have analysed is parlayed in a way that reads somewhat like a conversation between two friends (or frenemies) over a beer or coffee where one friend (or frenemy) complains and gossips about families, acquaintances, comrades, and foes while the other listens and—in what does depart from an ordinary conversation—then records. A veneer of discursive intimacy arises. Informing can assuage loneliness: the recording gives it a social work or therapeutic angle in which the StB steps into an *in loco parentis* moment.[15] The StB officer becomes a *compadre* to whom to vent, to secure validation, to prove relevance, and to seek advice.

Some informers came forward because informing satisfied their 'amusement' and 'enjoyment'.[16] Some informers simply wished to be heard. Others wanted to be seen, wanted to matter, and to count for something, somewhere, somehow. Goldfus, for instance, pleaded with the StB to let him continue informing so that he could feel affirmed and useful. Informing offered Goldfus friendship, people to

[14] Barbara Miller, *The Stasi Files Unveiled: Guilt and Compliance in a Unified Germany* (Routledge 2017) 48 (in the case of East Germany, noting that 'evidence does seem to suggest that refusing to agree to work for the Stasi . . . rarely led to any negative repercussions for the person concerned').

[15] ibid 60 ('Some informers claim that they regarded their [Stasi] officer as a colleague and, therefore, as an equal.'). See also Timothy Garton Ash, *The File, A Personal History* (Flamingo, 1997) 225 ('Sometimes—quite often, in fact—the Stasi comes as a substitute father. . . . Your case officer is the father you never knew.').

[16] See eg Luděk (n 12).

talk to, and some kind of camaraderie. It is as if he was looking for a buddy. Goldfus fancied digging up stuff and reporting it, whether journalistically or straight into the StB's hands. Informing secured Goldfus an audience for his poetry. Goldfus appeared like an addict. He endured the pain that informing caused him (iterated jailing) because he could not stop (or stop himself from) informing. Informing on others seemed to 'feel good' for some informers: as a way to get back at someone, to get even, and to sooth and brag about the power to haunt others. Informing may have delivered peace of mind.[17] Other informers wished to do something exciting. Some—such as Goldfus—saw themselves as adventurous spies.[18]

Tedium, ennui, and disillusionment also can be gleaned from the archived files, along with collaboration fatigue on the part of informers. Many informers abandon informing based on their own volition. They tune out and somewhat freely exit the informing role. For example, in the case of agent Inženýr, in 1976 her StB officer complained about her mediocre results: two years later her file states that 'lately she was indifferent and uninterested in meetings with the StB'.[19] Beginning in 1979, Inženýr seemed to avoid the StB altogether, claiming to be 'really busy' or feeling unwell. Some informers who became disinterested or bored or conflicted managed to drift away, either momentarily or for good. They weaned themselves off informing. On the one hand, the StB forced some citizens to collaborate. Yet, on the other hand, the StB seemed to flail when (some) informers hedged or retreated. Other informers were rather duplicitous and handled their StB officers deftly while integrating their own moral compass into the relational contract of their informing.

The StB officer, too, may 'catch the feels', so to speak. This kind of caring, for example in the interactions that emerge between officers and some informers, can manifest in the StB officers' guiding the informers, nudging them away from 'parasitic' lifestyles, and offering informers professional, matrimonial, and familial advice.[20] In these instances, there is more going on than just hunting and gathering

[17] Or not. On this contrarian note, one example is Vladimír Boudník, a Czech factory-worker artist and correspondent with celebrated Czech author Bohumil Hrabal. In *The Tender Barbarian*, Hrabal compiles and delivers a touching portrait of the stormy and intense friendship he and Vladimír shared. Bohumil Hrabal, *The Tender Barbarian* (Twisted Spoon Press 2019) 144 (the remainder of the quotations in this footnote derive from this source). We learn from Vladimír's 1963 letter to Hrabal that Vladimír suffers a great deal emotionally because his artistic 'endeavors were misrepresented [by the StB] to outrageously malign him'. The StB leaned on Vladimír to become an informer. Vladimír however remained resolute. He never wavered from his path as an artist. For Vladimír, this path 'is infinitely more gratifying than any peace of mind snitching might offer'. Vladimír does not become an informer. He writes that cooperating with the StB would 'at most' be 'an official form of satisfaction with fleeting psychological impact on my life'. In the end, however, Vladimír commits suicide.

[18] cf Miller, *The Stasi Files Unveiled* (n 14) 46 (concluding that while '[m]uch of the daily life of an informer was undoubtedly staggeringly banal, and the majority of informers were themselves the complete opposite of James Bond, ... this is not to say that the thrill of feeling just a little bit like an exotic spy was not sometimes influential in a candidate's decision to agree to work for the Stasi').

[19] File No TS-710172 MV, registration No 909 (Inženýr) (the rest is illegible). Inženýr is not included among our twenty-three summarized informers.

[20] Miller, *The Stasi Files Unveiled* (n 14) 60 (noting that the Stasi was focused on 'the well-being' of its unofficial employees and pursued a 'genuine human bond').

information. However controlling and self-serving these 'carings' on the part of the officer may be to avoid de-conspiration and trouble, our impression from the files is that they evince streaks of congeniality. An informal conversation we had with the Director of the ABS highlighted how close relationships between informers and their StB officers at times extended well into post-Communist days.[21]

In sum, based on our research, we deconstruct acts of informing to secret police within Communist Czechoslovakia as laced with threads of conversation, expiation, interlocution, coercion, loyalty, social navigation, a search for stability and security, and opportunism. Barbara Miller's observation from the context of East Germany—namely, that 'many informers were recruited because it proved relatively easy to do so'[22]—resonates in Communist Czechoslovakia; so, too, does Miller's finding that '[i]n some cases, the relationship between the informer and the officer went beyond that of colleagues and was perceived, at least on the part of the informer, as a friendship'.[23]

Informing was normalized by the operational politics of Communist Czechoslovakia. People lived in a fishbowl. Family disputes became primed for public fodder.[24] The politics of the state festered these spaces of distrust to corrode personal bonds so as to fritter away the private and in turn centralize the state. Lying, dissembling, and pretending became omnipresent.[25]

We nevertheless believe that to reduce informing to a purely political act under the behest of the state is excessively parsimonious. We glean from the archived files that something livelier and humanistic is going on, to wit, a form of *intimacy*. Intimacies can be governmentally curated, and even created, without losing their idiosyncratic elements and dispositional hues. Indeed, the StB files reveal a place in which public life and private space blur, along with the personal and the political.[26]

[21] Informal conversation with the ABS Director, Prague, Czech Republic, 9 May 2022.

[22] Miller, *The Stasi Files Unveiled* (n 14) 95, 100 (remarking also that '[t]he Stasi seems to have experienced little difficulty finding willing sources').

[23] ibid 61 (in addition citing a study that says that 'ten out of twenty-one unofficial employees compared their Stasi officer to a friend or even best friend'). See also ibid 62 (noting that some women informers reported being physically attracted to their Stasi officers and as working much better with them than with individuals for whom this was not the case).

[24] See eg Carmen Bugan, *Burying the Typewriter: A Memoir* (Graywolf Press 2012) 129 ('Since I was twelve my life has been lived in public, scrutinized, reviewed, pondered, and recorded over and over again.'). See also Anna Burns, *Milkman* (Graywolf Press 2018) 25 (depicting a place like Belfast at the height of the Northern Ireland Troubles and wryly commenting that 'you created a political statement everywhere you went, and with everything you did, even if you didn't want to').

[25] Roman David, *Communists and Their Victims: The Quest for Justice in the Czech Republic* (University of Pennsylvania Press 2018) 43–45 (citing Milan Šimečka, *Obnovení pořádku* (Edice Rozmluvy 1984) and Václav Havel, 'The Power of the Powerless' in Jan Vladislav (ed), Paul Wilson tr, *Living in Truth* (Faber and Faber 1986)).

[26] For comparable discussion in the Hungarian context, see Sándor Horváth, 'Life of an Agent: Re-energizing Stalinism and Learning the Language of Collaboration after 1956 in Hungary' (2015) 4 Hungarian Hist Rev 56, 69 (noting that informers 'sought solutions to the problems of their private lives by presenting them as if they were communal issues' and 'attempted to veil their personal interests by overemphasizing their sense of responsibility to the community').

What do we mean by intimacy? We mean a closeness, a sharing (at times in secret), a bond of sorts, and a relational connection. Claire Forstie posits intimacy as a contrast to, and a 'warm retreat from', the 'affective coldness' that she ascribes to 'modern capitalist economies'.[27] We think, notwithstanding Forstie's placement of her understanding of intimacy within the neo-liberal context, that 'retreat[s]' can also arise in the context of the erstwhile Communist economies. We sense that informer–StB relationships were not characterized by emptiness but, rather, by an intensity. These relationships were charged, personal, and intertwined. Informers had 'their' StB officer and the StB officers had 'their' informers. Higher-ups in the StB in fact fretted about too much—or too little— amiability within informer-secret police interactions.[28]

Forstie places intimacy on a spectrum ranging from strong to weak. Mostly, her work focuses on friendships, same-sex relationships, and polyamorous arrangements that are often rendered invisible or marginalized by society. Forstie is piqued by love, commitment, and passion. Assuredly, there is scant evidence in the files of informer–StB police relationships that were of a sexualized, amorous, or passionate nature, but we find plenty of indications of amity and connection. At times, these indications are overt—for example, reports in the files of StB officers sending gifts for the informer's children and visiting for family events such as birthdays.[29] Mostly, though, these intimacies are discrete. In a sense, these intimacies are amplified because of the mutuality of secrecy[30] and the free-fall that could ensue if this secrecy were shattered. We found that among the greatest of informer concerns was that being outed or exposed. A peculiar medley of trust and deception arises.[31] Hence, Forstie's heuristic of intimacy, which rests on invisible and marginalized

[27] Claire Forstie, 'A New Framing for an Old Sociology of Intimacy' (2017) 11(4) Sociology Compass e 12467.

[28] See eg File No 599667 (previously 787243), registration No 16701 (Kongres). Kongres' 'cooperation renewal pledge' was to be signed on the day of his son's first birthday. Kongres invited his StB officer to a party to celebrate both occasions. Kongres had a good rapport with his StB officer. This connection, however, led to disenchantment within the StB. Initially Kongres' cooperation renewal meeting was supposed to take place at a different location, but upon Kongres' insistence his StB officer agreed to meet him at a restaurant where the son's birthday was celebrated. Top brass at the StB were displeased with this switch. A handwritten admonition appended to one of the reports chastised the officer, stating: 'Make sure that similar cases will never repeat.'

[29] ibid.

[30] Alison Lewis, discussing East Germany, dedicates considerable attention to 'secrecy' as a value and a challenge in relationships between the Stasi and their informers. Lewis observes: '[S]ecrets acquire their special value because others are excluded from their possession' and therefore 'bind those initiated into them in inexplicable ways'. Alison Lewis, *A State of Secrecy, Stasi Informers and the Culture of Surveillance* (Potomac Books 2021) xxiv (quoting Georg Simmel who studied sociological aspects of secrecy and secret societies in the early 1900s). Lewis discusses the 'thrill of secrecy' as one of the motivations of some Stasi informers. ibid xix.

[31] Steve Hewitt, *Snitch! A History of the Modern Intelligence Informer* (The Continuum International Publishing Group 2010) 35 ('Because of the regular meetings and the all-prevailing secrecy surrounding their assignation, close relationships, not dissimilar to an illicit affair, frequently develop between handlers and informers … [i]ronically, trust is all-important in a relationship built on betrayal.').

interactional encounters, seems to illuminate some aspects of the social dynamics of informer–secret police connections in Communist Czechoslovakia.

A potent instrumental angle assuredly arises as well. The StB may have legitimated its own bureaucratic existence by collecting and assembling large amounts of data even if these data were at best marginally relevant to any actual threat to the state (ie a tangible lead on political dissent, sabotage, or unrest). That said, the ceaseless vacuuming of even scurrilous tangents could bolster 'national security' since each tidbit of information provided leverage, or a foothold, to comb extensively for other tidbits and, ultimately, compromise an individual.[32] Alternately, and collaterally, StB officers may have relished the ongoing stream of informational minutiae because it meant that they could keep on comfortably working as civil servants.[33] StB officers may have created and woven intimacies so as to serve ulterior purposes, including placating their own bosses as to their work expectations and satisfying designated quotas. Exploiting embarrassing imbroglios drew more and more informers into the overall matrix. Informed-upons became informers. The web thickened. The perceived prevalence of informers throughout society stoked an aggregate climate of fear and suspicion. We clearly see this in certain informers—such as Volný—who believed the StB omnipotently 'knew it all'.[34]

In the end, then, what emerges is a culture of collaboration as commiseration (expiation and building affective bonds) and compensation (to ensure ongoing work as a police officer, promotions, status). Informing becomes an industry with its own political economy. The state and the Party plant deep social roots and paternalistic connections.

[32] In *The Tender Barbarian*, Hrabal recounts one day when Vladimír fell under StB suspicion. Hrabal, *The Tender Barbarian* (n 17) 31. This happens when Vladimír paints a 'bend in the river' and an old retiree sets the police on them because the retiree thought the bend in the river was a 'vitally important area for national security', and even though the artists 'showed them [ie the StB] that [the artists] were only interested in the trees, they hauled us in'. ibid.

[33] On this note, it may be that StB officers became overtaxed, or frustrated, when tasked with obtaining information about well-known dissidents in that pressure mounted and the stakes rose. See eg in the case of Romania, Bugan, *Burying the Typewriter* (n 24) involving a daughter's memoirs about growing up in a household where the Romanian Securitate invasively spied upon the family and neighbours because her father was an outspoken public dissident. Bugan reports that the local police and Securitate were angry with Ion (her dissident father) because he made their own lives difficult. In other words, Ion's intentional acts compelled them to have to spy on him and stay up all night harassing the family. Ion's prominence brought the scrutiny of the Securitate higher-ups into play. This exhausted the local police. A local village policeman, who both helps and hurts the family, bitterly complains to Ion:

> You must understand, I have also got a family and before you threw yourself into this shit I was having a peaceful life in this village, with food on the table and no one coming to inspect me. Now they torture me because you escaped my attention and did your unthinkable act in Bucuresti [ie his public political protest]. They practically live in my house, breathing down my neck. Everyone got in trouble and hates you, from the town Securitate boss to the district boss. I am not sure when this will end, but you surely destroyed my life too. ibid 159.

[34] See also File No 710067, registration No 19327 (Zuzana).

The archived StB files we reviewed present a portrayal of life in Communist Czechoslovakia in which nearly everyone is having an affair,[35] is stealing from the workplace, has alcohol or drug dependencies, and is otherwise in routine default and delict. These vignettes contrast with portrayals of life in Communist Czechoslovakia as refracted through *ex post* oral histories (among ordinary citizens, not informers) which elevate family life as sacrosanct and make no mention of affairs or endemic substance abuse,[36] but indeed emphasize that everyone to some degree was swindling the state.[37] Certain oral histories depict a more pleasant recollection of life during the Communist years, specifically, a more colourful imagery than the troubled, turbulent, truculent, and downcast imagery contained in the StB files. Another contrast between oral histories and StB file-stories is that in these oral histories narrators present the workplace, school, family, and circles of friends as safe refuges and generally as fun environments.[38] They do not present these venues as intractably poisoned with resentment, mistrust, infidelity, and backstabbing—this latter imagery, however, suffuses the StB file-stories. While the informers in the StB files overlap with the characters in oral histories when it comes to grifting stuff from the state for personal or private use, informers seem to diverge when it comes to the conduct of their conjugal relationships, their mental health, their overall levels of contentment, and their lifestyles.

What to make of this contrast? It may be that the oral historians did not steer the conversations in these directions nor ask such questions. Or that, if asked, oral history interlocutors simply did not respond. Or that these interlocutors told the oral historians what they thought the oral historians would like to hear and informers told the StB officers things that they themselves would find affirming. The StB files record and reveal a contemporaneous assessment, delivered in the authorial voice of the StB officer, whereas the oral histories—compiled many years

[35] Celebrated Czech author Ivan Klíma notes the same in his novel *No Saints or Angels*. Ivan Klíma, *No Saints or Angels*, Gerald Turner tr, Grove Press 2001. Klíma situated this novel in post-Communist Prague. Jan, one of the central characters, works to uncover StB collaboration. In his review of the StB files, Jan wryly observes: 'As I go through the old reports of secret police agents I'm amazed how much of them is taken up by accounts of infidelities and deceptions. It's as if they were all being unfaithful to each other.' ibid 35.

[36] Vaněk and Mücke, *Velvet Revolutions* (n 4) 57. This book compiles 'about 300' oral histories—open-ended interviews—of people who lived through Communist Czechoslovakia and, when interviewed, were older adults in the post-Communist Czech Republic. ibid 7. The family is presented as a bulwark against public life, a refuge, a place of love; no mention is made of family members resenting, undercutting, snitching, undermining, or being mean to each other. ibid 57.

[37] The oral histories recount low levels of theft from the public space, corruption, bribery, wheeling and dealing, and conversion as normal parts of life and not perceived as morally problematic. ibid 64 ('A man who isn't stealing from the state is stealing from his family.').

[38] Vaněk and Mücke's oral history narratives draw a stark line between morals in the private space of the family on the one hand, and morals in the public space on the other, in which hypocrisy is the norm. This seems to contradict the StB files, in which the family is revealed as contaminated by public life (specifically the tentacles of information gathering and reporting) and by private machinations. The oral histories present Communist-era workplaces as relatively convivial bases of friendship and solidarity. ibid 133–34.

after 1989—might be doused with nostalgia about the past. Another potential factor accounting for this contrast could be that the StB's focus was not on happy recollections but rather on extant or imaginary enemies, diversion, and antisocial behaviour. The contrast between the tenor of the oral histories and the histories encapsulated in the StB files suggests the very real possibility that the group of people who became informers differs in terms of lifestyles and happiness. This group may simply be more marginal and untethered. Moreover, the precarious positionality of informers continues following regime change.

III. Emotions as Catalysts and Drivers

How to conceptualize informer–StB interactions? How to grasp their hydraulics? We posit that an under-discussed analytic lens with considerable explanatory value is to construct the act of informing as motivated not only by cognitive rationalities but also as deeply nestled in the (e)motions.[39]

We identify four emotions that redound in our reading of the files. These are devotion (to the Communist ideology or the Czechoslovak state), desire (getting things), resentment (*ressentiment*, in the French sense, namely getting even), and fear. We contend that parsing these four emotions helps unspool the dynamics of informing.

In all the files we reviewed, informers demonstrated mixed motivations—thereby congregating in a place that lurks in between devotion and ambition, that straddles political good and private personal gain, and that inhabits a liminal zone between fear and intrepidness.[40] Making use of the StB as an institution through which to 'get even' in light of perceived slights and wrongdoings also appears as a recurrent driver.

We do not present these emotions as mutually exclusive. They often overlap and jumble. This quickly becomes apparent when reading the files. Within the same informer different motivations may pop up simultaneously or emerge to varying degrees over decades of informing. Some emotions may be more influential some of the time and others more influential at other times. We are not interested in coding these emotions, nor in putting informers in boxes or tabulating them as preponderant adherents to one sentimental driver or another; nor in calculating aggregate percentages. These emotions, moreover, may entwine.

[39] For introductory discussion of behaviour and emotions, see Chapter 1, Section IV, '(E)motions and Human Behaviour'.

[40] Discussing informing in East Germany, Espíndola Mata notes that 'distinguishing between convinced socialists and reward-seeking opportunists might prove difficult, as one can do things out of conviction but also expect to be compensated for a job well done'. Juan Espíndola Mata, *Transitional Justice After German Reunification* (CUP 2015) 48.

And, to be sure, these four emotions are not exhaustive. In our research, we came across other emotions and drivers: *coping*, namely getting by; *obedience*, to wit, following the expectations of the system as a good person or as a passive person, which in the latter case is how Volný's informing seems to have initially catalysed; or *gratitude*, which arose in Soukup's case, in that he was thankful to the StB that they kept him out of trouble and also in the case of candidate for secret cooperation Reza, an Iranian exchange student, who returned to Iran after completing his education and training.[41] While attending university in Czechoslovakia, Reza informed out of a sense of thankfulness for having been afforded an opportunity to study and complete an apprenticeship. Our impressions, however, are that this set of motivators is not as pervasive as the four we have primarily identified.

A. Fear

Life in Communist Czechoslovakia unfolded under the constant shadow of fear and coercion. On a systemic note, the amplitude and intensity of top-down constraint oscillated through time. It was far greater in the 1950s than in the 1980s, to be sure, with the 1968 crushing of the Prague Spring constituting a major intensification point before things stagnated following normalization in the 1970s. The embedded brutality of political repression in the 1950s was pervasive. During this phase of Communist governance, as some of the files reveal, long-term imprisonment, cruel torture, extensive interrogations, and slave labour abounded. Informing in those times must be placed within this baleful context. In this space, then, the differences between 'informing on someone' and 'being interrogated about someone' tended to meld.[42]

One tragic example of the harshness of life in 1950s Czechoslovakia is Lily, who seemed to respond to political pressures with a sort of defiance which, while courageous, also triggered the deterioration of her situation and her repeated ensnarement in the StB's tentacles. That said, even in Lily's case, her interventions against the StB to other authorities were such that she was able to obtain her elusive residence permit. Other informers—such as Věra—were sedulous, including from within prison. Věra began as a wayward youth who challenged social conventions. She turned to informing as a practice to stabilize her life and, as she aged, she became financially secure, in part through informing, and—in contradistinction to other informers—she seemed to grow old comfortably.

[41] Candidate for secret cooperation File No 801964, registration No 33015 (Reza). Reza informed on Afghans and Iraqis studying in Czechoslovakia.

[42] See also Bugan, *Burying the Typewriter* (n 24) 143. That said, Bugan also observes that many ordinary citizens also found ways to refuse to inform, to avoid saying anything, and even to mock and disparage the police officers.

Informing as a social practice persisted during normalization and remained pervasive throughout the 1970s and 1980s notwithstanding the blunting of statal repression.[43] Still, even in this seemingly more benign space, as Ivan Klíma—speaking through the voice of fictional collaboration uncoverer Jan—observes in his novel *No Saints or Angels*:

> Only here did I come to realize the logic of the regime I was born into. Very soon only a few people were subjected to real violence, just enough to ensure that everyone else lived in fear and submitted to control and humiliation as the only possible form of existence.[44]

Overall, our reading of the archived files suggests that, although fear was omniscient given the authoritarian and arbitrary character of the Communist regime, limits arose as to the extent to which informers predominantly were motivated by fear. The StB ginned up fear by threatening to reveal things (such as an affair,[45] petty crime, public drunkenness, professional incompetence, and minor under-the-table financial indiscretions), by threatening to initiate criminal charges (such as failure to report a crime,[46] parasitism,[47] breach of public order,[48] or speculation[49]),

[43] Spurný, Jareš, and Volná, 'Intellectuals between Collaboration and Independence in Late Socialism' (n 9) 171. ('The Normalization regime ... in Czechoslovakia ... led to a comparatively long period of stability ... [t]his stability must have had other foundations than merely fear.').

[44] Klíma, *No Saints or Angels* (n 35) 35. Jan's father suffered greatly in prison. He was beaten and tortured. The memory of his father seems to fuel Jan's desire to work to expose former Communist collaborators in post-Communist Czech Republic.

[45] Threatening such revelations was a broader practice of security police throughout Communist Europe at the time, not to mention also on a far more general note. See eg Dan McLaughlin, 'One in 10 Polish clerics spied for dreaded secret police' *The Irish Times* (Dublin, 6 April 2006) (reporting that if the Polish secret police discovered that a priest was having an affair (or was gay) then the police would blackmail that priest into giving information); Ron Dudai, 'Informers and the Transition in Northern Ireland' (2012) 52 Brit J Criminol 32, 40 (noting 'the practice of recruiting informers from among criminals or using blackmail based on marital infidelity or other behaviours considered deviant').

[46] According to § 165 of the Czechoslovak Criminal Code 86/1950, failing to report certain specified crimes, such as high treason (§ 78), association against the republic (§§ 79, 80), sabotage (§§ 84, 85), espionage (§§ 86, 87), and endangering of a state secret (§ 88) was criminalized. This provision applied to cases where an individual 'deliberately fail[ed] to report such an act to the prosecutor or national security authority without delay'. A failure to report was punishable by imprisonment for one to five years. Even though the substantive crimes enumerated in the provision were quite specific and textually implicated only grave offences, they were still open to interpretation and could be expansively construed. Rudolf Glogar (ed), *Trestní zákon: Komentář (1. vyd.)* (Orbis 1958) 281. According to another commentary: 'In other cases ... non-reporting is not punishable in criminal proceedings ... but it is clear from the letter of the law that non-reporting other crimes would be a violation of civil discipline.' František Rokůsek, *Nový trestní řád* (Právník 1950) 328. For further discussion of Czechoslovak laws regarding duties to report crimes, see Chapter 2, Section II, 'The StB: Its Structure, Standard Operating Procedures, and Connections to National Security'.

[47] This Criminal Code offence was deployed to prosecute jobless individuals or individuals without proper employment.

[48] On the abuse of public order 'creating a scandal' provisions, specifically § 202 of the 1961 Czechoslovak Criminal Code, see Václav Havel, 'Kicking the Door' *New York Review of Books* (22 March 1979).

[49] See eg 1961 Czechoslovak Criminal Code, § 117. This provision proscribed 'acquiring or retaining items of necessity in greater quantities or an item of greater value with the intent to sell or exchange

and by insisting upon denunciation as civic duty. It is not known exactly how often the StB followed through on any initial threats to prosecute individuals for violations of these criminal offenses.[50] In any event, one common thread we observed was that while fear often constituted the ignition that the StB leveraged to jump start the informing relationship, as time passed fear often idled and the informer began to exhibit a greater affirmation of other motivational sentiments.

Confidant/agent Zuzana is an example.[51] The StB gravitated to Zuzana in 1975 because of her language skills (German, English, French, Russian) and her professional contacts (she was an engineer) with foreigners which at times also drifted into personal spaces. Described in the file as 'an intelligent woman, who c[ould] evaluate a situation and make appropriate decisions', Zuzana had allegedly collected favours and bribes from partner companies in exchange for granting them better business conditions. To be clear, this was officially viewed as illicit conduct. Zuzana also socialized with foreigners without alerting relevant authorities or her employers. Zuzana's file is replete with her voluminous recounting of the most intimate details of her private life: her many extramarital affairs, her romantic liaisons with foreign men, and her challenges in breaking off one relationship with a married man in particular (on this latter note, she even turned to the StB for advice about how tactically to proceed with this man, to which the StB officer responded in a supportively avuncular fashion).

Zuzana's file also demonstrates the subjectivity of fear. Zuzana divulged so many details of her private life because she thought that the StB 'knew it all' anyway.[52] Yet, the StB did not 'know it all'. Far from it.[53] Indeed, Zuzana consistently

them for profit or to gain another advantage'. Threats to charge Soukup with speculation served as a basis for the StB to dig their tenterhooks into him.

[50] Threatened informers and possible informed-upons could also privately negotiate the terms of the informing in an *ex parte* fashion. Timothy Garton Ash reports an example of such an ad hoc arrangement in East Germany. An East German citizen was busted by the Stasi for having an affair. As a result, he entered the Stasi network. The Stasi sought information on Jens Reich, a renowned East German scientist and civil rights activist. So the busted informer approached Jens and proposed that he inform upon Jens (to spare his affair getting revealed), but made a side deal with Jens as to exactly what he would tell the Stasi about Jens so that no-one would be harmed. These kinds of arrangements—poignant examples of candour and trust—negotiated within the bowels of a surveillance state further attest to the agentic discretion of informers and their targets. Podcast *Cold War Conversations*, Episode 158, 'Witness to the Eastern Bloc Revolutions of the 1980s with Timothy Garton Ash', <https://coldwarconversations.com/episode158> accessed 8 July 2023.

[51] Zuzana (n 34).

[52] Miller reports similar perceptual dynamics in East Germany. She observes that 'in the minds of the East Germans, the Stasi functioned as though it were physically omnipresent'. Miller, *The Stasi Files Unveiled* (n 14) 3. Miller also observes that informers for the erstwhile regime may tend to overstate the power of that regime once they are caught in transitional spaces. According to Miller: 'The mightier the Stasi is seen to be, the more informers are justified in claiming that attempts to resist recruitment or to end the contact would have been futile. By exaggerating the Stasi's omnipotence, informers aim to impose an element of inevitability on their actions.' ibid 118.

[53] See also generally Spurný, Jareš, and Volná, 'Intellectuals between Collaboration and Independence in Late Socialism' (n 9) 186 ('The StB's awareness of certain people and certain relations … was profound when it came to some problems and some people, but the StB was definitely not omniscient.').

overestimated the StB's reach. Zuzana in fact volunteered informational details about herself of which the StB was unaware. She did so because she felt if the StB already knew the information then she was better off volunteering it since that way the StB might come to trust her more. The StB did not correct her mistaken belief. Indeed, the StB officer wrote in the report from their first interview that 'I [he] did not refute her idea of our absolute awareness' and stated, 'she will find out over time that even if she conveys information known [to the StB] she will not be notified of what we know'. From the perspective of this StB officer, Zuzana's major asset was that she 'conveyed information on her own initiative'.

While at the start Zuzana feared repercussions from her transgressions and interacted with the StB quite intensely, over time she nonetheless detached from the StB. In the end, Zuzana offered virtually no useful information over the course of her stint as an informer—which lasted until 1986 when the StB terminated contact with her—other than some scattered tidbits from her workplace (alleged cases of improper special treatment given to foreign companies by her colleagues). Her diaristic file intimates that she juggled many balls, including multiple (overlapping) relationships, productive work demands, and taking care of her daughter.

Zuzana also seemed to juggle adroitly in her relationship with the StB. Whenever she encountered the StB, her *modus operandi* was to 'volunteer' a piece of information about herself that she selected. Her strategy was to share kibbles about herself to placate the authorities while not really harming anyone else. Zuzana barely reported anything on anyone else. She disclosed her own (mis-)doings and her affairs (judging from the documents accessible in her file). Paradoxically, throughout her decade of informing, Zuzana persisted in a lifestyle (meeting foreigners privately, accepting gifts) that was considered unacceptable. She even de-conspired herself (and other StB informers) publicly. The StB gave up on her after several attempts to redirect her. Yet she seemed not to have faced any recrimination.

The StB also exploited individuals who intrinsically had fearful or passive personalities. Such was the case with Volný, who in his StB file is described as a reclusive, introverted person with only a handful of friends. He 'appeared as fearful and very frightened', and equally as 'undecisive' such that 'everyone g[ot] from him whatever they ask[ed] for'. Volný was easily swayed by others. According to the StB, Volný found it difficult to say no. The StB moulded him into collaboration by manipulating his fears and his submissive nature. In addition, the StB also had compromising information on Volný that related to one inculpating thing he had said to a planted informer (which involved Volný's running afoul of the duty to report), as well as evidence that, in his work, Volný committed 'fraudulent machinations with expensive medications' by prescribing imported drugs to his colleagues without conducting any examination. That said, in a pattern characteristic of many informers we have encountered, as time passed Volný became a more proactive informer who demonstrated considerable initiative in his final phase of cooperation.

Young people may have been pushed into informing because of the conduct of their parents; for example, that the parents were *bourgeois*, landowners, politically problematic, *kulaks*, or circulated among the rich people. Agent Eva,[54] for instance, had two big strikes against her which the StB exploited. First, that she was born into a well-off Catholic family (the Communists had expropriated their property). Second, Eva's father had routine affairs and himself was accused of collaborating with the Nazis. Assumed or proven collaboration with the Nazis was often leveraged to cajole people to collaborate with the StB (as was the case with Goldfus). Eva was branded 'a traitor's daughter'. Born in 1936, growing up comfortably in troubled times, hers became a riches-to-rags story following the Communist takeover of 1948.[55] Eva spent years endeavouring to recover from her tainted background. Czechoslovaks who were intergenerationally compromised and intrafamilially tainted, so to speak, could turn to the StB as a remedial mechanism. Eva's father's past seemed to have been Eva's curse, in particular at the beginning of her adult life and the start of her collaboration. Eva eventually informed on her very own father and in return gained personal benefits from the StB.

B. Devotion and Allegiance

Devotion and allegiance—loyalty, to invoke a related term—are multifaceted. Citizens in repressive regimes may endeavour to balance loyalties to their families, friends, and colleagues.[56] In this discussion we, however, mean *ideological devotion*, that is, evidence from the files that the information supplied and the impetus behind supplying it rooted in the virtue of supporting Marxist-Leninist ideology or, collaterally, *patriotic devotion* to Czechoslovakia as a state. Assuredly, allegiance to the state or to official ideology could conflict with other loyalties, such as bonds with friends and family. The files indeed reveal informers who were glad to inform on certain categories of individuals but very explicitly told the StB officers that they were unwilling to inform on others, thereby couching the ongoing nature of informing in a categorically contingent way. For instance, confidant Hájek notified his StB officer he never would say anything about his closest friends. The StB officer accepted this conditionality such that Hájek's informing continued with

[54] File No 622129, registration No 36431 (Eva).

[55] Eva's youth, however, did not actually seem to be blessed. She had a turbulent adolescence. She had close contacts with the Junák movement (the equivalent of a Czechoslovak Scouts organization, which the StB viewed with suspicion). Eva's file states that she was a victim of sexual abuse on the part of a Junák leader.

[56] Spurný, Jareš, and Volná, 'Intellectuals between Collaboration and Independence in Late Socialism' (n 9) 173 ('[P]eople were faced every day with decisions and were involved in serious struggles among themselves and within themselves, mainly among the various layers of often-contradictory forms of loyalty, including loyalty to the party, loyalty to the institution of the university, loyalty to one's profession, loyalty to what one considered one's mission, and loyalty to one's colleagues.').

this caveat.[57] Hájek remained resolute and transparent with his StB officer that he would not reveal anything at all about his closest friends. Over time, Hájek became increasingly reticent to inform even upon his colleagues, and other Czechoslovak citizens, and restricted his willingness to convey information only to foreigners. The file intimates that Hájek's StB officer sequentially accepted all of these restrictions in order to retain Hájek as an informer.

As noted earlier, nearly all the pledges—the start of the relational contract—between the StB and the informer identify patriotism or ideological support of the state as the driver for collaboration. That said, upon closer reading, this seems rather hollow, rote, and performative. The essentialized boilerplate references to patriotism and socialist devotion in the 'pledge' trigger intriguing questions about declarativeness and about the pledge 'ceremony' as ritual. In the 1950s, more Czechoslovaks may have been ideologically committed to the Communist cause than in the 1980s. Nevertheless, our survey of the files revealed no informer who consistently seemed motivated by commitment to Marxist-Leninism or some patriotic duty or allegiance to Communist Czechoslovakia as indicated by the content of anything they actually shared with the StB officer or as discernible from the records or dialogue with the StB. *Prima facie* the informer who comes closest is Vašek, who appears to be a committed Communist, rising through the ranks from a sailor to an economist to a bureaucrat and then a diplomat. Despite his clean record, cordial relationship with the StB, prosperity, and high social credit, Vašek nonetheless was perennially surveilled by the StB through his lengthy informing stint.

We have encountered individuals in the files whose informing seems to be motivated by commitment to a cause and devotion to political values of some sort. These values, however, are not necessarily rooted in Marxism-Leninism or in the promulgation of Communism. One telling example is Barium, a chemist employed at a state organ that controlled toxic waste emissions.[58] Barium was praised for his adherence to Marxist-Leninist principles following Operation Danube. He lectured on Marxism. That said, Barium also was a scientist devoted to the cause of environmental protection.[59] He focused on hazardous waste management. Barium was preoccupied with technical violations of safety rules and negligent conduct that he felt triggered toxic waste leaks. Many of Barium's meetings with StB officers involved his making long-winded and tendentious presentations

[57] File No 643796, registration No 1233 (Hájek). Hájek did inform on Junák members.

[58] File No 790247, registration No 20480 (Barium).

[59] The state of the natural environment was a constant concern—and legitimacy threat—to the Communist regime, notably in its later years. Oral historian Miroslav Vaněk discusses certain parts of the environmental reality in Communist Czechoslovakia, which he describes as '[a] lunar landscape, chimneys belching smoke, falling ash, the stench of burning coal, the land shrouded in mist and low-lying cloud, the sun visible for at most sixty days a year'. Miroslav Vaněk, 'Twenty Years in Shades of Grey? Everyday Life During Normalisation Based on Oral History Research' in McDermott and Stibbe (eds), *Czechoslovakia and Eastern Europe in the Era of Normalisation* (n 11) 161 (remarking also that '[i]t was estimated that around 28 per cent of the population (around four million people) lived in districts where the atmosphere was polluted').

about waste management. StB officers dutifully jotted all this down. Moreover, Barium authored detailed scientific reports which he shared with the StB. Barium fretted that the state agency for which he was working was not adhering to the best environmental practices nor insisting on their operationalization elsewhere. These concerns, as opposed to non-conformities with Communist dogma, filled Barium's file. Barium informed on his superiors and co-workers on this one narrow theme. With one exception—an engineer with whom he appeared to have a personal grudge—Barium did not inform on his colleagues' political opinions or private lives. Yet even in the case of this one exception, Barium directed the bulk of his reporting to this engineer's 'not know[ing]/understand[ing] his job', failure to distribute funding properly, and otherwise inserting scientific gaffes into research proposals.

Some informers may indeed reflect their pledge and commence patriotically in the classic sense of allegiance to state and Party, but this does not seem to last. Agent Velíšek, a veterinarian who was initially committed to upholding socialist ideology, also cared deeply about the wellbeing of animals and, in a journey that marked the path a number of informers, became increasingly and openly embittered towards the Communist state and its authorities as he aged.[60] Velíšek's fourteen-year-long collaboration (which began in 1957) illustrates how he underwent a journey from being a friend of the Communist regime, which in his own words 'suited' him, to a person who became increasingly contemptuous with and sceptical of the socialist establishment. Velíšek seemed, furthermore, to grow more disillusioned with his own (financial) situation. Due to relatively high alimony payments to his ex-wife and the accumulation of other debts, Velíšek was perennially under financial strain.[61] Allegedly Velíšek started to borrow money from his subordinates at work. As a result, his good reputation became tarnished. In 1967, according to another informer (Velíšek's co-worker), Velíšek reportedly tried to sell privately (ie illegally) some products (fodder) from the animal hospital for which he worked. The StB officers were aware that Velíšek was doing this under extenuating financial pressure and decided to prevent him from making the deal. Velíšek also travelled to the West. During his trips abroad Velíšek witnessed differences in comparative living standards and became critical of the situation in Czechoslovakia. In 1968 he reportedly criticized the regime and openly advocated for establishing political

[60] File No 645347, registration No 3536 (Velíšek). Velíšek's StB file repeatedly mentions his stuttering as a slight impediment to his currency as an informer.

[61] The file contains a balance sheet of Velíšek's incomes and debts. The StB seemed to be keenly interested in these figures. According to the StB, Velíšek had debts of Kčs 45,000 for a car, which he paid off monthly at a rate of 700 Kčs; he also had monthly alimony to his first wife in the amount of 650 Kčs. These expenses were tacked onto to his normal living expenses such as rent and groceries. Velíšek's monthly income was 2,600 Kčs. Interestingly, Velíšek only obtained scant financial rewards from the StB. According to one of the reports included in his file, over the course of his entire period of cooperation Velíšek was given 2,071 Kčs (in money and gifts together). He seemed pleased to accept these emoluments.

opposition to the Communist Party. In 1970, Velíšek was expelled from the Party. In 1971, the StB decided to terminate Velíšek's collaboration due to his 'arrogant criticism towards the current politics of the Communist Party'. The StB file further notes that any meetings that transpired with Velíšek after 1968 were solely about him 'verbally attacking the armies of the Warsaw Pact'.

The StB was nonetheless quite clement with Velíšek. Despite his skipping meetings and vociferating pointed critiques of the state, Velíšek seemingly faced little recrimination or retaliation from the StB (at least according to his archived StB file). Based on Velíšek's file (and others we have analysed), it seems that treatment of informers was not even-handed. Considerable variation arose in how, for instance, the StB handled a 'defective' cooperative. Some of the differences could trace to varying protocols in force over different time-periods; some perhaps to the relevance of each particular informer to the StB; and some to the personalities of individual StB officers and the specific connection they may have had with a particular informer.

C. Desire: Getting Ahead and Getting Things

Desire regularly surfaces throughout the files, which are chock-full of acquisitiveness and ambition whether for the informer directly or on behalf of the informer's loved ones. The things that are desired are nonetheless widely disparate. Money, yes: the StB frequently offered financial awards, gifts, and compensation (often seemingly meagre, but perhaps of great actual or symbolic value to the recipient). Travel possibilities were also routinely provided, along with facilitating promotions at work. Admission to university or wishes to continue pre-existing studies seems to be another catalyst. Release from prison, as well, in a more desperate context: political prisoners—often serving gruelling sentences—were promised freedom if they signed a pledge of collaboration with the StB.

Marcel, a candidate for secret collaboration, bartered information in exchange, according to the StB, for 'securing a better situation for him personally' and also to enhance his chances to travel abroad.[62] Some collaborators were 'helped' by the StB to secure a new apartment, like agent Martin, who, along with monetary rewards for her 'good results', was assisted 'in moving to her new place of residence'.[63]

[62] File No 796432, registration No 42004 (Marcel). Marcel's file is not included among our twenty-three summarized informers.

[63] File No 796909, registration No 796909 (Martin). Martin's file is not included among our twenty-three summarized informers. Martin was a single mother of a son. Her file is full of reports about her 'intimate relationships', including with married male colleagues. The file details her own eventual marriage. The file also specifies her grooming habits and predilection for expensive jewellery. One of the first evaluations of Martin's informing from August 1974 noted that her cooperation was initially hesitant and irregular (due to her caring for her sick son), but that it improved and she eventually fulfilled the given tasks with assiduousness and followed all directions. Martin informed mainly on her colleagues. The StB repeatedly gave her financial rewards for her collaboration.

Věra was animated by material gain and travel opportunities so she could visit her daughter.

StB files reveal parents who informed on their own children for various reasons,[64] and others who collaborated in order to secure a prosperous future for their children within socialist society. Agent Inženýr complained to the StB in 1958 (after the StB had approached her) that, due to 'her class origins, it is difficult for her to find a job' and for the same reason 'her daughter has troubles to get into a high school'.[65] The StB was cognizant of her struggles and her wishes to arrange for the best possible life for herself and her children. Inženýr's collaboration ended up lasting for twenty-two years. Inženýr expressed as her only concern that no-one from her circles could ever find out that she was an informer. Hence, she refused to file any written reports. Still, Inženýr provided information on her friends, foes, and foils (including her colleagues at work). She was also occasionally given some concrete tasks in ongoing StB operations; she completed some of these but left others unfulfilled. The StB chided her for her lingering 'bourgeois outlook' which the StB noted with concern.[66] In the late 1950s the StB assisted Inženýr in finding a job as a translator and her son was admitted to university. Whether the StB actually played any role in getting the son with 'an unsuitable cadre profile' into university is not discernible from the file. That said, in 1969 the StB intervened on behalf of Inženýr's son in an ongoing criminal investigation for fraud in which his prosecution was halted.[67]

Many informer desires are triggered by the repressiveness of the Party and the state as channelled through the StB. By balefully threatening or controllingly rationing out benefits, the StB generated a distorted marketplace in which

[64] See eg Luděk (n 12). Luděk's long-term and staccato cooperation with the StB—both formal and informal—seemed to persist for multiple reasons. Luděk liked being an informer. He fancied some small-scale rewards. He cherished his amiable intimacies with one particular StB officer. Luděk felt an allegiance to Communist values. Luděk also ventilated personal grudges especially when it came to his family members. Indeed, Luděk did not hesitate to inform on his relatives, particularly after the family fell apart: He informed on his ex-wife, daughter, and son-in-law, all of whom had permanently moved to settle in West Germany.

[65] Inženýr (n 19). Inženýr was born in 1915 into a 'bourgeois' family of a rich architect. According to her StB file, Inženýr was habituated to 'an expensive extravagant lifestyle'. When nineteen, Inženýr married a man who was fourteen years her senior. Inženýr's husband was a real estate owner, theatre lover, and frequent traveller. Another informer described him as 'a big spender'. Their marriage, however, was described in the files as unhappily 'opportunistic, arranged for material reasons'. The couple did not really live together. Inženýr spent most of her time with her parents in a provincial town, where she socialized with 'the former elite' circles, 'the crème de la crème' of local society, or 'the former people' as they were often labelled in StB reports.

[66] This haunting—namely that the present is tinged by the past—is a recurrent thread in the informer files. It appears in the ignition of Lily's informing trajectory as a 'former rich person', with declining social status and deteriorating prospects in the new Czechoslovakia of the time.

[67] During the 1970s, Inženýr's readiness to collaborate waned. In 1976 her StB officer complained about her mediocre results. Two years later it was stated in her StB file that 'lately she was indifferent and uninterested in meetings with the StB'. In 1979, Inženýr seemed to avoid the StB altogether as 'she [was] really busy' or ill. The StB terminated her collaboration in 1980 due to the fact that she essentially stopped responding to any invitations or calls.

hardscrabble people might have informed in order to scramble together whatever gains they could.

These gains could be existential, such as getting released from a labour camp, notably in the 1950s. Gains can also relate to less drastic wants or needs. On this latter note, Jiří Imlauf (a candidate for secret collaboration codenamed 'Hráč' ('Player') who later became an agent 'Vijan')[68] presents as an example. Jiří was born in 1966. Jiří does not remember ever discussing politics with his parents. He thinks that his parents wanted to spare him from these issues: 'I was a chubby boy with glasses, who only listened to music and read. That was my world.'[69] It was only at university that Jiří recalled meeting people who openly voiced disagreement with the socialist regime. Jiří's hobby was music. He played guitar in a local band and was a big fan of The Beatles. Jiří's contact with the StB began in 1987. In December of that year, Jiří went to Prague to join in a commemoration of John Lennon's death. He and his friend witnessed how the police intervened in this putatively 'illegal gathering of subversive elements'. Jiří and his friend were scared, excited, and took a train back home. The StB approached Jiří for interrogation one month thereafter. Jiří recalls that his interrogation

> was done by a bloke in civilian clothes. I zigzagged, said that I was in Prague because I like music, not because I wanted to protest against the regime. He asked from whom I heard about the meeting and to whom I talked about it.[70]

Sometime thereafter Jiří was summoned for another interrogation. This time around it was two men, 'the so-called good cop and bad cop … [a]nd [the bad one] was tough and directly told me that it could easily happen that as of next week I will not go to university [anymore]'.[71] Jiří recounted how the StB explained that he needed to tell them any time he learned of any anti-regime action and that divulging such information represented his only chance to complete his studies. During the next meeting, Jiří was given 'a paper' to sign. He does not recall where exactly the meeting took place, but he does remember that on a table there was 'a salami, a bread roll, and a bottle of vodka … [t]hey [the StB officers] were playing it light, as if nothing was going on'.[72] And so Jiří signed the pledge to collaborate with the StB. According to Jiří's StB file, which we also read, he unequivocally agreed to collaborate and inquired only about the duration of the time the StB expected

[68] Jiří came out publicly with his story. His actual name and biographical details are featured on the website of *Paměť národa*. His story including audio and video materials (in Czech) is available on line. 'Jiří Imlauf' (*Paměť národa*) <https://www.pametnaroda.cz/cs/imlauf-jiri-1966> accessed 20 May 2023. It was also published in Adam Drda and Mikuláš Kroupa, *Normalizované životy* (Post Bellum 2017) 68-95. Jiří's StB file is archived. File No 993372 MV, registration No. 26032 (Jiří).

[69] 'Jiří Imlauf' (*Paměť národa*) (n 68).

[70] Drda and Kroupa, *Normalizované životy* (n 68) 83.

[71] ibid 84.

[72] 'Jiří Imlauf' (*Paměť národa*) (n 68).

collaboration would last. Jiří was willing to cooperate during his studies, but did not wish to continue after graduation. Jiří's task was to inform on students and people he met at cultural events and at restaurants. His StB file contains information he provided on his fellow students and teachers. Jiří was also given active tasks by the StB such as making recordings during concerts. He was rewarded financially for his 'service'. As he relays in his contribution to the *Paměť národa* project, Jiří did not enjoy his studies. In retrospect, then, he remains puzzled as to why he would have agreed to cooperate with the StB in order to finish something he did not really fancy. Jiří muses:

> It is a mix of various influences. Ranging from the fact that my parents insisted that I had to graduate to my personal characteristics and a naïve conviction that I could somehow play the system. All that combined in a perverse dependency on the idea that I had to finish my studies at any price.[73]

Jiří insists that he did not want to harm anyone, and sought to provide information he thought the StB already knew. It was only after seeing his file did he realize that perhaps that was not always the case.[74]

Other informers seem to be motivated less by avoiding the threatened withholding of benefits but, rather, by direct financial acquisition, namely getting things and getting ahead in the rigid strictures of socialist society. One example is agent Rolf, who was born in 1922 to a working-class family.[75] After the end of the Second World War, Rolf worked as a labourer in various industries and firms. He did not have any political affiliation. Over two decades passed. Then, in 1969, Rolf responded to a job advertisement posted by the West German Embassy in Prague seeking a driver for its business representation department. He got the job. This meant that he was frequently required to travel to West Germany and was routinely tasked with handling deliveries of documents from the airport to the embassy. These aspects of his new employment rendered him of interest to the StB. The StB deployed its extant informers to profile Rolf before personally approaching him.

Rolf's file contains a number of reports in which he is reprimanded for trading with West German Embassy employees, specifically unauthorizedly selling them traditional Czech crystal products and *bijouterie* for profit and also smuggling

73 Drda and Kroupa, *Normalizované životy* (n 68) 93.

74 ibid 90.

75 Rolf (n 10). See also Sony (a foreign candidate for secret collaboration), File No 566432, 772956, registration No 11220 (Sony). Sony is described in his StB file as 'an enterprising businessman who did not make differences among nations nor borders'. Based on what can be gleaned from his file, Sony agreed to inform so as to pursue business deals and routinely enter Czechoslovakia so as to undertake such deals. Sony's file evinces no devotion, no resentment, and no fear.

items to West Germany where he impermissibly maintained a bank account. The StB seems to have seized upon Rolf's 'business deals' as a portal through which to ensnare him.

Rolf nonetheless seems to have eagerly approached his cooperation. In addition to 'operational information', he provided the StB with copies of various documents, lists of all employees of the West German Embassy, and with duplicate keys for closets in its buildings. After only four months and eleven meetings, in September 1971 Rolf was swiftly promoted to the rank of agent. The StB report notes that 'since he takes initiative and has a good attitude towards members of the StB, it is not appropriate to have him sign a pledge of collaboration. Rolf received monetary rewards as an appreciation of his 'service'. Until November 1984, when his informing ended as a consequence of his retirement and poor health, Rolf procured financial rewards on at least eighteen occasions 'to promote his initiative and, at the same time, [to] acknowledge his conscientiousness in fulfilling tasks'. In addition to providing monetary rewards, the StB also expressed a willingness to assist Rolf, if needed and considered appropriate, in private life matters. Rolf took the StB up on these offers. For example, in 1972 the StB assisted him and members of his family in gaining permission to travel abroad, including a holiday trip to Yugoslavia. During one of his meetings with his StB handlers in May 1973, Rolf solicited help to obtain a permit from the Ministry of Finance to buy an old BMW sedan from one of his colleagues at the West German Embassy. In October 1973 he mentioned to the StB that his daughter had been told that, because of his position with the West German Embassy, she would not be admitted to *gymnasium* to continue her studies. Rolf's StB officer responded that 'he will do all in his power so that [the situation] is resolved positively'.

Both Věra and Soukup are informers whose cooperation with the StB appeared to be fuelled by getting things in a manner similar to Rolf. Soukup, in particular, was an active informer who seemed to disavow any commitment to political or public life. Although Soukup was not a hardened criminal nor a hurtful person, he certainly presents as a schemer with many financial machinations. He was committed to his children, but he became hooked by his illegal conduct, his business scams, his *vechsl*, and his cross-border shenanigans. The StB wanted information on foreign intelligence from Soukup, but ironically he appeared to have mostly provided information on West German intelligence that was investigating his own illegal behaviour in West Germany. Soukup ginned up a circle that kept sustaining his status as an informer. His dealings appear different than Goldfus', whose acquisitiveness seemed far more related to a pursuit of validation and ego. Soukup lived in disdain of the state whether Communist or capitalist. Soukup seemed to weather a lot of investigations and smoke swirling around him, though in the end these caught up with him. His dual lifestyle simply seemed to wear him down. By the end of his life, he just disintegrated.

D. Resentment: Getting Even and Settling Scores

The StB can serve as interlocutor or listener when people wish to get things off their chest and settle a score. The airing of personal grievances to the StB could have repercussions depending on how the StB chose to respond. We have observed throughout the files how the StB is used as a tool to manage interpersonal relationships. Many reports abound from within families, and among neighbours and friends and co-workers, complaining about things that transpire within a household or apartment building or workplace. Reporting to the StB becomes a way of expiating spite. We find this motivation—getting even—to differ from desire and ambition, namely, getting ahead. In both instances, however, the airing of these wishes to the StB, with the expectation that the StB would rectify the situation, places the StB in the role of providing social services, mediation or dispute resolution of sorts.

Resentment has a long thread in psychological and philosophical thought. Friedrich Nietzsche elaborated this emotion under the French term *ressentiment*, which he saw as a vengeful and controlling mindset, namely not wanting others to have what one has and delighting in things not working out for others. For Nietzsche, *ressentiment* also meant directing anger towards someone else as blame for one's own personal failures, all of which Nietzsche traces to the resentful individual's inability to attain their own aspirations.[76] Now, *ressentiment* may not have the same exact meaning as 'resentment' but our purpose here is not to delve into the semantics of words in two languages nor initiate a broad linguistic and psychological discussion. Accordingly, we take the term resentment to mean *ressentiment* which we also extend to score-settling.

Jiřina, for instance, was initially drawn to informing out of enmity towards tenants who lived in her home.[77] The Communist regime considered it inappropriate for individuals to have personal wealth. So, if a person owned a large house, the regime would forcibly move another family (namely tenants) into the house. Such was the case with Jiřina, who owned a villa with rooms for guests. The regime relocated a few other people—strangers—into these rooms. Understandably, Jiřina did not like this. She had frequent dustups with these tenants. Jiřina began her informing stint in the mid-1950s. Although Jiřina seemed willing to inform on anyone—and was described in her StB file as ambitious, avaricious, and eager to obtain personal gain—her file demonstrates specific patterns of informing predominantly on individuals with whom she had personal grudges or interpersonal

[76] Friedrich Nietzsche, *On the Genealogy of Morality* (authored 1887, Douglas Smith tr, OUP 1996)). See also Bernard Reginster, 'Nietzsche on Ressentiment and Valuation' (1997) 57(2) Phil and Phenomenological Research 281.

[77] File No 732583, registration No 2128 (informer)/36422 (confidant) (Jiřina).

conflicts. In Jiřina's sessions with the StB, she aired tirades about the tenants. Simply put, the tenants irked her.

In 1955, Jiřina reported to local police that one of her tenants, Františka, was a member of the Adventist faith and often received visits by members of that religious group. Furthermore, Jiřina reported that 'suspicious items' were regularly brought to Františka's room in baskets or sacks covered at the top by cut wood. Jiřina declared her willingness to help investigate these alleged improprieties by informing. At the same time, Jiřina mentioned her ongoing personal disputes with other tenants residing in her house. She suggested that she would appreciate some help. The StB came onto the scene. Jiřina told the StB that her tenants were 'reactionists, who hate everything progressive, without any positive attitude towards the people's democratic regime'. She was once visited at her home by StB officers because she had failed to attend the scheduled meeting due to an illness (Jiřina suffered from chronic pain and ongoing rheumatism). Jiřina welcomed the StB officers for a coffee to show them her unbearable living situation and yet again grumbled about the tenants.[78]

Over her nearly three decades of informing, Jiřina's 'targets' gradually broadened to include religious sects, local residents, the 'rich people', and foreigners.[79] Jiřina was in regular contact with almost all residents of her town. According to her StB file, she was very talkative and social. Jiřina was well versed in almost all local events as well as the personal problems of each townsperson. Hence, she could report on them with relative ease. In 1982 the StB cancelled the cooperation on account of Jiřina's old age (she was born in 1908).

Agent Vlastimil is another example of a resentment-driven informer.[80] An administrative office worker, including at one point with the Czechoslovak Chamber of Commerce (*Československá obchodní komora*, ČSOK), Vlastimil routinely complained about his job to the StB (in particular about one of his bosses). Vlastimil bemoaned what he saw as widespread corruption in his office, rampant nepotism, and his boss' prioritizing his own personal interests over collective corporate ones. Panning colleagues, venting about job conditions, and muttering disgruntlement about his work became continuous themes throughout Vlastimil's interactions with the StB.[81] The StB formally recruited Vlastimil as an informer (specifically as an agent) in March 1978. They envisaged using him in an ongoing operation that

[78] It is highly anomalous that StB officers visited their informers at home due to obvious deconspiration concerns. The report from this particular meeting in Jiřina's file notes, however, that 'this visit of [StB officers] was not conspicuous because [she] lives in a remote area of the village [and] there was nobody on the street in the vicinity of [her] house'. ibid.

[79] In total, Jiřina had at least 200 meetings with her StB officers. She submitted over 300 reports. The StB nonetheless consistently expressed doubts as to the reliability and usefulness of the information she supplied and explicitly recorded their scepticism. Jiřina never made it to the status of agent.

[80] File No 808963, registration No 11688 (Vlastimil).

[81] Vlastimil frequently changed employers over the course of his career. In each new job he developed similar negative feelings, and hence informed about his impressions of goings-on in each of these work places.

targeted a former deputy of the Minister for Foreign Trade who was, according to the StB, 'a bearer of rightist-opportunistic opinions'. Furthermore, the StB intended that Vlastimil inform on certain ČSOK colleagues, some of whom were persons of interest to the StB and some of whom Vlastimil had previously implicated. The StB believed that Vlastimil would be quite pleased to accept their offer to collaborate, as in his previous role as a candidate for secret cooperation he always openly 'criticized the flaws of his colleagues in ČSOK leadership and noted increasing corruption'. The StB was going to 'give him trust to help remove deficiencies [at ČSOK], which he himself had criticized [,] and therefore [provide him] an opportunity to contribute to their elimination'. Judging from the information that remains in his file, Vlastimil's informing was motivated by his recurrent dissatisfaction at his numerous workplaces and the antipathy he felt towards some of his colleagues (either for being incompetent professionals or for being persons that he simply did not like).

Many other informer files we have reviewed reveal streaks of resentment, grudges, and score-settling.[82] Volný, for instance, appeared to be animated by resentment in the third phase of his cooperation, which involved informing on other university professors, in which he unloaded on a toxicologist with whom he had been working. Volný, who provided expert evidence on hygiene and science, reflects some similarities to Barium, who as mentioned earlier also proffered lengthy technical reports, and who also seemed to begrudge one co-worker in particular, an engineer. Lily, it seems, resented the Communist regime and, in a polar opposite to other informers, her bitterness propelled her defiance to the StB. The StB seems to have reciprocally resented Lily, which perhaps explains in part the severity with which she was treated whereas other non-compliant informers whose files we have considered did not face the same harsh consequences that Lily did.

E. Summary and Synchronicity

The file-stories reveal a dynamic cocktail of (e)motions as drivers and catalysts of informing as a social practice. We identify four primary emotions in this regard: fear, resentment, desire, and allegiance. Our goal in identifying these is to deepen aetiological understandings of informing with a view to 'get closer to' informers, namely to understand them better.

Along our archival journey and deep reading of the StB files, we observe overlaps and synergies with the work of other scholars who, through their own methodologies and sources, put their fingers on the complexity of the informer and the drivers that fuel informing. All these works epistemologically contribute to conversations

[82] See eg File No 809203, registration No 18747 (Redaktor).

about how to speak about informers whether in Communist Czechoslovakia or elsewhere. Koudelka, for example, concludes that some informers acted out of compulsion; others out of genuine concern that Czechoslovakia was 'threatened by world imperialists' and they believed in socialism and considered their collaboration to be 'a civic or even patriotic duty'; others considered informing to be an auxiliary activity pertaining to their jobs; some did it for the promise of foreign travels.[83] Bárta observes how citizens used informing to settle personal accounts.[84] Other Czechoslovak informers, according to Urban, sought adventure and thrill.[85] Krisztine Slachta in her case study of two informers from East Germany and Hungary notes that for certain individuals informing was a means of getting things and gaining opportunities to build careers, acquire better living conditions, or travel.[86] Our research, moreover, tends to support some of Barbara Miller's and Alison Lewis' findings in the case of East Germany, which suggest a level of comparability among Eastern European surveillance states and illustrate how a granular reading of secret police archives constitutes an important evidentiary source to supplement and advance extant research.[87] According to Hewitt, in his popular public book synthesizing research on informers across a variety of contexts (both repressive and democratic), 'numerous motivations for informing have emerged over the years'.[88] He lists, for instance, money (or some other type of reward), fear, revenge, gratitude, envy, love and hate, patriotism/ideology, or 'a simple thrill derived from trafficking in secrets'.[89] Patrick Bergemann, looking at one-off 'voluntary' denunciations in Nazi Germany, concludes that Germans denounced their fellow citizens to the Nazis not based on ideology but predominantly based on personal grudges.[90] Gellately, in his work on denunciations in Nazi

[83] František Koudelka, *Státní bezpečnost 1954–1968: Základní údaje*, vol 13 (Ústav pro soudobé dějiny AV ČR 1993) 64.

[84] Milan Bárta, 'Úvod' in Milan Bárta (ed), *Člověk v soukolí StB* (Ústav pro studium totalitních režimů 2020) 9.

[85] Jiří Urban, 'Pedagog, Agronom a Úředník Mlékárny: Agenti Státní Bezpečnosti proti odpůrcům kolektivizace' in ibid 194.

[86] Krisztina Slachta, 'Unofficial Collaborators in the Tourism Sector (GDR and Hungary)' in Apor, Horváth, and Mark (eds) *Secret Agents and the Memory of Everyday Collaboration* (n 2) 310.

[87] Miller, *The Stasi Files Unveiled* (n 14); Lewis, *A State of Secrecy* (n 30).

[88] Hewitt, *Snitch!* (n 31) 26.

[89] ibid 27–28.

[90] Patrick Bergemann, *Judge Thy Neighbor, Denunciation in the Spanish Inquisition, Romanov Russia and Nazi Germany* (Columbia University Press 2019). Bergemann concludes: 'Loyalty motives, which indicate clear support for the Nazi regime, range from 18 to 35 percent of the denunciations in each of the samples. Regarding personal motives, recall that denouncers did not receive any sort of benefit or compensation from the authorities for their reports, nor did they gain protection from future harm. Thus, personal motives were social motives: the desire to harm or remove a particular member of the community. These were denunciations motivated by social opportunism. In each of the five samples, personal motives were responsible for more denunciations (an average of 37 percent) than were loyalty motives. Put another way, about 50% more denunciations are attributable to the former than to the latter … [D]espite ubiquitous propaganda roughly three-quarters of denunciations had nothing obvious to do with expressly supporting the Nazi agenda. There appears to have been widespread adoption of denunciations for their own use by Germans all across the country.' ibid 148–49.

Germany and in East Germany, pithily observes that 'self-interest fuelled the self-policing system'.[91]

IV. Life Cycles and Changes

The files show some informers to be serial. In other words: they informed to the Nazis, to other agencies, and then to the StB. In this regard, they can be cast as equal-opportunity informers or fair-weather collaborators. Goldfus presents a harsh example of the life of a serial informer in that he endured great suffering as the political winds shifted. Goldfus was punished by the Nazis, with whom he collaborated, because he had assisted Yugoslav fascists (considered to be a breach by the Nazis), and the Nazis sent him to concentration camps. Once liberated, the Czechoslovak Communists rearrested him for his collaboration with the Nazis. Goldfus spent a lot of time in jail but other serial informers may fare better.

Some of the informers in our survey of the archived files are double agents, or flit on the edges of such entanglements (Lily and Soukup). Some informers, however, remain faithful only to the StB. In fact, this type of informer reflects the bulk of the archived file-stories that we reviewed.

Wide variation arises among the group of file-stories we selected when it comes to the length of cooperative informing periods, to wit, from three to thirty-seven years. Some informers were engaged on a short-term basis. Others, however, informed for much of their adult lives: their relationship with the StB definitively terminates only when the StB decides they are too old, too infirm, or no longer useful as sources. The motivational drivers of long-term informers may shift through time and among different phases in Communist Czechoslovakia. Some informer–StB relationships are largely uneventful, even keel, and calm. They seem to end amicably, even pleasantly, notwithstanding the changed circumstances that come with moving, age, retirement, and infirmity. Věra and Vašek are probative examples.[92]

František Kraus is another continuous informer.[93] When he recounts his life story—in his contribution to the *Paměť národa* oral history project—he often

[91] Robert Gellately, 'Denunciations in Twentieth-Century Germany: Aspects of Self-Policing in the Third Reich and the German Democratic Republic' (1996) 68(4) J of Modern Hist 945.

[92] See also Reza (n 41). Reza's informing to the StB resembles a simple, straightforward, and functional relationship. Reza complied, to the best of his abilities, with what the StB wished of him. At times he took initiative. He never asked for much. He never complained. The StB also matter-of-factly accepted what he offered. The StB never faulted Reza's work. The StB observed that Reza was doing the best that he could within the constraints of his position. As we mention earlier, Reza perhaps thought that without the StB he would not have been able to fulfil his desire to reside and study in Czechoslovakia and thus was grateful to the StB. And, indeed, the StB assisted him with various administrative affairs (such as travel visas and residence permit extensions).

[93] Similar to Jiří Imlauf, František went public with his story. 'František Kraus' (*Paměť národa)* <https://www.pametnaroda.cz/cs/kraus-frantisek-1925> accessed 20 May 2023. We were not able to locate František's StB file within the digital archives. Upon our request to ABS to access the physical file, we learned that the StB had destroyed František's file in 1989. The quotations in subsequent paragraphs

refers to himself as being 'lucky'. Kraus survived Nazi concentration camps, forced labour in Germany, war in Israel, prosecution as an enemy of the people in the 1950s show trials held in Czechoslovakia, and incarceration for almost ten years in forced labour camps (from which he was released early after signing a pledge to collaborate with the StB).

František was born in Prague in 1925 to Jewish parents, both of whom perished in Nazi concentration camps during the Second World War. František was arrested in August 1942 and transported to Theresienstadt and from there to Auschwitz in 1943. After returning to Prague in 1945, he ascertained that he was the only surviving family member (other than his cousin, who resided in Palestine during the Second World War). As he did not anticipate much from his future in Prague, František accepted an offer to fight as a volunteer in the 1948 Arab-Israeli war. After that conflict ended, he returned to Prague, where he found a job as a security guard at a factory that manufactured MiG airplanes. František was again arrested in 1952: 'They [Czechoslovak authorities] found out that there is a certain Kraus, who was in Israel, in the army. Allegedly they were surveilling me for three months', he says. František spent time in pretrial detention, mostly in solitary confinement, where he was subjected to ongoing interrogation, psychological torture, sleep deprivation, and harassment. As an enemy of the people he was in the end convicted of spying. František was sentenced in 1952 to twenty-two years' imprisonment and sent to Camp Nikolaj, one of the correctional forced labour camps (uranium mining operations) established by the regime. František did not have to mine insofar as he was, in his own words, 'not very handy'. Instead František was tasked with ancillary work—taking in cargo or measuring. František recalls that although in 1956 conditions in the camp improved significantly (following fallout from the Hungarian uprising), he became weary and did not want to spend his life as a forced labourer. In 1959, he agreed to an offer to sign a collaboration pact with the StB in exchange for the commutation of his sentence:

> I said to myself, I have already been here for eight years, so I will give it a try. I could not imagine what they could possibly want to know from me. The officer called me in three times, and the third time I signed.

And so began František's thirty-year stint as an StB informer. František collaborated in accelerating fashion with the StB into the 1980s. During that time, he worked in a bakery and in a factory. The StB did not show much interest in him, however: 'They called me once a year. We met in a café. They asked how I was, if I needed anything and that was it.' That said, at the beginning of the 1980s the situation recalibrated. Upon the invitation of a friend he had met in the forced labour

of this chapter discussing František derive from the online materials available in Czech at the *Paměť národa* website.

camp, František began to work with Jewish religious communities in Prague. He increasingly came to occupy higher functions in these faith groups. The StB began to ratchet up its requests to solicit information from František. He recounts: 'They were inviting me. They had their own rooms. A flat in Dejvice, in various passageways and former stores. They were interested in movement of foreigners at the Association.' František supplied information not only on the activities of Jewish associations and their members (he recalls that he was even asked a couple of times to fire his subordinates, which he did) but also from his numerous trips abroad.[94] Looking back retrospectively at his collaboration, František says he does not regret anything:

> For me it was a way out of misery. One wants to go home. Life is too short. I did not know that there would be an amnesty in two years. This is how the life went and how it was. I am not ashamed ... My whole life credo is Švejk, with it I survived everything.[95]

František's cooperation with the StB, while kindled in desperation to escape a harsh prison, morphed over time into a broader mechanism of social navigation, as exemplified by his very own invocation of the Švejk fictional character—a mainstay of Czech literature renowned for his bumbling good fortune, irresponsibility, naïveté, and apathy—to describe himself.[96]

Catalysing motivations that can be gleaned from the files of long-term informers shift and oscillate over and through time. Attitudes towards the regime tend to curdle, however, in many instances over the life cycle of informing.

Bohumil, a pastor, exemplifies these souring trajectories.[97] Bohumil commenced his informing journey as an enemy of the state and ended up much more like a friend of the state. His archived file demonstrates many motivations for informing throughout his life. Initially, a fear of criminal charges and devotion (not so much to the state, of which he was rather circumspect, but to his church); followed by devotion to the position he could play within the church and state and becoming less critical of the state; but also getting ahead, namely being able to rise in the ranks of his church; and then getting things, too, such as travel permissions, religious liberties, and money. Bohumil compromised his church in order to keep

[94] František remarked: 'I was going to many congresses around the world and [the StB] was very interested. They wanted to know what was going on there. I was giving them materials, which I received on my trips. They were giving me documents, which they prepared, to distribute abroad.'

[95] In 1960 a Presidential amnesty was issued and the majority of political prisoners convicted during the 1950s trials were rehabilitated and released from prisons and labour camps.

[96] Jaroslav Hašek, *The Good Soldier Švejk* (authored 1917, Cecil Parrott tr, Alfred A. Knopf, 1993). While no collaborator with the Austrians, Švejk certainly is a social navigator. See also Vaněk and Mücke, *Velvet Revolutions* (n 4) 20 ('Švejk himself is also ridiculous, incapable of being serious ....').

[97] File No TS-755716 MV, registration No 3442 (Bohumil).

his church going and to personally remain influential within it. Bohumil succeeded on both fronts.

As a young student of theology, Bohumil spent two years on an exchange in Bern, Switzerland, in the 1940s. According to one report in the file, although Bohumil had an opportunity to remain in Switzerland, he returned to Czechoslovakia and became a peripatetic pastor in the Unity of the Czech Brethren (*Jednota českobratrská*), which was one of the Protestant churches in Czechoslovakia at the time.

Immediately after they assumed power in 1948, Communists perceived all churches as among their biggest obstacles in building a 'progressive socialist society'. From its infancy to its very last days, the Communist regime cast religious entities as 'enemy number one'.[98] Bohumil was an active pastor focused on organizing and educating youth in his congregation and leading them towards God and a religious calling. Unsurprisingly, the StB kept a vigilant eye on him. Throughout the second half of the 1950s, the StB scrutinized Bohumil's activities and collected information through other informers. Bohumil was described by the StB as a reactionary pastor. He was earmarked for prosecution. He was suspected *inter alia* of 'tendentious preaching against the political establishment', 'distributing defective religious literature', and 'keeping relations' with foreigners and 'reactionaries'. Other informers (including even his parishioners and youth group members) reported on Bohumil's allegedly anti-state and 'defective' language and complained about him. However, despite the intense surveillance, the StB did not seem able or willing to gather enough evidence against Bohumil to initiate a criminal prosecution for subversive activities. Rather, Bohumil transitioned from an informed-upon to an informer and thereby became an information gatherer. Bohumil's recruitment process seemed very deliberate and careful. The StB called him for sequential interviews in order to ask probing questions to 'test his honesty'. After eight such interviews, the StB decided to recruit Bohumil as a collaborator on the basis of 'compromising materials'. Hence, it seems that initially Bohumil's informing was sparked by fear.

Right from the start Bohumil was an active informer. His file contains some of his reports and records of numerous meetings where he discussed internal matters and relations in his church, at times expressing discontent with how things were going, the political situation, his local or foreign colleagues, friends, and even family members (for instance, his son). Bohumil reported to the StB for nineteen years. During that time, he was able to continue to practise his religion and ascend to important responsibilities in his Church.[99] Bohumil's increasingly cosier

[98] Czech historian Petr Žáček, quoted in the documentary 'Černý a Černější' (directed by J Novák, 2007).

[99] Bohumil was elected into its leadership in 1967, where he remained until 1983 when he resigned due to health reasons (diabetes) and old age.

relationship with the StB arguably brought him some personal benefits as well. There are indications in the file that, before his 'pact with the StB', Bohumil was not authorized to sojourn abroad to visit his friends. Thereafter, however, Bohumil frequently travelled abroad with StB approval (and even encouragement), be it professionally as a representative of his Church for various congresses, meetings or lectures (to Germany in 1966, Sweden in 1967, Kenya in 1970, Belgium in 1971, and many others) or personally for holidays in the Netherlands, for instance, or to visit friends and his son in Switzerland. At times, Bohumil was financially rewarded by the StB.[100] By the 1980s, Bohumil's reports and meetings dwindled in frequency. His file ends with the evaluation of his collaboration for the year 1984, which noted his serious health issues and the irregularity of meetings; in 1986 Bohumil's cooperation was definitively terminated. Bohumil's informing journey was much like that of other informers in that the relationship with the StB shrank once he became elderly and retired.

While Bohumil was continuously in touch with the StB, contacts between the StB and other informers were not necessarily constant. We also noticed in the files that the interactions between some informers and the StB ebbed and flowed, blew hot and cold, and evidenced lengthy lulls in which there was no contact, thereby remaining abeyant, only then to reactivate.[101] Volný—who experienced a twelve-year hiatus—is an example. It seemed that an informer embedded with the StB could be ignored when no longer of use, remain quiescent, and then undergo a renaissance of sorts once the context changed or that individual informer entered new and different social circles.

Initially cajoled informers could come to play a 'cat and mouse' game with the StB in order to socially navigate fraught situations. Candidate for secret collaboration Dora offers an example.[102] Dora was a twenty-four-year-old single mother in 1978 when an StB officer wrote a proposal to create her file as 'a person of interest'. Dora is described as someone who 'keep[s] relations with many tourists and businessmen who come to Czechoslovakia from the BRD [West Germany]' and who has 'personal connections with employees at the BRD Embassy in

[100] In 1969 Bohumil was given a gift package of the value of 150 to 200 Kčs for Christmas; in each of 1974 and 1975 he was given a financial reward of 1,000 Kčs.

[101] See eg Luděk (n 12). Luděk was an StB confidant, then terminated, and then in 1983, after an eleven-year silent intermezzo, was renewed as an agent. See also File no 621489, registration no 14684 (Malíř). Malíř—an artist—informed in the 1960s, then was discarded by the StB after Operation Danube, and then was lured back again by the StB in the 1980s to report on artists, émigrés, foreigners, and members of Prague's Jewish community. Malíř's relationship with the StB had volatile dynamics. It started and ended; over a decade passed, and then it restarted and re-ended again. Overall, Malíř prospered as an artist under Communism. He organized and participated in many exhibitions both within Czechoslovakia and abroad. Malíř illustrated many books. He created posters for theatre plays while his collaborative relationship with the StB idled. During his career, Malíř earned many awards and prizes.

[102] File No 731052, registration No 29292 (Dora). Dora's situation also demonstrates that some candidates for informing did move up the ranks and become agents, while others seemed to have (intentionally) managed their interactions with the StB such that they never were 'promoted' and thereby remained candidates for quite some time.

Prague'. Scrolling through her file, it slowly becomes clear that Dora was a sex worker. During the Communist years, prostitution was prohibited; furthermore, prostitutes became susceptible to charges of parasitism. The StB manipulated these spaces to deploy prostitutes to gather information on clients in exchange for shielding them from police and criminal investigations. As Dora seemed to be particularly interested in foreigners from the 'imperialist' West, who (according to her file) she regularly met in high-end Prague hotels, the StB was in turn keen that she extract information from her clients. Clearly the undertones of possible criminal prosecution amount to a coercion of sorts.[103] Yet Dora's file also reveals the agency and autonomy that she flexed in her dealings with the StB. Her relationship with the StB brought her benefits and shielded her from the law. Assuming a paternalistic role, Dora's StB officer lectured Dora on the need to adjust her lifestyle towards more 'responsible activities, including the contact with the StB' and that she 'should avoid any public disturbances, excessive drinking and fluctuation in her jobs which characterized her earlier behaviour'. While the StB recruited Dora because of her work as a prostitute, they also seem disturbed by her doing this kind of work. Dora is repeatedly reprimanded that she should find 'a proper job' and take better care of her reputation. Throughout her interactions with the StB, Dora is often chided for her 'irresponsible' attitude towards the StB, as her officer found himself repeatedly unable to contact her and she did not show up for meetings.

According to the reports filed by her StB handlers, Dora was cognizant of the fact that her relationship with the StB was instrumentally helpful to her. The StB remarked that Dora did not want it to end as it would be 'a great personal tragedy for her as it would not last long until she has troubles with the ordinary police again'. Still, Dora regularly avoided the StB, while the StB seemed to pursue her and insist on further contacts. The conversations cycled around and around without really amounting to much; the file reads like a bit of a game. Dora seemed to have had the agility and skill to remain in that conversational zone. In July 1982, the StB openly threatened Dora with transferring her file to the ordinary police. Dora explained to the StB that, owing to her new relationship with a boyfriend, who was very jealous and who insisted on accompanying her anytime she left the house, her informing work had become almost impossible to undertake. The result? Her collaboration ended in September 1982 due to her 'unserious attitude', 'stagnating cooperation since 1981', and her growing inability to provide any useful information. Dora, according to the file, faced no consequences for her recalcitrance.

[103] Dora's StB file also contains a couple of police reports filed after she had been arrested drunk at public places.

V. Solicitude and Disappointment

The file-stories reveal that StB officers, too, expressed emotion. One recurrent emotion seems to be caring or solicitude. Our goal is not to romanticize this sentiment. Most likely it was strategically fuelled by the desire to keep the informer in line and to avoid de-conspiration. That said, we were struck by the 'advice' that StB officers provided to informers, routinely in some cases, such as with Dora. Soukup's StB handlers similarly tried to direct him away from committing more property crimes. In short, StB officers seemed to don a paternalistic mantle of care towards some of their informers.

Velíšek, the veterinarian discussed earlier, offers yet another example.[104] As early as his initial recruitment meeting in 1957, the StB discussed Velíšek's private life with him. Indeed, this became a thread throughout his whole period of co-operation. In this regard, Velíšek confided that his relationship with his then wife was not at its best. According to the file, the StB officers tasked with Velíšek encouraged him to overcome his tensions with his wife and to reorient himself back to his family. The StB chided Velíšek for spending most of his free time repairing cars and motorcycles at home instead of attending to his wife. Velíšek allegedly had affairs with other women: the StB openly disapproved of this. StB handlers tried to steer Velíšek towards a more robust family life. Here, as was the case with other informers, the StB officers become akin to a *consigliere* or life coach even in intimate family matters. Throughout the years, the StB continued 'guiding' Velíšek in his private life. In 1964, for example, on the note of Velíšek's deteriorating marriage, it turned out that he did in fact have an extramarital affair and was about to divorce his wife. The StB officer reported how he 'reasonably talk[ed] it over' with Velíšek and how after this conversation Velíšek reportedly backed off from getting divorced. Indeed, Velíšek's family circumstances 'temporarily stabilized'. Velíšek reportedly shared with his StB officer his feeling that his wife was not exactly his 'soulmate'. Velíšek ultimately did divorce notwithstanding the StB's routine interventions and counsel.

The StB could also be belittling when it dispensed such advice, much like a nagging or scolding relative. For instance, in 1966 Velíšek married one of his lovers, H., who was twelve years younger than him. H. worked at the same veterinary hospital as Velíšek. The StB considered her as *bourgeoise*: 'She smoked in public, was meeting people from higher circles, and looked down upon manual workers' according to one of the assessments the StB had made of her. H. was politically passive and not really trusted. She was 'haughty' and demonstrated 'no good attitude towards neighbours.' That said, the StB was well aware of Velíšek's 'tendencies' and monitored his personal situation in his new marriage. In a report, they described

[104] Velíšek (n 60).

his relations towards women generally as 'demanding'. The StB evaluated Velíšek in 'this respect [ie his personal life] as very bad'. It turned out that, according to the StB, even after his second marriage Velíšek persisted in having love affairs. The StB again planned 'to educate' Velíšek 'to avoid past mistakes in his family life'. In sum, then, throughout the informing relationship the StB intentionally attempted to guide and channel Velíšek—not only politically but also regarding his professional ethics and his personal, matrimonial, and family responsibilities.

The StB's solicitude extended to health matters, as well. Alcohol abuse was prevalent among informers.[105] This was of concern to the StB. Assuredly, this concern was in large part utilitarian and self-serving, insofar as the StB did not wish informers to be erratic, lose control, and de-conspire themselves. The StB preferred them sober. On the other hand, our reading of the files suggests that something deeper and more affective lurks in this space. Agent Redaktor, for instance, was a journalist and long-term informer who succumbed to alcohol abuse and a mental health collapse that the StB tried to 'manage'.[106] Redaktor's collaboration with the StB began after his exclusion from public affairs in 1968 when he was branded (like many individuals at the time) as anti-Soviet only to be expelled from the Communist Party in 1970.[107] It was Redaktor's quest for reinstatement in the Party, acute hunger for social and professional rehabilitation, and longing for reputational resuscitation that seemingly made him such an active and eager informer. He professed willingness to 'make up' for his offences. Redaktor provided extensive private and personal information on his friends and foes against whom he seemed to have held grudges. Indeed, his file oozes with his simmering resentment. Redaktor continuously complained about what he perceived as his excessive punishment (ie expulsion from the Party) for his previous offences. He was bitter towards persons in his district who he felt had misled and manipulated him. In December 1972, the StB decided to formally sign a cooperation agreement with Redaktor. The StB couched the cooperation as an opportunity for Redaktor to rectify his earlier missteps.

This all hummed along smoothly until Redaktor started suffering health and personal problems in the 1980s. Redaktor drank heavily and, moreover, mixed alcohol with sedatives. The StB was initially determined to make him stop drinking. His StB supervisor suggested rewarding him financially for good working performance. This supervisor hoped that such inducements would motivate Redaktor to continue informing. The StB seemed to stage an intervention. However, this effort proved to be of no avail. Redaktor's health was quickly deteriorating; he also started suffering physical problems (related to combining drugs with alcohol). His

[105] See eg Kongres (n 28); see also Sony (n 75).

[106] Redaktor (n 82).

[107] Redaktor was found to have 'entirely succumbed to anti-Soviet emotions and nationalist psychosis'.

driving licence was suspended. The StB report also affirmed that Redaktor was irrational, denialist in not coming to terms with his addictions, and, furthermore, the report deplored that Redaktor was becoming 'entirely illogical' in regard to his relationship with the StB. Still, Redaktor's supervisor repeatedly tried to contact him, to bring him back, and to motivate him financially. But all this was once again to no avail. In 1988, Redaktor ceased cooperating with (and started ignoring) the StB. The StB visited Redaktor at his workplace, endeavoured to arrange meetings, but Redaktor did not show up. Furthermore, Redaktor was caught driving a car while his licence was suspended. So the StB finally became resigned to the situation and formally terminated cooperation in late December 1988. The StB cited his alcoholism and health problems as the main reasons.

Bouts of anger, frustration, and disappointment on the part of StB officers also surface in the files. When Soukup ends up in a *záchytka* (detox facility in a police station—a 'drunk tank' in dated parlance), the StB officers became angry with him and expressed their frustration and disappointment. The StB moreover became vexed with Goldfus when he did not follow instructions. Yet another example is agent Karel, a scholar of German studies.[108] In an extensive report from an April 1980 meeting, the StB expressed their general dissatisfaction with Karel's performance: reportedly he provided only general information about his targets. The StB sent Karel to training to learn to wear a wiretap device so he could directly record a meeting he had with West Germans. But when this occasion arose, Karel was visibly nervous about the operation and made gaffes. He failed. The StB was unhappy with the result. Karel's StB officer seemed cross with him and put some pressure on him. The report describes how the officer reprimanded Karel for not following directions. The officer was frustrated with his passivity. Karel's behaviour disappointed not only his StB officer but also higher-up StB bosses. The StB officer told him that if he would not 'truthfully report about the materials he was getting . . . [the StB] will stop covering [Karel] and he will bear potential consequences'. Karel's StB officer was puzzled 'why always when push comes to shove [Karel] runs away' and he wondered why 'Karel was so nervous—because of us—or because of them [West Germans]'. This officer could not figure out why Karel collaborated, to wit, was it 'in order to legalize his stay at the [West German] Embassy or out of personal benefit?'

The StB invested considerable resources and energies into Karel throughout his informing career. Karel, however, was clumsy and hesitant. He almost always found a way out or flatly ignored StB technical instructions. These vacillations further reaffirmed the StB's suspicion of Karel's alleged foul play.[109]

[108] File No 789654, registration No 21213 (Karel).

[109] A report from September 1984, for instance, notes how Karel constantly endeavoured to 'outsmart' the StB. It turned out that Karel 'exaggerate[s] some information and . . . uses his knowledge of [the] methods and aims of the StB which he gained during his [previous contact with the StB]. By doing that, he attempts to make an impression of successfully fulfilling the tasks, by which he wants to create conditions for getting material rewards. It cannot be excluded that by doing this he is trying to divert attention from the real nature of his contacts [at the Embassy] which might be motivated by material gains.'

This is an area in which we suggest a need for further academic research, namely on the sentiments of the StB officers and the lives that they led (and lead), along with their own motivations for joining the secret police and for recording what they had been told and listening to what they endlessly heard.[110] This might help shift that analysis beyond caricature.

VI. Victims who Victimize: Marginals with (Some) Power

Our reading of the file-stories places informers into an interstitial space that stumbles between power and weakness. On the one hand, many informers present as compromised individuals, woeful characters, and troubled souls. The StB—in conjunction with the entire architecture of authoritarianism—lorded power over them. StB officers bullied them. A vast proportion of informers were themselves exactingly surveilled. On the other hand, some StB informers were adept at manipulating the informing system to extract benefits. A few seemed to be equal opportunity double agents. Some informers managed to be quite clear about their no-go zones, in particular, the people they would not inform on. Others perfected the art of evasiveness and avoidance despite living under a microscope. In the moment of saying what they said—and electing not to say what they might otherwise have said—informers exercise considerable power over other individuals. After all, while not all informed-upons endured responsive action by the StB, the StB certainly hauled some informed-upons into their offices, recruited them, or penalized them severely. Without the involvement of the informer, these informed-upons would not have become hurt or put at risk of being hurt. Informers constituted pivotal elements in causal chains that triggered considerable harm to befall upon others.

Overall, we feel it appropriate to conceptualize StB informers as tragic *victims who victimize*.[111] This category of character on the stage of endemic human rights abuses is one of the most understudied. We define 'victims who victimize' as circumscribed actors that oscillate between the reductive antipodes of 'victim' or 'perpetrator' that suffuse the vernacular of international criminal law and transitional justice. The industrialization of repression and authoritarianism relies upon the involvement of massive numbers of meek and weak individuals without whom the violence never can metastasize, normalize, and become bureaucratic. Indeed,

[110] In Czech popular culture, StB officers are often represented as the embodiment of evil—spineless conniving men in black leather coats with their faces overshadowed by hats and their eyes shielded by opaque sunglasses—spreading fear and harassing everyone and anyone who crosses their path. See eg the series 'Herec' (Actor), Czech Television, 2020, directed by Peter Bebjak, available (in Czech) at <https://www.ceskatelevize.cz/porady/12309723448-herec/> accessed 24 January 2024; and a film 'Ve Stínu' (In The Shadow), 2012, directed by David Ondříček, for more information (in Czech) see <https://www.csfd.cz/film/231602-ve-stinu/prehled/> accessed 24 January 2024.

[111] Mark A Drumbl, 'Victims who Victimise' (2016) 4(2) London Rev of Int Law 217.

power is profoundly situational: a person in a precarious position vis-à-vis one individual may exercise significant authority over another individual on the very same day and in the very same moment. One of us has thought about this category of characters amid collective violence quite a bit, whether in the frame of the role of very poor (often illiterate) peasants, child soldiers, persecuted persons who target fellow group members, and women in patriarchal societies.[112] And now we come to place informers into this same frame.

We have consistently been startled by the extent to which the StB hawkishly monitored their own supply chain, in other words how nearly all of the informers themselves were informed-upon by others.[113] Why did the StB do this? One reason would be so that the StB could corroborate the veracity of informer statements, another would be to create cultures in which all walls have ears. Vašek (one of the most privileged informers we encountered) was subject to the StB's peering into every nook and cranny of his life. In Věra's case, and in many others, the StB constantly assessed the 'quality' of her reports. Here, the StB acts like an examiner. This, too, suggests the occupational nature of being an informer—it is like a job—with performance markers, check lists, and evaluations. Although the command-and-control Communist economy was bloated and inefficient,[114] work remained central to self-worth in part because not working was seen as 'parasitical'. Hence, some individuals might plausibly have informed for such long durations because they saw it as employment, as being useful, and approached it in that fashion, namely occupationally. The fact that so much noisy information was being diligently compiled actually meant that the 'job' of informing and listening to informers—the StB's work—was not different than any other work in Czechoslovakia.

A large swathe of content about the informer in a typical informer's StB file comes from other informers. Based on the contents of their files, twenty of the twenty-three informers in our sample were 'informed upon' (at times extensively). Moreover, 'anonymous letters' sent to the StB also seem to populate the files: such was the case in Lily's file (during the so-called French Affair) and in Vašek's file (the so-called chocolate bar controversy). The prevalence of these letters unveils the culture of spying and denunciation that pervaded Czechoslovakia. This culture sires the perennial vulnerability of all citizens, but in particular those individuals already enmeshed in the surveillance system or who had a file opened on them. A thick distrustful spiderweb emerges of constant feedback loops. Hearsay evidence becomes ubiquitous, which fuels further needs to corroborate, verify, and scrutinize. In any event, condemnatory

[112] Mark A Drumbl, *Atrocity, Punishment, and International Law* (CUP 2007); Mark A Drumbl, *Reimagining Child Soldiers in International Law and Policy* (OUP 2012); Nicole Hogg and Mark A Drumbl, 'Women as Perpetrators: Agency and Authority in Genocidal Rwanda' in Amy E Randall (ed), *Genocide and Gender in the Twentieth Century* (2nd ed, Bloomsbury 2022); Mark A Drumbl, 'The Kapo on Film: Tragic Perpetrators and Imperfect Victims' (2018) 6 Griffith J of Law & Human Dignity 229.

[113] See eg Karel (n 108). See also Eva (n 54) (StB installing a wiretap in her own apartment because they were wary of her 'foul play' and her de-conspiration risk).

[114] Vaněk and Mücke, *Velvet Revolutions* (n 4) 117.

hearsay evidence may become irrefutable regardless of lack of verifiability. Citizens, burdened with duties to report, found eager audiences in the StB for denunciations and informing, whether made openly or anonymously. The culture of denunciation ran deep, with even children being encouraged to condemn their own parents for improper conduct or impermissible statements.[115]

We also have been struck by the susceptibility, haplessness, desperation, and mental health struggles that bob and weave throughout the files.[116] The file-story of agent Dvořák is illustrative.[117] Dvořák was born in the late 1940s. He became an electrical engineer after completing his studies. Dvořák initially is presented in his file as a well-functioning family man who carries himself in a calm and cheerful manner. Dvořák is depicted as a social person with considerable professional expertise. Married with two children, in his free time Dvořák loved to go to the cottage, this being a common pastime among Czechs.[118]

Dvořák spent time in West Berlin prior to his marriage in 1975. There, he fell in love with a West German woman. Indeed, Dvořák's StB file contains a tender request he made in January 1969 to the office of the President of Czechoslovakia beseeching permission to visit her as she was ill and could not visit him. It seems, presumably, that his heartfelt request was denied. This letter is so touching that we translate and present it as yet another example of the files as biopic. Our book is after all a story about stories. These kinds of passages recorded and sequestered in the files constitute historiographies of life amid the 'peaceful coexistence'[119] of the Cold War:

> [I]n the academic year 68/69 I was completely legally a regular student at the Technical University in Western Berlin. During my stay, my relationship to Miss [V.] [address redacted], whom I met in the summer of 1967, very much deepened.

[115] For discussion of child informers and denouncers in the Soviet Union and Czechoslovakia, Barbora Holá and Mark A Drumbl, 'Children as Informers and Denouncers' in Christelle Molima and others (eds), *Children's Fights: Commonalities and Differences Across Time, Space and Place* (Routledge forthcoming).

[116] See also in the context of Northern Ireland, Ron Dudai, *Penality in the Underground: The IRA's Pursuit of Informers* (OUP 2022) 131 (finding that when the IRA caught a tout, despite the IRA's rhetoric of killing touts, the actual practice was more complex in that at times the IRA was swayed by the image of 'the informer as a luckless dupe falling prey to sophisticated entrapment by the British state ... [informers are] often victims themselves ... whose vulnerability is used most cynically by Crown Forces to trap them into informing').

[117] File No 766578, registration No 7537 (Dvořák).

[118] Of note, intergenerationally: the file reveals that Dvořák's father was an StB secret collaborator between 1955 and 1963. Dvořák's father had been 'drafted' based on compromising material, which consisted of the fact that he in his function as a testing commissar for motor vehicles had illegally granted someone a permit. Such conduct amounted to the misdemeanour of dereliction of public duty. Dvořák's father's cooperation with the StB was terminated in 1963 because he changed his job and moved from one city to another. The Ministry of the Interior lost interest in him as an informer.

[119] This is the Soviet phrase for the Cold War. For more discussion, see Mark A Drumbl, 'The Sights, Sounds, and Silences of International Law During the Cold War' in Mark A Drumbl and Caroline Fournet (eds), *The Sights, Sounds, and Sensibilities of Atrocity Prosecutions* (Brill forthcoming).

> Currently Ms. V. is seriously ill and therefore cannot visit me so often/practically almost not at all, as we would both wish for.
>
> Ms. V. is now in a very serious situation, as it is still not excluded that she has cancer. My visit would help her overcome the worst depression.
>
> Money for the journey was immediately sent to me to Prague. Therefore, I kindly ask you if you can review what can be done in this case. It also certainly is a complication that I would need to get to West Berlin more frequently than once a year, because as anyone can surely acknowledge it is very cruel for two persons to be separated for such a long time, in particular if one of them is not doing so well.
>
> I realize that my request can sound suspicious, as if I would like to get out at any price. I do not deny it, as I really need to get to Berlin but only for a short visit.
>
> I know that my request might not be suitable given the overall situation but I would not burden the Republic in any way and I think that even in the most complicated situation one should not forget 'little' human problems.
>
> I sincerely hope that you will take my letter as seriously as it was written, I can prove all the facts. I would kindly ask you for a very swift reply and I would very much like to discuss this problem with someone competent/authorized. Thanks in advance. Success to peace.
>
> Signature

Dvořák's informing began in 1976 while he worked at International Business Machines (IBM). The StB sought to deploy him in matters of 'Computer Technology', focusing also on the day-to-day happenings of the IBM office in Prague, notably, rustling up information on Czechoslovak citizens and foreigners who came to the office. Dvořák informed to the StB as well as to his bosses within IBM about his IBM colleagues. By the end of his stint at IBM, it appeared to have been widely known that Dvořák was an informer. Dvořák also reported on distant relatives of his wife in West Germany (a different woman than Miss V. referenced in Dvořák's letter reproduced earlier).

By November 1985, however, a report by informer (codenamed Vašák) revealed that Dvořák's relationship with his IBM bosses was steadily deteriorating. Dvořák apparently began drinking in excess, became unpresentable in public, arrogant at work, and his mental health crumbled. Dvořák spent two weeks in a psychiatric hospital. Dvořák's immediate boss at IBM remarked during an interview with the StB that Dvořák was very money-oriented. Apparently, according to his StB file, Dvořák had sticky fingers and skimmed funds off expense reports that he himself had filed. In his boss' words, Dvořák 'was after money as the devil'. In December 1985, a proposal was made to terminate collaboration with Dvořák.[120]

Overall, we were surprised by the number of informers who—like Dvořák—suffered mental health struggles, substance abuse, or other forms of social maladjustment (often worsening as they aged)—all of which intimates their largely marginal place in society. Eight informers (which is over one-third) in our sample of twenty-three faced such challenges. These informers were vulnerable and lonely, meek and weak, primed to be exploited, and, as a result, demonstrated limited agency and were easily pushed around by the StB.

Vulnerability, however, did not manifest only in mental health issues. Věra was initially blackmailed into cooperation because of accusations of breaching the duty to disclose and other alleged crimes. As a wayward young woman perhaps scared of ruining her and her family's lives, she agreed to the StB's offer. Věra was in and out of trouble with the law. The fact nonetheless remains that Věra really hurt other people through her informing. Věra also demonstrated considerably agency, as well. Věra proved to be an assiduous operative. She maintained a good relationship with her StB officers. On the basis of her informing, which lasted on and off for over thirty years, individuals were arrested, precluded from emigrating, or disciplined. Her words triggered deleterious consequences for others. Věra experienced no mental breakdowns.

Other informers do not seem to present so neatly as victims at any point in their lives. Vašek is a good example. He is one of the few informers among those whose files we have reviewed who did not hail from a marginalized group or began as a disenfranchised individual. He seemed to have been a consistently successful member of socialist society. He did not appear to need the StB to fulfil his professional ambitions or to save him from personal or professional downfall. He did not drink, he did not smoke, he barely even drank coffee, he led an ascetic life, and he focused on being in good physical condition. Vašek was a highly regarded informer. Yet he too was constantly surveilled and vetted by the StB.

Some informers became broken by the system that corralled them into decades of informing. Much like torture scars the torturer along with the tortured, so too does informing scar the informer as well as the informed-upons and the StB officers. Some informers may fare well over and though time, but many others self-destruct. The StB inflicted moral injury on the people it vacuumed into its informing bureaucracy. Informers were weaponized by the state. Assuredly, informers, in turn, contributed to the pervasive infliction of moral injury upon others. The StB polluted society with cultures of lying and deceit and made it risky to trust anyone at all or to form intimate relationships.[121] Yet values of loyalty, love, and trust still endured. Joys were not eviscerated.

[120] In sum, 107 meetings took place between Dvořák and the StB. Dvořák filed 157 reports. He was routinely rewarded financially in a total sum amounting to 11,000 Kčs.

[121] Spurný, Jareš, and Volná, 'Intellectuals between Collaboration and Independence in Late Socialism' (n 9) 186('A fundamental result of StB activity thus appears mainly to be the tangible (and

VII. Conclusion

The StB files offer a constellation of informer biographies. File-stories brim with passion, struggle, doubt, venality, and escapism. They are skeletal in places, while burgeoning with reams of details in others. The files beguile with their revelations. When carefully studied, the StB files put on tap a trove of micro-narratives in small-scale tales that in turn illuminate a broad history. The file-stories reflect the quotidian. They attest to the role of ordinary people in sustaining and navigating the Communist regime.[122]

Presenting the centrality of emotions—notably, fear, desire, resentment, and allegiance—to the act of informing conduces a frame that grasps the centrality of emotions to the process of transitional justice generally. On this note, post-1989 Czech Republic cascades with emotion: betrayal, anger, relief, excitement, shame, recrimination, nostalgia, longing, and trepidation. Vaněk and Mücke observe that whereas in the Communist years Czechs struggled with social and political constraints stemming from the surveillant state, despite being 'free' following 1989 Czechs now grapple with economic fears, notably losing their job.[123] Konrad Niesner, a narrator in Vaněk and Mücke's oral history project wryly intones:

> Once again, everybody's afraid today. People just grumble in the pub. It's the same as it was under Communism. You're afraid to open your mouth because today work is scarce, and if you open your mouth, you might as well get out, because there are three hundred other unemployed people waiting outside the gate.[124]

Chapter 6 faces the question of what, specifically, our reading of the files suggests can be learned for transitional justice mechanics in the Czech Republic and beyond. Ron Dudai notes that informers tend to occupy precarious positions in transitional spaces, in particular when the transition arcs away from a repressive

in some cases outright destructive) intervention in the lives of other people, the lives of the people who were being followed and, usually to a greater extent, the lives of the cooperators. This intervention and the awareness of the presence of an StB network helped to exacerbate the atmosphere of mutual suspicion.').

[122] Apor, Horváth, and Mark, 'Introduction' (n 2) 13 ('[S]ecret police files can be used to produce more-subtle social and cultural histories of the socialist dictatorships.').

[123] Vaněk and Mücke, *Velvet Revolutions* (n 4) 139–40 ('Unemployment has become a nightmare for many people. A number of narrators openly confessed in the interviews how much the mere thought of losing their jobs troubles them and gets in the way of their enjoyment of life ... [d]ozens of narrators compared waiting in line at the unemployment office to waiting in line before the revolution for bananas, tangerines, and, especially at Christmas time, oranges for their children.').

[124] ibid 197. See also ibid 117 ('Narrators described their experiences from both sides of the Velvet Revolution. On the one hand, the socialist regime guaranteed employment, even if it bordered on artificial over-employment, and required everyone to work; on the other hand, the post-revolution return to the market economy offered almost unlimited choice of employment, including the possibility of unemployment, whether by choice or unwanted.').

government which they may have aided and abetted.[125] Informers can be easily blamed for everything, dismissed, and cast as repugnant.[126] Yet this means—as was the case in post-Communist Czech Republic—that transitional justice produces a coarsely reductive depiction of informing as a social phenomenon. For us, this is a reason why we feel it crucial to augment the epistemology of informing—what do we know about informers, and from where? —by considering secret police files as a valuable data source. Our goal is neither to exculpate informers nor to condemn them. Rather, it is to *understand* them.

[125] Dudai, *Penality in the Underground* (n 116) 8.

[126] Apor, Horváth, and Mark, 'Introduction' (n 2) 2 (noting that collaboration 'became most commonly conceptualized as an individualized act carried out by the morally deficient, who can now be blamed, rather than a phenomenon with a history and a broader societal context').

6
Transitional Takeaways

Our journey thus far has involved a deep read of selected file-stories. This immersion prompted our extrapolative inquiry into what motivated individuals to speak to the StB and what kept them speaking. We identified emotions as key drivers, specifically fear, devotion, resentment, and desire. Since our case study is Communist Czechoslovakia, and rupture from a repressive regime declared illegitimate by its liberal capitalist successor, *transitional justice* constitutes a natural frame of reference.

Transitional justice—the reckoning with past human rights abuses[1]—has taken myriad forms in the Czech Republic. We set these out in Chapter 3. How do we connect what jumps out at us from the file-stories with how Czech transitional justice actually engaged with informers? Now that we have pulled out the *why*, what does this say about *what was* done and also about what *ought to be* done?

This chapter proceeds through two sections.

While Section I begins with the place of informers in transitional justice in the Czech Republic, it ends on a broader note that ruminates about the limits of transparency and gingerly explores the possible virtues of secrets. Section I contends that the implementation of transitional justice in the Czech Republic failed to grapple with the multifaceted nature of the informer and the subtleties of the reasons why people informed on others. Czech transitional justice did so in the case of informers by caricaturizing them as dangerous devotees to the old regime, as fuelled by ideological and patriotic motivations, and as still endorsing repressive Communist practices. This led to excessive simplification. It also constructed a *conveniently cosmetic* leitmotiv. Instead, we argue for an *aetiological expressivist function* of transitional justice, namely to tell it as it was. Aetiological expressivism can educate the public about how a social phenomenon came to be and then articulate that nuance in transitional settings. Section I further argues that this failure to appreciate the aetiological complexity of informing, while cocooning *comfort* for some Czechs, paradoxically led to *cruelty* for others through the opening of the StB files. Transitional justice settlements created winners and losers. Some losers, moreover, became scorned scapegoats.

[1] See generally Ruti G Teitel, *Transitional Justice* (OUP 2000) (positing 'transitional justice' as the concept of justice associated with periods of political change, notably shifts to liberal democracy in which responses are developed to confront the wrongdoings of predatory predecessor regimes while also constructing a new political identity for the successor state).

Informers Up Close. Mark A. Drumbl and Barbora Holá, Oxford University Press.
 DOI: 10.1093/oso/9780192855138.003.0006

Section II introduces an interrelated, yet broader, line of inquiry, namely a conceptual interrogation whether informers *should* map onto transitional justice frameworks when repressive regimes crumble and, if so, *how* that might look in light of the key role that varied emotions play as drivers in the industrialization of informing. While transitional justice may tend to call for modalities other than criminal trials, the fact remains that punitiveness can creep into accountability modalities such as truth commissions, reparations, lustration, transparency measures, and civil sanctions. This leads to *condemnation*, a somewhat ironic outcome since transitional justice prides itself in articulating justifications of promoting reconciliation, cooperation, and reintegration. These goals may become lost, however. Such was the case in the Czech Republic, where reconciliatory goals were left unfulfilled.[2] In response, we propound a vision that we believe can help foster reconciliation and cooperation while promoting a more accurate depiction of why ordinary people were drawn into, or at times pursued, discursive interactions with the StB. We differentiate aetiological expressivism from condemnation and posit that an aetiologically expressivist lens can vivify the reconciliatory aspects of transitional justice while also guard against occlusion and distortion, moderate public pressures to scapegoat and condemn, minimize the false comfort of reductive simplicity, acknowledge harm, and promote a paradigm of reintegration. Czech transitional justice was under-inclusive in that it ignored the multivalent provenance of informing and was over-inclusive in that it shoehorned former informers into the box of Communist loyalists who after the Velvet Revolution imperilled liberal democracy. Instead, we call for an embrace of granularity. We delineate a heuristic that can help promote this quest. This heuristic can help transitional justice become more informed about informing and thereby better 'get' where informers come from and how to speak about them following regime change.

Section III briskly concludes by starting something new. We query whether there is anything to be learned from informing in repressive times for informing in quotidian life amid liberal democracy. Any cross-overs? Here, we make a wink-link to the pitch on which we wish to conclude our book as a whole, namely to continue to wonder about informing as it transpires in *all* spaces and places.

[2] Muriel Blaive, 'An Impossible Reconciliation: National (Heroic) Memory and Individual Identity in the Czech Republic' (*Politika*, 2 April 2022) <www.politika.io/en/article/an-impossible-reconciliation> accessed 12 March 2023, para 4; Roman David, 'Transitional Justice Effects in the Czech Republic' in Lavinia Stan and Nadya Nedelsky (eds), *Post-Communist Transitional Justice: Lessons from Twenty-Five Years of Experience* (CUP 2015) 101.

I. Czech Transitional Takeaways

We begin by reflecting upon what our research has to say about the process of transitional justice undertaken in the Czech Republic. We centre our analysis on the hydraulics of comfort and the pneumatics of cruelty.

A. Comfort

After the Velvet Revolution, StB informers found themselves purged and excluded from jobs and public institutions.[3] Already marginalized and often facing serious personal crises and health issues, many informers were re-marginalized. As part of this process, Czech transitional justice initiatives flattened the myriad motivations of informers into one dominant explanatory vector. This reductive vector constructed informers as largely inimical to the successor state because of their devotion to the Communist regime, allegiance to the erstwhile ideology, and patriotism to the former state. Informers were imputed with a sinister fealty to the erstwhile regime. According to the transitional narrative, even if individuals did not believe (from a virtue ethics standpoint) in Communist ideology, by cooperating with the StB they willingly and actively buttressed (in a manner far more egregious than others) a system of norms, values, and behaviours that violate democratic principles and the rule of law. That alone was taken as proof of their loyalty to the old regime and its 'wrong ways' incompatible with the newly democratic polity.[4] To be sure, such imputations could be fatuously overdrawn insofar as in Communist society interactions with state officials and routine (often rote) incorporation of Communist vocabulary and nomenclature formed part of quotidian social practice.[5] In this regard, Communist ideology may have shaped mass behaviour even if only few (if any) people sincerely believed in this ideology.

Our research indicates this reductionism already began with StB officials who, as a matter of standard operating procedure, routinely and mechanically categorized informers as coming forth for ideological and patriotic reasons regardless of actual motivational diversity and even when the content of what was reported arguably presented scant evidence of tangible threats to ideology or *patria*. The apex

[3] Martin Tichý, 'Tři rozdílné osudy' in Milan Bárta (ed), *Člověk v soukolí StB* (Ústav pro studium totalitních režimů 2020).

[4] For more details, see Chapter 3, Section III, 'Exclusion and Lustrations'; see also Nález Ústavního soudu (pléna) ze dne 5 prosince 2001 (ÚS) [Decision of the Constitutional Court of 5 December 2001], sp zn Pl ÚS 9/01 (Czech).

[5] Michal Pullmann, 'The Ideological Face of Normalisation: Socialist Modernity and the "Quiet Life' in Kevin McDermott and Matthew Stibbe (eds), *Czechoslovakia and Eastern Europe in the Era of Normalisation 1969–1989* (Palgrave Macmillan 2022) 66 ('The hyper-normalised usage of communist language was of great importance. Paradoxically, it enabled many Czechoslovaks … to adopt and legitimize a fairly broad range of non-conformist stances … while at the same time regarding themselves as loyal socialist citizens.').

of this performativity was the 'pledge'. The StB largely squeezed informing into the imagery of devotion, thereby constructing informers as loyal citizens of the time faithfully committed to a higher order set of political values and to the state.

This caricatural categorization, moreover, persisted within subsequent transitional justice interventions. A continuity thereby arose despite the putative rupture and notwithstanding the supposed transition. While the heterogeneity of informers' motives tends to be noted in scholarship and public discourse,[6] and radiates through our encounters with and readings of the StB files, the fact remains that this heterogeneity has not been acknowledged by post-Communist transitional justice mechanisms. That particular kaleidoscope became monochrome.

We argue that this elective choice of narrative framing, initially by the StB and subsequently by the post-Communist state, leads to (and itself may be driven by) the pursuit of an assuaging sense of *comfort*. This comfort operated on a number of entwined levels.

We posit that StB officers turned to patriotism to stylize informers because it *looked* and *felt* much better aesthetically and for their own sensibilities, while also mechanically putting in place the buzzwords of the time. Presenting informing in this fashion made the informing process seem less unseemly, less coerced, and more palatable. The StB did this even in cases of serial informers, such as Goldfus, who informed to all kinds of different authorities (Nazis, Communists, West German intelligence).[7] In response, informers may have played the very same linguistic game. After all, as Michal Pullmann notes, in Communist Czechoslovakia 'ideological phrases, slogans and clichés were unthinkingly reiterated in everyday life … the performative quality of the official language, its form, prevailed in everyday usage over the constative one, its meaning'.[8]

Similar dynamics arose as part of the newly emergent liberal democratic state. Transitional justice in the Czech Republic did not entirely ignore these diverse motivations but overall it caricaturized informers as loyalists, so that ideological commitment to the erstwhile state (and its ways) came to dominate the disseminated imagery of the informer. Hence, the successor regime consolidated its legitimacy in part by depicting informers as traitorous, treasonous, and treacherous.[9] This

[6] Our research therefore supports scholarly findings about the diversity of informer motivations; cf František Koudelka, *Státní bezpečnost 1954–1968: Základní údaje*, vol 13 (Ústav pro soudobé dějiny AV ČR 1993) 64; Libor Bílek, 'I Undertake Voluntarily … Residents, Agents, Informers and Others: The State Security's Secret Collaborators, 1945–1989' in Alžběta Medková (ed), *Behind the Iron Curtain: Review of the Institute for the Study of Totalitarian Regimes*, vol 4 (Ústav pro studium totalitních režimů 2016) 100; Milan Bárta, 'Úvod' in Bárta (ed), *Člověk v soukolí StB* (n 3) 8–9; Jiří Kozák, *Právo Na Pomezí Diktatury a Demokracie* (Auditorium 2014) 113. See also Chapter 5, Section III.E, 'Summary and Synchronicity'.

[7] Serial informers may have ended up becoming repurposed to inform for the successor state (the Communist state in this case), but generally they first were punished and often harshly so.

[8] Pullmann, 'The Ideological Face of Normalisation' (n 5) 65.

[9] See generally Sharika Thiranagama and Tobias Kelly (eds), *Traitors: Suspicion, Intimacy, and the Ethics of State-Building* (University of Pennsylvania Press 2012) (arguing that treachery is a constant, essential, and normal part of the processes through which social and political order is produced).

strikes us as the prioritization of the political over the personal, the hegemony of structure over disposition, and the eschewing of Fulbrook's assessment of the salience of individuality even within participatory dictatorship.[10] The only nuance that was evinced in the post-Communist Czech Republic arose in the case of presumably unknowing informers—confidants and candidates for secret collaboration—in other words, informers who might have been unaware they were registered by the StB as such (though they may well have been aware that they were informing to someone).[11]

Czech transitional justice sterilized interactions between informer and the StB that, based upon our read, displayed emotive streaks of intimacy, solicitude, and camaraderie. In the end, it was convenient to portray informers as ideologues and loyalists rather than as petty, frightened, avaricious, apolitical, and grudging individuals. Informing became inordinately revised into an ideological box because—once again—it *is easier and helpful to see it that way*. Such a construction favours a soothing position in which informers could for a variety of reasons be scapegoated and excommunicated as irredeemable dangerous threats to the new state, thereby building community and validation through excision so as to fulfil political expediency. Resentful or desirous informers became presented as ideationally 'dangerous' to the new democracy and ostracized (irrespective of what they did, how and why they did it, or whether they cared about Communism) as poisonous pathogens, often through lustration, but also in broader public discourse animated by charged media portrayals and the Institutes of Memory. Ironically, but unsurprisingly, the marginalization of certain informers may be driven by similar personal vendettas, aims, goals, wants, or needs that prompted informers to implicate others in wrongdoings in the past.[12] To be sure, not every single informer was ostracized; some

[10] Indeed, transitional justice has elsewhere separated and suborned ideological motivations from material or private ones. In South Africa, for example, an amnesty was only available to those who disclosed information to the Truth and Reconciliation Commission related to 'political' crimes, whether in support of the apartheid state or oppositional entities such as the African National Congress. Disclosures involving crimes that were not political in nature were ineligible for amnesty because they were constructed as materialistic or as ordinary common crimes.

[11] To be sure, the StB was not the only official (or quasi-official) entity to which people informed in Communist Czechoslovakia. People informed to the ordinary police, to teachers and supervisors, and to other individuals who may have been seen as wielding social capital. That said, in Czech transitional justice, informing networks outside of formal StB channels did not much matter. The focus was on the StB, which in any event activated the fulcrum of the repressive state apparatus.

[12] David Kosař, 'Lustration and Lapse of Time: "Dealing with the Past" in the Czech Republic' (2008) 4 Eur Constitutional L Rev 460, 470 (explaining that the lustration laws have been 'abused for political motives and [have] led to witch hunts'). Indeed, politicians were accused of manipulating the lustration processes to discredit their opponents. For instance, a former Czech Member of Parliament and Minister of Foreign Affairs who faced accusations of collaboration and successfully challenged these claims in lengthy court proceedings claimed that he was publicly and unjustifiably discredited mainly because he had opposed the economic reform programme of the then Prime Minister Václav Klaus. Jan Kavan, *Spravedlnost s Náhubkem* (Doplněk 1999). As Hillary Appel notes, 'an accusation of secret police collaboration was a quick and dirty way to discredit opponents, even those with long histories battling communism'. Hillary Appel, 'Anti-Communist Justice and Founding the Post-Communist Order: Lustration and Restitution in Central Europe' (2005) 19 East Eur Politics and Societies 379, 398.

indeed were repurposed in light of their utility to the new regime, though overwhelmingly informers were denounced and cast aside including for the purposes of public service. In the end, in the Czech Republic as has been the case elsewhere, the practice of transitional justice can be massaged and subverted by powerful political actors to pursue their own ends.[13]

Branding informers as monolithically motivated by ideology breeds yet another form of Pyrrhic comfort, namely the comfort of simplification. It is assuaging to view the world binarily in silos of good or bad, unsafe or safe, and wicked or decent. Granularity, after all, can be exhausting.

The depiction of informing as dangerous public politics obscured one of the most painful parts of informing, namely *personal betrayal.* In many instances informers betrayed others for the most materialistic, pedestrian, rancid, envious, immature, or spiteful reasons.[14] In these instances, informing had nothing to do with placing trust in the higher order of the state. Rather, it had all to do with getting things, being weak, being insecure, being greedy, or being opportunistic. When the successor state classed such informers as treacherous betrayers of correct liberal democratic principles, this taxonomical move meant little to informed-upons who may have felt that the betrayal (breach of trust) was deeply personal *to them* and not to the amorphous collective or well-being of the new state.[15]

[13] See generally Cyanne Loyle and Christian Davenport, 'Transitional Injustice: Subverting Justice in Transition and Postconflict Societies' (2016) 15(1) J of Human Rights 126; Sidney Leclercq, 'Injustice through Transitional Justice? Subversion Strategies in Burundi's Peace Process and Postconflict Developments' (2017) 11(3) Int J of Transitional Justice 525; Siwach Sripokangkul, 'Subversion of Transitional Justice in Thailand: Transitional Injustice in the Case of the "Red Shirts"' (2019) 23(10) Int J of Human Rights 1673.

[14] Svetlana Alexievich, winner of the 2015 Nobel Prize in Literature, captures the deep betrayal of informing in her oral history *Second-Hand Time* through the character of Mama Anya. Svetlana Alexievich, *Second-Hand Time: The Last of the Soviets* (Bela Shayevich tr, Fitzcarraldo Editions 2017) 73. *Second-Hand Time* delivers polyphonic reportages about life in the Soviet Union. Among the stories Alexievich relates is one of Elena Yurievna, forty-nine years old—third secretary of the district party committee—within a section Alexievich entitles 'Ten Stories in a Red Interior'. This story is particularly gutting. It is a story of a neighbour who tattles in order to rattle about in a bigger space. Elena recounts: 'A regular communal apartment ... Five families live there—twenty-seven people in total. Sharing one kitchen and one bathroom. Two of the neighbors are friends: one of them has a five-year old daughter and the other one is single with no kids. In communal apartments, people were always spying on one another, listening in on each other's conversations. The people with ten-square metre rooms envied the ones with twenty-five. Life ... That's just how it is ... And then, one night, a Black Maria, a police van, shows up... They arrest the woman with the five-year-old daughter. Before they take her away, she has a chance to cry out to her friend. "If I don't come back, please look after my little girl. Don't let them take her to an orphanage". So that's what happened. The neighbor took the child in, and the building administration gave her a second room ... The girl started calling her Mama ... Mama Anya ... Seventeen years went by ... And seventeen years later, the real mother returned. She kissed her friend's hands and feet in gratitude. If this were a fairy tale, this is where the story would end, but in real life the ending was very different. Without a "happily ever after". When Gorbachev came to power, after they unsealed the archives, they asked the former camp inmate whether she wanted to see her file. She did. So she went down to look at it, opened the folder ... and the very first page was an informant's report. Familiar handwriting ... it was her neighbor's, Mama Anya's ... She'd been the one who'd informed on her ... Do you understand any of this? I don't. And that woman couldn't, either. She went home and hanged herself...' Alexievich, *Second-Hand Time* (n 14) 113–14.

[15] Barbara Miller, *The Stasi Files Unveiled: Guilt and Compliance in a Unified Germany* (Routledge 2017) 135 (noting that in East Germany the informer debate 'seemed not to be an abstract legal or

Betrayal is among the least addressed emotions in human rights and transitional spaces.[16] Branding the informer as a dangerous political toxin (and scarlet-lettering that individual) may bring little relief to an informed-upon who has been hurt because the informer betrayed him, like Judas, for thirty pieces of silver (or the German grudge informer, namely the unfaithful wife who wanted to get rid of the husband because she came to prefer her lover).[17] After all, in such instances informers do not have to address, face, or redress the actual reasons why they betrayed another as all can be chalked up to ideology. In the end, then, public comfort with ostracizing informers can lead to the private pain—or frustration—for informed-upons of not being properly listened to nor properly acknowledged.[18] Informed-upons, as well, became poignantly suborned to political expediencies.

The Czech social rejection of informers stands in contrast with the official approach to many other lower-level Communist-era functionaries, office-holders, teachers, and bureaucrats. Individuals in such capacities who were determined to be of utility to the new liberal capitalist state remained ensconced in their positions. In this vein, Jan Frolík, a former director of the archival services at the Czech Ministry of the Interior, remarks that the demonization of the StB and its informers 'served to exculpate all remaining state apparatus, which [had] also consistently served Communists'.[19] Milan Bárta concurs how in the wake of the Velvet Revolution, informers in the Czech context have largely been seen in negative light, subjected to condemnation, shunning, and stigmatization by society at large.[20] Indeed, the fact that informers could so readily be tarnished—thereby attracting the ire of the public and generating a target for fulmination—effectively shielded many of these other officials. Herein lies yet another form of comfort generated by transitional justice, namely the comfort of selective continuity. These other individuals could simply be seen as deformed products of their time who could become re-engineered after being transitionally vaccinated (thereby permitting their utilitarian repurposing whether in public life or in private enterprise). This led to *cosmetic* outcomes much like the cosmetics of the architectural repurposing discussed in Chapter 3, to wit, new paint jobs and subway station name changes.

political discussion, but one concerning the most basic of interpersonal issues, such as trust and betrayal').

[16] Writing in the context of informers, Dudai concludes that the 'inherently relational act of betrayal ... is considered "parochial" in the human rights framework and does not register as an international crime or human rights abuse in itself'. Ron Dudai, *Penality in the Underground: The IRA's Pursuit of Informers* (OUP 2022) 9 (additionally observing that '[t]he very reasons that make betrayal so attractive for fictional narratives—fluid identities, ambiguous categories, the human drama—appear to render it less amenable to academic research').

[17] For more discussion, see Chapter 1, 'Introduction' n 2.

[18] On the pain of not being properly listened to after having suffered an abuse, see generally Jill Stauffer, *Ethical Loneliness: The Injustice of Not Being Heard* (Columbia University Press 2018).

[19] Francoise Mayer, *Češi a Jejich Komunismus. Paměť a Politická Identita* (Helena Beguivinová tr, Argo 2009) 206 (citing Jan Frolík).

[20] Bárta, 'Úvod' (n 6) 8.

The repurposing of certain buildings is like the repurposing of certain people. Treacherous informers—these lowest of the low, so easy to despise—were banished from public service: much like the toppling and sequestration of certain statues and the erection of new commemorative monuments in their place.

Indeed, it does not take much effort to whip up abhorrence of informers. After all, '[t]he tradition of retaliation against informers spans centuries'.[21] Ron Dudai, writing within the context of Northern Ireland, concludes:

> Informers... are ... despised, with few political actors, if any, willing to challenge their status, and are easily blamed for setbacks. While political reality dictates compromise and even reconciliation with erstwhile enemies as an unsettling yet necessary part of the transition, the reviled figure of the informer remains constant ... [22]

The informer, therefore, is shoved into an infernality that precludes the possibility of reconciliation. Dudai notes how '[t]he rich vocabulary of abusive terms used to describe informers—such as rat, snitch, grass, squealer, stool-pigeon, sneak, snout or narc, and in the Irish context, tout—is but one indication of the contempt in which they are often held'.[23] In Czech, a similar opprobrious vocabulary with largely negative connotations has been used to refer to informers: *udavač*, *bonzák* (both can be loosely translated as tattle-tale), *donašeč* (stool-pigeon), or *fízl* (snoop).[24]

Václav Havel famously opined that 'the line between victim and oppressor ran through each person'.[25] It goes without saying that Havel's admixture of collective involvement and collective responsibility for history may have discomfited many Czechs. In response, turning informers into 'fall guys' could have expiated (or at least eased) that disquiet. Scapegoating could give full effect to the 'We are not like them' slogan of the Velvet Revolution. Fingering informers as vile toxins deflects the need for all individuals to reflect upon their own personal responsibilities for whatever they may have done to sustain Communist governance.

[21] Dudai, *Penality in the Underground* (n 16) 37.

[22] ibid 151. '[I]nformers provide a safe and "economical" target ... no political actor has demanded better treatment for informers.' ibid 149. Dudai notes that in Northern Ireland 'informers provided several functions: a fitting target for hostility and resentment within the post-conflict landscape, a "lightning rod" for various frustrations, a safe outlet for aggressive emotions, a source of identity and legitimation and a useful focal point for the self-definition of ethos and values'. ibid 148.

[23] ibid 37; see also ibid 2 ('Loathing informers, along with the related fear of being labelled an informer ... [r]emains a cultural trope in post-conflict Northern Ireland.'). Dudai goes on to conclude that, in Northern Ireland, the informer is seen 'as enduring enemy'. ibid 136.

[24] Bárta, 'Úvod' (n 6) 7.

[25] James Krapfl, 'Building the Normalisation Panorama' in McDermott and Stibbe (eds), *Czechoslovakia and Eastern Europe in the Era of Normalisation* (n 5) 27, 46 (citing Václav Havel). See also Miller, *The Stasi Files Unveiled* (n 15) 140 (explaining, in the context of East Germany, '[t]he Stasi's informers had been an extremely important part of the machinery, but these mechanisms would never have functioned without the silent conformity of the vast majority of East Germans').

The depiction of informers as loyalists comported with and cemented the anti-Communist agenda of liberal democracy's new elites. As Matěj Spurný, Jakub Jareš, and Katka Volná note:

> The politics of history and the forms of collective memory that were dominant after 1989 have exerted a strong influence on how individual stories have been and are being constructed and remembered. The prevailing image of a criminal, or at least degenerate, regime has produced an opposition between people who helped run the system and collaborated with it, on the one hand, and those who resisted, on the other. People who were adults in the 1970s and 1980s generally want to belong to the second category, and they seek to hide acts which cannot be interpreted as a form of resistance ... and even blame themselves for having failed to resist in such cases. This interaction between collective and individual memory produced an extremely black-and-white image of post socialist society and politics, which makes it difficult to talk about moral dilemmas or the different strategies adopted by historical actors.[26]

In sum, anti-Communist advocacy seems to replace accuracy in the epistemology of why people speak to secret police,[27] thereby attaining political purposes.

While the post-Communist regime may seem intrinsically legitimate, it too was (and remains) routinely concerned with maintaining its own status. Vaněk and Mücke's assembled oral histories ooze with the fears of ordinary citizens thirty years into life under liberal democracy.[28] They note 'popular disenchantment' with neo-liberal capitalist Czech Republic. Many ordinary citizens in the before-times do not perceive those Communist years as all 'grey'.[29] Indeed:

[26] Matěj Spurný, Jakub Jareš, and Kateřina Volná, 'Intellectuals between Collaboration and Independence in Late Socialism: Politics and Everyday Life at the Faculty of Arts, Charles University, Prague' in Péter Apor, Sándor Horváth, and James Mark (eds), *Secret Agents and the Memory of Everyday Collaboration in Communist Eastern Europe* (Anthem Press 2017) 171, 185.

[27] For a discussion of the challenges (epistemological, historiographical, and reintegrative) that arise when advocacy positions replace accurate assessments of the agency of child solders, see Mark A Drumbl, *Reimagining Child Soldiers in International Law and Policy* (OUP 2012).

[28] Miroslav Vaněk and Pavel Mücke, *Velvet Revolutions: An Oral History of Czech Society* (OUP 2020) 4; see also 'Press Release on Public Opinion Survey: Thirty Years from the Velvet Revolution in the View of the Czech Public' (*CVVM*, 29 October 2019) <https://cvvm.soc.cas.cz/en/press-releases/political/democracy-civic-society/5030-thirty-years-after-the-velvet-revolution-in-view-of-czech-public> accessed 22 January 2023 (according to a public opinion poll conducted in 2019 at the time of the 30th anniversary of the Velvet Revolution by the Public Opinion Research Centre (*Centrum pro výzkum veřejného mínění*, CVVM) of the Institute of Sociology of the Czech Academy of Sciences, only 49 per cent of Czechs evaluated life conditions as better compared to pre-1989, 12 per cent preferred the conditions under the previous regime, and 32 per cent felt half and half, ie certain things were better during Communism, certain things were better after).

[29] Matthew Stibbe and Kevin McDermott, 'Czechoslovakia and Eastern Europe in the Era of Normalisation' in McDermott and Stibbe (eds), *Czechoslovakia and Eastern Europe in the Era of Normalisation* (n 5) 1, 4 (discussing Vaněk's scholarship and emphasizing the need of 'developing new, less starkly binary perspectives on the post-1969 Soviet bloc').

> Many narrators did not feel it was contradictory that their working years were a constant drudgery (at work, in a second job, and at home); they had lots of fun with their friends, whether pursuing sports or recreation organized by their trade union, or just sitting down for a beer, even during work hours. The physical grind of work in many professions was in a way compensated for by the state's paternalism, which rid the narrators of their worries (so widespread today) and their own responsibility to make decisions.[30]

Vaněk and Mücke additionally note that many members of 'the public never suspected that neoliberal capitalism had a dark side':[31]

> Ordinary Czechoslovak citizens did not know much about capital, nor did they think much about the capital market or financial investments. Not only did they lack the requisite financial knowledge and skills, they had no savings or contacts with people who did own free capital. As ordinary people reveled in public squares in their newly acquired freedom, entrepreneurs with the necessary connections were already poised at the start line, waiting to spring forward. These were the front runners with the right connections and a clear idea about the prize ... The race was uneven from the start: while most Czechs did not even make it to the starting line, others were pushed off the track.[32]

Indeed, '[t]he environment in post-Communist countries ... connected the (often merely formal) logic of the market with patterns of behavior established in times of real socialism'.[33] These continuities (that benefitted powerful elites and adroit navigators) arguably necessitated an overdrawing of the differences as between past and future and ensconcing an exaggerated firmness of successor ruptures. Transitional justice mechanisms, broadly speaking, served this purpose well, and the vilification of informers generated further grist to that mill. This select number of gerontocratic elites, moreover, channelled generational anger to consolidate select elite continuity while discrediting peers in their same age cohort. This in turn opened the door to an influx of younger individuals into public life, while retaining positions for selected 'former people', to ironically use (our own word choice) the StB's language from the 1950s. On this note:

> [P]eople who were born around 1968, and were in their twenties in 1989, are in the overwhelming majority status staunch advocates of anti-Communist politics, because part of their story has to do with the end of Communism and the

[30] Vaněk and Mücke, *Velvet Revolutions* (n 28) 142–43.
[31] ibid 193.
[32] ibid.
[33] ibid 195.

> establishment of democracy and a market economy, processes in which they took over the positions of their grandparents and parents. Such generational positioning (against parents, the older generation, the authorities) is typical of great social shifts.[34]

The official depiction of informers and collaborators as allegiant political actors also nourishes a revised social history of life under Communism as a gloomy antagonistic binary between warped supporters and valiant resisters.[35] This historical framing presents the regime as the major driving force in life in the miserable before-times. Czech oral histories suggest, however, that many people lived joyfully in this time period—with touches of irony, trying to make the most of it—apolitically focusing on friends, family, work, love, hobbies, the cottage, and their own individual small-scale life.[36] The messaging of the new establishment that life 'back then' was awful indeed vexed many of Vaněk and Mücke's interlocutors, who actually felt hemmed in and hamstrung by this narrative requirement.[37]

In sum, then, the reductively binary transitional justice fulcrum assumed that informers were unable to function properly in the new liberal democracy and, even, that they posed a revanchist threat to it. All of this belies the question whether the informers to be purged were ideologues who cared about Communism or democracy, or (and) were just scaling the system, or (and) were just vindictive or meek souls. Their humanity was flatly erased.

We believe this framing, however expedient, is problematic for a number of reasons. These reasons include: The (in)accuracy of the historical record, state control over how people remember their own lives, dismissal of moral injury, shifting transitional justice for informers away from social reconciliation towards power

[34] ibid 202.

[35] ibid 3 ('It has become increasingly evident that a purely schematic story of an evil, totalitarian regime versus a good, oppressed society is no longer defensible.').

[36] See generally ibid. See also Miroslav Vaněk, 'Twenty Years in Shades of Grey? Everyday Life During Normalisation Based on Oral History Research' in McDermott and Stibbe (eds), *Czechoslovakia and Eastern Europe in the Era of Normalisation 1969–1989* (n 5) 145, 164–65 ('The formerly unprivileged citizens of Czechoslovakia have been caught in a trap set for them by other "judges of history". Today, these arbiters persuade the public that political activism is "highbrow", while realizing oneself in one's family, with friends, in the community, in work, in sport is "lowbrow"—that without political activism it is impossible to live a meaningful life. But narrators have no reason to perceive their lives during normalisation as boring, grey or lowbrow; it would be against the nature of their lived experiences.').

[37] Vaněk and Mücke, *Velvet Revolutions* (n 28) 170 (noting that, as 'ordinary people', these individuals hesitated to speak and 'made embarrassed statements and apologized when their own memories were not in line with the matrix of popular memory'. '[W]hile some people remembered life before 1989 as images of barbed wire, foreign currency vouchers, mandatory celebration of national holidays instituted by the Marxist doctrine, others spoke about the purchase of their first car, their first date with their partner, or happy May Day celebrations.'). One of Vaněk and Mücke's interlocutors, Milena, specifically says: 'I'm sorry, but real life back then was exactly as it is today. Those people had their loves, they had their grievances, their passions. There were good people and bad people, and the same thing repeats itself in every generation . . . Our everyday life wasn't much different from that of our grandparents and our children, under different conditions of course.' ibid 170.

consolidation, and funnelling political malleability.[38] We suggest that candidly recognizing the *mélange* of situational and dispositional elements presents a more accurate aetiology of collaborative informing. Surely the Czech experience might offer lessons learned for transitional justice elsewhere, even if just to be attentive to the diversity of motivations amid the human condition and not to privilege convenience or comfort over robustness and candour.

Roman David points out that transitional justice in the Czech Republic was a 'power game' with new actors occupying exclusionary roles; reconciliation, moreover, was not among the priorities of these new actors.[39] David adds that '[t]he predominantly collective character of the [transitional justice] measures suppressed the complexity of each individual's life story under the weight of the totalitarian regime.'[40] Yet each 'Little Czech'—to deploy David's caustic but insightful language[41]—had his or her own story, and the archived files brim and burst with all of these stories along with the pain they wrought and the hurt they induced. Obfuscating and revamping these stories leads to an incomplete and distorted compendium of collective memory.

Acknowledging the diversity of drivers as among individuals, and longitudinally as over time within the same individual, helps clarify the realities of what people do and how they act, often opportunistically or at times even thoughtlessly, within the repressive structures of an authoritarian state. This exercise contributes to what one of us has elsewhere described as *aetiological expressivism*,[42] namely in this specific instance, to explain how and why informing occurs and how it sustains itself as a social practice.

B. Cruelty

> '[O]ur only immortality is in the police files.'[43]
>
> Milan Kundera, 1978

Transparency—specifically, the publishing of informers' names and the opening of the StB archives—generated multiple winners and beneficiaries while also spawning losers and collateral damage. The blinding blight of light caused by the

[38] Kozák, *Právo Na Pomezí Diktatury a Demokracie* (n 6) 109 (arguing that '[t]he pragmatic aim of lustrations was a defence of democratic institutions[,] not a search for the truth about the past and about real contributions of individuals to the past crimes').

[39] David, 'Transitional Justice Effects in the Czech Republic' (n 2) 114.

[40] Roman David, *Communists and Their Victims—The Quest for Justice in the Czech Republic* (University of Pennsylvania Press 2018) 203.

[41] ibid 43.

[42] For a discussion of aetiological expressivism in the context of international criminal law, see Mark A Drumbl, 'Victims Who Victimise' (2016) 4 London Rev of Int Law 217.

[43] Milan Kundera, *The Book of Laughter and Forgetting* (Aaron Asher tr, Faber & Faber 1996) 120.

opening of the files humiliated many people. This massive public vernissage, so to speak, exposed a large number of informers and their perhaps hapless informed-upons to the eyes of anyone who cared to read about them, including gossip, salaciousness, personal shortcomings, infidelities, mental health issues, embarrassments, powerlessness, and misdeeds. The files, then, became akin to tabloid newspapers.

We contend that transitional justice can lead to cruelty.

What do we mean by cruelty? We take a broad definition. As a starting point we recognize an influential thread in the literature that links cruelty to intentionality and motive. Judith Skhlar, for example, associates cruelty with the worst evil. Skhlar buttons up the commonly held view by defining cruelty as 'the deliberate infliction of physical, and secondarily emotional, pain upon a weaker person or group by stronger ones in order to achieve some end, tangible or intangible.'[44] Other writers equate cruelty with enjoyment, in other words, sadism.[45] Similarly to Skhlar, however, this view centres the existence of cruelty on mindset and intentionality.

We instead choose to approach cruelty in terms of *harm and effects*, to wit, from the perspective of the affected and afflicted. Hence, our construction of cruelty includes intentional and unintentional acts, acts that satisfy the inflictor, planned acts as well as careless or thoughtless or reckless or ignorant acts, deliberate imposition of pain as well as collateral damage. As we see it, great hurt may arise inadvertently. Hence, when we speak of the cruelties of opening up archives—and the cruelties of surfacing long stashed-away secrets—we are not intimating or suggesting that transitional justice activists who exhort such openings-up do so while knowing or intending (or wishing or wanting) to be emotionally cruel. As we see it, cruelty can arise even out of the pursuit of otherwise good intentions. But that does not make it any less cruel, or painful, for those outed or outlawed by transitional justice efforts.

Ironically, the outing or outlawing of individuals by transitional justice modalities may implicate characters who the StB had elected, for whatever reason, not to out or outlaw at the time. The StB, after all, buried a lot of information in the files and thereby submerged all that content among the seams and reams of tissue paper. The StB destroyed many files and reports, as well. The StB did so, amid the heyday of Communism, because significant time had passed after a file was archived following the end of cooperation. In other instances, files were destroyed because the informer grew stale and useless, or emigrated, or passed away, or the conspirational arrangement just petered out. In the twilight of the Communist regime, the StB

[44] Judith Shklar, 'The Liberalism of Fear' in Nancy L Rosenblum (ed), *Liberalism and the Moral Life* (Harvard University Press 1989) 21, 29.

[45] Brent J Steele, '"The Cruelty of Righteous People:" Niebuhr on the Urgency of Cruelty' (2021) 17 J of Int Political Theory 203, 205 ('There are, thus, two core features that define cruelty: the pain of others and the enjoyment in an of such pain.'); see also Shklar, 'The Liberalism of Fear' (n 44) 29 (disclaiming, also, any necessary link between cruelty and sadism).

destroyed files because they feared the recrimination that would arise were the files to be discovered as flotsam and jetsam from the soon-to-be *ancien régime*.

The imperative of transitional justice is to preserve files, safeguard information, and in legal terms to avoid any spoliation of the evidence. Indeed, with the intervention of contemporary technology, the modern transitional justice impulse transcends preserving the physical product and extends to make the contents thereof iron clad through digitization and to render this purificatory content accessible from afar through virtual platforms.

To be sure, clarity and revelatory laws can promote justice interests. Moreover, such laws can surface redemptive things. Informers, after all, could also act generously, graciously, and courageously. They could—and did[46]—subtly or overtly refuse to inform on some people. They could—and did[47]—attenuate the StB quicksand through delaying tactics or obfuscation. The opening of the files reveals all this. Transparency can provide relief by dispelling suspicion that someone close at hand may have been surreptitiously duplicitous.[48] It can show love and commitment. It can highlight gumption and pluck. The closing scenes, heart-warming, of the film *The Lives of Others* come to mind.[49] Here, the flamboyant surveilled author peruses his compendious file and learns that Hauptmann Gerd Wiesler—the Stasi officer tasked to monitor him—had blatantly fabricated pages and pages of transcribed 'recordings' so as to protect the author and his loved ones. The author ultimately dedicates one of his books to the Stasi operative. The demoted operative, dejectedly delivering mail in a hastily reunified Berlin, is too shy to speak to the author when they serendipitously cross paths on a busy street after the fall of the Wall. One is known to the other, one is unknown to the other. But the former Stasi agent peruses that book in the bookstore. He finds that it is dedicated to him, as an operative. He buys it. When asked by the clerk if it is a gift, whether it should be wrapped, he replies, 'no', it is 'for me'.

Yet those same clarity and revelatory laws can also publicize duplicity and backstabbing. We argue that opening the secret police files as archives to the public,

[46] For instance, informer Hájek refused to say anything about his closest friends, told the StB officer he never would do so, and the StB officer accepted this limitation. Indeed, Hájek's informing continued with this caveat. File No 643796, registration No 1233 (Hájek).

[47] For instance, agent Karel seemed to have disappointed his StB officer due to his subpar performance, his failure to deliver required information, and stymieing things in ways that stalled the operations he was supposed to perform. File No 789654, registration No 21213 (Karel). See also File No 731052, registration No 29292 (Dora) (noting how Dora dissembled, parried, and bought herself lots of time).

[48] In her work on the Stasi, Miller notes that opening the archives meant that people learned which of their friends, lovers, and family members did *not* inform on them, which could help relieve and allay suspicious minds. That said, it is unclear whether a chronically suspicious mind could ever truly be assuaged, as that mind could still think the person was indeed a treacherous informer but that the Stasi simply did not record it or that those records ended up getting destroyed. Miller, *The Stasi Files Unveiled* (n 15) 126.

[49] *Das Leben der Anderen* ('The Lives of Others', Florian Henckel von Donnersmarck (dir) 2006).

while vaunted and vaulted as an act of transparency and transition, also can present as an exercise in cruelty.[50]

Cruelty operates on multiple levels. First, to the informer, who is exposed. Indeed, the cycle of life has come back to 'get' him or her, together with oftentimes very private and intimate personal details including identities or life stories of family members. Second, there may be cruelty to the informed-upons, whose improprieties and indiscretions and inanities (rather than just heroic resistances) become matters of the public record, even in contexts where the StB officer decided that the information was not something worthy of official action.

Obversely, archival openings also may create 'false positives', in other words openings may problematically authenticate fabricated stories and legitimize vicious gossip. The files may reveal the (e)motions of informing, but they may not be fully factually reliable. The StB may have acted not only as stenographer but as storyteller recording 'facts' an officer heard independently of what may have actually been said. Many putative cases of 'false positives' have arisen in post-1989 Czechoslovakia and the Czech Republic during the private (and public) publishing of the informer lists. These assignations have triggered contestations and complaints, and at times also legal proceedings.[51]

At this juncture, it is worthwhile to ponder one possible role that the file openings could play, namely to mitigate the cruelty of lists and unjustified lustrations. One permutation is that publicization of a file, or demonstration that there was no file in the first place, could parry these accusations. In some instances, it certainly did. Indeed, some accused informers were able to counterattack and legally clear their reputations. Yet many others did not or tried but failed to do so.[52] What is more, the court of public opinion diverges from the results of court proceedings. Indeed, the stench and taint of a collaborative accusation often lingers socially and discursively. The scandalization of merely being placed on a 'list'—or declared to be a Communist acolyte—sufficed in some instances to taint the accused informer in perpetuity. And all this was before the advent of the Internet, under which the

[50] Conversations about the advantages and disadvantages of public access to collaborator files is not limited to regimes emerging from periods of illiberality. These debates also rage following liberation from periods of outside military invasion. For example, considerable controversy arose in the Netherlands regarding online access to investigators' reports related to the plentiful number of Dutch informers and collaborators during the Nazi occupation. For a detailed discussion, see Herman Zonderland, 'Dutch to Make Public the Files on Accused Nazi Collaborators' *New York Times* (New York, 25 April 2023) (noting that, in the aftermath of the Second World War, more than 300,000 Dutch people were investigated for having collaborated with the Nazis and questioning the effects of opening these files to the public at large—which is imminent, as the restricted access period of seventy-five years is coming to an end—and fearing the effects thereof on their children and grandchildren).

[51] See eg Zdena Salivarová-Škvorecká, *Osočení—Dopisy lidí ze senamu* (Sixty-Eight Publishers 1993).

[52] According to the Czech Ministry of the Interior, for instance, 1,057 individuals contested positive lustration certificates finding that they knowingly collaborated with the StB. In most of these cases —80 per cent—Czech courts found that the StB's registration of the person was unjustified. Obversely, the validity of some *negative* lustration certificates has been challenged. Email correspondence with the Czech Ministry of the Interior, 12 July 2022, on file with the authors.

tarnish of cancel culture is likely to be faster, even more indelible, and all the more conclusively puritanical. No matter whether a person may have been 'cleared' of the lustration or threat thereof, these accusations stick like filthy mud.[53] Lady MacBeth's *cri-de-coeur*—'Out out damn spot!'—now becomes all the more piercing in times of social media.

In his quasi-fictional novel *Two Murders in My Double Life*—partly based on the real-time ordeal endured by his real-life wife, Zdena Salivarová-Škvorecká, as narrated through the character of Sidonia—Josef Škvorecký captures the tremendous power and cruelty of 'the List'; how, regardless of its factual accuracy (even if 'a cocktail of fact and falsification'),[54] 'the List' for many becomes an abusable rod of truthfulness, righteousness, reallocation, and *revanchisme*. It can turn old friends into present foes. It can decimate the socio-economic prospects (and mental health) of those 'listed'. Sidonia, a writer and editor exiled in Canada, had published censored anti-Communist works. Václav Havel (to whom Škvorecký dedicates the book) awards her a prize (the 'Order of the White Lion') for her efforts. Yet soon thereafter it becomes revealed, on an unofficial List, that forty years earlier Sidonia had fleetingly been an StB informer. Following the Velvet Revolution, Mr Mrkvička, 'naive, or more likely vile',[55] published this List, which included Sidonia, in his weekly paper *Kill Kommunism*. Sidonia tries to scrub herself off the List and clear her reputation. She claims she was falsely included and never had informed to the StB, except for one aberration where she actually tried to help her friend and in essence misled the StB. She brings legal action to clear her name. She wins. Yet Sidonia is naïve. After all, 'the suspicion that had fallen on her was hardly disprovable by criminological technique'.[56] She obtained a legal victory, but this simply 'didn't count' with the journal *Kill Kommunism*, with the public, and even with her 'friends'.[57] So in the end, this turn to the law (and towards the authenticity of legal truth) is futile. The suspicion cannot be dispelled. In the end, Sidonia alcoholically succumbs to a 'deadly depression'.[58]

Sardonic and mordant—relating a poignant account that historian Muriel Blaive extensively addresses as historical fact in her own work[59]—*Two Murders in My*

[53] Kavan, *Spravedlnost s náhubkem* (n 12). On scandalization, see Thijs Bouwknegt and Bart Nauta, 'A Cage Went in a Search of a Bird, On the Politics of Condemnation, Compensation and Convalescence' (2023) 21 J of Int Criminal Justice 185.

[54] Josef Škvorecký, *Two Murders in My Double Life* (Farrar, Straus & Giroux 2001) 21. The novel's narrator pithily comments that '[n]obody, except maybe finks, liked the StB informers. ibid 146. This narrator speaks elegiacally (and beautifully) about his wife: her background; the poverty and sweater-sharing she swapped with her sisters; her tired corduroy overcoat and grey beret; her large brown eyes that smiled at him on their first date while she walked toward him from a trolley car; her brother who spent twelve years on state edict in the uranium mines; her father who the state 'chased off to America where he was buried in some pauper's grave' and her mother, 'a used-up woman'. ibid 149.

[55] ibid 7.

[56] ibid 112.

[57] ibid 141.

[58] ibid 7.

[59] Blaive, 'An Impossible Reconciliation' (n 2) (discussing Zdena Salivarová-Škvorecká, whose name appeared in real-time on a list of secret police collaborators in 1992, and noting that '[a]s a young

Double Life is a broiling indictment of the times, of *J'accuse*, and of transitional rancour and recrimination. In Škvorecký's book, those Czechs who weaponized the lists to purge and cleanse indeed presented their contents as accurate. These advocates 'demonstrated the complex and foolproof system of entries into the register, which excluded any possibility of falsification . . .'[60] And, ironically, individuals who challenged their accusations often turned to the StB files thereby also asserting the ostensible veracity of these very same archived documents.

Cruelty also may arise for those who are associated with the informer through family. This is the shame of the daughter or son (or granddaughter, nephew, and so forth) learning a parent (or relative) was an informer. Or, regardless of whether the parent was an informer or an informed-upon, file openings may be painful to children who learn about their parents' (real or invented) imperfect lives back in the time: love affairs, petty crimes, work incompetence, social misfitting, alcohol abuse, and health ailments. File openings can trigger yet another cruelty, namely for a person to learn the past was just a charade, that loved ones surreptitiously reported every private word that was exchanged, that gaslighting abounded all about and all around, that nothing was private, and that one's memoirs had already been written by others.[61] Once a file is publicly available, it may tempt and beguile. In other words, it may be very difficult to avoid opening it, scantily skimming it, perusing it, or even fully reading it. To be sure, not everyone flocks to the archives as some pilgrimage site. Not everyone wishes to read the files. Not everyone succumbs to curiosity. Many citizens, indeed, prefer not to know or are simply disinterested. However, the (al)lure of the files remains. The pull persists. What is more, the post-Communist state certainly encourages the public to learn about the past so as not to repeat it.

One ready response to our concerns over files and cruelty is to enact privacy protection. And, indeed, many jurisdictions have done this. German laws regarding access to the Stasi files come to mind.[62] We are sympathetic to this position. Drawing from the work of Juan Espíndola Mata, we argue that *dignity* and *respect* ought to become important principles to infuse the opening and presentation of records from the past, in this case informer files. These guiding principles

woman, she had indeed agreed to spy on a female friend who was dating a Bulgarian national . . . [s]he wrote two meaningless reports in 1958 in which she tried not to endanger her in any way, and thereafter was left alone—until 1992').

[60] Škvorecký, *Two Murders in My Double Life* (n 54) 155.

[61] On discovering after the fact that extensive moments of one's childhood had been surveilled by others, see Carmen Bugan, *Burying the Typewriter: A Memoir* (Graywolf Press 2012) 210 (discussing the author's childhood in Communist Romania and noting that she experienced her youngest years as bucolic and joyful—full of scents and food and family—only to souringly discover, when the Securitate files were opened, that those years of hers were meticulously scrutinized, yet at the time she had been blissfully oblivious to living in this fishbowl).

[62] Timothy Garton Ash, *The File: A Personal History* (Flamingo 1997) 18 (discussing privacy protection of Stasi victims and innocent third parties in accessing Stasi archives in Germany).

become all the more germane in this day and age when virtuality renders access to such information and the wide dissemination thereof just a click (or two) away.[63] Espíndola Mata makes a strong case that the value of respect—indeed, respect for all—should inform the practice of publicly exposing informers (and in his case collaborators more generally). Dignity and respect matter when it comes to informers who still are living, as well as those who have died and can no longer speak for themselves.

So, assuredly, some of these cruelties can be blunted through privacy mechanisms. Like Espíndola Mata, we would encourage this. Yet for the most part such mechanisms are constructed as exceptions (or caveats) to the broader messianic imperative of the 'right to the truth', which remains a favourite among transitional justice activists. The United Nations has gone so far as to designate a special day to this right—24 March.[64] While recognizing the appeal of the truth, we also are sympathetic to what Christine Schwöbel-Patel describes as the 'right not to be seen' and to her heartfelt plea for life beyond 'visibility'.[65] Hence, we hope to question the self-evident affection transitional justice has for transparency and its concomitant revulsion at secrets.

Martin Kovanic plainly identifies memory laws in the Czech Republic as expressing the conviction that the crimes of the Communist regime must not be protected through secrecy or forgetting,[66] both of which we add have become anathema to the increasingly professionalized best practices of transitional reconstruction. Indeed, transparency is advanced as a social good, namely as cleansing, repairing, salving, and offering an antiseptic for a rotten polity—in short, as pulling the snivelling worm out of the wholesome apple.[67]

But all of this normativity hinges on the premise, central to transitional justice, that secrets are bad and putrefying and that disclosure is proper and purifying. Is it really the case, though, that *all* secrets are bad? That *all* disclosures are good? Or is it just *some* secrets that are bad and *some* disclosures that are good?

[63] Juan Espíndola Mata, *Transitional Justice After German Reunification* (CUP 2015) 27, 32 (noting 'that collaboration with the Stasi as an unofficial informant was degrading, that is, an act of self-disrespect').

[64] 'International Day for the Right to the Truth Concerning Gross Human Rights Violations and for the Dignity of Victims' (*United Nations*, 21 December 2010) <https://www.un.org/en/observances/right-to-truth-day> accessed 12 September 2023.

[65] Christine Schwöbel-Patel, *Marketing Global Justice* (CUP 2021) 253.

[66] Martin Kovanic, 'Institutes of Memory in Slovakia and the Czech Republic: What Kind of Memory?' in Apor, Horváth, and Mark (eds), *Secret Agents and the Memory of Everyday Collaboration in Communist Eastern Europe* (n 26) 94.

[67] After all, Czechs are reminded that those 'who do not know their past are condemned to repeat it'. This language is taken verbatim from the preamble to the law creating the Czech Institute for the Study of Totalitarian Regimes and which opens the StB archives with virtually no public limitations, assuredly begging the question as to who constructs the past in the present. Zákon o Ústavu pro studium totalitních režimů a o Archivu bezpečnostních složek a o změně některých zákonů [Law on the Institute for the Study of Totalitarian Regimes and the Security Services Archive and on Change of Some Laws], Zákon č 181/2007 Sb (Czech) (adopted 8 June 2007).

Sometimes to tell the truth is its own form of disrespect. Such unalloyed sharings may devolve into their own forms of visiting indignities upon others. Lying, hiding, not disclosing: totally selfish, sure, but these acts may safeguard the dignity of others. A difference certainly arises between non-disclosure on the one hand, and active deception on the other.[68] What is more, the palatability of hiding conduct itself hinges upon the effects upon others (ie does it harm others or does it just cause others to take offence?).[69] Should there be a duty to tell? An obligation to reveal? Is it self-evidently desirable for the state to obliterate personal choice in this regard through publicity and exposure, both of which now can reach exponential heights through social media?

In some instances, not disclosing or actively lying about something can give rise to public criminal sanction. One example, in the case of interpersonal relationships, is the attaching of criminal sanction to transgender persons who fail to disclose their birth gender (their gender history) when commencing an amorous relationship with another individual, even when kissing another.[70] In the United Kingdom, such conduct has been criminalized as 'gender fraud'.[71] One basis for this is that the other party has a right to know. Disclosure becomes a prerequisite to consent in such interactions. In the starkly different context of the opening of informer archives to the public, the question still remains whether the state has an obligation to expose, namely, is there a legal *right* for the public to know that which, correlatively, would render official any social *demands* to know. Rights to know can transcend the pursuit of objective facts for epistemological reasons. These rights can also be massaged to secure state-centric political ends, including scapegoating, constructing deviance, and consolidating legitimacy. By making all collected information available, and by presenting the truth in salvatory fashion and exhorting access thereto, the post-Communist Czech state certainly encourages reading the files and learning the truth on the part of society.

Paradoxically, it can be graceful to cover things up. Such was the case with British women in the Channel Islands—the only part of the United Kingdom occupied by the Germans in the Second World War—who had relationships and children with German soldiers.[72] Roughly 60,000 British citizens lived under German

[68] And there is a third category, 'bullshitting', as explored by US philosopher Harry Frankfurt. Harry Frankfurt, 'On Bullshit' in H Frankfurt (ed), *The Importance of What We Care About: Philosophical Essays* (CUP 1988). Frankfurt distinguishes the lie from 'bullshit'. Whereas a lie is inevitably subject to 'the objective constraints of the truth' in order to be plausible, 'bullshit' on the other hand is 'panoramic' in focus, largely 'unconstrained by truth', less 'austere', and essentially indifferent to the fact that at least some of the audience know that they are being bullshitted too, so long as this 'suits the broader purpose.' ibid 59–61.

[69] See generally Joel Feinberg, *Harm to Others: The Moral Limits of the Criminal Law*, vol 1 (OUP 1984).

[70] Alex Sharpe, 'Sexual Intimacy, Gender Variance, and Criminal Law' (2015) 33(4) Nordic J of Human Rights 380, 391. Many thanks to Nikki Palmer for pointing us in this direction.

[71] ibid (discussing three cases, including *R. v McNally* [2013] EWCA Crim 1051).

[72] See generally Madeleine Bunting, *The Model Occupation: The Channel Islands under German Rule, 1940–1945* (Harper Collins 1995). The leader of the Jersey resistance (and a saboteur), Norman

occupation. The occupation years form the subject of a number of museums on the Channel Islands. The Jersey War Tunnels, located several miles north of the city of St Helier on the island of Jersey, now contain rooms that recount life under German rule. Exhibits include letters anonymously handwritten to the local Gestapo offices in which neighbours informed on other neighbours who hid interdicted wireless sets (to listen to the news coming from England) or otherwise circumvented declared rules.[73] A placard affirms that some Jersey postal workers surreptitiously steamed open all letters deposited with them in order to delay any correspondence that involved informing so as to tip off the target.[74]

Other museum exhibits detail the relationships between local women (whose husbands were on the warfront) and German soldiers (whose wives were on the home front). Couples formed. Children were born to such unions; indeed as many as 900. These British women were derisively and scornfully referred to by their co-citizens as 'Jerry bags' in the immediate aftermath of liberation when they endured ostracism and even attacks.[75] The children, however, were largely accepted in the community. The Jersey War-Times Archives (opened only in the 1990s) and other sources detail the births of these children and how some British husbands, after returning from the war front, stepped into paternal roles as they rejoined their wives who had in the interim become mothers. According to journalist Jojo Moyes, most residents of the Channel Islands, decades later, say these issues 'should be left well alone'.[76] Indeed, the opening of these archives triggered disquiet, discomfort, and awkwardness. Ignoring, concealing, and obscuring became a preferred societal route, in particular, as time ticked by and war memories faded. But even when those memories were fresh, collaborators and informers who helped the German occupiers never faced any official sanction by British authorities.

Le Brocq, was the founder of the Jersey Communist Party and lamented the fact that collaborators, including the leadership of the Islands during the occupation, never were punished. In 1966, Norman Le Brocq and nineteen other Islanders were awarded gold watches by the Soviet government (on display in the Jersey War Tunnels Museum) as a sign of gratitude for their role in the resistance movement. See also Mark A Drumbl and Barbora Holá, 'Becoming More Informed About Informers' 2023 17(2) Int J Transitional Justice 348, 353–56 (book review essay).

73 The consequences of being caught could range from fines to imprisonment to wretchedly severe outcomes, namely execution, deportations to concentration camps, and brutal forced labour.

74 Placard from the Jersey War Tunnels Museum, author visit on 22 October 2022 ('So concerned were a group of Post Office sorters who handled this despicable mail that they decided to steam open the letters addressed to the Commandant, warn those who had been informed against, and then delay the arrival of the mail for 24 hours. This gave time for the illegal wireless, bag of corn or whatever, to be got rid of before the search began.') Another placard in the Jersey War Tunnels Museum reveals quiet resistance of a different sort involving a local newspaper: 'The *Evening Post* continued to be printed throughout the Occupation. However, strict censorship was enforced and the Germans wrote their own articles of propaganda. Arthur Harrison, the newspaper editor, would leave the English uncorrected so readers could tell it was written by the Germans.'

75 As with the *femmes tondues* throughout France.

76 Jojo Moyes, 'How Jersey's Nazi Children Disappeared' *The Independent* (London, 23 November 1996).

Sustaining relationships, communities, and interactions may well necessitate the cultivation of secrets and omissions and lies. Beautiful things can grow out of secrets and ugly things can fester because of secrets. And sometimes secrets—and denials—just help people make it to tomorrow after a raggedly long night. Secreting can be a tactic of social navigation.

One of the greatest scourges of a surveillance state, such as Communist Czechoslovakia, is to sow endemic mistrust among citizens. Informers do this.[77] Czechoslovaks never knew whether they were interacting with someone who would report it all—every pitiful straggling word—to the authorities. Although Czech oral histories suggest that there may have been greater interpersonal trust in the Communist times than the official post-Communist narrative intones, it is clear that massive surveillance does not encourage candour or genuineness. The response of transitional justice to this pervasive mistrust is to endeavour to build trust through openness and transparency. Secrets are, to put it bluntly, seen as tasteless and vile. In the Czech transitional context, secrecy and secrets regarding informer conduct were additionally considered problematic as they could have been easily exploited and (ab)used in order to blackmail individuals, in particular those active in politics, in exactly the same way as the StB had done (including to informers).[78] Paradoxically, however, high-quality scholarly work demonstrates that transparency implemented through lustrations and lists—and didactically encouraged by the democratic state—either furthered suspicion and curried mistrust among citizens or was inconsequential in terms of promoting a culture of reciprocal openness. For example, Cynthia Horne, in her comparative empirical study, found that 'lustration is correlated with declining interpersonal trust or, depending on the model, has no relationship with trust'.[79] Horne's findings rebut the presumption that lustration nurtures interpersonal trust.

Transitional justice has an aversion to secrets and secreting. It largely constructs 'cultures of secrecy' as malignant and rotten. But is transparency and honesty necessarily a successful response to mistrust and duplicity? Imposed openness may become a blunt cudgel. Like informing, secreting is a tool of social navigation. Some secrets are beautiful (informers who demonstrated loyalty to some folks, protected them, hid things from the secret police, then never told anyone what they omitted from saying); some secrets are necessary; and some secrets are ugly. Cultures of secrecy, and secrets themselves, are indispensable for resistance to arise within an authoritarian state or oppressive society. There can be no just liberation without many secrets; nor can there be social justice against historically heinous manacles or any stealthy revolution that pluckily overcomes oppression.

[77] cf Miller, *The Stasi Files Unveiled* (n 15) 2 (noting that the Stasi informers 'deliberately exploited trust').

[78] Petr Pithart, *Po Devětaosmdesátém: Rozpomínaní a přemítaní* (Academia 2016) 264–82.

[79] Cynthia M. Horne, 'Lustration, Transitional Justice, and Social Trust in Post-Communist Countries. Repairing or Wrestling the Ties that Bind?' (2014) 66(2) Europe-Asia Studies 225, 243.

Perhaps secrets are another subject for transitional justice scholars and practitioners, including lawyers, to engage with. Little work has been undertaken in this area, certainly counter-intuitively in a fashion that hesitates categorically to denounce secrecies of any sort.

II. Whither Condemnation?

Should transitional justice theory and practice concern itself with informers? Perhaps the first step in answering this question is to identify the *goal* of placing informers within transitional justice processes. Transitional justice pursues a panoply of at times contradictory aspirations. These include retribution, deterrence, non-recurrence, rehabilitation, expressivism, reintegration, reconciliation, and the legitimation of the new regime. Transitional justice turns to a broad palette of modal interventions to achieve these outcomes. Tension has nonetheless arisen as between punitive and non-punitive remedies within transitional justice rubrics.[80] Over time, transitional justice has come to incorporate more of criminal law's retributive elements and to distance itself somewhat from remedies that focus on reconciliation and rehabilitation. For example, critical feminists have observed an at times disconcerting turn to carceralism to promote international human rights, including gender equality, including in the wake of mass violence.[81] This drift-shift may be explained by transitional justice's increasing intersection with neo-liberal economics. Transitional justice efforts are wedded to capitalism. Transitions are seen to be legitimate if they move towards (or support) neo-liberal economics and all its requisite political scaffolding.[82] Insofar as retribution and penal ordering is necessary to build and sustain such political economies, well, then it seems inexorable that such a drift-shift might occur. What is more, whereas judicialized and legalized outcomes (eg jail sentences and lustrations) may be easily quantifiable and hence computable to donors upon whom global civil society relies, social processes such as reconciliation and reintegration are not readily capable of handy measurability. As a result, they present as more vexing to the calculus of funding and determinations of return on investment. The encasing in the international legal imagination of criminal trials as the 'first-best' response to atrocity has further consolidated the power of penal process, as operationalized through

[80] See generally Mikkel Jarle Christensen, 'The Borderlands between Punitive and Non-punitive Transitional Justice: Distinct Elites and Diverging Patterns of Import/export' (2020) 14(3) Int J of Transitional Justice 464.

[81] Karen Engle, 'Feminist Governance and International Law: From Liberal to Carceral Feminism' (2017) 690 Public Law and Legal Theory Research Paper, University of Texas School of Law <https://papers.ssrn.com/sol3/papers.cfm?abstract_id=3091260> accessed 12 September 2023.

[82] Marcos Zunino, *Justice Framed: A Genealogy of Transitional Justice* (CUP 2019) (noting that those transitional justice initiatives that are 'remembered' are those that embrace neo-liberalism and safeguard market economics owing to their 'sympathy for capitalism').

the complementarity doctrine, such that modalities of justice that depart from the tenets of procedural liberal legalism are encouraged to mimic those tenets in order to retain currency and credibility.[83]

In the Czech Republic, the two primordial goals pursued by transitional justice interventions were retribution and the legitimation of the new regime. Assuredly, in the Czech Republic informers were not criminally prosecuted. This choice certainly must have angered some Czechs as being too lenient. This means that Czech transitional justice was not starkly retributive. However, other modalities of transitional justice also can have (or can be infused with) robust streaks of punitiveness, denunciation, and condemnation. So it has been in the Czech Republic in the decades since the Velvet Revolution. Professionalized, and increasingly ribbed by technical best practices, transitional justice becomes beset with political contingencies which means that it might perceive less and less accurately (a banal informer muddling through life becomes seen as appalling and dangerous).

Our presentation of informing as a conversational, intrinsic, and coping exercise cautions against zealously placing informers within the moralizing and condemnatory frames of transitional justice. The ordinariness and liminality of informers—to wit, their humanity—and their recurrent victim–victimizer status awkwardly interfaces with their becoming subject to extraordinary disjunctive ruptures and righteous reckonings. Hence, we argue that the reconciliatory, rehabilitative, and reintegrative goals of transitional justice interventions might be more suitable for informers in light of the social positionality informers tend to occupy during and after repression.

Our goal is to initiate a conversation oriented toward the development of mechanisms that can speak in a forthright sense about the nuance of the informer, respect the dignity of all involved, and dissipate the coercive power of those who run the newly emergent state so as to ensure inclusivity and fairness while also promoting redress for persons aggrieved by the acts of informers. At the same time, we aspire to restrain transitional justice's tendency to exercise empire over morality[84] and to curb the pursuit of comfort through cruelty.

Talking about informing really means reflecting upon ourselves, regardless of whether one has lived in a repressive society or a free one (or both). Indeed, as we elaborate further in the conclusion to this book, informing is ubiquitous. While very few people have killed or maimed someone, nearly everyone—well, we will just say it, indeed, all of us—has informed, betrayed, or gossiped on someone to authorities (parents, teachers, administrators, or supervisors). This project on informing is therefore intimate and personal. When we presented this book in

[83] See generally Mark A Drumbl, *Atrocity, Punishment, and International Law* (CUP 2007) ch. 5 on 'legal mimicry'.

[84] Many thanks to Diane Marie Amann for this insight, delivered as comments at the American Society of International Law Mid-Year Meeting on Research in response to a presentation by the authors of this book in draft.

seminars or workshops, listeners routinely responded that they saw themselves in this book, whereas, on the other hand, so much of international criminal law (and transitional justice) is 'othered' in that very few people have actually killed or tortured or ordered such violence. Christopher Browning famously unwinds how 'ordinary' men ended up in the German Reserve Police Battalion 101, which committed a terrifyingly large number of mass shootings of Polish Jews in 1942.[85] These men committed extraordinary acts that hardly anyone else has committed. So their ordinariness is quite circumscribed. Informers do far more ordinary things compared to Browning's 'ordinary' individuals. We have all informed at some stage of our lives, we have all deceived, we have all ratted someone out to an authority figure, nearly all of us have smeared someone for some purported advantage or because we felt we had to or that it was the right thing to do.

Informing and transitioning, moreover, both are practices that share in common conversational processes of social navigation. Perhaps a starting point, then, for transitional justice in the case of informers might be for it to imagine itself as conversational and constitutive rather than condemnatory and denunciatory. As pursuing cooperation and reconciliation, rather than subordination and exclusion. When it came to StB informers, transitional justice in the Czech Republic tended to be both underinclusive (beyond coercion it did not matter why an informer informed) and also overinclusive (when it came to who ended up in the net of lustrations, scalded by the web of the lists, or simply being badgered by anti-Communists). Crude measures such as the ones adopted in the Czech Republic lost nuance, complexity, and context; they simultaneously underperformed and overperformed; they painted too thinly and in other ways lacquered too thickly.

One response to the concerns that inhere in placing informers within transitional justice processes is that these processes are too intrinsically unwieldy and, hence, it might make sense to do nothing. In other words, perhaps informers should assumptively hover beyond the reach of transitional justice. That said, a society that does *nothing* about informers—a transition that completely unplugs—might trigger sentiments of injustice, emptiness, and anger. After all, as we have consistently demonstrated, StB informers inflicted, or were part of chains that inflicted, great pain on others. This pain ranged a gamut from demotions, job losses, evictions from homes, denials of livelihoods, arrests, imprisonment, beatings, and torture. In the absence of some formal accountability process, people may just take things into their own hands. It goes without saying that informers have always faced private consequences for their betrayals: Indeed, so goes the colloquialism,

[85] Christopher R Browning, *Ordinary Men* (Harper Collins 1993) (signalling the importance of group dynamics, deference to authority, role altering, reformulation of moral norms, and conformity); see also David Chandler, *Voices from S-21: Terror and History in Pol Pot's Secret Prison* (University of California Press 2000) (discussing *inter alia* the individual psychological dimension that conditions people to commit torture and executions).

snitches get stitches.[86] Hence, perils arise for a libertarian transition beyond the state insofar as such a transition might cultivate vigilantism, vindictiveness, and vengeance.

Martha Minow posits that it might be plausible to forgive entire groups of people (lesser serious offenders, to be clear) for certain offences as part of transitional justice.[87] We believe the value of forgiveness is important when it comes to informers, who already begin with the social premise of being disgusting. Minow, writing in 2019, laments that 'ours is an unforgiving age'.[88] Forgiveness, according to Minow, does not however mean that there are no consequences (or requirements) for group members who are to be forgiven.[89] Consequences, after all, can ease forgiveness. But scapegoating and vilification—which can be facilitated by transitional justice—precludes forgiveness as it leads to excommunication from the collective and the imposition of the insecurities of the group upon the outcasts' shoulders. Forgiveness may instead be nudged by careful and balanced intervention.

While we believe that, in principle, many informers could be left outside of the *condemnatory* purview of transitional justice, the fact remains that making all informers invisible—with no granularity or fine-tuned analysis—would mirror the practices we have critiqued throughout this book. This is because such *simplification in reverse* would afford comfort to some and impose cruelty on others, notably, the informed-upons who might have suffered great harms. Therefore, categorically overlooking informers would also seem fundamentally unfair. Such a move would also be unproductive insofar as it would sideline reconciliation and reintegration. If transitional justice proceeds with our vision of a light touch, we believe this can and should be a nimble and thoughtful touch at the same time. We believe it would be helpful for this touch to be principled. Hence, we distil some takeaways that could sharpen the lens to avoid the comfort and cruelty that arise from the antipodes of excessive condemnation or numbing silence.

Insofar as transitional justice in the Czech Republic was both underinclusive and overinclusive, we develop a heuristic to advance a more individualized and fine-grained approach. We sketch this heuristic to promote reconciliatory goals insofar as it is our belief that the more transitional justice individualizes and assesses details the less expediently condemnatory and reflexively derisive it would become. Therefore, we identify six factors to consider in any evaluation that transitional

[86] Thanks to Kieran McEvoy for emphasizing this point in the context of informers and touts during the Troubles in Northern Ireland. It may be that usurping this space through public law, or official policy, can attenuate some of these less controllable individuated responsive actions.

[87] Martha Minow, *When Should Law Forgive?* (Norton 2019).

[88] Sarah Lustbader, 'Making Room for Forgiveness' *New York Review of Books* (New York, 18 November 2021) (extensively discussing Minow's work in the US and international contexts); see also Minow, *When Should Law Forgive* (n 87) (contrasting specifically the lack of forgiveness in matters of human rights violations with the prevalence of forgiveness in matters of bankruptcy and debtor's law).

[89] Martha Minow, *Between Vengeance and Forgiveness* (Beacon Press 1998) 14–21.

justice interventions would make of an informer. We believe incorporating these factors would help return transitional justice to its non-penal roots. Care in this regard is all the more important since it is inherently combustible to put informers into transitional justice processes because informers are so easily maligned. Therefore, attentiveness to the heuristic we propose could mitigate political machinations and also promote justice for the aggrieved. Should state actors proceed with integrating informers into the mechanics of state-run transitional justice processes, then we believe our work can help develop a heuristic about how the human impulse to judge, after the fact, could constructively intersect with the seeming human impulse to inform in the moment.

In the Czech Republic, other than knowledge of speaking to StB, none of these factors mattered. Hence, Czech transitional justice became garish and fairly (though not fully) retributive. We envision a more supple frame that channels transitional justice toward a humanized inquiry that eschews the alluring comfort of bright lines and that welcomes Havel's withering observation how the lines of responsibility—of harmed and harm-doer—run through everyone. We include informers with meekly weak individuals (victims who victimize) who socially navigate the spaces available to them in times of metastasized repression which, at times, means they may come to exercise considerable situational power over others. In nearly all instances, informers suffered the harms they visited upon others insofar as they were constantly surveilled by others. A sticky web of monitoring arose.

We propose the following six elements, in no particular ordinality, to be considered in a heuristic framework applicable to the interpellation of informers into transitional justice processes: (i) harm; (ii) constraint; (iii) time; (iv) motivation; (v) content; and (vi) awareness. These elements overlap. Such is certainly the case as between harm and awareness, as well as constraint and motivation. But we believe there to be sufficient independence among these six elements—notwithstanding their interactive interdependence—to class them as we do. This heuristic exercise, moreover, might also help inspire conversation about what kinds of elements might lead to the acts of an informer being seen as more or less in need of placement within transitional justice modalities in order to merit forgiveness pursuant to Minow's understanding of the term. Prudent consideration of these elements could also favour the selection of (or weight attributed to) specific modalities of transitional justice over others in any given case. In any event, setting out these elements—derivative of our 'up close' look at informers—could contribute to understanding informing as a social practice. We briefly tease, in part through questions, some components of each element.

(1) *Harm*. An act of informing could be scoped *by the actual or anticipated harms it visits upon third parties*. The commission of that harm, to be sure, overwhelmingly lies with state agents. But the acts of the informer comprise

part of that invidious causal chain. If the informing, for example, ultimately leads to torture and death, then it might be seen as graver, and hence requiring much more work to earn forgiveness, than if the informing leads to nothing or to outcomes such as a transitory work demotion. Assuredly, one shortcoming with this factor is that the harm itself is contingent upon the independent conduct of the secret police or other state actors. Hence, one way to address this intervening factor is also to add an assessment of whether the informer *knew*, or *ought to have known, of the consequences of informing on that other person*, in other words, what the secret police likely would do with the information that was supplied. Still, the harm may be the same regardless whether the informer acted knowingly, cluelessly, or was unaware of what would happen. Another intermingled wrinkle here is whether the information the informer provided exceeded what was asked by the StB agent. Did informers implicate individuals the StB had not asked them to track? Also, how did the informer speak about the purported transgression—was the language denunciatory and firm, or presented in a way that could have mollified the authorities into inaction?

(2) *Constraint.* This factor considers *the degree of coercion and duress that state officials exercise over the informer*. Was the informer blackmailed?[90] Entrapped, as was the case with Volný? Presumptively, the higher the level of coercion (and the longer its duration) then deductively the informing might become less agentic and, hence, easier to forgive. On this note, perhaps the informer's own vulnerabilities could slide into the discursive rubric. By this we mean the subjectivity of fear: Zuzana, for example, was frightened because she erroneously believed the StB knew everything anyway, yet at the same time she offered very little in terms of useful information (which goes to our fifth factor, namely content), while Volný was just a fearful personality overall. Even if aggressively bullied, some informers—Lily, for instance—remain defiant in deeply repressive times and plausibly such exercises of agency could militate in favour of treating that informer less harshly or adopting different reconciliatory methods. What about informers who were both defiant and cooperative, such as Hájek (who openly refused to inform on his friends but readily informed on others)? Another element of the vulnerability of informers might be their mental and physical health, their addictions, and their dependencies. What if they were just incompetent and bumbling, like Karel, and hence ineffective?

(3) *Time.* Might it matter for how long the individual informed? Whether the informer acted serially or fleetingly in a handful of instances? Or only offered a single denunciation? It could be that the acts of a long-run

[90] The fact that an informer was blackmailed into informing was taken by the IRA as a mitigating factor, although culpability never was eliminated. Dudai, *Penality in the Underground* (n 16) 170.

informer (Věra, for instance) can cumulatively be seen as more troubling (and as more in need of transitional attention) than a one-off informer who then ceased informing. How do shapeshifters fit into the equation, that is, people who are equal opportunity informers through time—informing for the Nazis, then for the StB, and then also for Western intelligence (or other agencies), such as Goldfus? These individuals derive meaning or resources from informing to anyone who is in charge, and they ostensibly would inform to the new liberal democratic authorities as well. Time, moreover, can also involve directionality. Would it matter if over time the informer spoke less and detached from the StB as things soured? Instinctively, it would seem so. This was the case for a number of the informers we encountered—for example, Redaktor who, by the end of his decade-long encounters with the StB began to ignore them. Alternately, Kongres just wanted more and more over time and, hence, informed more and more. Does it matter if an informer, like Věra, started off pushed into informing but then excelled at it and ended up doing it regularly while aging in relative security and comfort?

(4) *Motivation.* Our central goal has been to identify *why* people spoke to the StB. We do so to understand informing better and to present a more accurate aetiology of the provenance of informing in Communist Czechoslovakia. A cognate question now arises. This is whether motivation should matter as a factor in the operation of transitional justice interventions. This question was not meaningfully explored (ie no-one 'went there') even in one of the iconic philosophical discussions about the morality of law as assessed through acts of an informer, namely, the 'grudge informer' who denounced her husband to Nazi authorities because she was having an affair and wanted to get rid of the husband after he returned from the front.[91] We believe that including motivation among the elements of a heuristic would guard against the deforming simplicity of casting all informers irredeemably as pariahs and, hence, as unforgiveable. We believe that including motivation in any evaluative assessment would dilute the reactionary tendency to scapegoat informers and to demolish their dignity. The irrelevancc of

[91] See Chapter 1 'Introduction' n 2. The wife reported the husband's comments on her own initiative. Factually, the husband had made the comments that insulted Hitler. And his comments indeed contravened Nazi law. The wife's motivation (personal, to get rid of the husband so as to pursue her affair) was not at all dispositive to the overall discussion, or judgment. It could be speculated whether the German Court of Appeal's response may have been different were she to have been compelled by the state to disclose the insult, or whether she informed for the good of preserving Nazism. In another permutation, it could be conjectured whether her adultery infiltrated the Court of Appeal's perception or her status as wife (would the same have been the case were the gender roles to have been reversed?), or if she wanted to 'get rid of' the husband because he had abused her. As an aside, the Nazis found the husband guilty 'and sentenced [him] to death, though it seems that he was sent to the front in lieu of execution'. David Dyzenhaus, 'The Hart–Fuller Debate at Fifty: The Grudge Informer Case Revisited' (2008) 83 NYU L Rev. 1000, 1004. The German Court of Appeal did note that the wife knew that her report would lead to a possible range of deleterious outcomes for her husband, which ratchets back to our first identified factor, namely, the harm principle.

actual motivation in extant transitional justice processes leads to a problematic malleability that allows the informer to be restyled in ways that suit the interests of powerful actors and, in a sense, denies official historical accuracy to the informed-upons which, in turn, negates the betrayal they may have felt and precludes forgiveness and empathy. We noted when we first presented the file-stories that details do matter. This is not to say that the (e)motions of informers are static. Hence a supple and longitudinal lens is beneficial. Indeed, individual motivations change through time, in particular in cases where the informer was longer-term and drivers varied as the years passed. Also, some informers were animated by multiple motivations at the same time.

(5) *Content.* Another possible factor to be considered implicates the content, salience, verifiability, veracity, or pertinence of the information generated to the sustainability or existence of the regime. Hence, the gossipy informer sharing affairs and petty theft from the accounting department could be differentiated from the informer who proffers incontrovertible information that relates to sedition, threats to national security, resistance, or upcoming revolt. Just as with the harm factor, issues of the causal chain arise (namely, for the StB even scurrilous information was used to blackmail and cajole others into informing, or face consequences, in the putative interests of 'national security'). Furthermore, it is ultimately the decision of the secret police to verify the information—to test it, assess its pertinence through corroboration or some kind of process—and then decide to discard it, bury it, or act upon it.

(6) *Awareness.* The final element of our heuristic relates to whether informing was done knowingly, in other words, did informers know (or ought they to have known) that they were speaking to secret police who could have (ab)used the information for its authoritarian and arbitrary practices.[92] Some informers were candidates for secret collaboration and may not have fully known what was going on or that what they were divulging was being recorded. In this respect, *awareness of audience* bears upon, but is distinguishable from, the *cognizance of harm* which we mention as the first factor. *Awareness* could be imputed when an informer signed a written pledge to collaborate (which does not necessarily mean that knowledge of harm can be assumed from this performatory act). For *awareness*, therefore, in our understanding it is not solely determinative whether an informer's reporting contributed to or caused harm. The gist of this element is that the informer knowingly cooperated with the secret police and thus contributed to the repressive apparatus.

[92] 'Knowing collaboration' was the only differentiation recognized by transitional practice in both Czechoslovakia and the Czech Republic.

In sum, then, we believe that the preceding heuristic derived from our research could help guide—or, more realistically, initiate a guiding conversation—about how to structure transitional justice interventions for informers.

III. Conclusion

State legitimacy is temporal and historical. States initially appreciated as popularly legitimate can curdle into popular illegitimacy, often through their sustained deployment of coercion and repression. Our book is about informing in repressive times, curried by a state which, following revolution and channelled by processes of transitional justice, shrivels and is supplanted by a newer and presentable successor. We offer some observations rooted in the Czech experience and extrapolate from these to gaze beyond.

One goal of transitional justice is deterrence and non-recurrence of the problematic harmful conduct. So let's say that transitional justice succeeds in stamping out informing. Is that desirable? Do people really want to live in a society where informing as a social practice never occurs? Or barely happens? Or is illegal? In such a context we wonder what that society would look like. Where would the whistle-blowers be? How would law enforcement function? Public health protocols be enforced? Without informing, how to sustain a *nomos* that excludes misogyny, homophobia, transphobia, racism, and hate?

If people do not want to live in a society where the practice of informing is eliminated, a need arises to separate desirable informing from undesirable informing. We do not believe the answer is as facile as to say that some states (and rules) just inherently are bad, so supporting them is bad, while other states (and rules) inherently good, so supporting them is good. Bad states may make some good rules, and good states may make some bad rules; rules may be good for some and bad for others; and the need for rules change. In the end, things are more nuanced. All cannot hinge on the perceived legitimacy of the state or rule.

All this leads to another line of inquiry. Is anything that we uncover in our book of any use to understand informing *outside* illiberal contexts? Is there any crossover value? What motivates informers in so-called healthy states? Admittedly, the self-evident divide between liberal and illiberal contexts can also be fuzzy, as there are plenty of repressive and desperate spaces within purportedly free societies, many of which are fertile grounds to cultivate informers. Still, we wonder about the implications of how transitional justice *thinks about* informers in extraordinary times for how informers *are thought about* in ordinary, routine times in liberal societies. We pursue this conversation a bit further in Chapter 7 which also concludes our book.

7

Informers Here, Informers There, Informers Everywhere

We wind up by recapping, and then wind down by wondering whether our ruminations about what we have learned about informers in Communist Czechoslovakia might have any cross-over value for thinking about informers in liberal societies.

I. Recapping this Book

This book's journey begins in Chapter 1 with placing the act of informing within the broader context of collaboration. We define the informer as an individual who gathers and supplies information to authorities. Informing can occur in multiple contexts: to occupying powers, to non-state actors, to repressive autocracies, and to liberal regimes. Insofar as this book nests in Communist Czechoslovakia, the informers that we centre in our analysis are those who informed on citizens to authorities of a repressive regime—their own state—and, in light of the *dénouement* of that regime, who then became caught up in transitional justice processes. Our focus is on 'everyday informing', and on the construction of Czechoslovak state–society relations as interactively webbed and as evincing both participatory dictatorship and social engineering. The source data we principally rely upon are the StB files. In Chapter 1 we elucidate the limits and opportunities presented by secret police archives as knowledge sources to better understand informers and construct a history of quotidian life in Communist Czechoslovakia. In Chapter 1 we also introduce what we mean by (e)motions and their role in human decision-making. On this note, we hope to underscore the salience of an ontological perspective in reckoning with behaviour, in other words to set out and grasp the nature of being, and then to reflect upon how institutions can respond to innate human nature.[1]

Chapters 2 and 3 of this book respectively provided background on the history of the StB in Communist Czechoslovakia and also the modalities of transitional justice that were pursued following the Velvet Revolution. These chapters help situate readers. Each of these chapters describes the ways in which the governing state endeavoured to reset society—initially into Communism and then from

[1] For a similar approach rooted in ontological critique, see Alan Norrie, *Criminal Justice and Moral Psychology* (forthcoming, manuscript on file with the authors).

Informers Up Close. Mark A. Drumbl and Barbora Holá, Oxford University Press.
 DOI: 10.1093/oso/9780192855138.003.0007

Communism into liberal capitalist democracy. These transformative cycles recall Bohumil Hrabal's short story, 'Ingots',[2] in which Hrabal envisions a large foundry staffed with citizens who stuff the furnaces full of 'scrap'. This 'scrap' arrives in railway car wagons from all over the country. One wagon bursts with 'cylinders and pistons, a glass disc, the crushed remains of Leyden jars, twisted compasses, metal hoists with weights and counterweights, a bundle of iron rods and electromagnetic coils, an upright galvanoscope, a spectroscope, and a sextant with mirrors'.[3] A second wagon, once its latch is pried loose, reveals 'a sump pump, an old blower, pieces of a threshing machine, a farm gate that had been dismantled with a cutting torch, a paper cutter, a seed drill, a field mower, an old weigh scale, and parts of a plough'.[4] All these contents are tossed into the hopper that leads to the foundry's furnace. This flotsam and jetsam of daily life in the former regime exits from the furnace as new ingots, and these ingots that 'pour out of those furnaces are meant for a different era'.[5] In Hrabal's short story, the foreman instructs the workers: 'What'll become of you? The same as all this scrap, the tools of your trade, you'll be ingots too. This new age is melting you all down . . . '[6]

Political transitions are much like Hrabal's foundries. The rubble of the past becomes cleared off and melted down, citizens are recast into ingots of the new era (whether Communism in 1948 or liberal democracy in 1989) amid cyclical processes of change, belying the pyrrhics of the 'end of history' and the illusion of the 'last man'.[7]

Chapter 4 highlights the file-stories of six informers: Věra, Vašek, Lily, Goldfus, Volný, and Soukup. The file-stories demonstrate the complexities of the relationships between state and society in Communist Czechoslovakia. They reveal the social engineering effects of the state and the individually agentic contributory role of individuals. Each file-story showcases a cocktail of (e)motions that pulled informers towards and pushed informers away from the StB and vivifies how these sentiments morphed over time.

Chapter 5 identifies what jumps out at us from our 'up close' look at twenty-three StB file-stories, additionally buttressed by secondary sources, oral histories, literary accounts, and professional conversations. The chapter offers a number of key conclusions about the social practice of informing in Communist Czechoslovakia. For us, concepts such as intimacy, power, and exchange colour the relationship between StB officers and 'their' informers. Lenses such as relational contracting, bureaucratic justification, conversational expiation, and social

[2] Bohumil Hrabal, 'Ingots' in *Mr. Kafka and Other Tales from the Time of the Cult* (authored 1965, Paul Wilson tr, New Directions 2015) 55–76.
[3] ibid 56.
[4] ibid 57.
[5] ibid 73.
[6] ibid.
[7] See generally Francis Fukuyama, *The End of History and the Last Man* (Free Press 1992).

navigation are integrally helpful to elucidate the nature of the rapport between StB handlers and informers. Informing blurs the line between the political and the personal. Many informers turned to the StB to leverage their private wants and actualize their immediate needs. Informing thereby fulfils goals of commiseration and compensation. Chapter 5 sheds light on the question why people speak to secret police by examining the role of emotions as catalysing and then sustaining such interactive exchanges. Four emotions in particular stand out: fear, resentment, desire, and allegiance. This chapter invokes the file-stories to illustrate these emotions in the life stories of informers, while also noting that StB officers, as well, expressed sentiments such as solicitude and disappointment as part-and-parcel of their interactions with 'their' informers. The emotional drivers of the interactions between StB handlers and informers were not static. Indeed, one trend we noticed was that whereas fear may have triggered the initial pledge, over time informers began to turn to informing to get ahead, to get things, to get even, and to settle scores. Certain cooperative relationships between informers and the StB lasted for decades; over the course of all these years informing assumed varying rhythms. In the end, informers occupy liminal spaces between being victimized (often marginal, beset with personal struggles, health challenges, vulnerable, and perennially surveilled) and being victimizers (betraying others, harming others, lording power over others, and inflicting considerable pain on persons regarding whom they funnelled information to the StB). Informing quite simply broke a number of informers, shattering their souls and spirits.

Chapter 6 sets out normative takeaways for transitional justice in the Czech Republic and also beyond. Pressure arises for post-authoritarian successor regimes to 'do something' about their abusive predecessors and whoever is determined to have supported those abuses. Chapter 6 argues that, following the Velvet Revolution, Czech informers were scapegoated and vilified. They were officially cast as dangers to the new liberal democracy. They were thus stylized in a distorted fashion, with little justification for such an assessment based on what they actually did during the Communist years or why they did it. This scapegoating fulfilled pivotal regime legitimation functions while also enabling other 'former people' to flow relatively seamlessly from Communist times to post-Communist times. Rather than reflexively appreciate this comfort, Chapter 6 interrogates it and unpacks its problematic aspects. This comfort, moreover, became tethered to the cruelties that inhere in Czech transitional justice's opening of the StB files to the public in a largely unadulterated and at times lurid fashion. Here, too, the chapter critiques what may otherwise be seen as a salutary practice by taking an unconventional second look at secrets and their possible upshots. Chapter 6 then pivots from the Czech experience to broader normative questions about the place of informers in transitional justice modalities. Urging circumspection in this regard, this chapter argues that the liminal place of informers offers an inflective moment to curb the increasingly retributivist tendencies that infuse transitional justice best practices.

Encouraging transitional justice to embrace goals of rehabilitation, reconciliation, and reintegration in the case of everyday informers, rather than ostracism and rejection, this chapter proposes a heuristic that could serve as a guide for transitional justice mechanisms in how they speak to and engage with informers. The lens we suggest embraces and refracts the humanistic complexities and nuances that inhere in the act of informing so as to promote aetiological expressivism. We contend that it is important to present informing as it is and not as it is soothingly (or self-servingly) wished to be.

II. Uncorking New Directions

Are informers in repressive illiberal places *like* informers in democratic liberal places?[8] Epistemologically, is any of the work we have undertaken germane to the act of informing beyond the shadow of autocracy?

To be clear, there is a deep selectivity in the kinds of informers who are thrust into Hrabal's transitional foundry. Individuals who betrayed others so as to inform to the successful resistance rather than against the successful resistance would not be seen as troublesome informers requiring excommunication (or reconciliation) regardless of why they did so (or the harm occasioned, or any of the other indicative elements we suggest in Chapter 6). These individuals would be retrospectively heralded as heroes. Similarly, in the very different context of a nation being militarily occupied by an invidious foreign power, individuals who inform to occupying forces are seen as strikingly different after liberation than those who informed to the resistance. Such was the case pervasively in Europe during periods of Nazi occupation.

Informers are eternal. No state, no authority, no orthodoxy—regardless of how just, legitimate, or virtuous—can maintain power and protect the deemed public good without informers. Informing after all is 'inherent in the conditions of human society'.[9] Informing and collaboration are essential for any regime to sustain itself.

[8] We use the terms illiberal and liberal in their most rudimentary sense. By this we mean that illiberal places are ones in which the state (or presumably a non-state state-like actor in the case of entities that are not formally states) is repressive and authoritarian (often with command-and-control over economic structures), whereas liberal places are ones that are democratic with free markets. See eg Fareed Zakaria, 'The Rise of Illiberal Democracy' (1997) 76(6) Foreign Affairs 22, 22–23 (defining liberal democracy as 'a political system marked not only be free and fair elections, but also by the rule of law, a separation of powers, and the protection of basic liberties of speech, assembly, religion, and property'); see also Thomas J Main, *The Rise of Illiberalism* (Brookings 2022) (defining illiberalism as the repudiation of liberal democracy, to wit, a state which rejects electoral democracy, human rights, the rule of law, and tolerance). To be sure, the lines between these poles are fuzzy, permeable, and porous. As we note, illiberal societies can be 'participatory dictatorships' and can embody elements of capitalist markets. Zakaria and others observe the rise of 'illiberal democracies' in recent decades, and place certain former Warsaw Pact countries in this category (eg Hungary). Liberal societies also can evidence deep pockets of repression.

[9] *Hoffa v United States* 385 US 293 (1966).

All regimes require informers to identify persons suspected of contravening the *ordre du jour* and the *idée(s)-fixe(s)* of the moment: such contraveners are construed as renegade, insidious, ill-fitting, worthy of cancellation, or intransigently contrarian.[10] Informers, moreover, are essential to identifying criminals and antisocials and may become deployed to prosecute delinquents for their problematic conduct. Indeed, the United Nations Convention against Transnational Organized Crime formally encourages states to use persons 'who participate or who have participated in organized criminal groups ... [t]o supply information useful to competent authorities' and suggests that such cooperation should mitigate punishment or even merit immunity.[11] International criminal trials rely extensively on insider witnesses as indispensable for the provision of information and to serve as informers in ongoing investigations and prosecutions (notably of high-ranking suspects).[12] What is more, informers described as whistleblowers also are invaluable to manage improper conduct, including when undertaken by state officials who fail to respect the values that the state ought to maintain.[13]

Informing is an act. Informers can be perceived as brave heroes revealing dark and dank behaviour, or informers can be—to return to Dudai—the lowest of the low, to wit, traitors, tattlers (many of us might recall the admonition 'don't be a tattletale'), rats, and moles.[14] How often has the public imagination been suffused with the courage of the person from whom the barbarous state police wants information and who defies (eg in Ariel Dorfman's *Death and the Maiden*)?[15] Obversely,

[10] Steve Hewitt, *Snitch! A History of the Modern Intelligence Informer* (The Continuum International Publishing Group 2010) 4 (presenting a general analysis of informing and spying in democratic times and under authoritarian regimes).

[11] United Nations Convention against Transnational Organized Crime (opened for signature 12 December 2000, entered into force 29 September 2003), 40 ILM 335, art 26.

[12] Gabrielė Chlevickaitė, Barbora Holá, and Catrien Bijleveld, 'Suspicious Minds? Empirical Analysis of Insider Witness Assessments at the ICTY, ICTR and ICC' (2023) 20(1) European J of Criminology 185, 207.

[13] 'Deep Throat', a whistleblower, breached protocols and leaked US President Richard Nixon's wiretaps to the press. This act ultimately triggered the Watergate scandal and Nixon's downfall. 'Deep Throat' is seen as a good informer for having exposed the most senior US state official at the time.

[14] Elizabeth Bruenig, 'The New Moral Code of America's Elite' *The Atlantic* (New York, 28 July 2021) <https://www.theatlantic.com/ideas/archive/2021/07/amy-chua-yale-law-school-real-story-dinner-party/619558/> accessed 13 September 2023 (discussing a Yale University law student who informed to administrative leadership that two other students had impermissibly gone to the house of a professor, which infringed COVID-19 protocols, leading the author to recall her childhood memories of her chain-smoking grandmother who, whenever confronted with the author's complaints that some other child had done this or that, perfunctorily dismissed her and admonished her not to 'be a tattletale').

[15] Ariel Dorfman, *Death and the Maiden* (Nick Hern Books 1991). This play, written in 1990, features Paulina, a political prisoner, who had been raped and tortured by a doctor while under arrest for her dissident activities during the country's dictatorial regime. After this repressive regime fell (the play is ostensibly set in Chile—Dorfman is Chilean—though no country is named), her husband Gerardo encounters a stranger by chance in heavy rain along an isolated road near their cottage who helps bring Gerardo (whose car has a flat tire) to safety. The stranger is Dr Miranda. When Miranda arrives at their cottage, Paulina identifies him through his voice and mannerisms as the man who had raped and tortured her (she had always been blindfolded while in captivity). Gerardo serves as the head of the fictional country's truth commission. The play proceeds with Paulina accusing and Miranda denying. Gerardo for his part equivocates, but ultimately extracts a forced confession from Miranda at this

how often has the public imagination dismissed the person who refuses to cooperate with investigators as complicit in the wrongdoing (obstruction of justice can be a criminal charge) and as furthering evil (for example, cops whose laconicism maintains the 'blue wall of silence' or other forms of 'bro culture')?

A. Just or Unjust Informing

Is the rub the *betraying act of informing* or is it the *cause for which someone betrayingly informs*? Is it the *context*, specifically, to whom the informer speaks? The fact that public approval of (or disdain for) informing remains so contingent suggests that cause and context greatly matter.

Let us assume it to be a social *desideratum* to preserve 'good' informing and stigmatize 'bad' informing (and to deter people from engaging in 'bad' informing even in illiberal times, should such times come to recur in the future, namely to say 'no' to repressive secret police should they again come knocking at the door). So, how best to do that? How to differentiate? One way, of course, is through the trans-historical imposition of the filtering funnel of transitional justice intercessions. To look back and say: 'Hey, you were a bad informer so you should face consequences!' But what if this inhibits 'good' informing in the present? How does an individual know that their 'good' informing of today will not become the 'bad' informing of tomorrow or of the next decade? Why bother to share anything with the state if it can hauntingly come back to bite afterwards when that state might change, flail, then fail and fall? Of course, this discussion hinges on the assumption that transitional justice's evaluations of past informers actually matter in the future. Do police informers—and let's say environmental whistleblowers—in today's Czech Republic ever think about the ultimate fate of their predecessors (Barium, for instance) in Communist Czechoslovakia? If so, then, stigmatizing bad informing might lead to the dwindling of good informing because, in the end, 'good' and 'bad' often are determined retrospectively.

Let us begin with *context*. One self-evident distinction between the informer in Communist Prague and the informer in, say, liberal democratic Stockholm is that the nature of the state to which the informer informs is different. In a nutshell: one state seems more coercive—and with far fewer checks and balances—than the other, thereby leading to greater or lesser exercises of arbitrary power, deployment of violence, and human rights violations. This is an evident answer. But we do not feel this distinction qualifies for Occam's razor.[16] Surely the concept

isolated sea-side cottage. One of the subthemes in *Death and the Maiden* is that Paulina and Gerardo both were dissidents in the dictatorship, and Paulina never disclosed Gerardo's identity despite the torture. Dorfman's play was made into a film in 1994 by Roman Polanski.

[16] Attributed to William of Ockham, a fourteenth-century English philosopher and theologian, Occam's razor (*novacula occami*) is a problem-solving principle that roots in parsimony such that the simplest explanation is typically the best one.

of the state can and must be disaggregated. In repressive states many informers come forth on their own, providing tips (or denunciations) whether anonymously or with attribution, while in liberal states many informers inhabit highly constrained social spaces (accused of crimes, caught up in investigations, incarcerated, living in the precarity of insufficient income, beset by housing woes, facing work fragility, migrants without proper documents, individuals residing in impoverished over-policed neighbourhoods, and persons subject to racial (and other) forms of structural profiling and discrimination). It goes without saying that policing agencies in liberal states turn to entrapment and infiltration to secure information.

Assuredly, a liberal democracy with constitutional separation of powers offers more safeguards against police abuses. But, still, it is naïve to be too sanguine about the gentleness of liberal states. Liberal states can be awfully mean; the consequences they unleash can be harsh. Nowadays the consequences of informing can also reverberate through internet technologies, thereby piling on shame, harm, ostracism, bullying, and bankruptcy. Unlike in the days of Communist Czechoslovakia, the ubiquity of the iPhone and the instantaneity of social media compound the cruelties that might arise through the exposure of the informed-upons. Now anyone can be a denouncer and –through Twitter, Instagram, or TikTok—broadcast directly into the virtual ether with a rapidity and reach unheard of during the Cold War. On another note, the personal nature of informing in Communist Czechoslovakia contrasts with the automaticity of mass surveillance (eg through modern depersonalized algorithmic technology, cameras recording automatically everywhere) that may not implicate individual orchestration and cultivation (or exploitation) of intimacy. What is more, being exposed for allegedly dubious conduct can lead to banishment from virtual citizenship and virtual spaces that, for many, are the *sine qua non* of communication, *polis* membership, and belonging. Social media become the modern 'streets'. To be exiled therefrom is akin to being a shut-in, under house arrest, outlawed as in ancient Rome or the American Wild West: shoved into exile and stripped of access to 'the city on the hill',[17] for, after all, 'what is the city but the people'.[18]

[17] Attributed to John Winthrop, Puritan preacher and governor, to describe the new Massachusetts Bay Colony in 1630.

[18] William Shakespeare, *Coriolanus* (Wilder 2013). In Act 3, Scene 1, set amidst the bustle of daily life at the Roman Forum, Sicinius asks 'what is the city but the people?'; the Plebians reply, 'True/The people are the city'. ibid 71. Earlier in the same scene, Coriolanus is prosecuted by 'the tribunes of the people/ The tongues o' th' common mouth' who 'prank ... in authority'. ibid 63. Later, in Act 3, Scene 3, once again at the Forum, after Sicinius declares Coriolanus to be 'a disease that must be cut away', the 'noble tribunes' decide to banish Coriolanus from Rome. ibid 75–76. In Act 3, Scene 3, Coriolanus replies: 'You common cry of curs ... I banish you ... There is a world elsewhere.' ibid 89. That said, if one's world is virtuality, then there may simply not be another world elsewhere. So, banishment from such a world may be worse than exile from the city.

So, in the end, it strikes us as inadequate to conceptualize the normativity of informing entirely on the basis of *to whom it was made*, namely to agents of a stylized good state or agents of a stylized bad state.

What about *cause*? Let us begin anecdotally. Amid the many workshops we have given related to this book, sparks recurrently arose when we asked academic interlocutors whether they saw any possible parallel between the act of informing on COVID-19 lockdown violators (eg persons who called off a police hotline to tip off that so-and-so had one too many people over in the neighbouring flat, or was walking outdoors past curfew),[19] on the one hand, and persons who exposed rule violators in 1970s Prague on the other. The vast majority of our interlocutors perceived these two acts as incomparable, if not downright incommensurable. But when we probed academic interlocutors about informers who reported violations under the whistleblower provision that the US state of Texas enacted in 2021 to report individuals who assisted women in procuring abortions after six weeks of pregnancy,[20] the response was utterly different. There was a greater tendency to see such latter acts of informing as comparable to those undertaken to the StB, in other words as disturbing and undesirable.

[19] Examples abound. The government of Northern Ireland set up a dedicated web page for people to report breaches of COVID-19 restrictions. The police encouraged people to report. Lauren Harte, 'Coronavirus: Jim Allister "Uneasy" over Covid-19 Snitch Society as Police Encourage NI Public to Shop Neighbors' *Belfast Telegraph* (Belfast, 15 September 2020) <https://www.belfasttelegraph.co.uk/news/health/coronavirus/coronavirus-jim-allister-uneasy-over-covid-19-snitch-society-as-police-encourage-ni-public-to-shop-neighbours/39534542.html> accessed 13 September 2023. Violators could face fines of £60 to £1,000. Similarly, the UK Policing Minister said that 'residents should "absolutely" call the police if they see neighbours holding gatherings of seven or more next door.... Home Secretary Priti Patel said she would report breaches of the "rule of six" coronavirus restrictions.' ibid. In the end, then British Prime Minster Boris Johnson and members of his leadership team personally failed to respect these very same rules, leading to long-running public outrage and derision. Harte, 'Coronavirus' (n 19). See also 'In Lockdown, "Desperate" Swiss Turn to Snooping and Snitching' *Reuters* (London, 30 April 2020) ('One resident complained to police about a neighbourhood choir intended to cheer people up. The choir got off with a warning and responded by reducing the show's length and placing chalk markers to encourage spectators to social distance.'). Corporations and agencies also set up internal systems to report rule breaches among co-workers.

[20] On 1 September 2021, the Heartbeat Act went into effect in Texas. This legislation banned performing abortions after the detection of embryonic or foetal cardiac activity (determined normally to be after six weeks of pregnancy). This legislation permitted residents of the state to sue clinics, doctors, nurses, and also families, friends, counsellors, pastors, and drivers who had helped a woman get an abortion. It did not permit the woman seeking an abortion to be sued. The Heartbeat Act deputized the public to privately enforce through civil sanction, rather than the state through criminal penalty. Hence, it became permissible to create a website to permit people to anonymously report violations of the Heartbeat Act. One such website generated considerable controversy. It crashed after backlash, spamming, and the filing of a large number of scurrilous and fake reports; prank calls also were deliberately placed; and webhosts eventually denied service on the basis the website impermissibly collected private information about third parties. Meryl Kornfield, 'A Website for "Whistleblowers" to Expose Texas Abortion Providers Was Taken Down—Again' *Washington Post* (Washington, DC, 6 September 2021); see also Caitlin O'Kane, 'Texas "Whistleblower" Website Used for Snitching on Abortions Shut Down' *CBS News* (New York, 7 September 2021). In the end, the reported information simply became redirected to yet another website, this being of a group called the Texas Right to Life. Following the United States Supreme Court 2022 decision declaring there to be no constitutional right to abortion, the Texas government enacted even more restrictive legislation banning abortion and introducing direct criminal sanction. *Dobbs v Jackson Women's Health Organization* No 19-1392, 597 US ___ (2022).

Yet in the end it is the same *act* to call a lockdown hotline as it is to enter a tip on an abortion website. It is the subjective *justness of the cause* that appears to be viewed as different. The repugnance or desirability of an act of informing seems to hinge upon idiosyncratic perceptions of the political legitimacy of the law that is being affronted. Assuredly, different constituencies of interlocutors to ours (our interlocutors were mainly university academics) might respond differently to the goodness or badness of informing in these contexts. There are plenty of constituencies that would invert the reaction—finding the COVID lockdown informer to be a pathetic, virtue-signalling snitch and the abortion-provider informer to be gallantly saving the lives of the preborn.

How does this *selective cause–justness* interface with broader trends in international law and transnationalized best practices?

One example of cause–justness in international law is just war theory, this being an ethical framework to determine when it is permissible to go to war. Just war theory is complex and diverse. It has a lengthy philosophical, moral, and religious provenance and bears connections to natural law. The righteousness of war fermented in Ancient Egyptian cosmological theory, in Confucian ethics, and in the Hindu epic the *Mahabharta* with its introduction of *dharma-juddha*. Augustine of Hippo in *De civitate Dei contra paganos* (early fifth century AD) and Thomas Aquinas in *Summa Theologica* (late thirteenth century AD) addressed just war theory in the Christian tradition. Just war theory reverberates in modern philosophical thought as well.[21] In a nutshell, this theory posits that if the cause (and intention) is right, then as a last resort it is legitimate to declare war even if some people get hurt.[22] Of course, what is 'right' is contingent. Just war theory has been trotted out to legitimize the Crusades, White Supremacy, as well as postcolonial liberation struggles against oppressive governments and enslaver states.

Just war theory, however, has shrunk over the course of its contemporary migration from the dominion of ethics to the empire of international law. The modern *jus ad bellum* has narrowed just war theory. Going to war now only is justified if the United Nations Security Council procedurally (in other words, positivistically) says so, or if it is inherently in a state's self-defence (and, even then, only in as much as to minimally ensure self-defence). Everything else in the case of international armed conflict is an act of aggression, which can trigger individual penal responsibility.[23] Humanitarian armed intervention has not crystallized into conventional

[21] See eg Laura Sjoberg, 'Why Just War Needs Feminism Now More Than Ever' (2008) 45 International Politics 1; Seth Lazar and Helen Frowe (eds), *The Oxford Handbook of Ethics of War* (OUP 2018); Michael Walzer, *Just and Unjust Wars: A Moral Argument with Historical Illustrations* (4th edn, Basic Books 2006); Jeff McMahan, 'Just Cause for War' (2005) 19(3) Ethics and International Affairs 1.

[22] It is also required to adhere to the law in war, the *jus in bello*, namely how to fight and which tactics and what weapons to use.

[23] Rome Statute of the International Criminal Court (entered into force 2002) 2187 UNTS 90, art 8*bis* (detailing that the crime of aggression means the planning, preparation, initiation or execution, by a person in a position effectively to exercise control over or to direct the political or military action of a state, of an act of aggression which, by its character, gravity, and scale, constitutes a manifest violation of

or customary international law.[24] While reaching a discursive apex with NATO's aerial bombing of Milošević's former Yugoslavia in the late 1990s, the momentum to harden humanitarian armed intervention into international law ebbed thereafter, notably, once US President Bush invoked it as among the rationales to justify the 2003 Iraq invasion, and has now plummeted to a nadir after Russian President Putin referenced it as a basis for the Ukraine invasion (namely to protect ethnic Russians purportedly subjugated in eastern Ukraine).[25]

A similar tack arises with terrorism. There once was a time when 'freedom fighters' were heralded even if they deployed violent tactics. This was coloured as a necessary (and just) way in which abusive state power—including the yoke of colonialism and ethnic oppression—could be repelled. If violence was needed to secure a virtuous goal, then that violence could be justified, accepted, and legitimated. But this space, too, is shrinking. Terrorism is increasingly construed as a 'a method of coercion that utilizes or threatens to utilize violence in order to spread fear and thereby attain political or ideological goals'.[26] It is approached as an act (ie a method). In terms of law, while there is not yet a core customary international law definition of terrorism, Ben Saul notes that 'there is now a basic legal consensus that terrorism is criminal violence intended to intimidate a population or coerce a government or international organization'.[27] Reflecting this logic, the political offence exception in extradition law, in which a requested state may refuse to extradite a suspect to a requesting state for prosecution if the charges are political,

the Charter of the United Nations; an 'act of aggression' means the use of armed force by a state against the sovereignty, territorial integrity or political independence of another state, or in any other manner inconsistent with the Charter of the United Nations).

[24] Both humanitarian armed intervention and the responsibility to protect reflect the notion that there is an obligation to safeguard those who cannot protect themselves against violence committed by or within the territory of their own state. This means that under certain conditions other states can unilaterally use armed force to protect persecuted peoples (whether persecuted by their own state, by another state, or by other actors). 'The Responsibility to Protect: Report of the International Commission on Intervention and State Sovereignty, 2001' (*Global Centre for the Responsibility to Protect*, 1 December 2001) <https://www.globalr2p.org/resources/the-responsibility-to-protect-report-of-the-international-commission-on-intervention-and-state-sovereignty-2001/> accessed 13 September 2023.

[25] For more regarding Ukraine, Heather Ashby, 'How the Kremlin Distorts the "Responsibility to Protect" Principle' (*United States Institute of Peace*, 7 April 2022) <https://www.usip.org/publications/2022/04/how-kremlin-distorts-responsibility-protect-principle> accessed 13 September 2023. For more regarding Iraq, Rosa Brooks, 'Humanitarian Intervention: Evolving Norms, Fragmenting Consensus' (*Georgetown Law Scholarly Commons*, 2014), <https://scholarship.law.georgetown.edu/facpub/1464/> accessed 13 September 2023; Kerry Boyd Anderson, 'How the Iraq war undermined the Responsibility to Protect doctrine' *Arab News* (Riyadh, May 20, 2018); James Turner Johnson, 'Humanitarian Intervention after Iraq: Just War and International Law Perspectives' (2006) 5(2) J of Military Ethics 114.

[26] United Nations Office on Drugs and Crime, *Introduction to International Terrorism* 1 (2018) <https://www.unodc.org/documents/e4j/18-04932_CT_Mod_01_ebook_FINALpdf.pdf> accessed 13 September 2023 (an instructional manual).

[27] Ben Saul, 'Defining Terrorism in International Law' (*GlobaLex*, November/December 2021) <https://www.nyulawglobal.org/globalex/Defining_Terrorism_International_Law.html> accessed 13 September 2023.

is inapplicable if that person had deployed certain violent means (including kidnapping, malicious wounding, and placing or possessing or using an explosive).[28] These means are, to return to Saul, determined to be intrinsically criminal regardless of their goals.

International criminal law's aspirational even-handedness offers another example. The operational enforcement of international criminal law aspires to prosecute all sides to a conflict for impermissible conduct notwithstanding their respective causes (though such enforcement is not always politically or practically successful and sentences too may vary). The Nuremberg proceedings have been chided for neglecting the carpet-bombing of Dresden; the Tokyo Tribunal has been castigated for ignoring American use of atomic weapons at Nagasaki or Hiroshima. The Special Court for Sierra Leone—tasked with adjudicating individual criminal responsibility for internecine violence that wracked that country in the 1990s—went out of its way to build war crimes and crimes against humanity cases around brutal rebel groups and also a group (the CDF) which assembled to support the embattled Sierra Leonean government.[29] The South African Truth and Reconciliation Commission featured—to different degrees, to be sure—the conduct of both the apartheid government as well as of the anti-apartheid African National Congress.

In sum, then, just (or unjust) informing theory might help explain the contingent and deeply bimodal positioning of informers (ugly or heroic) that pervades in settled, ordinary times in liberal societies. The justness of a cause seems to operate as a barometer of acceptability. Yet, if perceptions of informing were to reflect broader movements in international accountability regarding the salience of *cause* as validating the impugned act, this is thinning ice. The directional momentum of international law and related best practices is shying away from cause justification. Accordingly, relying on cause justification to legitimize some acts of informing while condemning other acts of informing (in other words, a 'just (or unjust) informing theory') presents somewhat as a counter-current.

B. Informers in Liberal Times

Another interrogative opportunity opens. This is to apply the question we asked and sought to answer in the case of Communist Czechoslovakia to modern liberal societies. What do we know about *why* people speak to state police in settled times

[28] See eg US-UK Extradition Treaty art 4 (19 April 2004) <https://www.congress.gov/108/cdoc/tdoc23/CDOC-108tdoc23.pdf> accessed 13 September 2023 (exemplifying general practice among international extradition treaties).

[29] *Prosecutor v Fofana*, Appeal Judgment, Case No SCSL-04-14-A (28 May 2008) para 554 (regarding sentencing in this case, the Appeals Chamber of the Special Court for Sierra Leone explicitly noted that 'considering "just cause" and motives of civic duty as a mitigating factor' amounted to 'an error of law').

in liberal societies? If people are motivated to speak to police in liberal democracies because of similar (e)motions that prompted people to speak to the StB in Communist Czechoslovakia, then the act of informing would—according to our research—be largely driven by fear, desire, getting even, and, indeed, by some residual devotional adherence to the state and the cause. Perhaps the informer in liberal democracies turns to the cause the way that informers turned to ideology in Communist Prague, namely to palatably frame acts of informing that were really motivated by other considerations. If so, then, deploying cause justification (or the contextual differences between repressive and liberal governments) to distinguish the legitimacy of informing in Communist Czechoslovakia from informing today in the modern Czech Republic (or elsewhere) becomes a bit fatuous, since the cause (or the nature of the police) becomes a pretext for other motivations.

What does informing 'look like' in liberal societies? Here we class informers into a number of categories. Some informers may assist state intelligence organizations (such as the CIA and FBI (United States), National Intelligence Service (South Korea), CSIS (Canada), NIA (India), SIS (United Kingdom)) and accordingly be slid into and surveille groups considered dangerous at the time (eg in the United States, suspected espionage agents in the First World War,[30] White Supremacist organizations, secessionist or terrorist groups, civil rights groups, or alleged Communist sympathizers between the 1930s and 1970s).[31] Informers were also extensively used in other environments that US officials considered problematic, such as student power movements and LGBTQ+ and women's liberation movements.[32] Informers also are nurtured to surveil organized crime syndicates, smugglers, and narco-traffickers. Interestingly, as an aside, Hewitt discusses that '[t]he FBI Director made it clear that American informers performed out of a sense of patriotism, raising the controversial practice to the level of a proper citizen's duty', which indicates a clear parallel between how the FBI depicted informers and how the StB depicted informers, in both cases ostensibly to encourage them and assuage their sensibilities.[33]

Another category comprises ordinary criminal informer. This category includes persons with ongoing relationships with regular police officers in their neighbourhoods who report on crime more generally. This category can also include jailhouse informers and persons who share information with the state in individual

[30] The US government initiated an extensive domestic campaign to drum out putative spies and supporters of Germany during the First World War. One media report indicates this campaign was abused by many citizens; indeed '[t]he opportunities the espionage campaign offered for paying off private scores were untold, and there were many persons who gratified long-standing grudges'. John Sleicher (ed), *Leslie's Illustrated Weekly Newspaper* (vol CXXVIII, No 3318, New York, 17 April 1919) 540.

[31] Hewitt, *Snitch!* (n 10) 52–54.

[32] ibid 55.

[33] ibid 54 (as comment was made in 1955, it is interesting to note that the FBI director did so to differentiate US informers from informers to secret police forces in repressive regimes.).

criminal cases in which they themselves may be suspects in exchange for immunity or reduced punishment (or because they simply are scared).

And a third category involves denouncers, often regular citizens, who act on their own initiative: for instance by making an anonymous call to a COVID-hotline or reporting someone on an abortion website; tipping off the boss about misdeeds in the office; students who report improper conduct of their peers on campus (eg cheating, sexual violence and harassment, bullying);[34] employees who report the offensive, racist, or homophobic speech of their colleagues.

Are informers in liberal societies motored by drivers that are much different than informers in repressive societies? Epistemologically, we do know something about informers in liberal societies.[35] And what we do know suggests considerable commonalities with the individuals now 'immortalized', *pace* Kundera, in the Prague archives.

Gary Marx authored a seminal article about informers in the United States in the 1960s and 1970s who were deployed to monitor political organizations the US government deemed to be extremist and to expose individual members of such organizations.[36] As to motivations, Marx found

> [s]ome are patriotic Middle Americans and/or those insecure about their status. Others come from an urban criminal milieu where rewards of various kinds may be most important, while others seem to be otherwise typical members of the group they inform on ... who have become disenchanted with their group or get hooked into the role by the police. There are also, no doubt, some described by a police manual as 'demented, eccentric, nuisance types'.[37]

Marx also mentions 'that informers can be nudged by coercion and also "to avenge a loss ... personal vendettas"'.[38] Informing for some 'may be mainly a question of the need for money'.[39] Marx observes that '[t]he use of agents can be seen as

[34] Many thanks to Melina Bell for sharing this point with us.

[35] For a summary of a variety of informers' motivations, Hewitt, *Snitch!* (n 10) 28–29 (including such motivations as financial rewards, fear, revenge, gratitude, thrill, egoism, envy, disgruntlement, prejudice, and patriotism). Hewitt relies on literature that explores informing to criminal police or to intelligence agencies in democratic and authoritarian contexts. Coercion, duress, and blackmail also are noted in both democratic and non-democratic states, though it appears that, very similarly to the StB internal practices we presented in Chapter 2, coercive measures largely are discouraged insofar as coerced informers are seen as not as effective as those who inform freely. If compulsion is deployed initially as a tool of recruitment the handler may seek to alter the nature of the relationship in order to encourage more effective assistance—the idea being that those who willingly participate will supply better content than those who do so under duress.

[36] Gary T Marx, 'Thoughts on a Neglected Category of Social Movement Participant: The Agent Provocateur and the Informant' (1974) 80(2) American J of Sociology 402.

[37] ibid 413.

[38] ibid 413–15.

[39] ibid 415.

an example of … "dirty work"', and remarks 'that societies have a need for "dirty workers"'.[40]

What about police or jailhouse informers in contexts of ordinary common crimes? In the United States, the predominant motives for working with law enforcement agencies in such capacities have been identified as fear, revenge, and personal gain.[41] Fear is a frequently encountered motivation. Informers can be frightened of state punishment for criminal acts or of retaliation by criminal associates.[42] A 2011 study that interviewed eighty-four informers found that 'agreeing to become an informant provided temporary relief from the intense stress associated with being busted and the fear of immediate incarceration'.[43] These interviewees shared that the police usually deployed scare tactics, including overcharging and seizure of property, while also exhorting targets to 'do the right thing'.[44] That said, fear was not the only motivation for informing. This study identified 'mercenary informants', namely those motivated by money. Unfair drug deals, reactions to rumours that the target tried to snitch on a friend, scorned partners in intimate relationships, revenge seeking, and desire to eliminate criminal competition also arose as motivations for informing. Police *aficionados* (including persons who had sought but ultimately failed to secure employment as police officers) represent another motivational category. Another study found that some informers claimed they cooperated in order to repent for past crimes.[45] Other discerned motivations included vanity, civic mindedness, and gratitude.[46]

In one study, researchers asked US detectives to list up to three reasons why their primary registered informers started informing.[47] From the perspective of these detective handlers, informers evinced a wide variety of motives ranging from a sense of public duty (8 per cent) to enjoying the thrill of being an informer (15 per

[40] ibid 436 (citing Everett Hughes, 'Good People and Dirty Work' (1962) 10 Social Problems 3).

[41] James T Reese, 'Motivations of Criminal Informants' (1980) 49(5) FBI Law Enforcement Bulletin 23, 24 <https://www.ojp.gov/ncjrs/virtual-library/abstracts/motivations-criminal-informants> accessed 13 September 2023. See also Hewitt, *Snitch!* (n 10) 28 (according to Hewitt, 'criminal informers are distinct from intelligence informers, with money being even more important for the former, along with other, unique factors such as reduced sentence and revenge against rivals').

[42] Gregory D Lee, 'Drug Informants Motives, Methods, and Management' (1993) 62(9) FBI Law Enforcement Bulletin, 10, 10–11 <https://www.ojp.gov/pdffiles1/Digitization/144681NCJRS.pdf> accessed 13 September 2023.

[43] J Mitchell Miller, 'Becoming an Informant' (2011) 28(2) Justice Quarterly 203, 211–12. See also Robert M Worley, 'To Snitch or Not to Snitch, That Is The Question: Exploring the Role of Inmate Informants in Detecting Inappropriate Relationships Between the Keeper and the Kept' (2011) 25(1–2) Int Review of Law, Computers & Technology 79, 81 (noting that prison informers sometimes supplied information without any encouragement from correctional staff members as they believed they could curry favour with supervisors by providing unsolicited information, while in other cases informers had committed disciplinary infractions and more than likely believed they could improve their situation by notifying supervisors).

[44] Miller, 'Becoming an Informant' (n 43) 212.

[45] Lee, 'Drug Informants Motives, Methods, and Management' (n 42) 11.

[46] Reese, 'Motivations of Criminal Informants' (n 41) 24.

[47] Colin Dunnighan and Clive Norris, 'The Detective, the Snout, and the Audit Commission: The Real Costs in Using Informants' (1999) 38(1) The Howard J of Crime and Justice 67.

cent).[48] However, the most significant percentages cluster around: money (70 per cent), some sort of concession in relation to present and future charges (30–35 per cent), and revenge (22 per cent).[49] Criminal informers also evince mental health woes, much like many of the Czechoslovak StB informers back in the day.[50]

And ad hoc citizen informers? Why do people call the Texas abortion whistleblower line and implicate a specific alleged rule-breaker? Why, against whom, and for which reasons did people call COVID hotlines anonymously to report violators of public health ordinances? Or chose not to do so? Why do people blow the whistle within organizations?

Academic research sheds some light on these questions. For example, Patrick Bergemann and Brandy Aven conclude in their study of US federal employees that, when it comes to whistleblowing, a difference arises between group insiders (less likely to be outed for non-compliance) and group outsiders (more likely to be outed).[51] In other words, loyalty to potential targets matters. This means that when it comes to informing, heterogeneity and contingency arise in terms of responses to the very same wrongdoing.

Comparable findings have been reported in the context of informing to police regarding COVID-19 enforcement in New York City.[52] As a starting point for this compelling research, it must be noted that 'residents of New York City were directly encouraged by officials to call the city's 311 hotline if they observed others not following health guidelines, i.e., highly visible behaviors such as not social distancing or not wearing a face mask'.[53] These researchers begin with the premise that '311 calls—particularly for "uncivil" behavior—have been found to reflect normative responses of enforcement'.[54] That said, calls that reported such 'uncivil' behaviour were unevenly made. Neighbourhoods with higher levels of territoriality were more sensitive to norm violations, such that individuals in such neighbourhoods were more likely to report rule violations especially when more 'visitors' came from outside those neighbourhoods. Territoriality means increased homeownership,

48 ibid 78.

49 ibid.

50 See eg the documentary film *Inside the Mind of a Snitch: 'Tony'* (PBS Frontline) <https://www.pbs.org/wgbh/pages/frontline/shows/snitch/etc/tony.html> accessed 7 June 2023.

51 Patrick Bergemann and Brandy Aven, 'Whistleblowing and Group Affiliation: The Role of Group Cohesion and the Locus of the Wrongdoer in Reporting Decisions' (2022) 34 Organization Science 1, 1 ('When an individual observes wrongdoing committed by a person affiliated with the same group, higher group cohesion decreases the likelihood of blowing the whistle because of potential whistleblowers' greater loyalties toward group members and a desire to protect the reputation of the group. When an individual observes wrongdoing committed by a person not affiliated with the same group, higher group cohesion increases the likelihood of blowing the whistle, as potential whistleblowers feel they have the support of fellow group members, lessening fears of retaliation.').

52 Patrick Bergemann and Christof Brandtner, 'Territoriality and the Emergence of Health-Protecting Norms in Response to the Covid-19 Pandemic' (unpublished paper 2023, on file with the authors).

53 ibid 18–19.

54 ibid 19, 24 (noting 'the sheer number of complaints filed', thereby suggesting broad-based public involvement in reporting and informing on other citizens).

residence longevity, and building permits which correlate to three components of psychological ownership (namely control, familiarity, and investment).[55] Being a 'regular' made one more inclined to inform. More complaints were brought in neighbourhoods with higher territoriality, in particular when more outsiders entered those communities in perceived rule-breaking ways. In sum:

> Given the internalization of one's territory as part of the extended self, violations of that territory serve as personal affronts, which likely strengthen emotional responses and spur sanctioning. In this sense, sanctioning becomes less of a rational decision and more of an emotional reaction . . . .[56]

Journalistic accounts—however anecdotal—also are indicative when it comes to motivation for reporting COVID-19 rule-breakers. Melissa, in the United Kingdom, 'reported her neighbours to the police three times', stating:

> '[One] neighbour never seemed to do any exercise before and now he's training for The Olympics, out two or three times a day.' Melissa suspects another neighbour has had 'different lovers round.' [Melissa] says she is proud to be following the rules and feels it's right to shame those who don't.[57]

In 2020, in the United Kingdom '[p]olice [were] receiving thousands of reports a day of lockdown rules being broken' such that the 'police's professional standards body ... ask[ed] the public to curb "deliberate false reporting" and the spread of "misinformation" to target nuisance neighbours or to settle long-running feuds'.[58] One British observer was reported as being 'unsurprised about how quickly "a Stasi-like" narrative had emerged'.[59]

In sum, states need informers and some people turn to that need for their own personal ends. Informing can serve as a tactic and strategy in difficult (and not so difficult) circumstances. Informing might simply constitute a hardwired element of the human condition.

Indeed, while differences can be intuited between why people inform (or elect not to) in liberal societies from why they do so in repressive societies, on a very preliminary note carry-overs and parallels also seem to emerge. Emotions are key.

[55] ibid 47 ('Neighborhoods with higher levels of territoriality engaged in more compliance and more enforcement of behaviors intended to mitigate the spread of the virus. These findings support our proposition that when individuals experience a sense of ownership over a physical space, they feel empowered to make rules regarding the use of that space and to maintain and defend that space against violations.').

[56] ibid 48.

[57] Nosheen Iqbal and Mark Townsend, 'Duty or Score-settling? Rights and Wrongs of Corona Shaming' *The Guardian* (London, 18 April 2020).

[58] ibid.

[59] ibid.

Enforcing the official cause in question, then, might matter less to the informer than it does to the perceptions of others whether that informer is acting in a laudable or lamentable fashion. This might be one further explanatory reason why it was so easy in post-Communist Czechoslovakia to malign informers by stylizing them as dangerous and hostile to the new regime. Even if someone is driven by ulterior pettiness but the cause is seen as good (public health enforcement, for example), then an effect-based analysis could say that such informing—and the concomitant exposure and sanctioning of informed-upons—is just.

All this resurfaces the question of placing so much weight on the perceived justness of the cause as assessed in a temporally distanced moment. After all, there were times—plenty of them—when Czechoslovak Communism and Marxist-Leninist strictures were broadly seen as 'good': these -isms, after all, fought (and helped vanquish) the Nazis, countered private greed, and strove to build a just and equitable society. European Communist governments retained considerable public support for protracted periods of time, including from Western sympathizers comfortably ensconced in their Western sinecures.

To be sure, today's just causes can become tomorrow's failed orthodoxies and the next generation's historical ignominies. So the cycle goes, over and again, again and over. Such is the wheel of history. Throughout, it seems, informers abound. The informer is as timeless as change: always here, always there, everywhere, never nowhere.

Index

For the benefit of digital users, indexed terms that span two pages (e.g., 52–53) may, on occasion, appear on only one of those pages.

Figures are indicated by *f* following the page number